Between *Mysticism* and *Philosophy*

SUNY series in

Jewish Philosophy

Kenneth Seeskin, *editor*

Between *Mysticism* and *Philosophy*

Sufi Language of Religious Experience in Judah Ha-Levi's *Kuzari*

Diana Lobel

STATE UNIVERSITY
OF NEW YORK PRESS

Published by
State University of New York Press

Printed in the United States of America

For information, address the State University of New York Press, State University Plaza, Albany, NY 12246

Cover design by Marjorie Corbett. Original papercut, "Open the Gates of Righteousness," by Risa Mandelberg © 1992 The Paperdoll Company.

Marketing by Anne Valentine • Production by Bernadine Dawes

Library of Congress Cataloging-in-Publication Data

Lobel, Diana.

Between mysticism and philosophy : Sufi language of religious experience in Judah Ha-Levi's Kuzari / Diana Lobel.

p. cm. — (SUNY series in Jewish philosophy)

Includes bibliographical references.

ISBN 0-7914-4451-1 (hc : alk. paper). — ISBN 0-7914-4452-x (pb : alk. paper)

1. Judah, ha-Levi, 12th cent. Kitāb al-ḥujjah. 2. Spiritual life—Judaism. I. Title. II. Series.

BM550.J84L63 2000

296.3—dc21 99-31812

CIP

1 2 3 4 5 6 7 8 9 10

To Albert, Francine, and Janet Lobel,

with love

And to the memory of Professor Twersky *z"l*,

in spirit

Contents

Acknowledgments

This project began to take shape in the spring of 1987 in dialogue with Professor Bernard Septimus, and came to its first phase of completion in the spring of 1995 through conversations with Professor Isadore Twersky *z"l*. I am grateful to Professor Twersky for his patience and trust in the project, for his invaluable insights and Socratic guidance, for encouraging me to ask large questions and meet challenges I would not otherwise have considered. I feel fortunate not only to have received these gifts, but to have been able to thank him for them.

The book evolved further in my ongoing conversations with Professor Septimus, who has shared so generously of his rich scholarship and broad-ranging interests. A critically sensitive reader, he is a rare jewel of a scholar who has enriched my understanding in every area our exchanges have touched. I hope I can express my appreciation in deeds as well as words.

I would like to thank Professor Wolfhart Heinrichs for his careful and incisive reading of my dissertation, from which this book evolved, and for giving so generously of his time reading Arabic texts. His judicious comments and suggestions, and the genuine interest he brought to it were invaluable. I am also grateful to Professor Wheeler Thackston for his generosity in reading Arabic texts over the years, for sharing his erudition and original perspectives. Professors William Graham, Hava Lazarus-Yafeh *z"l,* and Everett Rowson were extremely helpful in reading texts and offering suggestions, as was Ahmad Atif Ahmad. Professor Bezalel Safran patiently launched and inspired my studies many years ago.

I am especially indebted to Barry Kogan, who has so generously shared his ideas and translations of the *Kuzari*. I have also enjoyed the fruits of rich intellectual exchange with Steven Harvey, Daniel Lasker, and Kenneth Seeskin. Warren Zev Harvey has been a fountain of knowledge, insight, critique, and guidance.

I would like to thank my colleagues during academic year 1996–97 at the University of Maryland at College Park, and from 1997 to present in the Religious Studies Department of Rice University, for warm intellectual community and support for my scholarship and teaching. Matthias Henze has been more than a colleague: a fellow teacher, collaborator, and dear friend. My many gifted students have been a deep and ongoing source of inspiration.

There were many whose reading of this manuscript and discussion of it in its various phases were of great benefit, including Linda Barnes, Miriam Bronstein, Jim Curry, Ted Kaptchuk, Jim Robinson, Joel Rosenberg, and Janet Zimmern. Betsy Bunn Kaptchuk offered the gift of clarity and wisdom. Ellen Birnbaum has been a colleague and mentor throughout this project; I have learned from her scholarship and from our exchanges in so many ways.

Naava Frank, Ken Kronenberg, Tom Ross, Ken Russell, and the staff at the OIT Computer Lab were of great assistance in the material production of the manuscript. I am grateful to the Memorial Foundation for Jewish Culture, which supported the early stages of my research. I would also like to thank my editors at the State University of New York Press, James Peltz, Bernadine Dawes, and Kenneth Seeskin for their warm assistance throughout the project.

Don Galbreth offered valuable editorial assistance, including incisive critique, suggestions, and a crisp writing and editorial style. Andrea Frolic read and edited the entire manuscript twice in its final stages, helping to bring it to synthesis and completion through her gifts of exquisite clarity, precision, and insight. Her expertise and support are deeply appreciated. Miriam Bronstein added several final touches to the manuscript, in a friendship that is steadfast and growing. I thank Martin Kavka for his expert indexing, and for much more.

For their inspiration and support over the course of this project, I would like to thank Dana Anderson, Meri Axinn, Nancy Barcelo, Sarah Braun, Debi Carbacio, Elaine Chapnik, Sandra Daitch, Stan Dorn, Mrs. Shirly Goodman, R. Moshe Holcer, Debbie Kagan, Judy Kates, Efraim Krug, Naomi Lake, Ellen Lim, Tina Mulhern, Marilyn Paul, Tony Rivera, and the Spinoza study group.

For their indefatigable support and good humor, I would like to thank my sister and parents, and grandparents to whom this book is dedicated.

Finally, to Christine Hoepfner, Walter Ness, R. Yonah, and the Source of all blessings—thanks go far beyond words.

Between
Mysticism
and
Philosophy

Introduction

1. The Genesis of the Kuzari *and Its Frame Story*

Twelfth-century Spain was alive with spiritual possibilities. A new language of religious experience was taking hold in medieval Islam; philosophers and Sufi mystics, legal scholars, theologians, and poets all sought to capture the experiential dimension of religious life and were reinventing Islamic vocabulary to do so. Each of these groups was engaged in appropriating and redefining a common set of terms for religious experience.

Despite their intersecting discourses and vocabulary, these communities of scholars were not necessarily talking with one another. It was only the rare polymath, fluent in each of these cultural dialects, who could engage the disparate voices in a common conversation. Weaving these worlds together required a scholar equally conversant in philosophy, law, poetry, theology, and mysticism, one whose talents and sensibility enabled him to perceive common threads and forge innovative connections.

Interestingly enough, the person in twelfth-century Spain who was able to do this was not himself a Muslim, but a Jew. R. Judah Ha-Levi (1075–1141) was one of the foremost medieval Hebrew poets, a revered figure among a circle of Spanish intellectuals, who at the end of his days shocked his contemporaries by abandoning life in Spain and setting sail for the land of Israel. Ha-Levi is renowned not only as a poet, but as the author of an influential philosophical dialogue, a work written in Arabic but popularly known by its Hebrew title, *Sefer ha-Kuzari* (*The Book of the Khazar*).[1]

In the *Kuzari*, Ha-Levi adapts and transforms this new language of inner experience to fit the Jewish context; he presents classical Judaism using the new experiential language emerging in medieval Islam. Ha-Levi thus describes unique Jewish experiences with vocabulary from the wider Islamic culture, using language which would capture the imagination of his contemporaries. At the same time he forges a broad cultural critique, weaving together layers of discourse with the artistry of a laureate poet and polymath. Ha-Levi's achievement in bringing together these conversations was not merely an exercise in erudition, but an act of creative imagination.

From a letter written by Ha-Levi to his friend Ḥalfon b. Netanel and found in the Cairo Genizah, we learn that Ha-Levi began his dialogue in response to questions from a Karaite in Christian Spain.[2] The Karaites—a sectarian group of Jews who emerged some time during the eighth century as opponents of rabbinic oral law—were a living presence in twelfth-century Spain, and Ha-Levi's work began in conversation with a Karaite.[3]

The work as it stands today, however, is much wider in scope, as is reflected in Ha-Levi's full description of his work: *The Book of Refutation and Proof in Defence of the Despised Religion.*[4] Written in the form of a fictional dialogue between a Khazar king and a philosopher, a Christian, a Muslim, and a Jew, the completed work is a broad-based defense of Judaism as the revealed religion par excellence; the principle adversary of the work is no longer the Karaite but the Aristotelian philosopher. The *Kuzari* was composed over some twenty years and completed shortly before Ha-Levi's departure for the land of Israel in 1040, an event taken by the Jewish intelligentsia of Muslim Spain as a devastating rejection of their ideals and way of life.[5]

Surrounding the dialogue is a frame story based on a real tenth-century correspondence between the Jewish courtier Ḥasdai Ibn Shaprut—principal minister to ʿAbd al-Raḥmān III, the Caliph of Cordova (912–961)—and Joseph, the king of the Khazars.[6] The Khazars were a central Asian tribe who converted to Judaism some time during the eighth century. Joseph's letter tells the story of that conversion. A certain Khazar king, Bulan, had a dream in which an angel appeared to him who praised him for his works and promised him blessings if he would observe God's statutes. The king and his people immediately accept divine rule, but are subsequently approached for conversion by Muslims and Christians. Bulan therefore invites representatives of the monotheistic faiths to discuss their doctrines. Not only the testimony of the Jews, but that of the Muslims and Christians as well, convinces him that Judaism is the best and truest faith.

Ha-Levi uses this historical account as the setting for a dialogue between the pagan Khazar king and representatives of various faiths. However Ha-Levi adapts this story for his own purposes. Whereas in

Joseph's telling King Bulan is informed that his works are pleasing to God, Ha-Levi's King is told that although his intentions are pleasing to God, his behavior[7] is not. Ha-Levi's King thus sets out in search of the religion whose way of action is itself pleasing to God. A key theme in the *Kuzari* as a whole is the importance of action for drawing near to the Divine.

According to the letter of Joseph, the Khazars convert to Judaism before a religious debate takes place. Ha-Levi, in contrast, first engages his King in a dialogue with four interlocutors—a philosopher, a Christian, a Muslim, and a Jew. Only through this conversation does the King become convinced of the truth of Judaism and accept upon himself the yoke of the commandments, taking the Jewish scholar (the *Ḥaver*) as his tutor.[8] Ha-Levi's dialogue thus sets out not only to prove which of the various monotheistic religions is the most worthy, the focus of the debate according to Joseph's account, but also to demonstrate the necessity and validity of revealed religion per se. Against philosophy's claim to possess truth through pure reason, the *Kuzari* sets forth a vigorous argument for the necessity of divine revelation, an argument that becomes the foundation stone of his defense of the despised faith.

2. *Ha-Levi's Arabic Terminology for Religious Experience*

In the history of Jewish philosophy, Ha-Levi stands out as a particularist thinker; he stresses the uniqueness of the Hebrew language, the Jewish nation, and the land of Israel. Whereas Maimonides opens his code of Jewish law by appealing to the universal God of creation, the First Cause of all existence, Ha-Levi's *Ḥaver* grounds Judaism in the unique history of the Jewish people. His God is not the God of the philosophers, but the God of Abraham, Isaac, and Jacob.

Surprisingly, this most particularist of Jewish treatises is written not in Hebrew, but in Arabic—more precisely, Judaeo-Arabic, Arabic written in Hebrew letters. Ha-Levi composed the *Kuzari* for the Jewish intelligentsia of twelfth-century Spain, educated in both Hebrew and Arabic. Like the student for whom Maimonides wrote his *Guide of the Perplexed*, Ha-Levi's intended reader is the philosophically educated Jew, tempted by the spiritual cornucopia of the medieval Islamic world. The temptations of that milieu included not only philosophy, Karaism, Christianity, and mainstream Islam, but also Islamic mysticism. The Sufi movement had arisen prior to the eighth century in the East, but was transplanted throughout the medieval Islamic world and flowered in Muslim Spain in the tenth century.[9] Sufi mysticism was thus known to

Jews in Spain not only through the text, but through its living embodiment, practicing Sufis in their midst, offering the promise of real religious experience.[10]

Our most striking testimony that Jews were reading Sufi texts is Baḥya ibn Paqūda's celebrated spiritual manual *The Book of Guidance to the Duties of the Heart* (*Kitāb al-hidāya ʿilā farāʾiḍ al-qulūb*; *Torat ḥovot ha-levavot*). While there has been much debate about the precise Islamic sources of Baḥya's work, it is clearly modeled on Sufi devotional manuals. We see this vividly in the structure of the book itself: the reader is led through ten gates, each representing a quality to be embodied in the soul's journey toward love for God.[11]

Among possible Sufi influences on Baḥya are the writings of the early Sufi teacher al-Muḥāsibī, whose works were eagerly copied and studied in eleventh-century Spain.[12] In fact, in the Cairo Genizah we find Sufi texts copied in Hebrew letters for the benefit of Jewish readers. These include mystical poems of the Sufi martyr al-Ḥallāj, the final chapters of Avicenna's *Book of Directives and Remarks* (*Kitāb al-isharāt wa-l-tanbihāt*), which investigate the path of the Sufis; and the writings of al-Ghazzālī, especially his spiritual autobiography, *Deliverer from Error* (*al-Munqidh min-al-ḍalāl*), in which he recounts his embrace of the Sufi way. The intimacy of this Jewish-Sufi nexus is seen vividly in a late Genizah text that weaves together rabbinic and Sufi terminology for stages on the spiritual path.[13]

It is thus clear that Ha-Levi would have had access to Sufi texts and ideas. He responds to the Sufis only indirectly, however. Ha-Levi does not mention the Sufis by name, but makes extensive use of Sufi terminology, appropriating and refashioning it to show his Jewish audience that the spiritual fruits promised by Sufism exist foremost within the living Jewish tradition. Our study will show that images and vocabulary from Islamic mysticism form a prominent subtext to the *Kuzari*. The Sufi is a background figure, an absent speaker whose presence we feel throughout the dialogue.

Like Sufi-influenced Islamic thinkers such as Avicenna and al-Ghazzālī, Ha-Levi asserts that sensory experience, direct and irrefutable, is more reliable than logic. Ha-Levi also appropriates both Sufi and philosophical terms for union to describe the Jewish relationship with God. Formerly these terms depicted an individual, isolated, disembodied quest for union with the Divine. In Ha-Levi's usage they describe a concrete, mutual, covenantal relationship, both individual and communal. Using Sufi language of passionate love and service, Ha-Levi depicts Abraham as the ultimate knower, lover, and servant of God.

A thorough study of Ha-Levi within his Islamic cultural context will thus shed new light on the *Kuzari*. In these pages, we will explore a paradox: that this apparently inner-directed book, written exclusively for members of the Jewish community, was in fact in active dialogue with contemporary currents in the Islamic world. Ha-Levi wrote in a charged climate of debates among Jews and Muslims on the varieties of religious experience, and amidst the promises of competing schools of law, philosophy, and mysticism. These debates form a crucial backdrop to Ha-Levi's religious project: to show his contemporaries that the spiritual promises of medieval Islamic culture are truly fulfilled at home in the classical Jewish tradition.

My focus in this study will be the way Ha-Levi uses and transforms Arabic terminology to present his unique view of Jewish religious experience. Because he is writing in Arabic, Ha-Levi is forced to use certain Islamic religious terms. As a Judaeo-Arabic writer, however, he also has the choice to introduce Hebrew terms and phrases. It is thus fruitful to ask why he chooses the Arabic terms he does, to investigate the Islamic context of these terms, and to analyze the way he builds upon or subverts their contextual meaning. We will discover that Ha-Levi Judaizes his Islamic terms, transforming them in the process. Nevertheless their origins in Islamic mysticism and Neo-Platonism would have a powerful impact on his educated reader, as he undoubtedly intended.

Various groups in the Islamic sphere—philosophers, theologians, Sufi mystics, legal scholars—were each laying claim to a common set of Arabic terms for religious experience. In the following chapters, I will show how Ha-Levi adapts and transforms these Arabic terms in an original way to reflect his unique view of religious experience, which he conceptualizes through language of relationship, human striving, sense perception, prophecy, and love. We will explore several groups of terms, some joined conceptually, others clustered around Arabic roots. These groups of terms are:

1. The Language of Relationship: Connection and Arrival: *w-ṣ-l*: *ittiṣāl*, *waṣala*, *wuṣūl*
2. The Language of Human Striving: *qiyās*, *ijtihād*, *taqlīd*, *istidlāl*
3. The Language of Perception: *sh-h-d*: *mushāhada*, *shāhada*, *mashhād*; *dhawq*
4. The Language of Prophecy: *mushāhada*, *nubuwwa*, *ilhām*, *ta'yīd*, *waḥy*

5. The Language of Longing, Intimacy, and Love: *shawq*, *uns*, *ʿishq*.

Our discussion will not be purely terminological, however. As Harry Wolfson noted, concepts ride on the back of terms.[14] In the course of our analysis we will find that Ha-Levi tackles major issues in the history of Jewish philosophy, including the nature of prophecy and revelation, the purpose of divine commandments, the problem of suffering in Jewish history, the role of asceticism in religious life, and the value of rationalizing the faith. While focusing on Ha-Levi's conception of the nature of religious experience, our exploration of his terminology will shed light on these related issues in the history of philosophy as well.

3. *A Brief Review of Scholarship on the* Kuzari

In the modern period there have been two major approaches taken to Ha-Levi's *Kuzari*: a philological approach, which traces the Arabic and Hebrew sources of Ha-Levi's terms and doctrines and explores their philosophical significance; and a literary approach, which investigates the dialogue as a carefully constructed work of religious literature. This study will unite these interpretive pathways. An overview of scholarship on the *Kuzari* will therefore set the stage for our analysis.

The *Kuzari* was translated from Arabic into Hebrew soon after Ha-Levi's lifetime. With the awakening of interest in philosophy in Christian Europe in the late twelfth century, Jews living in Christian lands needed the Judaeo-Arabic classics translated into a language they could understand. Judah Ibn Tibbon translated the *Kuzari* in 1167; thereafter it was read, commented upon, and quoted in Hebrew translation, often without reference to the Islamic context in which it was born. Ha-Levi was embraced as a foil to Aristotelian rationalism, which prevailed in Jewish thought from the twelfth century on through the towering influence of Maimonides. The *Kuzari* asserted great influence throughout Jewish history. In periodic revivals, it was hailed for bringing out the distinctiveness and particularity of Judaism.[15]

The Islamic background of the *Kuzari* was rediscovered by the historicizing *Wissenschaft* movement in the nineteenth century. David Kaufmann first drew attention to the Islamic context of Ha-Levi's work and to significant parallels between Ha-Levi's ideas and those of Abū Ḥāmid al-Ghazzālī (1058–1111), who is well known for challenging the sovereignty of Aristotelian philosophy in the medieval Islamic world. His *Refutation of the Philosophers* (*Tahāfut al-falāsifa*) is a carefully structured exposition and critique of the thought of Ibn Sīnā (Avicenna) (980–1037), a leading Aristotelian. Like al-Ghazzālī, Ha-Levi challenges some of the main tenets of Aristotelian philosophy, particularly its claims to certainty in metaphysical matters.[16]

The parallels go further. Ghazzālī is also responsible for bringing Sufi mysticism into the mainstream of Islamic thought, particularly through his elegant synthesis, the *Revival of the Religious Sciences* (*Iḥyā' 'ulūm al-dīn*). Even in his popular spiritual autobiography *The Deliverer from Error* (*al-Munqidh min al-ḍalāl*), Ghazzālī is not reticent about his mystical convictions; he asserts unequivocally that prophets and mystics possess an inner eye which sees what human reason cannot. For Ghazzālī a key function of the intellect is to expose reason's limitations and to deliver human beings safely to the guidance of the prophets, who see by the light of Truth.[17]

Kaufmann noted that Ha-Levi, too, speaks of the inner eye of prophecy. While acknowledging the vital role of reason to a point, Ha-Levi shares with Ghazzālī a pietism which points out the limits of reason. In the opinion of many later scholars, beginning with David Neumark, Kaufmann overstated Ghazzālī's influence on Ha-Levi; he viewed the *Kuzari* as essentially a translation of Ghazzālī's ideas into a Jewish framework. Nevertheless Kaufmann's achievement in bringing the Islamic context of Ha-Levi's thought to the fore should not be underestimated.[18]

Ignaz Goldziher followed Kaufmann's lead in his 1905 essay on the Islamic context of a key term in the *Kuzari*—the *'amr ilāhī,* literally, the divine thing, order, or command. According to most recent scholars, Goldziher erred in his conclusion that Ha-Levi's *'amr ilāhī* was the first in a series of hypostasized emanations, akin to the role of the *Logos* in Neo-Platonic and Christian thought. I will argue that scholars continue to reify the *'amr ilāhī* far beyond what Ha-Levi intended. Nevertheless from a historical perspective, Goldziher played an important role in locating Ha-Levi squarely in the world of Islamic mysticism and Neo-Platonism.[19]

Julius Guttmann in 1922, and subsequently David Baneth in much greater detail in 1924, presented a more nuanced picture of Ha-Levi's relationship to Ghazzālī and to the Islamic intellectual world. Baneth is careful to point out significant differences between Ghazzālī and Ha-Levi. Ghazzālī embraces Sufi asceticism and withdrawal; his doctrine is universalistic, and stresses a quietistic, individual communion with the Divine. Ha-Levi, in contrast, is particularist, and celebrates the this-worldly, communal, and active character of Jewish life.[20]

Israel Efros in 1941 and Harry Wolfson in 1942 added important nuances to our understanding of the Islamic sources of Ha-Levi's thought. Efros noted that in place of the philosophic goal of union with the Active Intellect, Ha-Levi introduces a religious goal of union with the *ʾamr ilāhī*, which Efros took to be the divine essence itself. He commented that Ha-Levi describes the aim of religious life in precise terms drawn from the sphere of Islamic mysticism.

Efros observed, moreover, that in his use of Sufi terminology, Ha-Levi actually goes beyond Ghazzālī. While Ghazzālī rejects use of the term *wuṣūl* (union or arrival) as theologically inconsistent with the unique oneness of God, Ha-Levi makes liberal use of the term *ittiṣāl* (union, connection, or conjunction), which is etymologically related. Efros noted, too, that Ha-Levi rejects the intellectual way of knowing God through logical reasoning (*qiyās*), and extolls the way of direct experience, which he describes in Sufi terms as taste (*dhawq*), witness (*mushāhada*), and mystical vision (*baṣīra*, *baṣar*, *ʿiyān*). While my analysis will show that Ha-Levi's use of terminology is more fluid than Efros realized, his work was nevertheless an important groundwork for this study.[21]

Harry Wolfson in his 1942 essay "Hallevi and Maimonides on Prophecy" continued along this path, tracing the sources of Ha-Levi's Arabic terms and concepts to shed light on his theory of prophecy. Rejecting the conclusions of Goldziher, Wolfson maintained that the term *ʾamr ilāhī* is used in the *Kuzari* in at least nine different ways. In addition, he traced the history of several Jewish terms Ha-Levi uses in connection with prophecy (Holy Spirit, divine light, Glory of God, kingdom of God, and *Shekhinah*), finding key sources of Ha-Levi's thought in Arabic Neo-Platonism. In his *Repercussions of the Kalām in Jewish Philosophy*, Wolfson also traced the Islamic and Jewish roots of Ha-Levi's understanding of the word of God.[22]

Later in this century, scholars turned to Ha-Levi's literary craftsmanship. Leo Strauss, Isaak Heinemann, and Eliezer Schweid drew attention to the careful structure of the *Kuzari*. Schweid's incisive literary analysis shed light on the *Kuzari*'s philosophical artistry, while Heinemann also revealed the philosophical dimension to Ha-Levi's poetry.[23] Herbert Davidson continued the path of philosophical analysis. Like Efros and Wolfson, Davidson situated Ha-Levi's doctrines squarely in their Islamic philosophical context, analyzing in masterful detail Ha-Levi's understanding of the Active Intellect, causality, and the complex concept of the *ʾamr ilāhī*, which Davidson identified with direct divine causality.[24]

In 1980 Pines published his groundbreaking article, which uncovered roots of Ha-Levi's thought and key terms in a series of Ismāʿīlī texts. In these texts, Pines found the sources of the term *ʾamr ilāhī* and of the doctrine of the *ṣafwa*, a chosen elite, whose prophethood is conferred by the divine *ʾamr*. Pines also suggested a historical development to Ha-Levi's thought. Earlier scholars were already aware that Book Five, section 12 of the *Kuzari* contained an early treatise of Avicenna; Pines postulated that the work of Avicenna became known to Ha-Levi between the time he composed Book One and Book Five. He conjectured that Ha-Levi was very impressed with the work of Avicenna, and may have tried to rework his own ideas and terminology in the light of Avicenna's system.[25]

The publication of the critical Baneth-Ben Shammai edition of the *Kuzari* in 1977 was itself a major breakthrough in scholarship, as was the discovery and analysis of autographs and letters of Ha-Levi from the Cairo Genizah. Goitein and Baneth used this significant material to piece together a biography of Ha-Levi and a sketch of the genesis of the *Kuzari*, tracing the book's origins to an exchange with a Karaite from Christian Spain.[26]

Yochanan Silman arrived at a somewhat different model of the genesis of the *Kuzari*. Based on the historical evidence of the Genizah documents, Silman agreed with Goitein and Schweid that Book Three was composed prior to the rest of the work. However Silman took this chronological framework one step further, using it to speculate on the development of Ha-Levi's thought. Silman suggested that Ha-Levi's ideas developed dialectically, responding to tensions inherent in each stage of their evolution. While my analysis diverges from that of Silman,[27] I will call attention to some of his interesting exegetical points.

Daniel Lasker not only traced the origins of the *Kuzari* to a conversation with Karaites, but also brought to light the major influence of Karaism on Ha-Levi's thought. Lasker highlighted Ha-Levi's use of legal terminology from the Islamic and Karaite spheres, including the terms *qiyās*, *ijtihād*, and *taqlīd*. His work has been groundbreaking and pivotal for my study.[28]

4. *The Literary-Philological Approach of This Study*

The last several decades have thus produced significant breakthroughs in our understanding of the *Kuzari* in its cultural context. However, while we have been shown the literary genius of the *Kuzari*, and have learned the sources of specific terms and doctrines, these two paths of investigation have not been brought together.

It is crucial that these two approaches converge, as each method taken on its own is insufficient for study of the *Kuzari*. Ha-Levi, even in his philosophical writing, is ultimately a poet; he is both deeply learned and genuinely creative. Because he is well versed in philosophical sources, one must be aware of the meanings of the terms he uses in their historical setting. A literary analysis alone can misrepresent the sense of a passage, if one is ignorant of the technical meaning of Ha-Levi's terminology; one must be aware of what these terms would connote to Ha-Levi's learned audience.

However, philology alone is insufficient; one cannot understand the words of a poet by consulting a dictionary. As a philosophical poet, Ha-Levi uses words in radically new ways. To understand the genius of the *Kuzari*, one must be sensitive to Ha-Levi's creative transformation of vocabulary and the ways his terms function in their literary context.

This study will therefore engage in a literary-philological approach, a global analysis of Ha-Levi's Arabic terminology in its literary setting. My analysis will show that Ha-Levi not only creatively reshapes Islamic terms, but constructs his argument through sophisticated rhetorical strategies, which daringly cross boundaries between particular terms and disciplines. The two methodological paths will thus illumine one another. Philology is incomplete without literary analysis; literary analysis is incomplete without philology. Philological analysis will bring to light Ha-Levi's creative use of terminology; awareness of his reinvention of terminology will reveal the literary twists that shape his argument.

5. *The Argument of the* Kuzari

The *Kuzari* consists of five Books. Book One describes a dialogue between a pagan king and a philosopher, a Christian, a Muslim, and a Jew. The King is on a spiritual quest for the correct way to serve God. Finding the answers of the philosopher, Christian, and Muslim inadequate, he engages in an extensive dialogue with the Jew, who bases the claims of Judaism not on universal philosophical grounds, but on Jewish religious experience and the events of Jewish history. The King is won over early in the debate; in Book Two he and his people convert to Judaism and he takes the Jewish sage (the *Ḥaver*) as his tutor. The *Ḥaver* teaches him the true meaning of divine names and attributes, the uniqueness of the Hebrew language and the centrality of the land of Israel.

In Book Three, the *Ḥaver* presents the life of the ideal Jew in distinctly anti-ascetic terms. He then launches a polemic against the Karaites, defending rabbinic tradition as the foundation of Jewish life. Book Four explores the philosophical significance of the divine names and the centrality of prophecy and religious experience. Finally, in Book Five, the *Ḥaver* explains and critiques Aristotelian philosophy and systematic theology (*kalām*). He closes by presenting his own views, culminating in his decision to leave Khazaria for the land of Israel.

Why does Ha-Levi choose the conversion story of the Khazar king as a setting for his defense of Judaism? As Leo Strauss and Eliezer Schweid have pointed out, the pagan king is a disinterested party, an adherent of none of the three monotheistic faiths. In fact, the King appears somewhat antagonistic to the Jewish nation. What greater testimony could be given to the truth of the Jewish faith than this: that such a critic chooses to join the Jewish people, knowing that his status as a convert will never equal that of someone born Jewish.

Ha-Levi appoints as religion's judge not the learned philosopher, but the pious person of common sense. He thus dethrones philosophy from its self-proclaimed position as universal arbiter of truth. The King's encounter with the philosopher sensitizes and sharpens his perspective, but it is ultimately the common sense of the Jewish sage that wins his allegiance.[29]

Leo Strauss emphasized the disjunction between Ha-Levi as author and his chief spokesperson, the *Ḥaver*. In the dialogue's opening remarks, the narrator asserts that he finds some of the scholar's arguments convincing. This suggests to Strauss that some of the *Ḥaver*'s arguments are not convincing to Ha-Levi; the author and the *Ḥaver* cannot simply be conflated. In fact, Strauss took this dis-identification as the key to the dialogue. In Strauss's view, the law of reason is the ultimate bearer of truth, but this is not a truth to which the person of faith can adhere. For this reason, the philosopher and the *Ḥaver* never speak to one another directly; the *Ḥaver* would be no match for the philosopher. However, while the *Ḥaver*'s arguments cannot be accepted by a true philosopher, they can be accepted by the genuine person of faith. Strauss portrayed Ha-Levi as valiantly defending religion—necessary to the moral order of society—against the more powerful and dangerous truth of philosophy, which must be hidden from the masses.[30]

I will certainly not follow Strauss's esoteric reading to this degree. Nevertheless, the distinction between Ha-Levi and the *Ḥaver* is instructive. Ha-Levi's views unfold dialectically through interchange between his characters; we cannot identify Ha-Levi's position with that of one speaker in the dialogue. The *Ḥaver* is not simply the mouthpiece for Ha-Levi; the *Kuzari*'s craftsmanship is more subtle and complex.

Ha-Levi shows the King gradually convinced by the arguments of the *Ḥaver*. As in the dialogues of Plato, what emerges is not so much objective truth, as the awakening of understanding on the part of a unique human being.[31] Ha-Levi's truth thus issues from the dialogue as a whole, not simply from the mouth of the *Haver*. In this study, therefore, I will identify the views of the *Ḥaver* as such, and will attribute to Ha-Levi the perspective that emerges from the dialogue as a complete work. This will include nuances of terminology, rhetorical strategies, and the argument as it unfolds through discussion between characters.

A few words should also be devoted at this point to Silman's developmental approach. Perhaps Silman's most interesting thesis is that in his earlier thought, Ha-Levi had not yet come to make a radical distinction between the two names of God: *Elohim*, representing the universal God known by the human intellect, and the Tetragrammaton, representing the God known through prophetic experience.

This thesis is central to Silman's developmental model. Silman argues that whereas in his early thought Ha-Levi conceives of God as essentially intellect, and thus knowable by human beings, in his late thought he conceives of God as radically transcendent and unknowable, reached only by means of intermediaries. However, III:17 (which he ascribes to the early period) and IV:3 (which he sees as the late Ha-Levi) describe the paradox of God's transcendence and immanence in almost identical language.[32]

When discussing III:17, Silman asserts that Ha-Levi's juxtaposition of the two aspects of God—transcendence and immanence—signifies that he sees them as complementary. When discussing IV:3, however, he suggests that the juxtaposition points to a radical disjunction between the transcendent God and the God known in experience. I would argue that Ha-Levi is consistent: in both passages, he describes in nearly identical language the paradox of God's transcendence and yet absolute nearness to humanity.[33] Therefore there is no reason to ascribe the two passages to different periods, or to deduce from them an evolution in his thought.[34]

6. *The Argument of the* Kuzari: *Part Two*

Before turning to my analysis, a more complete summary of the argument of the *Kuzari* may be in order. As historians of ideas, we often read works of medieval philosophy in parts, thereby losing a sense of the whole. Readers new to the *Kuzari* may find the following summary of the dialogue particularly useful, while readers familiar with the *Kuzari* may wish to proceed directly to Part One.[35]

Book One

Book One opens with a brief account by an anonymous narrator, who explains how the book came to be. The narrator explains that he was asked to bring forth arguments defending Judaism against the attacks of philosophers, sectarians (Karaites) and members of other religions. This request brought to mind the story of the king of the Khazars who converted to Judaism under the tutelage of a Jewish scholar (*Ḥaver*). Finding many of the arguments of the *Ḥaver* convincing and in harmony with his own views, the narrator decided to write them down, presumably as persuasive arguments in defense of the despised religion. The author then winks at his audience, acknowledging an element of fiction in both the frame story and his own remarks, noting that "the wise will understand."[36]

At this point, the narrator's voice for the most part disappears, and we are left with the interlocutors. Told by an angel in his dream that his intentions are pleasing to God but not his way of action, the King first turns to a philosopher, a character not appearing in the historical records, but invented by Ha-Levi. The philosopher offers a standard medieval philosophical account of the origins of the universe: he describes a chain of strictly determined cause and effect, which emanates eternally from a First Cause.

The First Cause is not a personal Creator, does not know individuals and cannot hear their prayers. The goal of human life is to purify oneself in order to become like the Active Intellect, a spiritual emanation from the First Cause which governs our sublunar world. As a means to that goal, one may follow any one of the rational religions, or invent a religion of one's own (I:1).

The King rejects this account, for the philosopher does not discriminate between various modes of action, while a specific way of serving God is precisely what he seeks. He is equally dissatisfied with the accounts of the Christian and Muslim, which as an outsider he finds inaccessible. However, he notices that both Christianity and Islam are founded on the accounts of the children of Israel. He therefore resolves to speak to a Jew, although he had once dismissed the Jews as downtrodden and of unpleasant disposition (I:2–10, 12).

The Jew does not begin his account with the universal God of creation as did the philosopher, Christian, and Muslim. Rather, he begins with the God of history, who led the Israelites out of Egypt with signs and wonders, who revealed the law through Moses, and sent subsequent prophets to confirm that law. The *Ḥaver* observes that in addressing the people of Israel, God did not say, "I am the Creator of the world and your Creator," but rather, "I am the God whom you worship, who brought you out of the land of Egypt."[37] The *Ḥaver* likewise speaks, as does all of Israel, not on the basis of theoretical reason, but of personal experience and uninterrupted tradition (I:11–25).

When the King protests that this faith seems exclusive to the people of Israel, the *Ḥaver* does not disagree, arguing that Jews are the select (*ṣafwa*) of humankind.[38] He alludes to a natural hierarchy, a chain consisting of minerals, plants, animals, humans, and then prophets, who exist above ordinary human beings as a separate, angelic species (I:26–47). The prophets passed down a true tradition regarding creation and the chronology of the world. The Greeks, in contrast, while they have an impressive heritage of philosophy, are forced to rely on their intellects precisely because they lack divine tradition (I:49–65). Had Aristotle possessed a true tradition that taught the creation of the world, he would have used his logical arguments to document creation, rather than to prove that the world is eternal.

According to the *Ḥaver*, there is decisive proof neither for creation nor for an eternal world order. The Torah does not contradict anything patently clear or decisively proven by reason. However, the words of the prophets are more reliable than the conclusions derived by reason alone. Given that the Torah teaches creation, the arguments for creation are to be believed over those for eternity. Historical experience and prophetic tradition prevail over mere human logic (I:65–67).

Whereas philosophy ascribes the wisdom of creation to nature, the Torah denies that nature is inherently intelligent. Rather, nature bears the marks of its wise Creator, who alone can teach humankind the means to receive traces of the Divine (I:69–79). Human beings who try to control the Divine are like an ignorant person who dispenses drugs from a pharmacy without knowledge of medicine. This person is more likely to harm than to heal, for the healing properties lie not within the jars of medicine but in the wisdom of the physician who prepared them. Just so, we can only reach God through practicing the regimen of commandments prescribed by God.

Pagans forgot the true physician and guide, following instead intermediate causes such as astrological constellations, which left them wandering from god to god and from law to law (I:79). In contrast, the true religion did not arise gradually, but all at once. Through the plagues in Egypt, God demonstrated that the Divine acts directly in nature, with no need for intermediate causes or astrological help (I:80–83).

However, despite all the miracles they saw, the Israelites continued to doubt whether God had in fact spoken to Moses. Perhaps, they reasoned, the law was merely a human invention. Perhaps Moses was inspired in a vision or a dream; perhaps the Torah was the creation of his human intellect, only later confirmed by divine support. In order to refute such philosophical theories of prophecy, God orchestrated the event at Mount Sinai; only direct experience of revelation could remove all doubt from their minds. Without being able to explain how it was possible, all who were present at Sinai knew the revelation came directly from the Creator, with no intermediary (I:87–91).

How then could the nation descend so swiftly to the sin of the golden calf? Worship of idols was widespread at the time; idolatry was the universal language of religion. Even a philosopher setting out to prove the unity and sovereignty of God would point to an image, which he would argue was connected to a divine presence (an *ʾamr ilāhī*). Thus did the Israelites point to the pillar of cloud and fire that accompanied them in the wilderness, and to the cloud which spoke with Moses in the tent of meeting. The people's goal in making the golden calf was to have an object to which they could point when relating the wonders of God. Their sin consisted not in building an image per se, but in attributing an *ʾamr ilāhī* to something they chose and created themselves, without the guidance of God (I:97). This, says the King, confirms the angel's message in his dream: one can only reach the Divine (*ʾamr ilāhī*) through a command of God, an *ʾamr ilāhī* (I:98).

The *Ḥaver* agrees, explaining that the law articulates precisely how one should approach the Divine, including detailed laws of prayer, sacrifice, and ritual purity (I:99). The King, however, protests the exclusivity of such a law, given in the Hebrew tongue to one particular people. Would it not have been better if all humankind had been guided in the right path? (I:102). To this plea, the *Ḥaver* responds by reiterating his vision of sacred history: the spirit of divine prophecy rested upon one individual per generation, until the twelve sons of Jacob, each of whom either achieved the degree of prophecy or "became spiritual" through contact with prophets (I:103). While the King presumes that one who had achieved such a level would surely long for death, the *Ḥaver* assures him that the Torah promises connection with God in this very life. One who tastes immortality in this world does not need to fasten hopes on the world to come (I:108–9).

However, the King challenges this point, arguing that if we judge a person's chances for the afterlife by their closeness to God during this life, we should judge the status of the Jews in the next world by their station in this world. The King here articulates the standard Christian argument from history, which deduces the falseness of Judaism from the Jews' lowly station. The *Ḥaver* counters that Christians and Muslims cannot legitimately level this argument against the Jews, as both Christianity and Islam glorify humility and lowliness (I:112–13). However, he agrees with the King in one respect: Jews should take on their degradation and exile in a spirit of submission to God's will. If they do so, they will hasten the arrival of the Messiah (I:115).

Book Two

At the opening of Book Two, the King and his people convert to Judaism and the King takes the *Ḥaver* as his tutor.[39] He begins with a lesson on God's names and attributes. The *Ḥaver* explains that all of God's names are adjectives describing the way creatures are affected by God's actions. While God appears merciful and compassionate at some times, jealous and vengeful at others, God is simply a just judge, who does not actually change from one attribute to another.

The *Ḥaver* classifies divine attributes as attributes of action, attributes of relation, and attributes of negation.[40] Attributes of action describe God through actions proceeding from him: God makes poor and makes rich, acts mercifully or with strict judgment. Attributes of relation describe God in language through which humans exalt the Creator: blessed, praised, glorified, holy, exalted, and extolled. Negative attributes—such as living, only, first, and last—negate their contraries, without being established in their ordinary sense. For example, we call God "living" in order to deny that God is inanimate or dead; in truth, however, God is beyond life and death, which apply only to material bodies (II:2). God's will made the heavens revolve continually; the same will adapted the air to the sound of the divine word in the giving of the ten commandments, fashioned the two tablets out of stone, and engraved the writing on the tablets. The spiritual forms called God's Glory—those forms that are visible to the prophets—are produced from an ethereal, created substance known as Holy Spirit. Like material bodies particularly affected by sunlight, the land of Israel is especially benefited by the Glory of God, which is like a ray of divine light (II:4–8).

The *Ḥaver* thus reaffirms that God acts directly in nature, with no need for intermediary causes (II:6), and explains how the light of the Divine can manifest as Glory or *Shekhinah*, and in one land more than another (II:6–24). From discussion of the land and the Temple, the *Ḥaver* turns to the sacrificial order (II:25–28). Since its destruction, the Jews have missed the heart of the nation, the Temple; however, they still connect with God through commandments such as circumcision and Sabbath (II:29–34). Even today, Israel is among the nations like the heart amidst the organs of the body. It is the organ that is most sensitive, reflecting the sickness and health of the whole (II:36–44).

The King is surprised, given Israel's spiritual sensitivity, that there are not hermits and ascetics among the nation. The *Ḥaver* explains that attitudes such as humility and submission alone do not draw one near to God; divinely commanded actions are necessary. Love and fear of God are aspects of the rational law, which precedes the divine law in character and in time. However, it is ultimately the divine law which connects the nation with the *ʾamr ilāhī*. This divine law does not demand asceticism but rather moderation, giving each faculty of the human being its due. God is approached equally through awe, love, and joy (II:45–50). The chapter concludes with an excursis on the superiority of the Hebrew language (II:67–81).

Book Three

As Book Three opens, the *Ḥaver* reiterates his anti-ascetic stance: the pious person[41] among Israel is not someone who detaches himself from society, but one who disciplines his life in this world so as to merit life in the world to come. Those who attempt asceticism today are in danger of self-delusion and of distancing themselves from—rather than drawing closer to—the Divine (III:1). The good person is obeyed by his or her senses as a prince is obeyed by his people. Pious Jews are aided in self-discipline and purification by the rhythm of *mitsvot*: three daily times of prayer, weekly Sabbaths, and the yearly cycle of festivals (III:5). The *Ḥaver* explains in detail the meaning of the Jewish liturgy, including the advantage of communal prayer over individual worship (III:11–19). This completes the argument begun in Book Two that Jewish communal life provides a taste of the world to come, and thus requires no ascetic isolation or monasticism (III:20–22).

The second half of Book Three offers a detailed response to the Karaite critique, building on the anti-Karaite polemics of Saʿadya Gaon. The *Ḥaver* argues that there are two crucial ingredients for drawing near to God: divine command and true tradition. Legal dialectics, for which the Karaites are known, are no substitute for true tradition, which the rabbis possess. The tradition of the rabbis is grounded in divine inspiration; rabbinic authority traces back to the Sanhedrin, which was graced with the presence of the *Shekhinah* (III:22–41). Moreover the rabbis maintain necessary safeguards to preserve the unity and integrity of divine law (III:42–53)

Divinely commanded actions are ultimately like works of nature: they are not under our control, we do not understand how they work, and yet they miraculously bring us into contact with the Divine. We can only draw near to God through actions commanded by God. Knowledge of these commands comes through prophecy, not through human reason. Our link to prophecy, and thus to divine commandment, is rabbinic tradition (III:53). The *Ḥaver* affirms and traces the chain of tradition from the prophets of the First and Second Temple to the rabbis of the Mishnah and Talmud (III:54–67). He defends rabbinic interpretation of Scripture and rabbinic *aggadot*, conceding that the rabbis may have possessed canons of interpretation that we have lost (III:68–73).

Book Four

While Book Three focuses on law and interpretation, Book Four turns to prophecy and religious experience. The book opens with an analysis of the names for God in the Torah. The *Ḥaver* observes that *Elohim* functions as a common noun—a generic term for God, which can even take a definite article—whereas the Tetragrammaton functions as a proper noun, the personal name of the God of Israel. *Elohim* is the governor of the world whose existence we deduce through logical argument; the Lord is the God human beings know through prophetic experience (IV:1–3).

The prophets are endowed with an inner eye; through this eye, they witness visions which teach profound truths about the Creator. Whereas Greek philosophy doubts whatever it has not encountered, prophets cannot doubt what they have witnessed directly through their inner eye. Living in many different generations, the prophets testify to one another about the truths they see, forming a community of corroborating witnesses (IV:3). Prophetic vision can see in an instant what volumes of philosophy cannot grasp. The prophetic experience gives birth to love and awe; these are natural responses to standing in the presence of God. Moses brought the people to Mount Sinai to see the light that he had seen; the hours and direction of prayer were instituted so people could continue to behold this divine light (IV:4–11).

Once one has known the Lord through direct witness and taste, one becomes a servant of God, passionately in love with the divine beloved, ready to die for God's sake, rather than lose the sweetness of God's presence. Abraham was such a lover of God; once he has tasted God's presence, he scoffs at the indirect way of reason, by which he had once sought to prove God's existence. The Lord is called the God of Israel because Israel is the people of this seeing, and the land of Israel provides the climate that makes seeing God possible. Common people sense that the rabbis possess an authentic teaching not found in the words of the philosophers, however sophisticated (IV:15–17). The divine law in fact transforms one who practices it. Just as a seed transforms the soil in which it is planted, so will Israel transform the nations among whom she is dispersed, which is God's wise design (IV:23).

Book Four concludes with a detailed interpretation of *Sefer Yetsirah*, a book of numerical speculation, taken to demonstrate the achievements of the Jewish people in natural science (IV:25–31).

Book Five

In Book Five, the *Ḥaver* agrees after protest to provide a detailed explanation of the principles of the *kalām*. He begins, however, by explaining principles of cosmology, metaphysics, and psychology according to the philosophers;[42] his discourse on psychology in V:12 is in fact a treatise of Avicenna's. However, once he has thoroughly impressed the King with this philosophical explanation, the *Ḥaver* launches into a trenchant critique of the philosophical world view, a critique that has much in common with Ghazzālī's *Incoherence of the Philosophers*. The *Ḥaver* rejects the philosophers' notion of four constitutive elements of nature as a theoretical construct with no empirical proof. He points out flaws in the suggestion that philosophical learning brings union with the Active Intellect and immortality of the soul. If this is the case, he asks, how do we account for people who lose their learning; do they have two different souls? Why do various philosophers not conceive their ideas simultaneously, hold identical views, or know what one another is thinking? In fact, what little consensus exists among philosophers is not due to theoretical agreement, as in mathematics and the demonstrative sciences, but because individuals belong to the same philosophical school (V:14).

As for *kalām*, he insists it is dangerous. It cannot endow a soul with the simple faith that comes naturally, like a poetic gift, and can in fact raise doubts where none existed before (V:16). Nevertheless, he outlines a system of *kalām* metaphysics, which proves the creation of the world in time, and the eternal, non-corporeal nature of the Creator. *Kalām* metaphysics portrays God as living, omniscient, and possessed of an eternal will (V:18).

Finally, the *Ḥaver* outlines his own beliefs. He affirms both human free will and active divine providence, asserting that events work through divine, natural, and accidental causes. God creates all with wisdom, endowing every substance with its perfect form. However, intermediary causes are also necessary to bring beings to their perfect formation. The *Ḥaver* insists on the existence of a natural hierarchy consisting of minerals, plants, animals, and humans, who are nearest to the First Cause, which—somewhat surprisingly—he describes as reason itself. The divine law brings one even closer to reason, and practice of the commandments leads one to an angelic degree, the degree of prophetic inspiration (V:20).

The *Ḥaver* thus suggests an interesting dialectic between freedom and providence. Human beings have freedom to choose their actions; the possibility of repentance is ever present, and reproof is therefore effective. From another point of view, however, everything can be traced back to the First Cause, either directly or indirectly. The highest we can reach is to perceive supernatural causes in natural events; since we cannot grasp the nature of the Divine itself, we dwell on God's works. On a national level, the divine will guides Jewish history. Although providence was more evident when the *Shekhinah* dwelt among them, divine guidance continues and is manifest for those with eyes to see (V:20–21).

The *Ḥaver* closes by expressing his intention to set out for the land of Israel. Although the visible *Shekhinah* has departed, he affirms that the invisible *Shekhinah* is present with every Israelite of pure heart, and that the land of Israel is pervaded by the Divine Presence. The divine law comes to full fruition in the land. The *Ḥaver* affirms he seeks only the freedom to serve God; service of God is true freedom, humility before God is true honor (V:25).

He stresses, however, that intention on its own is not enough; intention must be united with action. Only when it is impossible to act is one rewarded for intention alone. The holy land stands as a reminder and stimulus to the love of God; when all of Israel yearn passionately for Jerusalem's restoration, only then will she be rebuilt (III:27). In face of such a plea, the King concedes it would be wrong to hinder the *Ḥaver* from his journey, and bids him well (III:28). This brings us full circle, for the King was admonished in his dream to seek the way of action pleasing to God. The implication is that this way of action is ultimately fulfilled in the land of Israel.

Our summary concluded, let us turn to analysis of the specific terms Ha-Levi uses for religious experience, and the way these terms shape his argument on behalf of the Jewish faith.

PART 1

The Language of Relationship

Religious Experience as Connection or Union (Ittiṣāl) *and Arrival* (Wuṣūl)

As we have noted, various rival groups in the medieval Islamic world—philosophers, theologians, Sufi mystics, legal scholars—were each laying claim to common Arabic terms. Ha-Levi adapts and transforms these Arabic terms in an original way to reflect his distinct perspective on religious experience.

One way Ha-Levi speaks of the religious path or goal is in relational terms—as union, communion, contact, connection, or conjunction (*ittiṣāl*); as well as attaining, arriving at, or reaching the Divine (*wuṣūl*). Both terms stem from the Arabic root *waṣala. Waṣala* means to connect, join, unite, combine, or link; and also to arrive at or reach, perhaps through a process of connection. These terms were the subject of great controversy in twelfth-century Muslim Spain. Because they describe the very goal and purpose of religious life, these key terms reach to the heart of each group's identity: philosophers, mystics, and mainstream legal scholars each felt the need to define a position on the possibility of *ittiṣāl*.[1]

The terms *ittiṣāl* and *wuṣūl* are in fact the focus of a central debate in the Middle Ages: in what sense is it possible for human beings to achieve union with the Divine, and how does one attain such union?[2] While some groups assert *ittiṣāl* is possible and they map out a detailed program for its attainment, others object strongly to this concept. Ha-Levi plays with the terms *ittiṣāl* and *wuṣūl* in a way that reframes the problem and offers a unique resolution.

Ittiṣāl is central to the *Kuzari* from the very outset; the term is featured in the King's opening encounters with his three interlocutors. We will thus begin by examining Sufi and philosophical senses of *ittiṣāl* and their role in the opening dialogue, the dialogue's use of Shīʿite terminology, and the place of *ittiṣāl* in the *Ḥaver*'s chronicle of Jewish history. We will see that the *Ḥaver*'s narrative includes an account of *ittiṣāl* among founding figures, various levels of *ittiṣāl* (individual and communal, elite and non-elite) and the covenantal dimension of *ittiṣāl*.

We will then consider the importance of *mitsvot* and Jewish communal life for Ha-Levi's concept of *ittiṣāl*, and examine the relationship between *ittiṣāl*, immortality, and the afterlife in Ha-Levi's thought. The final section will explore several dimensions of Ha-Levi's argument: the *Ḥaver*'s response to Christian and Muslim critiques of Judaism, his defense of Biblical asceticism despite Ha-Levi's anti-ascetic religious ideal, and his unique interpretation of Jewish national suffering.

A. Sufi and Philosophical Terminology: Use of the Term *Ittiṣāl* in the Opening Dialogue

We have noted that the Islamic mystical movement known as Sufism (*tasawwuf*) flowered in Muslim Spain from the tenth century on. Sufis and philosophers in medieval Spain each described a form of union with the divine realm which they called *ittiṣāl*. For Sufis, the goal of spiritual life was clear: union with God. For scholars like the philosopher depicted in I:1 of the *Kuzari*, the more modest goal of the human quest was union with the Active Intellect, the tenth celestial intelligence emanated from the Divine, which governs the sublunar world and brings human thought from potentiality to actuality.[3]

The philosopher in I:1 speaks of this achievement as *ittiṣāl ittiḥād*, a conjunction of union. He advises the King to liken himself to the Active Intellect, and to pursue the virtues of contentment, quietism, and humility;[4] he also suggests that the philosophic path leads to prophecy. While his speech is thoroughly in keeping with the medieval philosophical quest, the vocabulary and images he uses have Sufi overtones. The Sufi is therefore a background figure in the dialogue, the missing interlocutor whose language and presence we feel throughout.

With respect to the individual who has achieved perfection (the Perfect One),[5] the philosopher asserts that

> there conjoins with him [*yattaṣilu bi-hi*] from the divine nature a light which is called the Active Intellect. His passive intellect conjoins with it [*yattaṣilu bi-hi*] [in] a conjunction of union [*ittiṣāl ittiḥād*], to the point where the individual regards himself as that Active Intellect, with no distinction between them. (I:1: 4)

The phrase *ittiṣāl ittiḥād* in fact represents two ways in which union with the Divine had been depicted in Sufi thought: as *ittiṣāl*—contact, communion, or union—and as *ittiḥād*, an identification of natures. In the Sufi model, the seeker divests himself more and more of his own human attributes, gradually taking on the qualities of the divine beloved until he or she becomes that beloved, perceiving an identity or unification (*ittiḥād*) of the two natures. Some Sufis argued that such talk was heresy, for it implies there are two independent entities that could be united, an affront to the absolute unity (*tawḥīd*) of the one divine Reality.[6] Here we see the philosopher using the phrase *ittiṣāl ittiḥād* to suggest a less embracing union. The passive human intellect unites not with God, but with the Active Intellect, thereby becoming a fully actualized intelligence, knowing all that it is possible for a human mind to know.[7]

We see that while using the same terms, philosophers and Sufis were living in radically different worlds. There were bridges between these worlds however. There was a common striving for union which united intellectuals in the Islamic world, and much common ground existed despite clear differences.[8] In particular, the experiential dimension of Neo-Platonic philosophy created a bridge between philosophy and Sufism. Plotinus, the third-century father of Neo-Platonism, had described divine emanation as an initial "downward" path, whereby the unknowable One emanates through Mind, Soul, and Nature into this world; this is the philosophical dimension to his thought. However, he also prescribed an upward, religious path by which a soul yearning for return to the One could strive to attain reunion.[9]

Plotinus described his own experience of mystical oneness in a passage frequently quoted by medieval philosophers of Judaism and Islam. For Plotinus, union was not simply intellectual, but experiential and ecstatic:

> Often I have woken up out of the body to my self and have entered into myself, going out from all other things; I have seen a beauty wonderfully great and felt assurance that then most of all I belonged to the better part; I have actually lived the best life and come to identify with the divine; and set firm in it I have come to that supreme actuality, setting myself above all else in the realm of Intellect. Then after that rest in the divine, when I have come down from Intellect to discursive reasoning, I am puzzled how I ever came down, and how my soul has come to be in the body when it is what it has shown itself to be by itself, even when it is in the body.[10]

Plotinus's account of his own experience provided a bridge between a purely cognitive approach to *ittiṣāl* and the experiential approach of the Sufis. It is true that this passage was known to medieval Islamic and Jewish philosophers in a slightly different form: the Arabic version was found in an apocryphal work known as the *Theology of Aristotle*. This translation softened Plotinus's language of union by speaking of his being "attached" to the divine world rather than united with it. Nevertheless, the experiential nature of Plotinus's journey remains clear:

> Sometimes, I was as it were alone with my soul: I divested myself of my body, put it aside, and was as it were a simple substance without a body. Then I entered into my essence by returning into it free from all things. I was knowledge, knowing, and known at the same time. I saw in my essence so much of beauty, loveliness, and splendor that I remained astonished and confused, and I knew that I was a part of the exalted, splendid, divine upper world, and that I was endowed with an active life. When this became clear to myself, I rose in my essence from this world to the divine world, and I was as it were placed there and attached [*muta'alliq*] to it. I was above the whole intelligible world, and saw myself as if I stood in that exalted divine position, and beheld there such light and splendor as tongues are unable to describe and ears are impotent to hear.[11]

Elsewhere, moreover, the *Theology* translates Plotinus using the term *ittiṣāl*, as in the following passage: "When the soul leaves this world and enters the higher world . . . it unites with (Intellect) without its essence perishing. . . . It is both thinker and thought[12] . . . because of the intensity of its conjunction (*ittiṣāl*) with Intellect"; soul and Intellect are then "one thing, and two."[13] Avicenna and other medieval philosophers thus evoke both sides of Plotinus when they describe the goal of religious life as *ittiṣāl*, a union that is both cognitive and ecstatic.[14]

Avicenna's language of union cannot be wholly ascribed to Neo-Platonic philosophy, however. He and other medieval thinkers were also seeking to make sense of claims to religious experience by Sufis in their midst. Avicenna devotes a section of his *Book of Directives and Remarks* (*Kitāb al-ishārāt wa-l-tanbīhāt*) to a phenomenological description of the path of the Sufis. In it, he describes *ittiṣāl* as one stage of contact or uniting on the way to final arrival or union (*wuṣūl*) with the Divine.[15] The fact that there was already an ecstatic component to the philosophical model of *ittiṣāl*, and that the term was current in medieval Neo-Platonic texts, solidified the bridge to Sufi thought. The language of *ittiṣāl* was common to the worlds of Sufism and philosophy, so much so that it is not entirely clear in which sphere the term originated.

The twelfth-century theologian al-Ghazzālī, too, devotes attention to the path of the Sufis and to their language of union (*wuṣūl*). An orthodox thinker well versed in philosophy, Ghazzālī was a crucial link between worlds, one who found in Neo-Platonic metaphysics language to express the unitive nature of Sufi *ittiṣāl*.[16] Ghazzālī varies in his degree of comfort with the terminology of union. He is critical of such language in his well-known spiritual autobiography, in which he recounts his conversion to the Sufi way. Ghazzālī asserts that the only path to true knowledge of God is the path of the Sufi, and he describes with conviction the disciple's ascent on the way (*ṭarīqa*). However, of the final stage on the path, he warns: "The matter comes ultimately to a closeness to God which one group almost conceives of as indwelling [*ḥulūl*], and another as union [*ittiḥād*] and another as arrival [*wuṣūl*], but all this is wrong."[17]

In the *Niche for Lights*, however, Ghazzālī describes in lyrical Sufi language the state of those who attain to the Divine (*al-waṣilūna*). They are annihilated in God; "nothing remains any more save the One, the Real." Nevertheless, Ghazzālī is careful to distinguish between consciousness of God's absolute Unity (*tawḥīd*)—the recognition that there is no real Being other than God—and certain Sufis' claims to *identity* with God (*ittiḥād*), a claim he rejects. Ghazzālī is aware of both the mystical possibilities of the language of union and its dangers, and expresses both dimensions in his writings.[18]

As we have seen, Baḥya ibn Paqūda, author of the eleventh-century classic *Duties of the Heart*, is also a maker of bridges; Baḥya unites the worlds of the Sufi, the philosopher, and the Jew. He structures his work exactly like a Sufi manual, with various gates teaching Sufi ideals such as absolute trust in God (*tawakkul*), introspection and spiritual self-reckoning (*muḥāsaba*), humility (*tawāḍuʿ*) and surrender to God's will, even ascetic self-denial (*zuhd*). The opening chapter, in which Baḥya demonstrates the absolute unity of the Divine (*tawḥīd*), blends Sufi spiritual ideals with those of Neo-Platonic philosophy.[19] In the last chapter, Baḥya explains that love of God is the soul's essential yearning to conjoin (*tattaṣil*) with God's light; in Baḥya, *ittiṣāl* assumes a Sufi, devotional flavor.[20] Whether or not Ha-Levi is responding directly to Baḥya, Baḥya's very presence attests to the strong attraction Sufi ideals of union held for the Jewish community of medieval Spain.

We thus hear both Neo-Platonic and Sufi overtones within the language of union used by the philosopher in I:1. The philosopher describes an intellectual path to union with the Active Intellect that mirrors the experiential path of the Sufi. Unlike the Sufis or Plotinus however, Ha-Levi's philosopher—like other medieval Neo-Platonists—holds that union with God or the One is not possible. He therefore makes intellectual perfection, rather than mystical union, the goal of his quest.

Moral virtues are crucial for the philosophical path, Ha-Levi's philosopher teaches, both as an aid to intellectual perfection and as a fruit of union with the Active Intellect. The philosopher's moral vocabulary also carries Sufi overtones; he associates the philosophical path of moderation ("the most just and balanced of ways")[21] with central Sufi virtues of contentment, quietism, and humility. The philosophers' limbs become like limbs of the Active Intellect, just as the Sufi who reaches union becomes an instrument of the Divine.[22]

Like Al-Fārābī, Avicenna, and other Islamic philosophers, Ha-Levi's philosopher portrays prophecy and true dreams as the ultimate fruit of the philosophical quest. Here, too, we find echoes of Sufi teachings, for Sufi *ittiṣāl* with God is said to result in dreams, visions, and prophecy. Al-Ghazzālī describes prophecy as an offshoot of the Sufi path, and states categorically that "the properties of prophecy beyond those just mentioned can be perceived only by tasting (*dhawq*) as a result of following the way of Sufism."[23]

Ha-Levi's philosopher advises the King to follow the philosophical path to perfection so that he may achieve his ultimate goal:

> You will be able to arrive at your desired goal[24]: making contact [*ittiṣāl*] with that spiritual [entity], I mean the Active Intellect. And perhaps it will cause you to prophesy, and instruct you in the hidden knowledge[25] through true dreams and accurate images. (I:1: 5)

The philosopher speaks with a note of irony; by suggesting that true dreams and prophecy occur only after a long and arduous journey, the philosopher in effect dismisses the "prophetic" dream that had prompted the King's quest.[26]

From the outset, however, Ha-Levi challenges the philosophical claim to prophecy. He has the King argue that despite their contact (*ittiṣāl*) with the spiritual realm, philosophers are not known for prophecy, while people without philosophical or spiritual preparation receive veridical dreams. This, concludes the King, proves that between the Divine (*'amr ilāhī*) and souls there is some connection, which he terms a secret (*sirr*), beyond the philosophical.[27] The King thus defends both the revelatory nature of his dream and the possibility of a kind of *ittiṣāl* beyond that promised by philosophy. Moreover, by using the term *sirr*—a Sufi technical term for the secret, innermost part of the human soul—Ha-Levi once again plays the philosopher against an absent Sufi interlocutor and the promise of Sufi *ittiṣāl*.[28]

By using Sufi terminology, Ha-Levi sets up implicit contrasts between philosophy and Sufism, not in order to hold up Sufism as an alternative, but to point out weaknesses in both ideals. Ultimately, Ha-Levi plays both Sufi and philosophical *ittiṣāl* against what he sees as a more direct, concrete, and powerful religious experience found in the relationship between the Biblical God and the people of Israel.

The King explicitly extends the term *ittiṣāl* to signify such concrete divine-human contact when he expresses a philosophical skepticism, perhaps inspired by the philosopher's argument, about the possibility of this kind of *ittiṣāl*:

> The [human] soul is not at ease admitting that the Creator has contact [*muttaṣīl*] with flesh [and blood] [humanity] except by a miracle that changes the natures [of things], by which we know that only the One who created [all] things from nothing was capable of it. This event must take place before masses who witness it directly—it should not come to them through a report or a chain of tradition—so that it can be studied and carefully examined, lest it be thought that it was a phantasm or magic.
>
> [And even then] it is [30] [only] with difficulty that the soul [can] accept this great thing, that the Creator of this world and the next world and the heavens and the heavenly bodies makes contact [*yattaṣilu*] with this dirty piece of mud, I mean a human being, and that God talks to him, and fulfills his requests, and does his will. (I:8: 9)

The King poses this objection still more trenchantly to the *Ḥaver* in I:68:

> But how did your souls become convinced of this great thing,[31] that the Creator of the bodies, spirits, intellects and angels, who is too high, too holy, too exalted for intellects—much less for the senses—to perceive, makes contact [*ittiṣāl*] with this low creature, sunk in matter, even if he is great in form. For in the smallest of worms there are mysteries of wisdom that the understanding cannot grasp. (I:68: 18)

The King is clearly impressed by the strength of the philosopher's argument; he is not impressed, however, by the philosopher's attempt to co-opt the term *ittiṣāl*. For the King realizes that while exalting philosophical *ittiṣāl*, the philosopher implies that real contact with God—what the King would call true *ittiṣāl*—is impossible.

The King's use of *ittiṣāl* thus prepares us for Ha-Levi's new twist to *ittiṣāl*, which we hear in the Christian's speech in *Kuzari* I:4:

> The Creator has concern for [providence over][32] creatures, and contact with [*ittiṣāl bi*] human beings,[33] and anger and compassion and speech and

appearance and revelation to prophets and pious ones[34] and dwelling[35] among those who please him among the masses.

As the first voice for Biblical religion in the *Kuzari*, the Christian introduces the Biblical God who has a personal relationship with human beings; Ha-Levi uses *ittiṣāl* here in a new way to describe the corporate and individual contact between God and humanity attested to in the Bible. The Christian states his belief in "all that is mentioned in the Torah and in the records of the children of Israel." The Christian thus testifies to the veracity of the Biblical record. The Christian goes on to claim that God's continual *ittiṣāl* is specific to the nation of Israel. Christians, he asserts, "believe in [God] and in [God's] dwelling [incarnation][36] among the children of Israel as an honor [distinction] to them, because the divine [*'amr ilāhī*] never ceased to be attached [*yattaṣilu*] to them until the masses rebelled against this messiah and crucified him"(I:4: 7).

The Christian, like the philosopher, appropriates the term *ittiṣāl* for the form of *ittiṣāl* he believes is the highest; for the Christian, this is divine incarnation. Beyond this specifically Christian claim, however, the Christian in Ha-Levi's text has also introduced the broader notion of *ittiṣāl* as God's providential relationship with the people of Israel. In attesting to God's specific connection with the people of Israel and describing it as *ittiṣāl*, the Christian prepares the reader for Ha-Levi's new twist. The *Ḥaver* will expand upon the Christian's words by tracing the entire history of the Jewish people as a history of *ittiṣāl*.

In summary, Ha-Levi's philosopher uses the term *ittiṣāl* in the standard medieval philosophical sense, to describe conjunction of the Active Intellect with the perfected intellect of the individual philosopher. The King introduces the term *ittiṣāl* to portray concrete, divine-human contact when he describes the philosophical problems in positing such a personal relationship between God and human beings. The Christian, as the first witness for Biblical religion, uses the term to depict the specific relationship between God and the people of Israel.

This play among the various senses of *ittiṣāl*—including that of the absent Sufi—serves as a fitting introduction to the dialogue. The frame story prompts readers to ponder the problem of divine contact and the conflicting ways it had been posed by rival factions in the medieval world. Ha-Levi's readers, medieval Jews educated in the intellectual terminology of Judaeo-Arabic culture, would be attuned to the various ways Ha-Levi has used the term *ittiṣāl* in framing the debate. Ha-Levi's readers will thus be especially conscious of the new twists Ha-Levi introduces, chiefly through the person of the *Ḥaver*, to the language of *ittiṣāl*.

B. Shīʿite Terminology

We have seen that in the opening dialogue, Ha-Levi's Christian brings a new nuance to the term *ittiṣāl* by using it to describe the Biblical relationship between God and Israel. When we come to the *Ḥaver*'s use of *ittiṣāl* and *wuṣūl*, we discover that Ha-Levi's usage is also a creative adaptation and transformation of Shīʿite language.

Whereas Sufis and philosophers by and large used *ittiṣāl* to describe the goal of a human-initiated quest for union, in certain tenth-century Shīʿite texts we find God reaching to unite with the human rather than human beings reaching out to the Divine.[37] In these Ismāʿīlī texts, which Shlomo Pines brought together, God chooses to attach to a series of prophets, the best individual in each generation.

The Shīʿite authors link three terms we also find at the center of the *Kuzari*: *ʾamr*, *ṣafwa*, and *ittiṣāl*. The term *ʾamr* literally means thing, matter, order, or command. In the Qurʾān, the term *amr* signifies God's command; in Shīʿite thought, the divine *ʾamr* came to signify God's commanding word, the divine will, or what Pines terms "a divine influx conferring prophethood."[38]

In the Shīʿite texts to which Pines called attention, *ʾamr* (or *ʾamr Allah*) denotes that aspect of the Divine which comes down to select human individuals and signals God's choice of them.[39] The term *ṣafwa* in these texts denotes either the fact of divine election, or the people who are the select of God.[40] Variants of the verb *ittaṣāla* (conjoin) and *ittaḥada* (unite) are used in these texts to describe the conjunction of the divine *ʾamr* with the line of prophets, beginning with Adam.[41]

Unlike the Sufis and philosophers, for whom *ittiṣāl* had come to indicate the goal of a human-initiated quest for union, Ha-Levi, like the authors of these Ismāʿīlī texts, sometimes uses *ittiṣāl* to indicate contact initiated by God.[42] Ha-Levi also adapts and transforms the Shīʿite complex of terms: we find in the *Kuzari* the term *ʾamr* for the Divine—most often in the phrase *ʾamr ilāhī*, commonly translated divine "power," "influence," or "order"—and the term *ṣafwa* for the line of individuals to whom the divine *ʾamr* attaches (*ittaṣala*). However, whereas the *ʾamr* of the Shīʿites is a divine influx that comes down through a series of emanations, Ha-Levi detaches the term from its elaborate Neo-Platonic framework, and uses it as a fluid way to point to the Divine.

Many scholars have tried to pin down the precise ontological status and function of Ha-Levi's *ʾamr ilāhī*; my sense, however, is that Ha-Levi likes the flexibility of this moniker for the Divine.[43] While Ha-Levi does often use the term *ʾamr* or *ʾamr ilāhī* to describe God's interaction with creation, he uses these ambiguous terms precisely so that this interaction not be reified; it is doubtful that he conceived of the *ʾamr ilāhī* as an intermediary with a specific ontological status.[44] I have thus opted to translate the phrase simply as "the Divine," and not pin down the *ʾamr ilāhi* as a specific order, influence, influx, or command.[45] Ha-Levi's adaptation of the terms *ṣafwa* and *ittiṣāl* likewise resists being reduced to any rigid theoretical framework. Ha-Levi seeks to capture the simple, mysterious relationship to God he sees in true Biblical religion, and adapts this complex of Shīʿite terms to explain the unique connection of the Jewish people to God.

Of course, Ha-Levi's interest in the term *ittiṣāl* as used by the Shīʿites stems precisely from the term's prestige among Sufis and philosophers. Ha-Levi's appropriation of Shīʿite language does not then imply a complete rejection of Sufi and philosophical models. Throughout the *Kuzari* the sense of a human-initiated quest for union will remain in a tense dialectic with historical, God-initiated *ittiṣāl*. Ha-Levi is keenly aware that both elements vie for attention in the Biblical story.[46]

C. The History of the Jewish People as a History of *Ittiṣāl*

In Book One of the *Kuzari*, the *Ḥaver* lays out for the king his basic conception of Jewish history. Our focus on the verbal root *w-ṣ-l* will reveal this to be a history of God's encounter with humanity, a history, in effect, of *ittiṣāl*.

1. Ittiṣāl *among Founding Figures*

The *Ḥaver*'s sacred history of the Jewish nation sets forth a prophetic elite beginning with Adam. The *Ḥaver* describes Adam using motifs available in his Islamic intellectual milieu—in particular, Sufi and philosophical models of perfection. In I:95, he calls Adam the Perfect One (*al-kāmil*), a term that calls to mind the philosopher's description of the perfect human being (*al-insān al-kāmil*) in I:1. Like the Sufi Knower of God[47] who has entered into union with the Divine, Ha-Levi's Adam "knows the Truths without instruction, by simple reflection" (I:95: 28).[48]

The *Ḥaver* describes Adam's capacity for an individual connection with God as the crowning perfection of the father of the human race;

Adam, he says, received "the divine power[49] beyond the intellect, by which I mean (that he was at) the level at which one connects (*yattaṣilu*) with God and spiritual beings" (I:95: 28).[50] Adam is untutored, yet has a natural capacity for *ittiṣāl*, a gift that Sufis and philosophers only attain through an arduous path of development.[51] The original relationship between human beings and God is a spontaneous connection, not one cultivated by following the steps of a program.

Like the Sufis, and unlike the philosophers, Ha-Levi wants to situate Adam's capacity for *ittiṣāl* beyond the realm of the intellect, and to claim that it makes possible communion not only with the Active Intellect or the realm of spiritual beings, but with the Divine itself. Perhaps Ha-Levi wants to hint that this is the "secret" between the soul and God to which the King alluded in I:4—a connection with the spiritual realm different from that spoken of by the philosophers, and one whose existence the King is seeking to verify.

Unlike the Sufis, Ha-Levi's use of *ittiṣāl* nowhere hints of *unio mystica*.[52] However, Ha-Levi does suggest the human soul has some connection to God that philosophers have failed to acknowledge, a connection that makes possible a personal relationship with God and intense religious experience.

Drawing upon the Shī'ite theory of the *ṣafwa*, Ha-Levi suggests that Adam's capacity for *ittiṣāl* makes him the forebear of an elite line of humanity. Adam's sons also have contact with the Divine, but Ha-Levi explicitly portrays this *ittiṣāl* as originating not with the sons themselves but with God. God singles out some of Adam's sons as the select (*ṣafwa*), especially suited for divine contact, while the rest are regarded as secondary and superfluous:

> After Cain his brother killed [Abel] in jealousy over this level, he was replaced by Seth, who was similar to Adam, being his quintessence [*ṣafwa*] and core,[53] and others were like husks and rotten fruit. The quintessence of Seth was Enosh, and thus the *'amr* made contact [*ittaṣala*] until Noah, with individuals who were the heart, similar to Adam, called sons of God, perfect of physical constitution and temperament, long of life and of knowledge and of capacity. . . . Perhaps there were among them those to whom the *'amr ilāhī* did not attach [*yattaṣilu*] like Terah. But Abraham his son was a disciple of his grandfather 'Ever; moreover he had known Noah himself. And so the *'amr ilāhī* was linked[54] from grandfathers to grandsons. (I:95: 28)

The select sons are apparently distinguished from birth; the *'amr ilāhī* chooses to make contact with them because of characteristics they inherit from their father Adam, who was created perfect. Their siblings with whom God did not make *ittiṣāl* simply failed to inherit a trait—to use a modern genetic term—which would render them fit for *ittiṣāl*. However the genetic comparison is imperfect, as Ha-Levi allows for both nature and nurture. Abraham is able to receive contact from the *ʾamr ilāhī* not only because he inherited the recessive gene from his grandfather ʿEver, but also because he was a student of his grandfather, and had known his righteous ancestor Noah as well. The early ancestors passed down both a tradition and a capacity for connection with the Divine; thus, the capacity for prophecy is both inherited and learned.

In each generation the *ʾamr ilāhī* continues to make *ittiṣāl* with one individual whom God finds worthy—as we saw in the Shīʿite texts—from Adam down to the twelve sons of Jacob. Finding all twelve sons fit to link with, God makes *ittiṣāl* with all of them, forming what the *Ḥaver* calls "something of an angelic elite, almost a different species of humanity" (I:103: 35). Speaking of the prophetic line from Adam to Moses, the *Ḥaver* asserts:

> These, on account of[55] their contact [*ittiṣāl*], are the quintessence of Adam and his select [*ṣafwa*].[56] And each of them had progeny like husks, not resembling the[ir] fathers, and [therefore][57] the *ʾamr ilāhī* did not make contact [*yattaṣil*] with them, and the chronology continued with the[se] divine ones, who were individuals, not a group, until Jacob begat the twelve tribes, all of them fit for the *ʾamr ilāhī*, and the Divine came to a group,[58] through whom [continued] the chronology. (I:47: 14)

Ha-Levi's use of the term *ittiṣāl* in this passage may be deliberately equivocal; as a poet he may in fact delight in the texture and ambiguity of the term. The *Ḥaver*'s assertion that these, "on account of their *ittiṣāl*, are the heart of Adam and his select" is unclear. Does this indicate that some of Adam's descendents are the "select" of their father because of an innate capacity or worthiness, or that their actual *ittiṣāl*—God's relationship with them—makes them an elite? Are the *ṣafwa* special because they are chosen, or are they chosen because they are special? The *Ḥaver*'s equivocal language leaves room for an arbitrary quality to the choice. One might argue that the rejected sons' status as "husks" derives at least partially from the fact that God did not actually connect with them, that for Ha-Levi *ittiṣāl* is ultimately an act of God, who chooses to initiate contact with certain descendents of the primordial Adam.

While in this passage the *Ḥaver* speaks of fitness for *ittiṣāl* as if it is innate, elsewhere he uses language of striving or aspiration for contact with the Divine. For example, the *Ḥaver* states that all twelve sons of Jacob strove for prophecy and most of them achieved it; those who did not reach the level of prophecy nevertheless were able to draw near to God through acts of holiness and encountering prophets (I:103: 35). In his speech on the characteristics of the pious Jew, the *Ḥaver* asserts that one who joins together in prayer certain affirmations of the Jewish faith with pure intention[59]

> is a true Israelite, and it is fitting for him to aspire to[60] *ittiṣāl* with the *ʾamr ilāhī*, which is connected to [*al-mutaṣṣil*] the Children of Israel to the exclusion of the other nations.[61] He finds no difficulty in standing in the presence of the *Shekhinah*. And when he asks, he is answered. (III:17: 105)

Ha-Levi here portrays *ittiṣāl* as a connection to which a person may aspire. The *Ḥaver* indicates that sincere worship through the traditional halakhically prescribed service is a component of, or makes one fit for, aspiration to *ittiṣāl*.[62]

We also see elements of both divine election and human striving in Ha-Levi's telling of the Abraham story. Ha-Levi was obviously fascinated with the rabbinic narrative in which God comes to Abraham the iconoclast, the first human being to reject idolatry and discover the existence of one God.[63] This is not an arbitrary selection process, but the choosing of one who is himself a seeker; Abraham takes some initiative and is met half-way. Ha-Levi's portrait of Abraham attempts to do justice to what he finds in the classical Jewish tradition.[64]

Ha-Levi depicts the *ʾamr ilāhī* as eagerly awaiting an individual such as Abraham with whom it will be fitting to connect:

> See how Abraham—since he was distinguished [excellent] and his *ittiṣāl* with the *ʾamr ilāhī* was necessary,[65] he being the core of that select [*ṣafwa*]—was moved from his land, to the place where his perfection could be completed . . .
>
> For the *ʾamr ilāhī* is, so to speak, waiting for whomever is worthy to attach to him [*ʿan yattaṣila bi-hi*] and become a God to him, such as the prophets and pious friends of God; just as the intellect, so to speak, waits for the one whose natural qualities have become perfected and whose soul and moral qualities have become temperate, that it may dwell in him perfectly, like the philosophers; just as the soul waits for one whose natural powers have become perfected and prepared for increased excellence so that it may dwell in it, like the animals; and just as nature waits for the mixture which is temperate in its qualities in order to dwell in it so that it may become a plant. (II:14: 49–50)[66]

Here, too, however, Ha-Levi's language is equivocal. An equally valid translation would be: "when Abraham became distinguished (excellent), *ittiṣāl* with the *ʾamr ilāhī* became necessary." It is not clear whether *ittiṣāl* comes to Abraham because of his inherent fitness or because he has perfected himself. Ha-Levi chooses Arabic verbs that accomodate ideas of both innate excellence and struggle.

The *Ḥaver* develops a biological metaphor combining nature and nurture: natural fitness and the need for certain environmental elements. Like the root of a good tree that must be transplanted into richer soil in order to thrive, Abraham must be brought to the land of Israel in order to be made fit for *ittiṣāl*: "It was not fitting that Abraham connect [*li-yattaṣila*] with *ʾamr ilāhī*, and that he [should] enter into and conclude a mutual covenant [with God] until he had reached that land in the vision[67] between the pieces" (II:16: 50).

Beyond natural fitness and environment, however, Ha-Levi emphasizes Abraham's spiritual struggle, his willingness to make great sacrifices for this God with whom he seeks to be in obedient relationship:

> See how syllogistic reasoning [*qiyās*] declares circumcision absurd! It has no entry into political life,[68] and yet Abraham submitted his person and children to it despite the natural difficulty of the command, he being one hundred years old. And it became a sign of the covenant, that the *ʾamr ilāhī* would connect [*li-yattaṣila*] with him and with his descendants. (III:7: 96)[69]

God chooses to connect (*li-yattaṣila*) with Abraham and his descendents because Abraham willingly submits himself to the commandment of circumcision. Abraham merits *ittiṣāl* because he is a spiritual pioneer, developing a relationship with God based upon obedience and trust. We thus see in Ha-Levi's story of Abraham a foreshadowing of themes he will develop in tracing the nation's relationship with God—specifically, Ha-Levi links *ittiṣāl* with the language of covenant.

In summary, Ha-Levi gives a complex and even contradictory portrait of the role of divine choice and human initiative in the unfolding of Biblical history. The sources of Ha-Levi's terminology reflect tensions within his thought. Shīʿite *ittiṣāl* seems predetermined. While Shīʿite thought depicts a natural elite with an innate capacity for *ittiṣāl*, Sufi and philosophical *ittiṣāl* make room for religious quest and struggle. Ha-Levi finds in the term *ittiṣāl* a subtlety which he uses to steer a middle course between the activism of the Sufis and philosophers and the passivism of the Shīʿites. The term *ittiṣāl,* which signifies union, contact, or connection, is itself ambiguous; it is not clear who initiates the contact or how union is achieved. Perhaps the ambiguity of the term *ittiṣāl* allows Ha-Levi to describe a mutual relationship—a collaborative effort, both between God and individuals and between God and the nation as a whole—made tangible through the divine commandments.

2. *Communal* Ittiṣāl

God's *ittiṣāl* with individual founding figures expands to a group phenomenon when the twelve tribes grow into a religious nation, solidified through the Exodus from Egypt and the revelation at Mount Sinai. This series of events establishes the unique religious status of the Jewish people:

> THE KING: Is your Law then confined to you?
>
> THE ḤAVER: Yes, but whoever from among the nations joins us, in particular (*khāṣṣatan*)[70] shares in our good,[71] although they are not quite the same as us (*lam yastawi ma'nā*). For if the obligation of the Law derived from His having created us, the white and the black would indeed share equally in it (*lastawā fī-hi*), for all of them are His creation. Rather the Law (is obligatory) because of His bringing us out of Egypt, and his attaching to us (*ittiṣāluhu binā*), for we are the select (*ṣafwa*) of humankind.
>
> THE KING: I see you quite altered, oh Jew, and your words are so poor, after having been so rich [1:25–27: 11] . . .

Up to this point, the King has gradually been won over by the *Ḥaver*'s arguments; here he is startled by the *Ḥaver*'s particularism. Like the King, readers may find several points jarring:

1. The exclusivism of this passage is heightened by other passages of the *Kuzari*. In III:17, for example, the *Ḥaver* asserts that God attaches to Israel *to the exclusion of* the other nations.
2. The passage can be read to suggest that God attaches to the Jewish people because they are innately special. Once again, we are struck by Ha-Levi's decided ambiguity. With respect to individuals, the *Ḥaver* asserts that certain sons on account of *ittiṣāl* are the select of humankind. Here, too, on a communal level, the King is told that God has attached to the Jewish people and that they are the select. Are the Jews

select because God has chosen them, or are they selected because they are God's best prospects among humankind?

3. For the modern reader, the *Ḥaver*'s reference to "the white and the black" calls to mind modern claims of innate racial superiority.[72]

We should not overlook or minimize the potentially disturbing implications of this passage. The King himself here and elsewhere expresses discomfort with the *Ḥaver*'s exclusivity; clearly, Ha-Levi wants to point out the provocative nature of his claims. As Schweid has emphasized, the King is brought in as a fair and impartial judge of Judaism. The fact that the King recoils from the *Ḥaver*'s particularism indicates that Ha-Levi is aware he is presenting problematic ideas, and expects his readers to respond accordingly. If we accept the *Ḥaver* as a simple mouthpiece for the author we oversimplify Ha-Levi's position.

However, we must carefully distinguish the problems this passage raises in a modern context from the way it would have been read by Ha-Levi's contemporaries. The medieval Islamic context of Ha-Levi's terms and arguments is crucial. By analyzing his rhetorical strategy within its Islamic context, we can discover a more complex, nuanced perspective than is apparent at first glance.

First, we should note a striking innovation Ha-Levi has made. In translating the Shīʿite theory of the *ṣafwa* into a Jewish context, Ha-Levi has shifted from speaking of *ittiṣāl* as an individual religious experience to *ittiṣāl* as a communal relationship.[73] By using the term *ittiṣāl* to describe God's historical attachment to the Jewish people, Ha-Levi draws on classical Jewish tradition to conceptualize religious experience in a way which is unprecedented in Arabic thought.

In rabbinic literature, the most intense metaphors for religious experience are reserved for corporate experience; for example, until the medieval philosophers, the Song of Songs is read as an allegory of the love between God and the nation of Israel.[74] Whereas Arabic religious thinkers used *ittiṣāl* to describe individual religious experience, Ha-Levi reinterprets the term to emphasize collective revelation. Moreover, by using one Arabic term to describe both individual and group communion, Ha-Levi unites the two under a single rubric; he invests Jewish communal experience with the aura surrounding individual religious experience in the medieval world.

Second, the passage features an ingenious rhetorical twist. In writing that "the white and the black would be equal to us" Ha-Levi is alluding to a well-known Islamic tradition (*ḥadīth*). In one of its several versions, Muḥammad lists five ways in which his prophecy differs from that of all the prophets who came before him; the ultimate difference is that "(every other) prophet was sent to his nation in particular (*khāṣṣatan*), but I have been sent to all, the red and the black.[75]

To the modern reader, red and black suggest simple racial categories, but the medieval picture is more nuanced. The Arabs describe themselves as black or dark- colored, in contrast to the Persians or other non-Arabs, whom they describe as red, yellow, or in general of lighter hue. The red and the black thus refers, in the words of Ignaz Goldziher, to "Arabs and non-Arabs, i.e. the whole of mankind or the whole world without special consideration of races."[76] This universalism is most explicit in texts which combine two parallel *hadīths*. For example, in the twelfth century Sufi allegory *The Conference of the Birds*, we read, "I was sent to the red and the black," and "I was sent to all creatures."[77] The red and the black—or white and black, in Ha-Levi's version—evoke Islam's claim to universalism, to be valid for all of God's creation.

Ha-Levi, in a characteristic turning of the tables, reverses the logic of the Prophet's claim. Muḥammad argues that as the seal of the prophets, he brings the Law that is most authoritative, because it is universal. Ha-Levi's *Ḥaver* argues just the opposite: the authority of the Torah derives from its claim upon a specific people. The Law is not incumbent on all human beings as creatures of God, but on the Jewish people, because God brought them out of Egyptian bondage. The Torah is not a high-minded, universal abstraction, but a concrete covenant, grounded in a personal relationship and unique historical events. Whereas Islam argues that it is superior because it offers a universal Law for all humankind, the *Ḥaver* asserts proudly the distinctiveness and historical particularity of the Torah.[78]

Ha-Levi's clear allusion to the *ḥadīth* may also shed light on his use of the word *khāṣṣatan* in this passage. The word in fact echoes the *ḥadīth's* remark that "every other prophet was sent to his nation in particular" (*khāṣṣatan*). The *ḥadīth* suggests that to send a prophet to one nation in particular is exclusive and limiting. The *Ḥaver*, in contrast, argues that particularism is a strength. Just as God chooses to send a prophet to one nation in particular, so a person may choose to join one nation in particular. Whereas the philosopher in I:1 claims it does not matter which way one serves God, the *Ḥaver* argues that there is reason to choose the practice of one community over another. Hence: "whoever from among the nations joins us, as a particular group, shares in our good."[79]

Notice, however, that in 1:27 it is unclear whether the Jews are given the Torah because they are inherently special, or whether they become *ṣafwa* through their acceptance of divine law. The nature of the collective specialness of the Jews is as opaque as the *ittiṣāl* of the prophets, discussed above. Ha-Levi appears to deliberately leave the precise nature of Israel's status as *ṣafwa* ambiguous. While many have interpreted Ha-Levi's notion of the *ṣafwa* as inherent, quasi-genetic superiority, akin to modern theories of racial supremacy, such a reading is anachronistic.[80] The Shīʿite background of his vocabulary shows that these terms cannot be reduced to modern racial categories.

In fact, close examination shows that Ha-Levi is once again borrowing an image from its Islamic context and cleverly transforming it. We have seen that the term *ṣafwa* was used in Ismāʿīlī texts to refer to an elite line of prophets. The sources Shlomo Pines gathered describe a distinct metaphysical hierarchy beginning with minerals and culminating in prophets, who constitute a rank above the human.

These ideas are present in the tenth century encyclopedia of the Brethren of Purity (*Ikhwān al-ṣafā'*), a circle of Muslim Neo-Platonists associated with Shīʿite and possibly Ismāʿīlī thought. In the famous debate between the animals and humans found in the second treatise, an Iraqi character claims for his people:[81]

> We are the *lubb* [heart, core, choice part] of the human beings [*al-nās*]; the human beings are the *lubb* of the animals; the animals are the *lubb* of the plants; the plants are the *lubb* of the minerals; and the minerals are the *lubb* of the elements. Indeed, we are the heart of hearts."

This character claims further that the Iraqi people bear the gift of prophecy and that Iraq is the center of all lands.[82]

The correspondences between this passage and the *Kuzari* are of course not exact. As Harry Wolfson noted, no parallel is found to Ha-Levi's doctrine that Israel among the nations is like the heart among the organs of the body, most sensitive and most easily affected (11:36–44: 66–68).[83] However, we do find a striking terminological parallel. The term *lubb* and its sister *lubāb* are keywords in the *Kuzari*; they are often found together with the term *ṣafwa*, and treated as its synonym. Ha-Levi, then, was not the first to claim for his people the status of *ṣafwa* and *lubāb*; his innovation is to apply these intra-Islamic claims to the Jewish people.

In the Islamic context, such ideas would have important sociopolitical consequences. The doctrine of the *ṣafwa* was used to justify an exclusive, hereditary imāmate, the central religious and political authority of the community. The claim that prophets and imāms are metaphysically superior—a divine species exclusively empowered to legislate matters of divine law—thus becomes an eminently practical matter of religious authority.

In Ha-Levi's subtle borrowing, the terms of the debate shift. The King is disturbed by the *Ḥaver*'s exclusivity not because of a debate over metaphysical hierarchy or religious authority, but because he is troubled by the notion of a revelation intended for a particular nation. The King's protest thus echoes the historic claims of Islam and Christianity that they are superior because they offer a revelation which is universal. In addition, the King has been pre-disposed by the philosopher's speech to favor universalism.[84] According to the medieval philosophical tradition, all human beings are endowed with intellect; the Active Intellect governs the world impartially, with no unique relationship to any one being, species, or nation.

The *Ḥaver* does not apologize for Jewish particularism, but draws upon the concept of the *ṣafwa* to explain it to the King. Already in 1:27, the *Ḥaver* suggests that the Jews' status as *ṣafwa* is not purely biological; it is connected with the historical event of the Exodus from Egypt and God's binding himself to the nation through the giving of the Torah. Nevertheless, there is a strong naturalistic component to his response to the King.

Indeed, Ha-Levi's theory of the select, which he creatively adapts from his Shīʿite sources, maintains a tense balance between the elements of nature and nurture. He accepts the notion of a metaphysical hierarchy, beginning with minerals and culminating in prophets, who constitute a level above the human. Ha-Levi fully exploits the theory's naturalistic metaphors. Abraham must be transplanted to choice soil before *ittiṣāl* can be achieved (II:14: 49); the Holy Land is distinguished by *ittiṣāl* (II:14: 48). Moreover, the Jewish people in exile will transform the world as a seed transforms the soil into which it is planted (IV:23: 172). Ha-Levi uses these natural metaphors—like the Shīʿite metaphysical hierarchy—to assimilate history to natural processes.

Ha-Levi does, then, imbue Jewish *ittiṣāl* with a universal purpose. The Jewish people's particular connection to God serves a vital function for the world as a whole, which needs one community that dedicates itself to *ittiṣāl*. The nation of Israel serves as a conduit through which God can send blessings, and establish a just social order:

> At the [daily morning] blessing "With eternal love," the excellent person[85] thinks about the *ittiṣāl* of the *ʾamr ilāhī* with the community who is prepared to receive it, as a smooth mirror receives the light; and that the Law is the outcome of his will, in order to establish his Law on earth, as it is in heaven. (III:17: 104)

We find here another prominent Sufi image which Ha-Levi has appropriated from the realm of individual religiosity and applied to collective religious experience. We find this image, for example in Avicenna's account of Sufi illumination: the soul is a mirror, which the adept polishes to reflect the one Truth. The Sufi gazes back and forth at the Truth and at him or herself; in arrival (*wuṣūl*), the Sufi merges with the Truth he or she beholds.[86] Ha-Levi transforms this image to capture Jewish communal experience, shifting the emphasis from the self-reflective to the interpersonal. Whereas the Sufi image of the soul as a mirror serves as an aid to self-transformation, Ha-Levi's mirror receives light on a communal level. Calling to mind Isaiah's vision of the Jewish people as a light to the nations, the *Ḥaver* suggests that the world needs one community to receive the light of God—perhaps even to reflect the light outward—and to mirror the Law of heaven on earth.

The *Ḥaver* suggests further that this function explains Jewish suffering. The tribulations of the Jews are necessary to purify the nation in order to render it a suitable link to *ʾamr ilāhī*:

> The trials that befall us bring about the soundness[87] of our faith, the purity of the pure-hearted[88]among us, and the removal from us of impurities.[89] And through our purity and our integrity[90] the *ʾamr ilāhī* connects [*yattaṣilu*] with this lower world. (II:44: 67)[91]

Ha-Levi here draws on the vocabulary of Muslim pietism common to Islamic authors of all bents, but especially prominent in Sufi thought.[92] Through this language Ha-Levi articulates a theology of suffering that goes beyond simple purification of the self or the nation. In his view, the Jewish nation exists to serve as a bridge between God and the world, through which the world as a whole can participate in *ittiṣāl* with God. Ha-Levi sees Jewish suffering as serving this larger extra-mural purpose of purifying the nation in order to enable the world as a whole to connect to the Divine. Defying Christian interpretation and Jewish reticence, Ha-Levi embraces Isaiah's image of the Jewish people as a servant whose suffering is redemptive for all humankind.

3. *Levels of* Ittiṣāl: *Individual and Communal, Elite and Nonelite*

Ha-Levi thus distinguishes three levels of *ittiṣāl*: The broadest level is universal *ittiṣāl*, facilitated through God's connection with Israel; the second level is God's guidance of and providence over the Jewish people; a third level is God's special relationship with the prophets and pious, who witness God directly.

As the *Ḥaver* tells the King:

> [While] [God's] *ʾamr* and governance[93] connect [*yattaṣilu*] with human beings [as a whole] . . . the select [*ṣafwa*] connect [*yattaṣilu*] with God to the point that they witness him by means of the Glory, *Shekhinah*, and other such manifestations by which he proves to them that they had been addressed by him on High. (IV:3: 149)

Ha-Levi's notion of communal *ittiṣāl* does not, then, supersede or replace individual *ittiṣāl*, either historically or conceptually. Just as the founding figures of the Biblical nation had individual encounters with God, so, too, the prophets and the pious continue to have moments of personal communion with the Divine.[94] In the event at Mount Sinai, moreover, the nation as a whole experienced this intensity of contact with the Divine.[95]

The individual and communal forms of *ittiṣāl* work hand in hand for Ha-Levi. Ha-Levi underscores this point rhetorically when the *Ḥaver* describes the pious person's prayers, in a passage cited earlier:

> One who unites all this with pure intention[96] is a true Israelite, and it is fitting for him to aspire to *ittiṣāl* with the *ʾamr ilāhī*, which is connected [*al-muttaṣil*] to the Children of Israel to the exclusion of the other nations. He finds no difficulty in standing in the presence of the *Shekhinah*. And when he asks, he is answered. (III:17: 105)

Participation in the regular communal prayer service with pure intention prepares one for a deeper, more personal contact with God. However, God is already connected to Israel as a whole; this *ittiṣāl* is indeed the basis for the religious life of the community. Those for whom individual *ittiṣāl* might be too powerful can take heart in knowing that the *ʾamr ilāhī* is already connected (*muttaṣil*) with all the Children of Israel, a gift that need not be earned by individual attainment. On the other hand, it is God's connection with the community as a whole that provides the structure and foundation for personal *ittiṣāl*. Communal prayer is not an impediment but a vehicle for individual religious experience.

4. Ittiṣāl *as Covenantal*

Ha-Levi's telling of the story of Abraham introduced an additional twist to his use of the term *ittiṣāl*: Ha-Levi uses covenantal language and imagery to describe both individual and communal *ittiṣāl*. While the philosophers and Sufis used the term to suggest ontological union, Ha-Levi stresses that the Jewish connection to God is a covenant—a relationship between two parties, requiring commitment, loyalty, and obedience. The *Ḥaver* tells the king:

> The *ʾamr ilāhī* found next to the stars and spheres only a few individual people between Adam and Jacob who accepted his command obediently [*qābilā tāʾiʿan*] and clung to the order he had decreed. When they had become a people, the *ʾamr ilāhī* rested on them out of love, "in order to be a God to them." (III:17: 104–5)

The obedience of the Israelite ancestors forges a connection for the entire community of Israel, among whom God chooses to dwell.

The notion of obedient acceptance (*iltizām ṭāʿa*; here, *qābilā tāʾiʿan*) is used in Islam to describe acts of devotion beyond the required five pillars of Islam; early handbooks of Sufism assert that the pious ones spent days in acts of obedience. Moreover Ha-Levi had Judaeo-Arabic precedents for adoption of this phrase: Saʿadya uses similar language in his Arabic translation of Biblical passages enjoining the Jews to cling to God. Unlike many later medieval thinkers, for whom the noun *devequt* (clinging) became an important mystical term, Saʿadya interprets the Torah's injunction to cling to God (*u-le-dovqa-vo*) in a decidedly non-mystical sense: Jews are commanded to cling in obedience (*lāzimīna ṭāʿa*) to God's ways.[97] Baḥya ibn Paqūda offers another Judaeo-Arabic precedent to Ha-Levi; he devotes a section of his Sufi-flavored manual to the importance of worshipful service (*iltizām tāʿa; ʿavodat Ha-shem*).[98]

Ha-Levi also echoes the phrase in a parable about a visit to the king of India (I:109: 37–38). Drawing on conventions of the vassal-lord relationship, Ha-Levi's parable demonstrates clearly that obedience to the King brings connection (*ittiṣāl*), arrival (*wuṣūl*), and ultimate happiness.[99]

Ha-Levi's parable abounds with Islamic terminology, which he uses to show that the Jewish path to *ittiṣāl* is wholly covenantal and based on obeying commandments. The king of India recognizes an early visitor to the king—whom the *Ḥaver* identifies as Moses—because his ancestors (the patriarchs) had been among the king's companions (*awliyāʾi*; sing: *walīy*—a frequent Islamic term for pious companions of God). Once the traveler has accepted obedience (*ṭāʿa*) to him, the king charges the traveler with commands and covenants;[100] he then sends the traveler off with messengers, the prophets.[101] The solicitude of these messengers, who guide subsequent pilgrims along the shortest and most direct path, allows the traveler's friends to more easily reach (*wuṣūl ʾilā*) India and see the king.

The terms *ittiṣāl* and *wuṣūl*, of course, are used by Sufis to describe final arrival in the Divine. Ha-Levi describes seeing the king using the term *ru'ya*, a standard Islamic term for the beatific vision of God. He describes the solicitude of God's messengers as *ʿināya*, the Arabic philosophical term for divine providence; he depicts their guidance along the path to the king with Qurʾānic roots declaring divine guidance (*h-d-y* and *r-sh-d*). The *Ḥaver* describes the path they travel to the king as the *ṭarīq*, a less common Arabic term for the Sufi path or way (*ṭarīqa*).[102]

The *Ḥaver* continues:

> All of them knew that it would be made easy [for] one who wishes to reach [*wuṣūl ʾilā*] India [if he would] take upon himself obedience [*iltazama ṭāʿa*] to the king and honor his messengers who bring him into contact [*muwaṣṣilīna*][103] with [the king]. And they did not need to ask: why go to the trouble to [take upon oneself] this obedience [*ṭāʿa*]? For the reason was clearly apparent: to make contact [*li-yattaṣila*] with the King—and that connection [*ittiṣāl*] with him is fulfillment. (I:109: 37)[104]

While Ha-Levi does use the term *tarīq*—reminiscent of the Sufi *ṭarīqa*—to describe the Jewish path to the king, much of the language in this parable is drawn from mainstream Islamic thought. Ha-Levi uses the common terminology of Islamic pietism to emphasize that it is the commandments themselves that bring *ittiṣāl*; this path is not superseded or replaced by spiritual exercises or antinomian mysticism, as it was among the more radical Sufis. As the *Ḥaver* explains, later Jews reach (*waṣala ʾilā*) the king by following the path forged by the prophets and obeying the covenant God establishes with them—ultimately, by obedience to the King (*iltizām ṭāʿat al-malik*).

What do we make of Ha-Levi's language of obedience? We have seen that Saʿadya uses the phrase "clinging in obedience" (*lāzimina ṭāʿa*) to translate the Biblical admonition to cling to God. However, other medieval thinkers went much further. The same Biblical language gave them a Hebrew term—*devequt*—to express direct cognitive and mystical union.[105] It is thus significant that Ha-Levi adopts Saʿadya's conservative rendering of *devequt* as clinging *in obedience* (*iltizām tāʿa*), particularly when speaking of those who finally arrive at (*waṣala ʾilā*) the king. Unlike Avicenna, for example, who describes Sufi arrival (*wuṣūl*) as unitive absorption in the one Truth that is God, Ha-Levi here describes arrival in a language of respectful obedience, rather than direct clinging.[106]

The *Ḥaver* uses similar caution when explaining the divine Name "*Qedosh Yisrael*," Holy One of Israel. *Qedosh Yisrael* he says is "a name for the *ʾamr ilāhī* which is attached [*muttaṣil*] to Israel [i.e., Jacob], and after him, to his descendants, an *ittiṣāl* of guidance and governance, not an *ittiṣāl* of clinging and contact"[107] (IV:3: 151).

The contrast drawn here reflects two conceptions of *ittiṣāl* debated in the Islamic world: an *ittiṣāl* in which God remains separate and above the individual soul—an *ittiṣāl* of governance and guidance—or an *ittiṣāl* which is a connection of absolute equality, union, and adhesion between the devotee and the Divine. Perhaps Ha-Levi wants to suggest that divine contact is most safe when it is distant and providential attachment, rather than direct and unitive adhesion, which is fraught with dangers, at least for most ordinary Jews.[108] Similarly, Ha-Levi uses the metaphor of the sun to describe *ittiṣāl* at a safe distance for the nonelite of Israel; the sun, whose light can mystically penetrate, can also scorch and burn. Providential *ittiṣāl* is safer than the more direct, intense form of *ittiṣāl* experienced by the prophets, but is no less to be accounted communion with the Divine.

Ha-Levi thus portrays Jewish *ittiṣāl* as existing on a continuum ranging from simple obedience to communion with the *Shekhinah*. By using the term *ittiṣāl* in such a broad-stroked fashion, Ha-Levi suggests that the entire continuum of religious experience is crucial for drawing the *ʾamr ilāhī* to dwell among the Israelites and for establishing God's Law on earth. The *ittiṣāl* of ordinary Jews who cling in obedience to God's ways—by observing God's commandments or imitating God's actions—is as necessary as the *ittiṣāl* of the prophets and pious of Israel, who bask in the presence of the *Shekhinah*.[109]

5. Ittiṣāl *as Union*

There is one passage in which Ha-Levi is less cautious in his approach to *ittiṣāl*. This is a key passage in the *Kuzari*: it leads to the King's epiphany in IV:16, where he articulates the difference between the God of Abraham and the God of Aristotle. Here Ha-Levi draws upon his Sufi lexicon to express the love, longing, and intimacy a Jew experiences in relationship with God. However, we will hold off our analysis of that passage until we have examined other terms with which it will come into dialogue.[110]

D. *Ittiṣāl*, Asceticism, and Mitsvot

1. Ha-Levi's Religious Ideal: Against Asceticism and Isolation

Colored as it is with classical Jewish thought, Ha-Levi's conception of *ittiṣāl* is integrally bound up with a covenental ideal of relationship within community. Traditional Jewish and Islamic thought in general did not see a conflict between human relationships and relationship to God, as both tended to view family and community as integral to religious life. However, with the rise of philosophy and Sufism in the Islamic world there arose a competing ideal of withdrawal from society to achieve a more intimate relationship with God. Moreover, traditional Jewish and Islamic views held that a person is a unity of body and soul; even resurrection was understood to include the physical body. Philosophers and Sufis, on the other hand, came to experience a tension between body and soul, and thus became attracted to asceticism as well as isolation.[111]

Baḥya's *Duties of the Heart* demonstrates that some of Ha-Levi's Jewish contemporaries were also attracted to this approach. But while Baḥya's work was closely modeled on contemporary manuals of Sufi piety, Baḥya did not go as far as the Sufi ascetics. Given the emphasis on community in traditional Jewish thought, there were limits to Jewish acceptance of ascetic practices. Even Baḥya, the most enthusiastic Jewish advocate of Sufism up to this time, shows reservations and sets boundaries to Sufi asceticism.

The strong attraction Sufi ascetic practices held for some contemporary Jews leads Ha-Levi to address at some length the question of asceticism, to which he takes a subtle, nuanced approach.[112] While admitting that in Biblical and rabbinic times there were certain individuals who successfully drew near to God through ascetic practices, he denies that such an approach can succeed today. Most importantly, Ha-Levi rejects isolation as a valid spiritual ideal; *ittiṣāl*, he contends, is to be found today in communal life.

Ha-Levi's reinterpretation of *ittiṣāl* in this way serves a polemical purpose. Sufi *ittiṣāl* is portrayed as the fruit of a path of self-denial and isolation. Sufism holds up asceticism,[113] humility and self-abasement,[114] and isolation as ideal virtues.[115] Philosophers, too, were commonly associated with asceticism. The *Ḥaver* notes that the ancient philosophers separated themselves ascetically from the world,[116] while the King points out that one who isolates himself ascetically[117] is called a philosopher.

Ha-Levi's creative reinterpretation of the term *ittiṣāl* counteracts Jewish attraction to these ascetic trends. Ha-Levi appropriates the term *ittiṣāl* and its attendant prestige, applying it to an engaged, communal way of life that is antithetical to the self-deprivation normally associated with *ittiṣāl*. In a brilliant move characteristic of his strategy of argument, Ha-Levi plays off the traditional, ascetic view of *ittiṣāl* held by both Sufis and philosophers against another philosophical ideal. Using the Arabic terms for temperance (*iʿtidāl*) and justice (*ʿadl*), Ha-Levi embraces the Platonic and Aristotelian value of moderation against the more dualistic Neo-Platonic trend of asceticism.

The term *ʿadl* is key in the Arabic philosophical lexicon, for *ʿadl* is the term chosen to translate *dikaiosyne* (justice), the concept under investigation in Plato's *Republic*.[118] What Socrates seeks ultimately is an adequate understanding of justice in the human soul. It is only for pedagogical purposes that he investigates justice in the state, justice writ large and thus easier to see.

For the Greek philosophers, justice is a balance of conflicting elements. Both Plato and Aristotle preach a moral and psychological ideal of moderation, achieved by learning to balance the needs of the various faculties of *psyche* or soul. Ha-Levi gives this ideal his own twist. The *Ḥaver* asserts:

> The divine law does not bid us to devote ourselves in service through asceticism[119] but rather through moderation [*iʿtidāl*], giving each faculty of the soul and body its just [*ʿadl*] share, without overburdening one faculty at the expense of another. (II:50: 69)

Ha-Levi thus embraces one prestigious ideal of the philosophers (*iʿtidāl*) to defeat another (ascetic *ittiṣāl*), arguing that the Torah teaches a path of moderation, balance, or justice. As a further extension of his anti-ascetic polemic, the *Ḥaver* tells the King that those who isolate themselves today do not enjoy *ittiṣāl* with the divine light; *ittiṣāl* is not available without the presence of the *Shekhinah*, the Temple, and the land of Israel. Those who experiment with asceticism today to achieve religious experience do so without direct divine guidance, and their efforts will come to nought (III:1: 91).

Ha-Levi's readers might therefore conclude that *ittiṣāl* is completely out of grasp for contemporary Jews. To counteract this notion, Ha-Levi insists that there exist institutions which make *ittiṣāl* available in exile—the *mitsvot*, and most specifically, prayer and Shabbat. After denying that *ittiṣāl* is possible today without the land and the Temple, where the divine Presence had its abode, the *Ḥaver* goes on to state that prayer and Shabbat are specifically reserved for *ittiṣāl* with the Divine (*ʾamr ilāhī*) (III:5: 94).

Ha-Levi is thus far from systematically consistent. Rather than creating a systematic philosophy of religious experience, Ha-Levi appears to be addressing Jews attracted to Sufi isolation and asceticism, whom he believes fail to recognize the spiritual value and significance of Jewish life in community.[120] In particular, Ha-Levi may want to guard against extreme attempts at *ittiṣāl* by those who think themselves far more spiritually advanced than they are. Ha-Levi thus denies that these attempts at ascetic piety will come to fruition in *ittiṣāl*. At the same time, he asserts that the very communion such Jews seek through asceticism and withdrawal is available through the practice of *mitsvot* and through Jewish communal life.

Ha-Levi is clearly concerned to counter philosophical and Sufi antinomianism or indifference to the Law. A major theme in his portrait of the philosophers' path is their indifference to religious law; law for them is just a matter of ethics, and one can just as easily follow a rationalistic ethic.[121] Certain Sufis, too, were well known for claiming that once one has reached an advanced level of spiritual development, religious law is unnecessary, and in fact may keep one mired in the temporal. Ha-Levi thus adds to his creative reinterpretation of *ittiṣāl* the notion that *mitsvot* are not only not antithetical to religious experience, they are in fact essential to the achievement of *ittiṣāl*. The way to experience communion with God in contemporary Judaism is through the practice of the commandments, a practice that requires community and that establishes a harmonious balance between action and contemplation.[122]

Ha-Levi returns again and again to the assertion that the way to *ittiṣāl* today is through *mitsvot*. The *Ḥaver* asserts, for example, that

1. circumcision is a sign of the covenant—that the *ʾamr ilāhī* would attach (*yattaṣila*) to Abraham and his descendents (III:7: 96);[123]
2. today Jews connect with God through the *mitsvot*, which God has placed as a bond (*ṣīla*) between Jews and the Divine (II:34: 65);
3. one comes near to God only through God's commands; God alone knows their measure, by whose fulfillment comes the pleasure of God and *ittiṣāl* with the *ʾamr ilāhī* (III:23: 112);

4. if love and joy bring singing and dancing, then this is worship and a bond (*ṣīla*) between the worshiper and the *ʾamr ilāhī* (II:50: 70);
5. all religious laws have as their promise drawing near to God and the angels in this life and the next, so that one who has reached (*waṣala*) this level need not fear death (I:109: 36).

Ha-Levi emphasizes that Judaism is life-affirming, not life-denying. Afflicting oneself is not the primary way to serve God; one serves God equally with joy. Nor is isolating oneself and denying the senses the best way to achieve religious experience. One can equally come to experience God in community, even while eating and drinking in fellowship with others. One's worship may even involve singing and dancing—a notion that may suggest some Sufi influence.

Ha-Levi rejects isolation as a valid spiritual ideal. Ha-Levi's conception of *ittiṣāl* is an engaged *ittiṣāl*, one which values the fabric of human relationships. On the other hand, Ha-Levi acknowledges the need for a certain withdrawal from everyday actions and time for quiet contemplation. The *Ḥaver* asserts that "the three times of [daily] prayer are the fruit of [one's] day and night, and the *Shabbat* is the fruit of the week because it is reserved[124] for *ittiṣāl* with the *ʾamr ilāhī*, to serve God with joy, not with submissiveness" (III:5: 94).

Ha-Levi maintains that Judaism is in fact the one religious Law through whose knowledge and practice one arrives (*yuṣilu*—related to *ittiṣāl* and *wuṣūl*) at experience of the Divine in this life (I:103: 35). *Ittiṣāl* is not only achieved without asceticism and withdrawal; it is achieved in this world, bringing assurance of *ittiṣāl* in the world to come.

E. *Ittiṣāl*, Immortality, and the Afterlife

1. *New Challenge: Christian and Orthodox Muslim Critiques*

Ha-Levi thus uses his reinterpretation of Sufi and philosophical *ittiṣāl* to respond to a challenge from another direction: the orthodox Muslim and Christian charge that Judaism is a this-worldly religion, one lacking the promise of an afterlife.

Orthodox Muslims by and large do not use the language of *ittiṣāl* when speaking of the afterlife. They focus on God's promise (*waʿd*, *mawʿid*, or *miʿād*) of a spiritual journey after death and reward for the faithful at the end of history.[125] Sufis and philosophers, on the other hand, focus upon a philosophical and mystical quest for immortality and union with God (*ittiṣāl* or *wuṣūl*) achieved in this life through spiritual development; it is assumed that union with the Divine achieved in this life will continue upon leaving the body. Ha-Levi cleverly throws one opponent against another: he upholds many of the Sufi and philosophical values associated with *ittiṣāl* and juxtaposes them against the Orthodox conception of an afterlife. He argues that the promises of *ittiṣāl* are themselves the greatest *mawāʿid*; however these are the promises of a specifically Jewish form of *ittiṣāl*, one that is communal, this-worldly, and achieved through the life of *mitsvot*.

The *Ḥaver* responds to the charge that Judaism lacks promises of an afterlife by arguing first that the fulfillment of Jewish promises (*mawāʿid*) is very much available in this life: for the elite, *ittiṣāl* with the *ʾamr ilāhī* by prophecy and prophetic inspiration; for all Jews, *ittiṣāl* of *ʾamr ilāhī* with the Jewish nation by providence and wonders and miracles (I:109: 36). Ha-Levi thus retains the sense of *maw'id* as the fulfillment of a promise, while stripping it of its otherworldly connotations as a reward at the end of time.

A motif appearing often in the Qurʾān is the inevitability of the day of judgment at the end of history: God has made a promise (set an appointed time) (*waʿda mīʿāda*) that he will not rescind.[126] Ha-Levi supports his point with an echo of this familiar Qurʾānic phrase when the *Ḥaver* asserts that Judaism ("this Law") assures the fulfillment of its promises (*al-mawāʿid*), so that their rescinding[127] need not be feared (I:109: 36).

Ha-Levi's contention, however, is that in contrast to the Qurʾān's appointed time of fulfillment (*mawʿid*), realization of the Jewish promise is to be found first of all within history, in the Jews' special relationship to God and in God's guidance of the Jews as a people. The *Ḥaver* asserts that a Jew need only reflect on such natural and historical wonders as the fertility of the Holy Land and the miraculous deliverance of the nation from its adversaries. Such reflection reveals that "an order [*ʾamr*] greater than the natural order [*ʾamr*] guides your order [*ʾamr*]; all this, and all these laws—their promises [*mawaʿid*] are assured, one need not fear that they will be rescinded"[128] (I:109: 36).

There is a special religious connection of *ittiṣāl* between God and Israel in nature and history, whether manifest or hidden, and this in itself constitutes the fulfillment of the Jewish promise. Ha-Levi suggests that religious experience may be subtle, historical, and cumulative as well as intense and dramatic, that there is a form of *ittiṣāl* whose true significance as religious experience is revealed only in hindsight, upon reflection.[129]

Moreover, the *Ḥaver* juxtaposes those who ascend to heaven and those who witness God's emissaries fighting for them on earth. The former most probably alludes to visionaries who visit the realm of the divine chariot; the latter, to Biblical theophanies and to midrashic images of God as a mighty warrior rescuing the Israelites at the Sea of Reeds:[130]

> There will be those among you who will come into my presence and ascend to heaven, like those who have moved about[131] among the angels. And there will also be those of my angels moving about on earth. You will see them, singly and in groups, guarding you and fighting for you. You will remain in the Land which leads to this degree—that is, the Holy Land. Its fertility or barrenness, its happiness or misfortune, depend upon the *ʾamr ilāhī*, according to your deeds, while the rest of the world will go according to its natural course. (I:109: 36)

In the same breath, the *Ḥaver* mentions heavenly journeys of *merkavah* mystics, Biblical theophanies, witnessing the fertility or barrenness of the Holy Land, and the victory of Israelites over their enemies. This juxtaposition of images and mixing of historical times suggests that all these forms of contact with the Divine are equally reflective of God's presence, equally to be accounted religious experience.

To those critics who charge that Judaism holds an impoverished image of the afterlife, Ha-Levi responds with a twist on the Sufi and philosophical view of *ittiṣāl*. Ha-Levi agrees with the Sufis and philosophers that connection with God experienced in this world assures an abiding connection in the next. The *Ḥaver* asserts that a good[132] person in prayer

> meditates on [prays for] *ittiṣāl* with the divine light in this life. And if he prays in the degree of prophecy—and there is nothing nearer for man to God than that—there is no doubt that he has prayed for more than the world to come, and if he achieves it, he also achieves the world to come.
>
> For one whose soul is attached [*ittaṣalat nafsuhu*] to the *ʾamr ilāhī* [while he is still] busy with the accidents of the body, it stands to reason that he will join [*yattaṣilu*] [the *ʾamr ilāhī*] when he withdraws and leaves this unclean vessel. (III:20: 109)

Ha-Levi maintains that all Jews experience some degree of *ittiṣāl* in this life through God's providential guidance of the Jewish people. He therefore suggests that Christian and Muslim boasting about the afterlife is superfluous to a people who experience connection with

God in this life. Ha-Levi adds that Jewish literature itself disproves his opponents' charge. Jewish sources hold many allusions to the afterlife, and it is in fact from Jewish literature, both Biblical and post-Biblical, that Christianity and Islam draw their images of paradise and hell (I:115: 40).

Finally, Ha-Levi contrasts the afterlife portrayed in the Qur'ān to Jewish this-worldly fulfillment, once again turning his opponents' critique on its head. Jewish this-worldly fulfillment, Ha-Levi suggests, is in fact more spiritual than the Islamic afterlife: "Thus what is promised in the Torah as a reward for keeping the Law is not beautiful gardens and great delights. God rather says, 'You will be special to me and I will be to you a God who will guide you'" (I:109: 36).

In Ha-Levi's view, the fact that Jewish fulfillment exists first of all in this world does not detract from its spiritual nature. The *Ḥaver* asserts:

> The promises [*mawāʿid*] of this Law are all included under one principle: the anticipation [expectation, hope] of drawing near to the Lord and his angels. One who has arrived [*waṣala*] at this degree need not fear death; our Law has demonstrated this plainly. (I:109: 36)[133]

2. *Explanation of Biblical Asceticism and Isolation*

Ha-Levi acknowledges, however, that certain great spiritual figures in the Biblical Age (Enoch and Elijah, for example) did fruitfully practice asceticism. They could profit from isolation—which Ha-Levi describes using Sufi terms[134]—because their isolation was not complete: ascetics had the companionship (*uns*) both of fellow seekers and of God and the angels. Since the Jews were still in their Land, true *ittiṣāl* with the divine was available. Moreover, those who practiced asceticism in the Biblical Age created communities, the schools of prophets[135] (III:1: 90). Ha-Levi maintains that even people who were not themselves prophets but who encountered prophets had experiences of the Divine that offered them a taste of the world to come (I:103: 35).

Today, however, people who attempt an ascetic path no longer achieve true *ittiṣāl*. To Jews attracted to Sufi asceticism, Ha-Levi argues that the Divine is not as accessible as when Jews dwelt in the Holy Land, the divine Presence rested upon the Temple, and Jews could achieve prophecy. To Jews attracted to philosophical asceticism, Ha-Levi adds that neither is wisdom as accessible today as it was to the ancient philosophers:

> Today [the would-be ascetic] does not connect [*yattaṣil*] with the divine light which would be his companion[136] like the prophets, nor does he have

> the learning that would enable him to be absorbed in it and enjoy it all the rest of his life, as the philosophers did. (III:1: 90)

While others might view him or her as genuinely pious, a contemporary ascetic would grow to hate this world—not because this world is not holy, but because the human body really longs to be active. Moreover, contemporary ascetics actually long for community. Ascetics today do not have the fellowship[137] of spiritual beings, whereas in ancient times ascetics—both prophets and philosophers—lived in community, aiding one another in the pursuit of wisdom and holiness. While asceticism may be mistaken by outsiders for the genuine humbling of oneself in submissiveness and contrition,[138] the ascetic actually reflects the misery of sickness[139] and pious fraud, making oneself ill in the guise of zealous piety: "One who brings himself into ascetic isolation[140] has brought himself into mental and physical sickness and suffering" (III:1: 90).

Ha-Levi thus suggests that excessive humility and self-abasement is actually a form of arrogance, a pretense to being more spiritual than the average person. In a beautiful play with the sound and rhythm of the Arabic language, the *Ḥaver* asserts that today ascetics do not enjoy the delight of isolation (*iltidhadh bi-l-tafarrud*), but rather experience the misery of sickness (*tadhallul al-amrād*).[141] While genuine religious experience might lead to a desire for asceticism, asceticism alone does not bring religious experience. Self-imposed isolation and suffering do not bring the authentic communion made possible through the balanced, communal life of *mitsvot*.[142]

3. *National-Historical Suffering and the Christian Argument from History*

While Ha-Levi rejects the Sufi virtues of submissiveness and self-abasement as a vehicle to religious experience if they are self-initiated, his position with respect to the historical, divinely appointed suffering of the Jews is more nuanced. Countering the standard Christian argument from history—which holds that the Jews' degradation and misery in this world are proof of the truth of Christianity—the *Ḥaver* maintains that if the Jews take their divinely appointed suffering in a spirit of submission to the divine will (*khuḍūʿan li-llahi*) it can indeed draw them closer to God (I:115: 39). The *Ḥaver* thus suggests to Jews attracted to the ascetic life that they already reap the spiritual reward of humility by submitting to their historical fate and remaining Jews. They can fulfill the Sufi virtue of submission as Jews, without taking on an additional path of ascetic self-abnegation.

The *Ḥaver* turns the argument from history on its head. To those who would deduce from the degradation[143] and misery[144] of the Jewish people that their spiritual light has been extinguished, he points out that Christians and Muslims themselves extoll the virtue of humility—exemplified in the persons of Jesus, Muḥammad, and their early followers—as a means to draw one near to God (I:113: 38). Those who extoll the spiritual value of suffering and lowliness cannot point to the Jews' degraded status as a sign of God's displeasure.

The King quotes from the Book of Isaiah to show that the Hebrew Bible declares that God dwells among the contrite and humble.[145] Moreover he explicates Isaiah using Sufi terminology; Isaiah's words show that lowliness (*dhilla*) and humility (*khuḍūʿ*) are more appropriate to the *ʾamr ilāhī* than are greatness and pride (IV:22: 171). By interpreting Isaiah in Sufi terms, Ha-Levi appropriates the Sufi language of humility, but refashions it according to Jewish experience. He reframes Sufi humility from an individual context to a national-historical one, and restricts the value of lowliness, submissiveness, and suffering to that appointed by God. While inappropriate as a self-initiated path to the Divine, these Sufi virtues are appropriate as a response to divinely appointed suffering and exile, and as such can draw Jews closer to God.

The *Ḥaver* concedes to the King that only a small minority of Jews do take on their degradation (*dhull*) in a spirit of submission (*khuḍūʿan*) to God and to the Torah; that more do not accept their lowly status willingly is the Jews' major weak spot, he concedes. However, for those who do accept suffering willingly, humility will reap its divine reward. Indeed, the *Ḥaver* goes so far as to say that if all the Jewish people were to bear their suffering in the spirit of submission to the will of God, the Messianic Age would come and the Jews would be redeemed (I:115: 39). The *Ḥaver* points out further that with one word, any Jew living under Islam could convert. Under such circumstances, a Jew's faithfulness to Judaism in itself attests to his or her surrender to the will of God (I:115: 39; IV:23: 172).

In literary terms, then, Ha-Levi can have it both ways. The historical degradation of the Jews is not a sign that they have been rejected by God. Jews are bidden to bear the burden of degradation gracefully, for it has been appointed by God. If God appoints exile and suffering upon the Jewish people, and if they take this period of exile on themselves willingly, they will both transform the world around them through the doing of *mitsvot* and hasten their own redemption.

PART 2

The Language of Human Striving

Qiyās, Ijtihād, Taqlīd

In chapter 1, we noted that various groups in the Islamic sphere were diversely interpreting common terms for religious experience. We saw that Ha-Levi draws upon a cluster of meanings associated with *ittiṣāl* and *wuṣūl*, co-opting and transforming these concepts by redefining them in a Jewish context. In the next two chapters, we will see that Ha-Levi adopts an even more daring strategy with other terms, including *qiyās*, *ijtihād*, *taqlīd*, *mushāhada*, and *dhawq*. Ha-Levi joins together the disparate meanings of each term, forging innovative links not made previously by Islamic thinkers, and in the process, builds a global critique of his contemporary culture.

For example, generalizing from his criticism of *qiyās* in several spheres—philosophy, theology, pietism, pagan religion and the occult—Ha-Levi portrays *qiyās* as illegitimate human striving (*ijtihād*), any attempt to reach the Divine by sheer human effort. He rejects such *qiyās* and *ijtihād* in favor of witnessing (*mushāhada*) and tasting (*dhawq*) the Divine, that is, direct experience not achieved by human effort, but granted by the grace of God. Ha-Levi transforms the terms *mushāhada* and *dhawq*—terms associated in the Islamic world with Sufi mystical practices—by employing them to describe Abraham's encounters with God and the Jewish nation's experience at Mount Sinai. These encounters, he will argue, bring us closer to God than any form of human *qiyās*.

To understand Ha-Levi's critique, we must first examine the various connotations of the terms *qiyās*, *ijtihād,* and *taqlīd* in medieval Islamic culture. We will then be in a position to discern the creative use Ha-Levi makes of these terms, forging a cultural critique more encompassing than its individual touchstones.

1. *Introduction: The Islamic Context of the Term* Qiyās

In Islamic legal theory, *qiyās* is a method of legal analogy whereby one extends law from cases known from the Qur'ān, the way of the Prophet (*sunna*), or the consensus of the community (*ijmāʿ*) to the many, varied circumstances that arise over time. *Qiyās* is considered a particular form of *ijtihād*, personal effort or diligent striving; more specifically, it means exerting oneself to form an independent opinion in law. A *mujtahid* is someone who by intellectual exertion forms his own legal opinions, whereas a *muqallid* (imitator) is one who adopts the opinion of another through reliance or imitation (*taqlīd*).[1]

Legal reasoning or juridical discretion in the broadest sense (*ra'y*) was practiced in Islam as early as the second Islamic century; its practitioners came to be known as the Party of Legal Reasoning (*ahl al-ra'y*) in contrast to the strict Traditionists (*ahl al-ḥadīth*). The Traditionists sought to find justification for any legal decision in the practice of the Prophet Muḥammad himself, discovered in statements which relate his words and deeds, when they are supported by a reliable chain of tradition (*isnād*). However, in practice, the Traditionists preferred a "weak" tradition (that is, one without concurrent chains of transmission) to a strong analogy (*qiyās*), such was their suspicion toward use of the human intellect in matters of religious law. The Party of Legal Reasoning, on the other hand, trusted individual intellectual striving (*ijtihād*) and the method of legal analogy (*qiyās*) to creatively derive rulings on new matters not discussed explicitly in the Qur'ān.[2]

In earlier twentieth-century scholarship it was often written that by the fourth Islamic century (900 C.E.), the gates of *ijtihād* were closed. A consensus was reached that jurists could no longer venture independent decisions, that all legal issues had essentially been satisfactorily decided. From now on all that was possible or necessary in the realm of religious law was imitation or reliance (*taqlīd*): the unquestioning acceptance of the authority and decisions of one's predecessors. No one in this day and age was thought qualified to exercise his own intellectual analogies (*qiyāsat*), to strive (to be *mujtahid*) by means of his own independent legal reasoning. Everyone was now an imitator (*muqallid*), bound to practice *taqlīd*, unquestioning reliance.[3]

However, more recent scholarship suggests that this commonly accepted view is inaccurate, that both in theory and practice, there continued to be scholars who met the qualifications of the independent jurisprudent (*mujtahid*) and actually exercised *ijtihād* in their judicial rulings, including the renowned eleventh-century theologian al-Ghazzālī.[4] For our purposes, what is significant is that the matter of independent judgment—who was qualified to be a *mujtahid*, the unfortunate necessity for *taqlīd*—was under debate in the tenth and eleventh centuries. Among the educated classes, *taqlīd* had a negative connotation; *taqlīd* was contrasted with the independent, innovative, creative spirit of *qiyās* and *ijtihād*.[5] This was particularly so among the philosophers who, as we shall see, adapted these terms to their own field of inquiry.

It is fair to say, nevertheless, that by the tenth century the terms of the debate had shifted. The great jurisprudent al-Shāfiʿī (b. 767 C.E.), called by some the "architect of Islamic Law," restricted the exercise of juridical discretion (*raʿy*) to the strict method of analogy (*qiyās*) alone. At the same time Shāfiʿī accepted the Traditions (*ḥadīth*) of Muḥammad's practice (*sunna*)—now regarded as divinely inspired—as a source of knowledge of the divine will equal to the Qurʾān. In a certain sense, the Traditionists had won, although by incorporating and subsuming the arguments of those who upheld independent judicial reasoning. The orthodox schools of law for the most part accepted individual judicial discretion as one of the four roots of Islamic law—along with Qurʾān, the practice of the Prophet (*sunna*), and the consensus of the community (*ijmāʿ*)—but they narrowly restricted its domain to strict analogy alone.[6]

Moreover, there continued to be vocal opponents of *qiyās*. Dāwūd al-Ẓāhirī (d. 884)—his moniker *Ẓāhirī* describes him as "the literalist"—avoided reasoning by analogy wherever possible, although even he recognized that recourse to analogy was sometimes necessary. As one of his predecessors had explained: "written texts are limited, but the incidents of daily life unlimited, and . . . it is impossible for something infinite to be enclosed by something finite."[7] Al-Ẓāhirī preferred, however, to rule based upon the literal content of Qurʾān and traditions alone. The influential orthodox theologian Ibn Ḥazm (d. 1064) upheld the tradition of the Ẓāhirī school, while the Ḥanbalī school and the Shīʿi jurists rejected *qiyās* absolutely.[8]

Because of its association with the use of the human intellect, philosophers extended the term *qiyās* from the realm of legal reasoning to that of philosophical reason. *Qiyās* was the term they coined for the Aristotelian syllogism; its meaning was thereby extended not only from legal analogy to philosophical syllogism, but in a broader sense, to any use of logic or human intellect to derive truth.[9] *Qiyās* was also indispensible in the literature of Islamic theology (*kalām*). The term *kalām* simply means "word"; in its technical sense, however, *kalām* refers to theology in contradistinction to jurisprudence (*fiqh*). *Kalām* discusses articles of faith, while *fiqh* discusses matters of law or action. The *kalām* theologians (*mutakallimūn*) were therefore those whose specialty was theological discussion. *Qiyās* was a prime tool of the *mutakallimūn*, for it enabled them to prove the existence of God inductively, arguing from the known world to the necessary existence of its unknown Creator.[10]

2. *Ha-Levi's Critique of* Qiyās

With this background, we can explore Ha-Levi's critique of *qiyās*. The debate between the Party of Tradition and the Party of Reason was focused in the sphere of jurisprudence, while the use of *qiyās* was debated in the discrete realms of law, philosophy, and theology. Ha-Levi's critique, in contrast, extends beyond these discrete spheres to reflect an entire religious orientation. Ha-Levi's critique innovates by viewing *qiyās* as any human-initiated attempt to bridge the gap between the human and the Divine. Ha-Levi thus capitalizes on certain negative connotations of *qiyās* now in the air and applies it to all the spheres to which he extends the term *qiyās*, including the legal, philosophical, mystical, and occult spheres. Ha-Levi's use of *qiyās* in various ways can be seen to form a coherent pattern:

1. In the *legal sphere*, Ha-Levi criticizes the Karaites for using their own individual legal analogies (*qiyāsāt*) to interpret revealed law. According to Ha-Levi, divine revelation of law, including the oral law, is transmitted by rabbinic tradition. Rabbinic tradition is assured both by the Sanhedrin's institutional authority and by divine assistance in its judicial decision making. The Karaite mistakenly believes that he can use his own legal reasoning to interpret divinely revealed law.

2. In the *philosophical sphere*, Ha-Levi, like al-Ghazzālī, seeks to prove that the claims of *qiyās* in Aristotelian philosophy are pretentious and overreaching. It is not necessarily that Ha-Levi finds nothing of value in philosophy, but he does consider the claim that *qiyās* uncovers absolute truth to be misguided.

3. In the sphere of *mysticism and pietism*, Ha-Levi innovates by using the concepts of *qiyās* and *ijtihād* to refer to any systematic or Sufi-like program for the cultivation of religious experience. Genuine religious experience may lead to a desire for asceticism; however, it is illegitimate and idolatrous to follow an ascetic program of one's own human invention. Ha-Levi also innovates by describing asceticism, monasticism, and isolation as supererogatory pietism, forms of worship not commanded by God. Ha-Levi thus includes all forms of extra humility and self-abasement under his global critique of *qiyās* and *ijtihād*: as self-initiated, self-invented attempts to draw close to the Divine.

Philosophers, like Sufis, used *qiyās* to achieve a unitive experience. Ha-Levi's critique of *qiyās* extends to any attempt to plan one's own regimen for the cultivation of religious experience, whether philosophical, mystical, or pietistic.

4. In the sphere of *the occult*, Ha-Levi also innovates by using the terms *qiyās* and *ijtihād* to extend his critique to magical and occult practices—astrology, alchemy, necromancy, and other methods of divination—through which individuals attempt to discern and influence the divine will, to bring down the *ʾamr ilāhī* into human experience.

The belief that human beings can force the divine will through their own self-invented formulas marks a common denominator between "sophisticated" forms of *qiyās*, such as philosophy, and the *qiyās* of pagan cults. Ha-Levi's rhetorical innovation is to discredit the *qiyās* of law, philosophy, mysticism, and asceticism by associating *qiyās* with the disdained formulas of pagan practices.

A. *Qiyās:* The Legal Context

1. R. Saʿadya's Critique of Karaite Qiyās

An anti-Karaite polemic was central to the *Kuzari* from its inception; we know from Ha-Levi's letter to his friend Ḥalfon that the *Kuzari* began in the context of a debate with a Karaite.[11] We know, too, that the Karaites adopted much from Islamic legal theory and were known for their use of *qiyās*. Whereas the Rabbanites had a large body of law upon which to draw, encompassing centuries of continuous legal development and theory, the Karaites, claiming to be pure Biblicists, were forced to rely much more on *qiyās* to decide cases not mentioned explicitly in the Torah.[12]

Prior to Ha-Levi, R. Saʿadya Gaon had already made a frontal attack on Karaite use of *qiyās*, most specifically, on Karaite use of *qiyās* to derive particular laws—the "branches"—from those revelational laws given in the Torah, the "roots."[13] Saʿadya frames his attack on the Karaites in Islamic terms derived from the debate within the Islamic legal community between the Party of Tradition and the Party of Legal Reasoning. He describes the rabbis solely as bearers (*naqalūna*) of tradition (*naql*), denying that they innovate legally (*yajtahidūna*) or set forth their individual opinions (*'arā'ahum*, sing. *ray*') as do the Karaites through their reliance upon the method of *qiyās*.[14]

Saʿadya thus denies outright that the rabbis actually use *qiyās*. He claims that even the thirteen hermeneutical principles—the principles of

Biblical interpretation by which the rabbis appear to derive laws from Scripture—are not methods of legal creativity at all. Saʿadya sketches a portrait of the rabbis that minimizes their use of legal reason, suggesting that the rabbis do not create law, but simply hand down law by tradition.[15] He argues further that God has ordained one law, and the role of rabbinic tradition is simply to transmit that law, not to elaborate or develop it.[16] Thus the Karaite use of *qiyās* leads to anarchy in *halakhah*, an affront to the will of God. Moshe Zucker has shown that both the general vocabulary of Saʿadya's polemic and the actual arguments he uses have close parallels in the Islamic world, in the arguments against the juridical use of *qiyās* by such Muslim traditionalists as Dāwūd al-Ẓāhirī, Ibn Qutayba, and Ibn Ḥazm.[17]

Saʿadya's critique of Karaite *qiyās* is organized around three major points:

1. One cannot use *qiyās* to discover details of laws given by revelation.
2. The rabbis do not in fact use *qiyās* to develop law at all; the thirteen hermeneutical principles are patterns the rabbis discover in the *halakhah*, rather than rational principles they use to derive law.
3. *Qiyās* leads to legal anarchy, whereas there is in fact only one true law commanded by God.

2. *Strategies of Ha-Levi's Critique of the Karaites*

Ha-Levi builds on Saʿadya's arguments and, responding to anti-Rabbanite polemics, develops his own nuanced critique of the Karaites. One of the standard charges in Karaite polemics is that rabbinic literature, while claiming to represent received tradition, is actually rife with unresolved controversies. Ha-Levi's response to this charge is to push back the question of consensus to the period of the Second Temple. Rather than focusing on the post-Sanhedrin period where the majority of controversies are found, Ha-Levi points to the absolute consensus that he maintains existed throughout the entire Second Temple period. Ha-Levi thus traces the source of rabbinic consensus and institutional authority to the period in which the Sanhedrin sat within the Jerusalem Temple, and attributes the breakdown of consensus to the loss of the Sanhedrin. Like Saʿadya, Ha-Levi maintains that disputes from the early

Mishnaic period on are just details which do not affect the main lines of tradition.[18] Moreover the fact that the Sanhedrin sat in the Jerusalem Temple is not incidental for Ha-Levi; the "place which the Lord shall choose" is the abode of the *Shekhinah*. Ha-Levi maintains that the Sanhedrin received divine assistance in their interpretation of law, which guaranteed the correct decision.[19]

A second Karaite charge to which Ha-Levi responds is one set forth by the tenth-century Karaite Qirqisānī specifically in response to Sa'adya's anti-Karaite writings. Qirqisānī points out that when Sa'adya attacks Karaite use of *qiyās*, he is actually rejecting an exegetical method of the rabbis, *heqesh* (analogy)—one of R. Ishmael's thirteen principles by which the Torah is interpreted.[20] A late-tenth-century Karaite author, Yefet b. 'Elī, argues similarly that while Sa'adya on the one hand rejects the use of analogy in *halakhah*, on the other hand he upholds the rabbis' teachings[21] in the Mishnah and Talmud, which are themselves built upon inference,[22] including the thirteen hermeneutical principles. "Thus," writes Yefet, "[Sa'adya] is like the person who says: The words of So and So are false, but I believe them because So and So said them."[23]

In several nuanced ways, Ha-Levi counteracts the Karaite argument that the rabbis themselves, like the Karaites, use *qiyās*. Ha-Levi's approach is a variation on a standard medieval defense of rabbinic exegesis: the assertion that rabbinic exegeses (*derashot*) are in fact just a support (*asmakhta*) for laws known independently by received tradition.

Ha-Levi makes this argument, however, using Islamic terminology. The Khazar King asserts that even if the Sages should appear to derive some legal opinions through the use of *qiyās*, these conclusions are supported by (*musnad 'ilā*) a tradition (*naql*) from the prophets (III:38). Ha-Levi's Arabic readers would be aware that in Islamic law, to verify the authenticity of a Prophetic tradition, one must invoke a chain of authority as a support (*isnād*). Through his Arabic terminology, Ha-Levi therefore suggests that the conclusions of rabbinic reasoning are in fact supported by sound tradition—tradition which meets standards of authenticity respected in the Islamic world.

This approach, of course, harkens back to that of Sa'adya. Sa'adya's attitude toward *midrash halakhah* had a decisive impact on the medieval Jewish tradition, particularly in the Islamic sphere. As we have seen, Sa'adya argues that details of the Law required for Jewish practice cannot be discerned from Scripture itself.[24] How then does he account for apparent rabbinic attempts to derive such details of law from Scripture? Drawing upon the Talmudic concept of *asmakhta*, he argues that such *derashot* represent mere supports or mnemonic devices (*asmakhtot*) for laws known independently by tradition.

However, Saʿadya has given the Talmudic concept of *asmakhta* a new twist. In the Talmud, the term describes exegesis used to support a law regarded as binding by the authority of the rabbis. Saʿadya, however, uses the term for the exegesis underlying laws deemed to have Scriptural authority as well. Saʿadya therefore denies categorically that the Sages use legal exegesis; the rabbis are simply bearers of tradition. The thirteen hermeneutical principles that the rabbis use to interpret the Torah represent patterns the rabbis discover in the *halakhah*, rather than principles they use to derive law.[25]

Ha-Levi is thus following in the footsteps of Saʿadya when he suggests that rabbinic *qiyās* is actually supported by a tradition from the prophets. His view is not simply a restatement of Saʿadya's, however, as becomes apparent in III:68–73, where he presents a two-fold position on rabbinic exegesis. The Khazar king protests that *qiyās* (here, probably something like common sense) rejects as absurd the rabbis' interpretation of verses. The *Ḥaver* replies that given the precision of the Sages' halakhic interpretation, can one imagine (*a-fa-yuqās*—related to *qiyās*) that they are ignorant of what we know about Biblical verses (III:71: 143)? In a clever rhetorical twist, the King protests with puzzlement that whereas the Talmudic rabbis' interpretation of laws[26] is always congruent with *qiyās*, their interpretation of verses in the Torah[27] rarely accords with *qiyās*. This leaves two alternatives: either we are ignorant of the rabbis' method of interpreting the Torah, or those who interpreted the Torah were not those who interpreted the *halakhah*.

The *Ḥaver* replies with two alternatives of his own. Either the rabbis possessed by tradition (*naqlan*) some secret methods for applying the thirteen hermeneutical principles, or their interpretations are just supports; they used the verses of the Torah as a mnemonic device for an interpretation they had received by tradition (*naql*) (III:73: 143). Whichever is the case, it is necessary to rely on the Sages,[28] given their knowledge, piety, diligence,[29] and their great number, which makes the notion of collusion impossible.

This picture is less rigid and more complex than that of Saʿadya. Ha-Levi's language might even open the possibility that the rabbis use *qiyās* to engage in creative legal decision making. Nevertheless, the *Ḥaver* makes clear that when the Sages appear to use *qiyās*, their *qiyās* is in fact supported by a tradition (*naql*) from the prophets (III:38: 121). The rabbis' comments on Scripture seem mysterious to us only because they are at times based upon traditions or principles of which we are ignorant.[30] We simply do not have all the evidence we need to understand rabbinic exegesis.

Ha-Levi's defense of rabbinic tradition thus contains several interwoven threads. Divine revelation of law is transmitted by rabbinic tradition. The main lines of rabbinic tradition can be traced to the early Mishnaic period, when the Sanhedrin sat within the Jerusalem Temple. There are four supports that assure the truth of the assertions of the Sages:

a. The *institutional authority* of the Sanhedrin.
b. *Divine assistance* in the Sanhedrin's judicial decision making.
c. *Consensus* of a full scholarly community both within each generation and across generations.
d. *Rabbinic traditions*, which support any legal opinions the Sages might arrive at independently through the use of *qiyās*. If we do not understand the rabbis' reasoning, it must be because we are lacking knowledge of some tradition (*naql*) that would explain their methodology.

Ha-Levi criticizes Karaite *qiyās* as lacking these four supports. In addition he argues that when it comes to interpreting divinely revealed law, *qiyās* is completely out of its league.[31] Finally, the *Ḥaver* points out that the Karaites achieve consensus only when they rely upon Karaite tradition.[32] However, if they must rely upon tradition, they would be best off accepting that of the Sages, which is the most reliable.

Saʿadya held a strict *asmakhta* theory of rabbinic exegesis: according to Saʿadya, the rabbis use the thirteen hermeneutical principles not to derive law, but rather to find support in the Torah for independently known traditions. Ha-Levi's version of the *asmakhta* theory expands upon that of Saʿadya, adding that the rabbis may have possessed traditions and methods of interpretation that are lost to us today. Ha-Levi thus echoes Saʿadya in pointing to the inadequacy of *qiyās* to interpret revealed law. However, Ha-Levi goes beyond Saʿadya's focus on tradition: he invokes as a source of authority not only rabbinic consensus dating from the period of the Second Temple, but actual divine inspiration of the Sanhedrin. Ha-Levi broadens Saʿadya's attack on the Karaites by grounding rabbinic law not only in received tradition, but in continued divine inspiration.

3. *Ha-Levi's Response to Karaite Legal Anarchy; His Ironic Use of* Taqlīd

The Karaites accused the rabbis of adding to the Torah through Talmudic legislation, violating the prohibition of Deuteronomy 13:1, "You shall not add to or take away from it."[33] In a clever rhetorical twist, Ha-Levi turns this Karaite criticism back against the Karaites. He argues that this prohibition was in fact intended to proscribe the use of *qiyās* by individuals other than the Sanhedrin, so that unauthorized individuals not "pretentiously exercise their intellects,[34] pretend to be wise [or: play the judge],[35] and themselves contrive laws by [their own] analogies (*qiyāsāt*) as the Karaites do" (III:41: 124).

The Karaites further challenged the authority of rabbinic tradition on the ground that there is no certainty in the Talmud, owing to the prevalence of unresolved controversies. Like Saʿadya, Ha-Levi argues that it is the Karaite free exercise of *qiyās* that in fact results in anarchy; even one individual "will not remain with one law, for a new opinion will appear to him every day as he increases his knowledge or meets someone with a new argument who converts him to his opinion" (III:38: 120).[36]

The King points out that when there is consensus rather than divergence among Karaites, one knows that "they are relying (*muqallidūna*) upon one or many of their predecessors" (120). Ha-Levi derives his terminology from Islamic legal theory, from the distinction between those qualified to formulate law independently (*mujtahidūna*) and those who are bound to rely on the authoritative opinions of others (*muqallidūna*, "imitators"), who are only permitted unquestioning reliance (*taqlīd*).

As we have noted, intellectuals had given *taqlīd* a pejorative connotation of servile intellectual conformity; *taqlīd* was contrasted with the independent, innovative, creative spirit of *qiyās* and *ijtihād*.[37] Ha-Levi uses the pejorative connotations of the term *taqlīd* ironically, arguing that although the Karaites criticize the Rabbanites for their reliance upon tradition, the Karaites themselves ultimately are bound to *taqlīd* as well.

Ha-Levi's dialogue builds upon arguments for the necessity of tradition found in rabbinic sources and formalized during the period of the gaonim, most particularly in the letter of R. Hai Gaon (939–1038).[38] The *Ḥaver* prods the Khazar King to concede that the Karaites, like the rabbis, believe the written Torah is authentic and trustworthy. In order to have a completely trustworthy text, the King admits, a community must rely upon the judgment of someone divinely assisted,[39] if not a prophet. If this is required for the correct punctuation and vocalization of the Torah, it is necessary all the more for the meaning[40] of the text. The community needs an interpretive tradition that is completely trustworthy because its source is divine, and must follow it faithfully.[41] The necessity of *taqlīd* for the written text of the Torah proves its necessity—for Karaites no less than Rabbanites—for the Torah's interpretation as well. The Karaites, like the rabbis, are bound to rely on the authority of their predecessors; it should come as no surprise, then, that historically this is the case.

4. *Ha-Levi's Critique of Karaite* Ijitihād

R. Saʿadya is intent on denying that the Sages exercise (*yajtahidūna*) their own opinions.[42] Ha-Levi picks up Saʿadya's critique of Karaite *ijtihād* and develops it. The Khazar King is initially impressed by Karaite *ijtihād*, but after hearing the *Ḥaver*'s critique of Karaite legal theory, he makes a startling concession. The Karaite can never be totally secure in his religious observance, the King admits, because as far as his diligence (*ijtihād*) extends, he knows the laws he practices are the result of his own pretentious analogizing (*taqayyus*)[43] and "playing the judge."[44] The Rabbanite, in contrast, knows that his Law is transmitted,[45] based upon a sound chain of tradition (*isnād*) from trustworthy individuals whose knowledge is from God (III:50: 131).

Ha-Levi thus plays off two senses of the term *ijtihād*: a nontechnical sense of zealous religious devotion, and its unarticulated echo, the technical sense of individually initiated legislation. Ha-Levi suggests that for all his religious devotion, the Karaite is haunted by the knowledge that the "commandments" he practices are in truth the product of his own intellect—a subtle form of idolatry.

Ha-Levi's foil to *ijtihād* is a standard Islamic foil: true, transmitted tradition (*naql*) supported by a chain of reliable authority (*isnād*). The Karaite knows there are many among the nations more diligent in striving (*mujtahidūna*) than he (III:50: 131). The King himself is said to be very diligent (*mujtahid*) in the pagan Khazar religion, but discovers diligence alone is not sufficient (I:1: 3). Ha-Levi has thus extended the term *ijtihād* beyond its strict legal context of freedom to innovate law creatively. By using the term in a less technically precise sense to signify any kind of religious striving, any human-initiated effort in religious matters, Ha-Levi has extended his critique beyond that of the Muslim Traditionists.

To the King's admiration of Karaite *ijtihād*, the *Ḥaver* responds that the Karaites are like wanderers in the wilderness who must always be vigilant and properly armed lest they be attacked by robbers, while the rabbis can rest content upon their beds of *taqlīd*, safe and secure.[46] The *Ḥaver* here explicitly calls the rabbis "those upon whom we rely" (or "those whom we imitate") (*al-muqalladūna*), in comparison with the Karaites, whom he concedes show greater individual initiative (*ijtihād*). However he sees the Karaites' greater *ijtihād* as a defensive anxiety, a sign of the weakness of their position rather than a sign of strength. With biting irony, Ha-Levi exploits the pejorative connotation of *taqlīd* as unthinking, slavish obedience. The lesser effort of the rabbis and those who rely upon them is not a sign of intellectual laziness but of certainty.

There are times, however, when Ha-Levi uses the term *ijtihād* positively; he praises diligence when it has a preservative, rather than an innovative function. The King affirms with the *Ḥaver* that the work of the Masoretes, who preserve the tradition of the text of the Torah, is not superfluous and idle work, but rather an effort (*ijtihād*) in that which is obligatory.[47] The *Ḥaver* also points to the Sages' diligence with reverence, as proof of their reliability as bearers of tradition: "What need is there for me to point out to you these (halakhic) details after I've told you the necessity for reliance (on tradition) (*taqlīd*), the trustworthiness[48] of those upon whom we rely (i. e., the rabbis) (*al-muqalladīna*), their greatness and their diligence (*ijtihād*)?"[49]

Elsewhere, he points to the Sages' *ijtihād* as proof of their reliability as Biblical exegetes, despite certain puzzling examples of rabbinic Biblical exegesis: "Relying on the Sages is necessary, considering the soundness of their wisdom, piety, and diligence [*ijtihād*] and their great number, which does not permit collusion. Therefore, we should not doubt their words, but our understanding." He points out that the very fact that we possess these traditions of exegesis is due to the *ijtihād* of disciples who recorded carefully the words of their teachers.[50]

Finally, the *Ḥaver* suggests that is need for a kind of spiritual *ijtihād* in private religious life, to be distinguished from the *ijtihād* which the Karaites exercise in the interpretation of law. The rabbis adhere to strict boundaries in religious law, to the parameters of legal study or investigation. At times this approach will yield legal loopholes that are off-putting to the religious sensibility. There is thus a need for the individual to exercise a kind of *ijtihād*, to exert him or herself beyond the letter of the law, so as not to take advantage in practice of every loophole that is permitted in theory.[51]

The *Ḥaver* maintains that the Karaites, in contrast, work primarily from *ijtihād* in their legal interpretation, with no respect for the boundaries of strict law. Their *qiyās* can thus lead them to overstep the limits of commandments as spelled out in the Torah (III:49: 128–29). While there is a place for *ijtihād* in personal religious life, legal *qiyās* must be always be bounded by the limits of tradition. The king errs, suggests the *Ḥaver*, by mistaking the Karaite's excessive legal striving for personal spiritual effort. The Rabbanites, who use both approaches—strict legal investigation (*naẓar fikhi*) and individual spiritual effort (*ijtihād dīnī*)—are held to be superior to the Karaites, who rely on *ijtihād* alone (III:50: 131).

The *Ḥaver* asserts that one should not follow one's own taste and opinion[52] in reasoning, that these are unique to the individual and will lead to the legal anarchy of the Karaites, whereby one finds in one house ten different opinions.[53] If one wants to undertake legal investigation for oneself, one should investigate the roots of laws known from tradition[54] and from the Torah,[55] using the traditional methods of rabbinic interpretation[56] (i. e., the thirteen hermeneutical principles) to trace the way specific laws are derived through analogies (*qiyāsāt*) used by the tradition.[57] Rather than embark upon one's own path of interpretation, one should follow the path of rabbinic logic, retracing the branches of rabbinic law to their roots in the Torah, and putting one's faith in these (III:49: 129–30).[58]

Finally, we should note that in his critique of Karaite *qiyās* and *ijtihād*, Ha-Levi may be drawing on ascetic as well as legal connotations of these terms. The Karaites not only innovated legally, but did so by making laws of purity more stringent, and by taking on ascetic practices of self-mortification. We know historically that the mourners of Zion (*avale tsion*) among the Karaites had admirers among the Rabbanites.[59] This may be what disturbed Ha-Levi even more than Karaite legal sophistry: the presumption that rabbinic Judaism was not sufficiently stringent and ascetic. Here too, Ha-Levi will argue, the appearance of *ijtihād* is deceptive. The moderation of the rabbis is a virtue, not a blemish.

In summary, the *Ḥaver* argues that Karaite *ijtihād* in the strict legal sense—the freedom to innovate law—is no virtue, but a sign that Karaites lack sound tradition. The Sages exert themselves to preserve the Law that God has given, not to out-do God by inventing laws of their own. It is true that personal *ijtihād* is sometimes necessary to correct for legal loopholes permitted by the Law. The *Ḥaver* argues, however, that whereas the rabbis respect the limits of tradition, the Karaites' excessive legal striving oversteps the boundaries of the Law. It is better to direct one's effort toward tracing rabbinic law to its sources in the Torah, thereby confirming one's faith in rabbinic tradition.

Ha-Levi extends his critique of *ijtihād* to include any human-initiated effort to reach the Divine. Zealous striving is impressive at first glance, but *ijtihād* can be misleading. Authentic spirituality is expressed not in excessive striving, but in quiet certainty, resting on the bedrock of God-given law and true tradition.

B. *Qiyās*: The Philosophical Context

Despite the fact that the *Kuzari* began as a result of questions from a Karaite, as the book stands now, its central opponent is the philosopher. The challenge issued by philosophy is set out in the philosopher's initial speech, and serves as a background for all subsequent discussion.[60] Though the philosopher does not explicitly mention *qiyās*, Ha-Levi's readers would associate *qiyās* with the method of philosophical reasoning and with the philosopher's raison d'être.

As Baneth and others have shown, Ha-Levi, like the Islamic thinker Ghazzālī, sought to prove that the claims of Aristotelian philosophy were pretentious and overreaching. It is not necessarily that Ha-Levi found nothing good in philosophy, but he did consider misguided the claim that *qiyās* could discover absolute truth.

Ha-Levi's attack on *qiyās* is a unifying theme throughout the *Kuzari*: his rhetorical strategy is to use the negative associations he establishes for *qiyās* in one area to taint other spheres. Ha-Levi's critique of *qiyās* in the legal sphere, which we have examined, will find echoes in the realm of philosophy. Moreover, the terminology of *qiyās* and *ijtihād* is a link that unifies the themes of the book.[61] Using these terms, Ha-Levi emphasizes that God reaches humanity through revelation and prophecy, while humans go astray when they approach the Divine using their own judgment and reasoning.

1. *Philosophical Reliance on* Qiyās

Ha-Levi turns the tables on those who would charge Judaism with a lack of philosophical sophistication. In fact, argues the *Ḥaver*, philosophers mistakenly turn to *qiyās* with questions that cannot be resolved by reason alone; they resort to this inadequate tool because they lack divine assistance and reliable tradition. We should not, then, be dazzled by the brilliance of philosophical proof, but should look deeper. The philosophers overcompensate because of a serious lack; they extend the intellect beyond its proper sphere precisely because they lack prophecy and divine light (I:65: 17; V:14: 212).

Ha-Levi thus establishes a parallel between the *Ḥaver*'s critique of the philosophers and his critique of the Karaites. Both philosophers and Karaites over-rely on *qiyās* because they lack authentic tradition based in revelation. However, *qiyās* is out of its proper bounds in metaphysical matters, just as it is in matters of religious law. The *Ḥaver* declares several times that the philosophers should not be blamed, for they did the best they could; since their knowledge only came by way of *qiyās*, their results could not but be flawed.[62]

2. *Inadequacy of the Method of* Qiyās

Ha-Levi takes shots at the philosophical method in a variety of contexts, showing that it is a less accurate tool than the philosophers have claimed. Philosophers can use *qiyās* to prove whatever they set out to prove.[63] For example, there is no decisive proof of whether the world is eternal or was created in time. The philosophers happen to give preference to those syllogisms (*qiyāsāt*) which argue in favor of eternity; they err in this case by seeking to resolve the question through reason alone.[64] If they had lived among a nation with an authentic, irrefutable chronology, they would have used their syllogisms and proofs to establish creation instead. Authentic tradition (*naql*) from the prophets testifies to the creation of the world, and prophecy is more reliable than *qiyās*.[65] We see here the parallel between Ha-Levi's arguments in law and philosophy: in both, the *Ḥaver* contrasts *naql*—authentic, reliable tradition—with unreliable human *qiyās*.[66]

Similarly, the *Ḥaver* argues that God has given prophets the ability to grasp mysteries of the universe[67] that God has not granted ordinary human beings to know by *qiyās* alone. The evidence of prophetic tradition on such matters therefore outweighs the speculation of *qiyās* (V:14: 211–12).

Not only can philosophers prove anything they set out to prove, but philosophers' criteria for what is acceptable as a premise or conclusion is what they have encountered in nature. The only reason philosophers did not affirm such accounts as the vision[68] of Elijah is because "those things (that are) not perceived by the logical method (*qiyāsan*), the Greek philosophers nullified—for *qiyās* declares absurd anything it has not seen the likes of." The *Ḥaver* goes so far as to argue that if Greek philosophers had witnessed the Hebrew prophets at the time of their prophesying and performing miracles, they would have confirmed them and sought means through the logical method (*qiyāsan*) to arrive at that spiritual level themselves. However, just because one has not encountered something does not mean it is impossible. The fact that a doctrine has or has not been proven by philosophy says nothing about its truth (IV:3: 157).

3. *The Need for Divine Assistance*

The *Ḥaver* insists that human beings cannot attain to all the branches of knowledge by *qiyās* alone, without divine assistance (II:64: 78). The members of the Sanhedrin were knowledgable in the sciences—presumably mathematics and astronomy, those necessary for matters of *halakhah* such as determination of the calendar—because they had such divine aid (III:41: 125). Just as human *qiyās* on its own cannot achieve truth in law or philosophy, so human *qiyās* on its own cannot achieve truth in science.

Even in scientific matters, then, *qiyās* cannot match what is seen by the prophets. The prophets themselves would not have believed the phenomena they report in their visions if they had not known them by way of prophecy, "whose perception[69] is clearer than *qiyās*" (IV:3: 156). Prophecy is the touchstone of truth in science no less than in law and metaphysics (V:14: 211; IV:25: 183).[70]

Once one has attained to prophecy, *qiyās* becomes superfluous. *Sefer Yetsirah*—ascribed by tradition to Abraham, and regarded as the pinnacle of Jewish achievement in natural science—Ha-Levi assigns to an early, philosophical period of Abraham's life that Abraham abandons when he receives prophetic revelation from God. Ha-Levi illustrates this point by taking off on a well-known midrash. Once Abraham had a personal encounter with God, the *Ḥaver* declares,

> how could he not deprecate his former *qiyāsāt*? [This is just] as the Sages explain, "And he brought him forth outside [to look at the stars]" [Gen 15:5] [as meaning] "Give up your astronomy!" That is to say, God commanded him to give up his scientific studies [*'ulūmahu al-qiyāsiyya*] of the stars and other things, and adhere obediently[71] to him whom he had come to perceive by taste, as it says, "Taste and see that the Lord is good." (IV:17: 169)

Similarly, after the *Ḥaver* has explained the complex theories of *Sefer Yetsirah* to the King, the King asks why one needs to posit a role for the Hebrew letters in creation rather than simply affirming creation by the divine will alone. The *Ḥaver* agrees, "When God revealed himself (to Abraham), he gave up all *qiyāsāt*" (IV:26–27: 184). Knowing

God through direct encounter makes Abraham's philosophical quest superfluous.

Only knowing God through direct encounter or authentic tradition can remove philosophical skepticism. When a person grasps the reality of God in a way that transcends *qiyās*, all previous doubts are removed, and one laughs at those *qiyāsāt* by which one had tried to attain knowledge of God and the universe (IV:15: 168). The experience of revelation and the tradition that follows from it establish unshakable belief (I:89–91: 26).[72] Direct encounter not only gives accurate knowledge of God; it establishes a personal relationship. One who has discovered God in a way that transcends *qiyās* becomes a loving servant, willing to make sacrifices, even to die for God's sake (IV:15: 168). Abraham is willing to be circumcized at a ripe age (and "how far is circumcision from *qiyās*!") and is even willing to suffer martyrdom[73] for the God he has encountered through the events of his life (III:7: 96).

In contrast, the relationship between a philosopher and the God discovered through *qiyās* is detached—an objective, nonemotional connection, similar to the relationship one has to any other object of knowledge. The philosopher is simply inclined logically (*qiyāsan*) to accept the truth of the proposition "God exists," rather than being passionately committed to the point of martyrdom. Philosophers, asserts the *Ḥaver*, only acknowledge God so long as their lives are not endangered (IV:16: 168–69).

4. *Philosophical* Qiyās *and* Taqlīd

The concept of *taqlīd* holds up a contrast between the philosopher and the religious believer as well. We have seen that rationalists in the Islamic world regarded *taqlīd* as a necessary evil, suitable only for persons of weak mental capacity, for those who lack the original mind to pursue truth through striving (*ijtiḥād*) and logic (*qiyās*).[74] Ha-Levi points out, however, that even philosophers operate with a kind of *taqlīd*.[75] Philosophical traditions are accepted on authority and parrotted just as are religious traditions.[76] The sole difference is that Aristotle is held up as the supreme authority rather than Abraham.

Philosophers hold many doctrines that are in fact contrary to *qiyās*, for example the nonexistence of the vacuum (III: 49: 130) and the notion that only philosophers attain immortality (I:110: 38). These views are accepted counter to logic on a kind of philosophical *taqlīd*. The common person, however, prefers reliance upon the tradition of the

Sages to that of Aristotle, the simple wisdom of the rabbi to the sophisticated, elegant proof of the philosopher (IV:17: 169). The common person is correct, in Ha-Levi's eyes. If *taqlīd* is necessary, one might as well rely upon those who are in fact reliable, namely, the Sages (III:39: 123).

Ha-Levi's argument here parallels his critique of the Karaites. Ha-Levi uses the term *taqlīd* ironically to show that philosophical *qiyās*—like Karaite *qiyās*—is less certain than reliance upon tradition, which both philosophers and Karaites disdain. Knowing God through logical demonstration is less certain than reliance upon authority (*taqlīd*)—a radical proposal for an intellectual to make, even in irony.

5. *Philosophical* Qiyās *and Immortality*

With biting sarcasm, Ha-Levi challenges the notion that philosophers achieve immortality through the intellect. The *Ḥaver* questions whether there is a particular degree of knowledge necessary to achieve immortality, and whether it is possible to lose one's achievement if one loses one's knowledge:

> [According to the philosophers' view], what are the limits of knowledge by which the human soul becomes separate from the body, without perishing? If it is the knowledge of all existence, there is much that remains that the philosophers do not comprehend of what is in heaven and earth and sea. . . . If it is inescapable that one penetrate deeply and grasp thoroughly [all these things] in logic and natural science, then [it is] a thing that cannot be grasped, and one will undoubtedly perish, according to their view. (IV:14: 211)

The philosophical doctrine of immortality is as absurd as the notion that one can save one's soul by a mere utterance, that one can achieve salvation through a confession of faith. We see here one of Ha-Levi's favorite rhetorical techniques: to play his opponents off against one another. Here, he plays the philosopher against the pious Muslim or Christian:

> It does not agree with *qiyās* that man should become nought in his nature, body and soul perishing, as is the case with animals, except for the philosophers—according to their view. [The same applies to] the statement made by believers in other faiths—that man, by the pronunciation of one word alone, may inherit eternal life, even if, during the whole of his life, he knew no other word than this, and perhaps did not even understand its meaning. Indeed, how great a word—that can raise one from the ranks of a beast to that of an angel! He who did not utter this word would remain an animal, though he might be a learned and pious philosopher,[77] who yearned for God[78] all his life. (I:110: 38)

Note how the *Ḥaver*, in playing the philosopher against the Muslim or Christian, suddenly depicts the philosopher as a pious soul yearning for God![79]

In addition to ridiculing the notion that one can achieve immortality through accumulated knowledge or a verbal confession of faith, the *Ḥaver* argues that speculation on the nature of immortality is unnecessary for two reasons: first, because *qiyās* alone cannot determine these matters with certainty, and second, because prophetic tradition has already revealed the nature of the afterlife, which *qiyās* is at a loss to grasp: "You have let yourself be deceived by destructive imaginings, and sought what your Creator has not made possible for you, and which the human disposition has not been given to grasp logically [*bi-qiyās*]" (V:14: 211).

It is union with the Divine, achieved through the doing of *mitsvot*, and not union with the Active Intellect as a result of *qiyās* that brings immortality. Speaking of divine commandments that from a logical point of view seem absurd—like sacrificing a lamb and sprinkling its blood—the *Ḥaver* argues:

> If this were not done from the divine command[80] one would belittle these actions and would think that they distance one from God rather than bring one near to God. But as soon as the whole is properly accomplished and you see the divine fire, or notice in yourself a new spirit, unknown before, or see true visions and great miracles, then you know[81] that they are the result of [that action] that preceded—and [of] that great *ʾamr* with which you have united [*ittaṣalta*] and to which you have arrived.
>
> Then do not care that you die. After you have united with it[82] your death is only the destruction of the body, while the soul having reached this level, cannot descend from it, nor can it be removed. (III:53: 134–35)

6. *Demonstration Leads Astray*

Ha-Levi epitomizes his critique of human reasoning in a clever play on words: logical demonstration (*al-istidlāl*) leads astray (*muḍallil*) (IV:3: 148). Ha-Levi thus includes *istidlāl* (from the root d-l-l, to show or prove) in his multifaceted critique of *qiyās* and *ijtihād*. Just as he has extended the terms *qiyās* and *ijtihād* beyond their original legal context, Ha-Levi extends the term *istidlāl* beyond its context in logic to criticize dualists, materialists, and other adherents of heretical beliefs.[83] All these schools arrive at their misguided metaphysical assumptions as a result of the same impulse that guides the philosophers: the desire to demonstrate truths about the Divine (148).

This impulse comes under the scrutiny of Ha-Levi's attack. There is no need to demonstrate God's existence, in Ha-Levi's view; God exists whether or not human beings acknowledge this fact.[84] The greatest proof of God's existence is simply God's presence. When Moses asks God for a name he can report to the Israelites, God tells him:

> Say to them "*Ehyeh*" whose meaning is "I am that I am," meaning the Present One, who is present when you seek me. Let them seek no greater proof [*dalīl*] than my presence among them, and let them name me accordingly. (IV:3: 150)[85]

The *Ḥaver* notes that proofs (*dalā'il*) for the creation of the world and for its eternity counterbalance one another; neither is proved decisively. God has a more powerful method of proof: God performs miracles to prove (*li-yadulla*)[86] that the Creator can do whatever he wills (I:67: 18). Ha-Levi's use of the root *d-l-l* for both methods of proof sets up an implicit contrast. Logical proof is inconclusive; the proof of experience is more convincing than logic.

The way to arrive at accurate knowledge of God is not through logic; we can neither obtain certainty nor accuracy through logical demonstration. Ha-Levi notes that the various methods of demonstration all arrive at results that contradict what is revealed in Scripture (IV:3: 148). However, while *istidlāl* on its own does not arrive at the truths of revelation, the assertions of the Torah are not refuted by *istidlāl*.[87]

The only way that one can discover God is illustrated in the Bible itself: through personal experience, or through true tradition based upon direct experience (V:14: 211–13).[88] Adam, gifted with supreme intellect, would have remained content to believe in a generic God with whom he had no hope for interaction. However when personally addressed by God, Adam verified that God is the unique Creator of the universe, a personal Deity aware of particular human beings—precisely the kind of information philosophers take pains to prove through logic. Adam then passed on these traditions to his children, who in turn verified them through personal experience (IV:3: 148–49).[89]

7. *Nuances to Ha-Levi's Critique of Philosophical* Qiyās

Like Ghazzālī, Ha-Levi acknowledges that philosophers' arguments in mathematics and logic offer authentic, irrefutable proof (*burhān*); according to both thinkers, however, it is a mistake to deduce from this that one can likewise attribute the status of *burhān* to philosophers' arguments in natural science and metaphysics.[90] In logic and mathematics, philosophers achieve consensus; in physics and metaphysics, we find doubt and disputes. If we do find certainty here and there, it is only because there exists a philosophical tradition (*taqlīd*) upon which others in that school rely.[91]

Ha-Levi maintains, however, that his is not an anti-rational position.[92] The *Ḥaver* insists that the Torah does not assert anything that flies in the face of logic, anything that can be refuted through clear, incontrovertible proof[93] or that the intellect declares absurd.[94] On the other hand, in any apparent conflict between reason and experience, Ha-Levi gives primary weight to experience; experience itself is an irrefutable proof.[95] The intellect would not accept certain events—such as the appearance of God's Glory and the consumption of sacrifices—if it were not for eyewitness and personal experience,[96] which there is no refuting (II:48: 69). The events of revelation outweigh the judgments of reason.[97] Similarly, Ha-Levi gives authentic, reliable tradition weight over pure reason.[98]

8. *Theological* Qiyās: Kalām *and* Taqlīd

Ha-Levi does not use the terms *qiyās* and *istidlāl* in his explicit attacks on *kalām* in Book Five. However the term *istidlāl* is itself a *kalām* term; it signifies theological proof, which Ha-Levi asserts "leads astray." Analogy and inference are the prime tools of theology, for they allow the theologian to derive that which is absent[99] from that which is present,[100] to find evidence for God's existence and attributes from their traces in the world.[101] Ha-Levi's biting remarks with respect to *kalām* are thus worth exploring at this juncture.[102]

Critics of *kalām* point out that its arguments are fundamentally apologetic and polemical: their purpose is to defend the faith and to refute charges as they arise, rather than to provide apodictic proof. The historian Ibn Khaldun, for example, writes that *kalām* "merely wants to refute heretics"; *kalām* is "a science that involves arguing with logical proofs in defense of the articles of faith and refuting innovators who deviate in their dogmas from the early Muslims and Muslim orthodoxy."[103]

The King and the *Ḥaver* agree that *kalām* is only needed for those who have already stumbled in their faith.[104] The King, however, begs the *Ḥaver* for an explanation according to the method of the theologians (V:1: 191).[105] He defends his request by admitting that he has already fallen into doubts and conjectures, debates with philosophers and members of other religions. Therefore, he argues, it would be best for him to have knowledge and expertise to refute corrupt views, as he has already forsaken the possibility of uncritical reliance (*taqlīd*):

> *Taqlīd* is only appropriate for one with pleasantness of soul.[106] However, for someone of a wicked soul, investigation[107] is better. All the more so if investigation brings one to the verification of that *taqlīd*. Then a person brings both levels together, I mean knowledge[108] and *taqlīd*. [V:1: 191]

The *Ḥaver* does not appear to disagree, qualifying the King's statement only by suggesting that the situation is even more grave than the King realizes:

> But who among us has a calm soul, which is not deceived by these views . . . of the natural scientists, the astrologers, the makers of talismans, the magicians, the materialists, the philosophers, and others. One does not [today] arrive at faith except after one has passed through many stages of heresy.[109] Life is short and the labor long. Only [unique] individuals have faith by nature, and these views are all repugnant to them, and their souls immediately detect wherein lie their errors. I hope that you may be among those singular ones.
>
> [However], if it be thus, and I can't avoid [acceding to your request], I will not travel the way of the Karaites, who ascended to metaphysics without levels. (V:2: 191)[110]

The *Ḥaver* argues that pure faith is a gift that argument can only poorly imitate. Just as the philosopher labors long to achieve what the prophetic inner eye sees in an instant (IV:3–6: 155–61), so the theologian employs dialectics to prove that which the calm soul accepts by nature (V:16: 213).

Like Ghazzālī and others in Islamic literature, the *Ḥaver* likens faith to the gift of poetry. In contrast to the "frightful babble" of poets who quantify meter according to prosody, the poetically gifted "sense"[111] the correct meter, not erring by the slightest syllable. Ironically, the highest goal of scholars who quantify meter is to become like the natural poet, who is ignorant of prosody. However, the gift of the natural poet can only be taught to someone naturally endowed, who can be taught by the slightest hint (V:16: 213).[112]

It is the same with the nation of Israel, argues the *Ḥaver*:

> Likewise the community that is endowed by nature [with a gift] for religious Law and drawing near to God on High. There ignites in their souls

> sparks from the words of the worthy ones[113] and there arise flames in their hearts. One who is not so endowed needs to study *kalām*; however sometimes it does not help him, but rather harms him (V:16: 213).

Jews should not need *kalām*, the *Ḥaver* argues, for they are endowed by nature with faith. *Kalām* is like the babble of those who try to compose poetry by rules; pure faith is like genuine poetry. However *kalām* is worse than bad poetry; it can actually lead one astray from the truth:

> The highest goal of that *mutakallim* in all that he learns and teaches is that he arrive in his soul and in the souls of his students at principles that are in the guileless one's soul by nature. And sometimes the knowledge of *kalām* harms and destroys many of the principles of truth for him, for they produce in him doubts and changing views. (213)

Like Ghazzālī, Ha-Levi believes that *kalām* can be a veil to truth. However, whereas Ghazzālī believes that blind faith can also be a barrier to truth, Ha-Levi here holds up *taqlīd* as an ideal, if an unattainable one in this age.[114] Indeed, in III:37 the *Ḥaver* suggests that it is only through unwavering reliance upon the rabbis that the soul can find true rest. Theologians had argued that one could never find peace of mind (*sukūn al-nafs*) in *taqlīd*; the *muqallid* falls into doubt at the slightest push. Only by proving the truths of faith for oneself can one find true certainty in which the soul can take rest.[115] Ha-Levi ironically inverts this concept: those who, like the Karaites, are ever inventing new arguments to guard their faith can never find peace of soul; there will always come along someone with another argument to challenge one's claim. If the Karaites are ever found agreeing, it is only because they have resorted to *taqlīd*, relying on one or another of their founders. Better then to simply admit the necessity for *taqlīd* and rely on the rabbinic Sages, who offer sound tradition and thus true peace of soul.[116]

While in III:38 the *Ḥaver* offers this argument in the context of Karaite law, his arguments in Book Five regarding *kalām*—for which the Karaites were also well known—reiterate this position. Like legal *qiyās*, *kalām* has little value; like Karaite legal *ijtihād*, Karaite *kalām* merely boasts an impressive appearance. Who becomes a practitioner of *kalām*? The simple, guileless believer does not answer questions by way of *kalām*; like the prophet or poet, he or she can rarely benefit another by instruction. The *mutakallim* however—like the philosopher who delights in elegant proofs—has an apparent "luster of knowledge" which fools his listeners into thinking that he is superior to the simple, pious believer. The irony here is that the goal of the theologian with his dazzling proofs is to arrive at precisely those principles which the simple person possesses by nature. And sometimes these complex arguments destroy the very principles he seeks, for they produce doubts and changing views not only in others, but in himself as well.

According to the *Ḥaver* the nation of Israel is endowed by nature with a gift for religious law and drawing near to the Divine. Jews, therefore do not need *kalām* arguments; they merely need to hear the words of the prophets and Sages, which ignite the sparks of faith dormant in their souls.

What ties III:37–38 together with the two passages in Part Five, then, is that Ha-Levi contrasts the superficial luster of *qiyās*—legal or theological—with the simplicity of *taqlīd*. In III:37 the *Ḥaver* bemoans the fact that people are fooled by the greater striving of the Karaites and mistake the calm of the rabbis for laziness. In V:16 he argues likewise that people are fooled by the theologian's "luster of knowledge," and mistakenly think the theologian superior to the simple believer.

The Karaites and *mutakallimūn* must run, as it were, to stay in place; Ha-Levi hints that they secretly wish for the peace of mind of those they scorn. Moreover, underneath the pyrotechnics of the Karaites and the philosophers, if not the theologians, one finds the specter of *taqlīd*. It is better, then, to rely in simple-minded "ignorance" than to partake in the *istidlāl* of the theologians, which truly leads astray.

C. *Qiyās*: The Context of Mysticism and Pietism

Ha-Levi's overarching theme is that worship of God cannot be derived by *qiyās*. Ha-Levi applies this critique to the context of mysticism and pietism by arguing that those who use their own human judgment to devise an ascetic path toward religious experience are simply using another form of *qiyās*. Ha-Levi's innovative use of the term *qiyās* taints mystics and ascetics with the negative associations he develops around the term through his critique of Karaites, philosophers, and practioners of the occult.

1. *Asceticism in the Islamic World*

We have seen in our discussion of *ittiṣāl* that a major theme in medieval Islamic civilization, particularly among Sufis and philosophers, was the value of withdrawal and self-abnegation as means to religious experience. Sufi hermits and ascetics regarded humility (*khushū'*) and self-abasement (*tadhallul*) as ways of tempering the human soul to return it to its divine Source. This led Sufis, and to some extent philosophers, to develop a disciplined path of ascetic exercises.[117] The example of Baḥya's *Duties of the Heart* has shown us that some of Ha-Levi's earlier Jewish contemporaries were also attracted to this approach.[118] In Part One, we explored Ha-Levi's rejection of asceticism as a component of his spiritual ideal. In this section we will take up Ha-Levi's critique of asceticism as another form of *qiyās*—a human tool for the cultivation of religious experience.

Ha-Levi extends his critique of *qiyās* to asceticism in a notable interchange between the King and the *Ḥaver* in II:44–50. The King initially expresses surprise that Israel—which had been described as the heart of the nations, intimate with the Divine—does not have more hermits and ascetics[119] (II:45: 68). Ha-Levi thus has the King express the view, apparently held by a number of Jews, that Sufi asceticism and isolation represent the pinnacle of spiritual life.

The *Ḥaver*, in contrast, challenges the notion that one can draw near to God through the ascetic life, through humility (*khushū'*) and self-abasement (*tadhallul*) alone; he argues that one can only draw near to God through the actions one has been commanded by God (II:46: 68). The *Ḥaver* thus includes the way of ascetic lowliness with other forms of *qiyās*, which he criticizes as attempts to draw near to God by self-invented, rather than divinely commanded, means.

In II:49 the King is won over to the *Ḥaver*'s view; he agrees that if one innovates ascetically, one is brought back to the situation of the philosophers and pagans, who sidestep the divine command through use of *qiyās*. The human impulse to ascetic self-denial, he suggests, is actually a form of egoistic self-assertion.

The *Ḥaver* associates asceticism with the philosophers' belief that a virtuous person can approach God by any moral path, whether it be Jewish, Christian, or one that he himself invents. In arguing thus, Ha-Levi taints asceticism with a host of terms that have come under his critique. The King declares: "but now we have returned to speculating,[120] analogizing [*qiyās*], pretending to be wise,[121] each person striving [*mujtahidīna*] to invent law by what their *qiyās* leads them to, and that is absurd" (II:49: 69). Ha-Levi thus innovates by associating the concepts of *qiyās* and *ijtihād* with any systematic or Sufi-like program for the cultivation of religious experience. Genuine religious experience may lead to a desire for asceticism; it is illegitimate, however, to jump-start the process by following an ascetic program of one's own human devising.

A Jew who has had a powerful religious experience—for example, through encountering a genuine prophet or in the great event at Mount Sinai—may witness the divine light and "become spiritual,"[122] which might lead him or her to seek an ongoing separation from the senses. The experience itself may invite asceticism: "separation from [the human] species by purity of soul, longing[123] for those [elevated spiritual] levels, clinging to humility [*khushūʿ*] and purity (I:103–108: 34–36).

Ha-Levi, using these Sufi terms, thus reverses the relationship between asceticism and religious experience presumed by the Sufi path of ascetic exercises and mystical states. Genuine religious experience might lead to a desire for asceticism; asceticism on its own does not bring religious experience. Philosophers who use *qiyās* to achieve a unitive connection are similarly misguided. Ha-Levi's critique of *qiyās* extends to any regimen for the cultivation of union, whether one's path be philosophical, mystical, or pietistic (II:49: 69).

Ha-Levi, it seems, is uncomfortable with setting up any step-by-step plan for spiritual growth outside the *halakhah*. The *Ḥaver* does describe the halakhic way of life as a discipline: the servant of God is one who disciplines his senses (III:5: 92), and diligent pursuit of the *halakhah* leads to the degree of prophecy (V:20: 223–24). However, Ha-Levi resists the notion of a systematic path such as those described by Avicenna and al-Ghazzālī in their writings on the Sufis: training of the will, ascetic exercises, a carefully mapped-out journey of specific stages and states.[124] Rather, Ha-Levi's focus is theocentric: it is contact with God, and not a willful path of ascetic training designed by humans, that enables one to transcend one's humanness.

Ha-Levi also resists the notion of *mitsvot* themselves constituting a step-by-step Sufi-like path. *Mitsvot* are efficacious, Ha-Levi asserts, but one should not spend time trying to trace the effects of specific commandments. Following *mitsvot* as commanded, rather than trying to delineate their effectiveness, brings one near to the divine Presence.[125]

The *Ḥaver* thus rejects submissiveness (*khushūʿ*) and self-abnegation (*tadhallul*) as a path chosen by individuals to reach the Divine. We saw above that Ha-Levi also uses these Sufi terms to discuss the issue on a national-historical level. The *Ḥaver* suggests that Jews are bidden to bear the burden of degradation (*dhilla*) in a spirit of submission (*khudūʿ*), for it has been historically appointed by God. However, it is God and not human beings who decides the appropriate measure of self-abasement. Humility and submissiveness "work" as a religious path only if appointed by God, not if chosen by humans as a theurgic path to reach the Divine by human will alone.

D. *Qiyās*: The Context of Paganism and the Occult

As we have seen, Ha-Levi innovates by extending the term *qiyās* beyond its context in law and philosophy to ascetic practices by which humans attempt to reach God. Ha-Levi further extends the term *qiyās* to pagan, magical, and occult practices by means of which human beings attempt to bring down the *ʾamr ilāhī* into human experience.

Ha-Levi acknowledges that a common religious quest unites pagans and adherents of true Biblical religion: both seek to make contact with the *ʾamr ilāhī*. What distinguishes the two for Ha-Levi is that while the pagan tries to make contact with the Divine through human *qiyās*, the religious believer aims for connection by obeying the divine command known through revelation. Ha-Levi's rhetorical innovation has two parallel functions. First, Ha-Levi critiques the attempt to connect with the *ʾamr ilāhī* through human-invented formulas. At the same time, he discredits the *qiyās* of law and philosophy by associating *qiyās* with the disdained formulas of pagan practices.

That Ha-Levi establishes such a continuum through the term *qiyās* is not surprising; occult practices were considered to be applied sciences. Occult books boasted formulas incomprehensible to the layperson, as did other scientific disciplines. Astrology, like astronomy and medicine, was one of the ancient sciences practiced by the "wise ones" (*ḥakhamim*) of Ha-Levi's day, often Jews employed by the court; Jews were also associated in the popular mind with the science of alchemy (*al-kimiyya*). Ha-Levi's innovation is to point out the common denominator between "sophisticated" forms of *qiyās*, such as those of law and philosophy, and pagan *qiyās*: the belief that human beings can connect with the Divine through their own self-invented formulas.

1. *Pagan* Qiyās *and Dualistic Theology*

As we saw in our discussion of philosophy, Ha-Levi maintains that a form of logical demonstration (*istidlāl*) led ancients into misguided metaphysical assumptions. What Ha-Levi had in mind presumably was a form of reasoning that looks at dualism in the world—day and night, light and dark, good and evil—and deduces two causes, or looks at the greatness and power of the sun or fire and deduces that they are to be worshipped. This *istidlāl* led dualists to believe in two eternal causes, materialists to believe in the eternity of the spheres, and other pagans to worship fire or the sun (IV:3 148).

While acknowledging that the *istidlāl* of the philosophers is more precise than that of other pagans, he notes that the philosophers' *istidlāl* arrives at a God who has no contact with individual human beings and is thus as far from the true God of the Bible as are pagan gods. By placing philosophical *istidlāl* on a continuum with the reasoning and formulas of pagan cults, Ha-Levi deprecates the philosophers' results; he points out that like pagan worshipers, philosophers believe in that to which their faulty human reasoning leads them. While pagan *qiyās* can lead to a dualistic theology, such *qiyās* is not different in principle from the *qiyās* and resulting theology of philosophers among the monotheistic nations.

In contrast to those who would seek to connect with God through humanly discovered formulas, Ha-Levi maintains that God alone is capable of creating conditions for connecting with the Divine.[126] No human science can formulate or fathom these; they do not in any way conform to human *qiyās*. Astrologers, makers of talismans, and other occultists are mistaken in believing that their *qiyās* provides true formulas for divine connection. The conditions for the appearance of the Divine are made known by God, and they are not detachable from God. One cannot simply steal or imitate the formulas and thereby gain control over the Divine Presence.

Ha-Levi suggests this through a rhetorical device, playing upon the ambiguity of the term *ʾamr*, which signifies both "command" and the more elusive "thing, matter, affair." The *Ḥaver* repeatedly tells the King that one can only approach the Divine (what he calls the *ʾamr ilāhī*) by that which is commanded by God (an *ʾamr ilāhī*).[127] This rhetorical motif suggests that there is something of God present, as it were, in the commands themselves, that the commands serve as a bridge between the human and the Divine. It is *qua* divine command—*ʾamr ilāhī*—that the *mitsvot* bring the Divine (*ʾamr ilāhī*) into the world.

Ha-Levi elaborates on this point through several illustrations: (1) the *Ḥaver*'s description of the building of the Tabernacle; (2) the parable of the ignorant person dispensing medicine from a pharmacy; and (3) the comparison of religious actions to works of nature.

The Building of the Tabernacle (III:23)

On first reading, this account might invite a theurgic interpretation. Ha-Levi's language almost suggests that fulfillment of the requisite conditions guarantees God's appearance; the *Ḥaver* asserts that the descent (*hulūl*) of the *Shekhinah* is bound up, necessitated by, or connected with[128] the human building of the Tabernacle (III:23: 113). This would seem to make the appearance of God in this world a purely mechanical affair, dependent upon performance of the necessary procedures.

The *Ḥaver* insists, however, that pure intention[129] is among the conditions that make possible God's appearance within the nation (III:23: 113). One cannot bring down the *ʾamr ilāhī* by formulas alone; one's worship must be in the correct spirit of devotion. This caveat tempers an approach that might otherwise appear to be theurgic, a magical formalism in which the requisite formula controls the divine will.

He also suggests here an intimate connection between the divine command and the divine presence:

> We have already stated that the only way to draw near to God is through the commandments of God [*ʾawāmir Allah*] themselves, for God alone knows their measure, times, and places, and what follows from[130] such requirements by whose fulfillment[131] comes the favor[132] [of God] and the attachment [*ittiṣāl*] of the *ʾamr ilāhī*, as we see in the building of the tabernacle. (III:23: 112–13)

The Parable of the Ignorant Person Dispensing Medicine from a Pharmacy (I:79)

The fact that the ignorant person dispensing medicine fails to heal proves that the source of healing—"that which is beneficial in itself"—is not contained in the medicine, but in the knowledge of the physician who prescribed it:

> [The ignorant person] kills people with the very medicine which used to benefit them. Should some of them by chance derive benefit from one of those jars, the people will turn to him and say that he was the one who gave benefit. . . . They did not know that that which is beneficial in itself[133] was the knowledge of that learned physician who prepared the medicines and explained the proper manner in which they were to be administered. (I:79: 20–21)

The *mitsvot*, then, are not beneficial in themselves as magic formulas, but because they are *ʾawāmir Allah*, commanded by the *ʾamr ilāhī*: "beneficial [useful] in itself[134] is the *ʾamr ilāhī*, its absence is hurtful in itself" (I:79: 21). This illustration can be interpreted in one of two ways: (1) God alone knows the correct "medicines" and precisely how they are to be administered; (2) that which is commanded by God has something of God in it; there is a *participation mystique* in God's commands.

According to either interpretation, practitioners of pagan arts are likened to the ignorant person who dispenses harmful medicine in the guise of benefiting others, whereas that which is commanded by God is without doubt beneficial.[135] Religiously prescribed actions are entirely determined by God; human beings are incapable of deducing them (III:53: 132–33). Like the mysteries of nature and life itself, the appearance of God is not fully within human understanding or control.

Alchemists believed they could discover and harness the mysteries of creation; spiritualists reasoned that just as the prophets had discovered how to harness the Divine through investigation, research, and *qiyās*, they too could conquer the Divine through *qiyās* alone:

> When the spiritualists[136] heard that the appearance of the divine traces from Adam down to the children of Israel was gained by sacrifices, they thought that the appearance was the result of investigation and research, that the prophets were but people pretending to be wise[137] who accomplished these wonders by means of their *qiyās*. They on their part were anxious to determine sacrifices to be offered up at certain times and astrological opportunities, accompanied by ceremonies and burning of incense which their *qiyās* prescribed. They even composed astrological books and other matters the mention of which is forbidden. (III:53: 133–34)

According to the *Ḥaver*, pagans thought they could imitate the prophets by contriving formulas to unite with the Divine. However it is not the words prophets say that accomplish their miracles; such words could be easily imitated. In fact, Ha-Levi includes Jewish magical formulas in his critique of human *qiyās*. Jews who perform magic using the divine names are no different from pagans using other magical formulas.

The Comparison of Religious Actions to Works of Nature (III: 53)

The *Ḥaver* makes a sharp distinction between magic, which is theurgic, and genuine obedience to divine command, which is not. He asserts that there is something divine, mysterious, and unfathomable at the core of religiously prescribed actions—as at the core of life itself—such that their power cannot be harnessed by human *qiyās*:

> The adepts of magical names [*shemot*], having heard that a prophet had been spoken to[138] [in this or that utterance] and that a certain miracle had occurred to him, imagined the words were the cause of the miracle. They therefore endeavored to accomplish a similar feat.

> The artificial [that which is made] is not like that which is natural. Religiously prescribed deeds[139] are, however, like the natural. Being ignorant of their designs one thinks it but play until one sees the results. Then one praises their guide and mover, and commits oneself to him. . . . [Like human sexuality, if one did not know about childbirth] if [the sacrifices] were not done from divine command [*ʾamr Allah*] one would think little of these actions and would believe that they would distance one from God, not draw one near.
>
> [However], when you have completed what is necessary and see the heavenly fire, or find within your soul another spirit which you had not known, or true dreams or miracles, then you know that this is the result of your preceding action, and of the great *ʾamr* with which you have connected [*ittiṣālta*] and to which you have attained. Then, do not care that you die. After you have connected[140] with this, your death is only the expiration of the body, while the soul that has arrived at this level cannot descend from it or be removed from this degree.
>
> This will show you that one can only come near to God by the commandments [*ʾawāmir*] of God, and there is no way to knowledge of the commandments of God except by way of prophecy, not by speculation [*taqayyus*] or cleverness[141] and there is no bond [*ṣila*] between us and those commandments except sound tradition.[142] (III:53: 134–35)

According to the *Ḥaver*, pagans looking at Judaism thought that the sacrificial system—indeed the entire system of *mitsvot*—was theurgic, a body of magical practices to manipulate the Divine. Ha-Levi wants to make it clear that Judaism is not theurgy, because the *mitsvot* are prescribed by God, not discovered through *qiyās* by clever human prophets, and we do not know the formula whereby they work. The *mitsvot* are a necessary but not sufficient condition for the realization of religious experience. True religious experience is not theurgic in nature; *qiyās* in all its forms is. The appearance of God is in God's hands; human beings can only obey God's will with earnest intention,[143] and hope to receive divine contact.

2. *Pines on the Question of Theurgy*

Shlomo Pines showed that in I:79 Ha-Levi uses the term *ruḥaniyyāt* (spiritual beings) as it is used in other Arabic texts, to describe a kind of theurgy whereby spirits are invoked and "brought down" to do the will of the worshiper.[144] In III:23, the *Ḥaver* includes spiritualists[145] among those pagans who strive (*mujtahidūna*) to draw near to God, whereas the *Ḥaver* asserts that judging for oneself, speculating, and conjecturing in the Law do not bring about the favor[146] of God.

He interprets these passages as suggesting that spiritualists are misguided in their theurgy because they are using the wrong formulas, whereas only a formula whose source is God can be efficacious. Judaism is superior to pagan systems not because Judaism stands above idolatry *per se*, but because it is the only theurgic system that is actually effective.[147] I would like to suggest that the texts Pines cites invite a different interpretation.

In I:97, he points out, the *Ḥaver* asserts that the golden calf was made "from the speculation[148] of those astrologers and makers of talismans among them, who thought that their actions from *qiyās*[149] were closer to the true actions, like the ignoramus who entered the physician's pharmacy and killed people [by that from which] they had previously benefited" (I:97: 31). This is a striking analogy; the *Ḥaver* suggests that actions done from *qiyās* can "kill" as can medicines prescribed in ignorance. Pines does not note, however, the significance of the *Ḥaver*'s key assertion: the astrologers believe their own actions from *qiyās* are more efficacious than those prescribed by God. Nor does he note an additional remark by the *Ḥaver* in the same passage: "Their sin was in the image which they had been forbidden, and then in that they attributed a divine *ʾamr* [*ʾamr ilāhīyya*] to something fashioned by their [own] hands and will[150] without the command of God [*ʾamr Allah*]" (I:97: 31).

The *Ḥaver*'s words demonstrate as close to a Biblical reproof of idolatry as one can find.[151] It is clear that for Ha-Levi, the sin of the astrologers is not that they lead people into ineffective theurgic practices, but that they seek to reach God through self-invented means—that they worship the work of their own hands. The *Ḥaver* argues that pagans believe they can outdo God, that actions discovered by human *qiyās* are more effective than actions prescribed by the divine physician.

According to Pines, Ha-Levi uses theurgic language of "usefulness" with respect to God and God's commandments, comparing the *mitsvot* to medicines that are beneficial because prescribed by a wise physician who knows precisely which medicines are intrinsically effective.[152] However, Ha-Levi does not argue that the divine commandments are to be practiced because they are beneficial; they are beneficial, rather, because they are prescribed by God. These passages may even suggest that God's command does not simply convey correct information about which actions are beneficial; God's command transforms actions in some intrinsic way. Ha-Levi does not say this explicitly and does open himself to a theurgic reading, one implying an almost necessary connection between correct action and the appearance of the *Shekhinah*. However, his repeated play upon *ʾamr ilāhī* as divine command and as

Divine presence suggests that something of the Divine lies within divinely prescribed actions.[153]

Pines argues that what disturbs Ha-Levi about the philosophers is that they fail to benefit from God, whereas followers of religious law derive great benefits from the God they worship.[154] It seems to me, however, that what truly disturbs Ha-Levi is what he sees as the philosophical attitude: for philosophers, God is merely an object of knowledge, rather than someone to love, serve, and obey (IV:15: 168). Ha-Levi's position is summed up in the *Ḥaver*'s statement in III:53:

> The approach to God is only possible through God's commands [*'awāmir*], and there is no road to the knowledge of the commands of God except by way of prophecy, but not by means of *qiyās* and cleverness. There is, however, no other connection [*ṣila*] between us and these commands except by means of sound tradition. (III:53: 135)

The key to authentic religious experience of the divine *'amr* is the *'awāmir*, the commands of God, known only by true tradition going back to authentic prophecy, which is itself the ultimate level of religious experience. Humanly developed means by *qiyās* and *ijtihād* are no substitute.

3. *Ha-Levi's Theory of the Commandments (Ṭa'ame ha-Mitsvot)*

The *Ḥaver* repeatedly points out the miraculous efficacy of the *mitsvot*: the people build the Tabernacle according to the command of God, and the *Shekhinah* miraculously descends (III:23: 113); the priests offer sacrifices as commanded and the divine fire consumes their sacrifices (III:53: 134). Ha-Levi's comparison of *mitsvot* to works of nature is highly suggestive: he portrays the *mitsvot* as a divine mystery, a gift to Israel that no other nation can boast, and that cannot be rivalled by any speculative science (III:53: 132–33).[155]

His portrait of the *mitsvot* seems designed to impress his readers, well aware of the claims of astrology, astronomy, and metaphysics, that the *mitsvot* themselves truly constitute divine science. The difference between human science and divinely prescribed action is that the latter—as an *'amr ilāhī*—is not within our intellectual grasp or control. Over against the flawed efforts of pagans and misguided Jews to reach God through human *qiyās*, Ha-Levi sets up the Jewish way of life. The practice of *mitsvot* alone opens the door to authentic religious experience. We will thus turn to Ha-Levi's alternative to *qiyās*: Jewish religious experience, depicted as witness (*mushāhada*) and taste (*dhawq*).

PART 3

The Language of Perception

Religious Experience as Witness (Mushāhada) *and Taste* (Dhawq)

In Part 1, we saw that Ha-Levi describes religious experience in relational terms as contact or connection (*ittiṣāl*), a term which figures prominently in Book One of the *Kuzari*. Part 2 described Ha-Levi's rejection of human-invented paths to achieve such contact with God, all of which he denigrates as *qiyās*. True religious experience is ultimately a gift of God. Ha-Levi thus weaves his critique of Karaite *qiyās* into a global critique of all human-invented paths of striving for religious experience.

In the following chapter, we shall explore Ha-Levi's alternative to human *qiyās*: religious experience described as sense perception, using the metaphors of witness (*mushāhada*) and taste (*dhawq*).

1. Experience vs. Knowledge

Among the most powerful claims of the *Kuzari* is Ha-Levi's assertion that direct religious experience and not logical demonstration stands at the heart of Judaism. Only a God known through direct experience, he argues, could have aroused the will to make the kinds of sacrifices made by Judaism's founding father Abraham. Hence the following epiphany in Book Four:

> *The King*: Now it has become clear to me the difference between God and Lord, and I understand what [the difference is] between the God of Abraham and the God of Aristotle. The Lord, may He be blessed, one longs for with a longing of taste [*dhawq*] and witness [*mushāhada*], while we [only] incline logically [*qiyāsan*] to God.

And this tasting prompts one who has attained it to be consumed in love for him, and to [prefer] death to being without him; while that logic [*qiyās*] [only] shows that veneration is incumbent as long as one does not suffer or bear hardship on account of it. . . .

The Ḥaver: Whereas Abraham bore justly [all that] he suffered in Ur of the Chaldeans, in emigration, in circumcision, in the removal of Ishmael, and in his distressing resolution to sacrifice Isaac—for he perceived [*shāhada*] the *ʾamr ilāhī* by taste, not by logic. (IV:16–17: 168–69)

A key to this passage, of which the Arabic reader would have been aware, is that Ha-Levi has borrowed a Sufi term for intense religious experience, *mushāhada*. Derived from the root *sh-h-d*—which also appears here as a verb to describe Abraham's sensing of the Divine—the term literally means "witness." Medieval Arabic writers of all shades use *mushāhada* to depict direct experiential perception of God and the spiritual world.

A second key term in the passage is *qiyās*. While I have translated the term here as "logic," we have seen that *qiyās* would carry diverse overtones for Ha-Levi's Arabic readers: for the lawyer, a method of legal analogy; for the philosopher, the Aristotelian syllogism; for the theologian, a tool that enabled one to prove the existence of God inductively, to argue that just as all things in this world have a cause, so must the world as a whole have a Creator.[1]

In the passage quoted here, the *Ḥaver* goes on to argue that someone who has directly experienced God's presence would forsake the way of *qiyās* as useless. He suggests that sensory experience, direct and irrefutable, is more reliable than logic. Ha-Levi's prime example is the patriarch Abraham, and he draws upon oral traditions about the life of Abraham to graphically illustrate his claim: Abraham withstands the test of being thrown into a fiery furnace in his early life in Ur of the Chaldeans;[2] later in his life, he composes the philosophical and scientific work *Sefer Yetsirah*;[3] finally, God tells Abraham unequivocally to give up study of the stars. Drawing upon a well-known medieval *topos*—that of the philosopher or poet who rejects secular pursuits in his old age[4]—Ha-Levi offers a revolutionary interpretation of the rabbinic traditions he has inherited. Once God touched Abraham directly, the *Ḥaver* argues, Abraham completely abandoned his philosophical quest:

For he [Abraham] perceived [*shāhada*] the *ʾamr ilāhī* by taste, not by logic [*qiyās*]. . . . How, then, could he not reject his earlier logical speculations [*qiyāsāt*]? This is the way the Sages explain [the verse] "He brought him [Abraham] outside [to view the stars]" [Gen 15:5]: He said to him: "Give

> up your study of the stars!" [*itstagninut*] [Shabbat 156a]. That is to say, God commanded him to give up his studies of the stars and other matters through *qiyās*, and adhere obediently to Him whom he had perceived by tasting, as it is said, "Taste and see that the Lord is good" [Psalms 34:9]. (IV:17: 169)

In the Talmudic passage from which Ha-Levi quotes, R. Yehudah cites Genesis 15:5—"He brought Abraham outside [to view the stars]"—in order to prove that constellations do not control the fate of Israel.[5] God tells Abraham, Give up your astrology; rely upon God and not the stars! Ha-Levi creatively reinterprets the mandate "give up your astrology (*itsṭagninut*)" to signal "give up your *astronomy*." That is to say, God commanded Abraham to abandon scientific study of the stars, but more significantly, to relinquish his quest to reach God through human reasoning (*qiyās*). The goal of his quest has already met him: Abraham has already experienced God's presence through taste.

It is tempting to read this passage from Ha-Levi as an extended exegesis of the verse from Psalms. The psalmist's cry, "taste and see that the Lord is good" suggests to the *Ḥaver* that intellectual pursuit of God is futile—that human beings have a "longing for taste and witness," a need to behold God face to face.

However, the picture becomes more complex when we realize that just as *mushāhada* is a well-known term for religious experience, so too is the Arabic word Ha-Levi uses for taste, *dhawq*. Furthermore, *dhawq* is often linked with *mushāhada* as an aspect or dimension of the same experience. As ʿAbd al-Razzāq al-Qashānī writes in his Dictionary of the Technical Terms of the Sufis: "*Dhawq* (refers to) the first levels in the witness (*shuhūd*) of the Truth. . . ."[6] Ha-Levi therefore injects psalm 34 with an original twist: he links the Hebrew verbs *ṭaʿamu* (taste) and *re'u* (see) of the psalm with the well-known Sufi mystical states of *dhawq* (taste) and *mushāhada* (witness). This Judaeo-Arabic link would completely transform the way an Arabic-speaking Jew read the psalm. "Taste and see that the Lord is good" was no mere rhetorical flourish. The psalm was intended to evoke a concrete, living experience.

2. *Mystical Knowledge as Sense Perception*

More than simply a coincidence of Hebrew and Arabic vocabulary, we find here a key motif in Arabic religious literature: the notion that knowing God is more akin to an act of sense perception than it is to intellectual knowledge. Ha-Levi suggests that just as eye-witness of an event is more reliable than hearsay, so religious experience gives first-hand knowledge which the intellect, knowing indirectly, can only approximate.

Ha-Levi, like many Sufi thinkers, chooses as analogies to religious experience two forms of sense perception that are direct and immediate. The sense of taste is by its very nature unmediated; no second-hand report, however eloquent, can convey the actual savor of a feast. *Dhawq* is not simply a kind of cognition, but an immediate experience accompanied by relishing and enjoyment.[7] Vision, too, shares this characteristic; whereas a person can hear a report second hand, one cannot see an event through another person's eyes.[8]

Ha-Levi realizes, however, that unlike taste, vision can have a collective as well as an individual dimension: many people together can witness the same event. In fact, the most rigorous evidence is the corroborating testimony of several eye-witnesses; collective visual testimony (*shahāda*) can be mutually reinforcing. Ha-Levi thus makes a startling innovation. Whereas Arabic thinkers had by and large used the verbal root for witness (*sh-h-d*) only with respect to individual religious experience, Ha-Levi—drawing upon the root's sense of testimony—broadens *mushāhada* to the historical and the collective. Ha-Levi uses the positive charge of the Sufi term to advance his case for the superiority of Judaism. Judaism has the strongest epistemological base of any religion, Ha-Levi argues, because the entire Jewish people were witnesses to the event at Mount Sinai, participating in a collective experience of *mushāhada*.

In this claim, Ha-Levi may be drawing upon similar gaonic arguments. R. Nissim ben Jacob of Kairouan (d. 1062), writing in Hebrew, had argued that the nation at Mount Sinai knew for certain that God had spoken to them because they were aware of the event through sensible knowledge [*be-yedʿiat ha-hargashot*]. R. Nissim contrasts this sensible knowledge, which leaves no room for doubt, with knowledge by proofs [*yedʿiat ha-reʾayot*], in which he believes the other nations engage. He even quotes Isaiah's words that the Jews serve as witnesses [*ʿedim*] to God.[9] Ha-Levi's argument is quite similar: the nation as a whole witnessed the Divine at Mount Sinai, and this sensible knowledge is far stronger than any intellectual proof of God's existence. Ha-Levi's innovation is to bring the prestigious Sufi concept of *mushāhada* to advance this notion. Ha-Levi makes the Jewish event of revelation concrete and vivid by depicting it as an experience of collective *mushāhada*.

Ha-Levi draws another innovative connection with respect to the Arabic root *sh-h-d*. The root was widely used by Islamic thinkers in the context of religious testimony. One becomes a Muslim by the simple statement of faith known as the *shahāda* (testimony), by declaring that there is no god but Allah, and that Muḥammad is his messenger.[10] Moreover the religious martyr, willing to die for the divine beloved, is called a witness (*shahīd*) to God. Sufi poets extend this sense of religious testimony by drawing upon a motif from secular Arabic love poetry: that of the lovesick individual who pines away for his beloved, sometimes even dying as a martyr of love. Indeed, for later Sufi poets the martyr Ḥallāj is revered as the ideal lover of God.[11]

Like Sufi literature, rabbinic texts, too, link the themes of love and self-sacrifice. The rabbis derive the duty to give up one's life rather than commit idolatry from the injunction to "love the Lord your God with all your heart, with all your soul and with all your might—even if he should take your soul."[12] Ha-Levi thus draws upon a classical Jewish theme with Sufi parallels when he describes Abraham's willingness to bear adult circumcision, the sending away of Ishmael, the binding of Isaac, and even the fiery furnace, where he was willing to give up his life for God, because he has witnessed God directly. The *Ḥaver* describes Abraham's painful but transformative tests using these Sufi terms:

> Whereas Abraham bore justly [all that] he suffered in Ur of the Chaldeans, in emigration, in circumcision, in the removal of Ishmael, and in his distressing resolution to sacrifice Isaac—for he perceived [*shāhada*] the Divine [*ʾamr ilāhī*] by taste, not by logic.[13] (IV:17: 169)

Like Sufi poetry in which the protagonist is depicted as both lover and martyr, the *Kuzari* shows Abraham, a lover of God, ready to be a witness/martyr to the God he has witnessed, a terminological association that may be original to Ha-Levi. The witness to God is willing to be a martyr (*shahīd*) because of his experience of *mushāhada*.[14]

3. *Witness at Mount Sinai as Public Testimony*

Ha-Levi thus creatively bridges the gap between the Sufi sense of *mushāhada* as individual religious experience and the broader Islamic notion of *shahāda* as public testimony. Ha-Levi connects these two senses most strikingly when he depicts the revelation at Mount Sinai as collective *mushāhada*, a religious experience to which the Jews offer mutually corroborating witness. The collective historical experience of the nation at Sinai plays a central role in the thought of Ha-Levi, and the Arabic root *sh-h-d* figures prominently in his description of it. The *Ḥaver* explains: "The masses did not [receive and] hand down these Ten Commandments from individual persons, nor from a prophet, but from God.

However, they did not have the capacity of Moses for witness [*mushāhada*] of that grand thing" (I:87: 24).

Ha-Levi here takes as his starting point the Biblical account of the event at Mount Sinai. The text tells us that after God speaks the Ten Words, the people out of fear ask that Moses and not God speak to them lest they be harmed. Ha-Levi follows rabbinic interpretation, according to which the nation heard at least some portion of the Ten Words directly from God and then desisted from hearing.[15] The *Ḥaver* thus explains that the people had a lesser capacity for *mushāhada* than did Moses.[16]

Despite the fact that the people did not share Moses' gift for an extended experience of *mushāhada*, the event at Sinai convinced them that the philosophical account of prophecy was completely misguided.[17] Ha-Levi reads back into the scene at Sinai a dispute among his contemporaries between philosophers and traditionalists. God's intention, the *Ḥaver* maintains, was to disprove the philosophers' claims:

> And from that day the people believed that Moses had been spoken to in words whose origin was God. Moses did not first have a thought or an opinion. For prophecy is not, as the philosophers claim, from an individual psyche that has purifed its thoughts and connected with the Active Intellect, which is called Holy Spirit or Gabriel, and thus been inspired. . . . These opinions were refuted at that great scene [*mashhad*], and the divine writing which followed the divine address, when he wrote those Ten Words on tablets from a subtle substance, and presented them to Moses; and they saw it to be divine writing, as they heard that it was divine address. (I:87: 24–25)

The people were direct eye witnesses of this great theophany[18] (*mashhad*—another derivative of *sh-h-d*); it was their own seeing and hearing that convinced them of Moses' claims.[19] They could no longer suspect Moses of being an imposter, presenting them with a Law that he himself had originated in his own mind, but sought to pass off as God's. Once the people of Israel had received God's direct address, they themselves had a taste of prophetic revelation; they knew experientially what Moses had undergone, and thus had no need to construct an elaborate theory of prophecy.[20]

Ha-Levi is not interested in substituting a "mystical" theory of prophecy for that of the philosophers with a new faculty of soul capable of perceiving the Divine.[21] Ha-Levi may have also sought to protect himself from potential attacks by philosophically educated critics when he hedges his explanation:

> I do not assert authoritatively that the thing was like this description, and perhaps it was in a way more difficult to comprehend than I could imagine.

> Nevertheless, the result of this was that whoever witnessed [*shāhada*] those scenes [*mashāhid*][22] had conviction that the thing was from the Creator, without an intermediary. (I:91: 26)

Ha-Levi shows here his dialectical relationship to Sufism. On the one hand, he borrows Sufi terms, drawing upon the prestige of Sufi mystical terminology to affirm that the revelation at Mount Sinai was a profound religious event. On the other hand, he does not want to suggest that such an experience could be the result of a philosophical or Sufi-like program. As we have seen, unlike many Sufi authors, Ha-Levi does not put forward a scientific path, a rigorous step-by-step process whereby one aims to achieve mystical states, and perhaps even prophecy.[23] Ha-Levi thereby protects the uniqueness of the Sinaitic revelation, denying that it is analogous to any experience that could be cultivated by human *qiyās*. Describing the event at Mount Sinai, Ha-Levi rejects the technical precision of the scientist, preferring the intuitive sketch of the artist.

4. *Knowledge as Sense Perception: The Philosophical Dimension*

We should not assume, however, that the contrast between *qiyās* and *mushāhada* was absolute in Ha-Levi's world. Ha-Levi was not a lone rebel against the philosophical method of *qiyās*; Arabic thinkers were in fact debating this issue and expressing the same disillusionment with *qiyās*—and with the way of intellect in broadest terms—as an adequate tool for knowing God. Philosophers in Spain were eagerly discussing experiences claimed by the Sufis, and how they could be cultivated through an intellectual or spiritual path. *Dhawq* and *mushāhada,* and how they could be achieved, were topics of lively debate among both mystics and philosophers. Ibn Ṭufayl's introduction to *Ḥayy Ibn Yaqẓān* offers us a vivid picture of the controversy in the Spanish culture of which Ha-Levi was a part.[24]

Al-Ghazzālī, for example, had written of his study with the Sufis:

> I knew with certainty that the Sufis were masters of states, not authors of words,[25] and that I had already learned all that it is possible to learn by way of theoretical knowledge.[26] What remained was only that which is attainable not by oral instruction and study, but by taste [*dhawq*] and [actually walking] the mystical path.[27]

Ibn Ṭufayl, too, describes his spiritual journey as a two-stage process, beginning with the way of the intellect and culminating in direct experience: "Finally I was able to see the Truth for myself, first by way of study and theory, and now in the taste [*dhawq*] that comes in witness [*mushāhada*]."[28] And Ibn Ṭufayl writes that when the philosopher Avicenna wrote about mystical states: "he only intended that they be [reached] by taste [*dhawq*], not by way of theoretical knowledge which is deduced by syllogisms [*maqāyīs*, plural of *qiyās*], with the prefacing of premises and drawing conclusions [from them]."[29]

Ha-Levi's claim—that the most accurate knowledge of God is more akin to sense perception than to intellectual knowledge—was thus shared among Arabic intellectuals. And it was not within the mystical sphere alone that this claim was gaining acceptance. Avicenna—a well-versed exponent of Aristotelian philosophy—advanced the same argument in the sphere of epistemology.

The term *mushāhada* itself had taken on a technical philosophical meaning which lent itself to such an analogy. Avicenna writes in his *Book of Directives and Remarks*:

> As for perceptions [*mushāhadāt*] they are like things known by the senses; they are the propositions whose assent we derive only from the senses, like our judgment that the sun exists and shines and that fire burns. [Or] they are like subjective propositions, like our witness [*mushāhada*] of forces outside sense perception, [for example] our knowledge that we have a thought, or that we are afraid or angry, or our knowledge of our own self and our actions.[30]

Avicenna also explains that dreams, the visions of sleep, are perceived by *mushāhada*.[31]

Mushāhada, therefore, is the direct awareness of an event, so immediate that it requires no reasoning and admits of no doubt. A.-M. Goichon, in her *Lexique de la langue philosophique d'Ibn Sīnā* thus renders Avicenna's understanding of *mushāhada* as "*vision* [*vue*], particularly vision in the sense of *immediate perception* without reasoning, *intuition*; [it] designates above all *sensible intuition* as opposed to *hads*, intellectual intuition."[32]

We can thus see that the link between the philosophical and the mystical senses of *mushāhada* lies in the immediacy of the experience. Witness of God is an experience as direct and irrefutable as awareness of our own inner states, emotions, and sensual experiences. One who witnesses God knows that he or she has witnessed God with the same degree of certainty that one knows one is thinking or afraid, or that one feels the burning of a fire.[33]

Avicenna makes this connection explicit. Louis Gardet notes that according to Avicenna, "that which is 'direct vision' [*mushāhada*] can only be grasped empirically. It is already thus with sensible intuition; discursive reason can only know globally, without precision."[34] For, writes Avicenna,

> most of what is grasped by *qiyās* is too obscure to be given in detail. It is likewise with intellectual delight[35] and the summit of the states[36] of witness [*mushāhada*] of the supreme Beauty. *Qiyās* informs you only that it is the most excellent splendor, but its singular quality—only direct contact[37] can inform you of that, and that is not within easy reach [of all].[38]

Discursive reason can make the statement "fire burns," but such global knowledge pales beside the direct experience of one's hand burning in the fire. As a favorite Sufi metaphor asserts, there is a world of difference between talking about the taste of wine and tasting the wine.[39] Reason can delight in discourse on the magnificence of God; in *dhawq* and *mushāhada* one directly "tastes" that magnificence, one sees the radiance of the Divine and is burnt by its fire.

Whether or not Ha-Levi was aware specifically of Avicenna's use of this analogy, the idea was certainly being discussed in his milieu, and he returns to it repeatedly. He even goes so far as to suggest that in a conflict between sense perception and reason, sense perception—direct witness of an event—wins out. It is Israel's collective historical experience that proves the validity of the Law Moses brings, including that of the non-rational commandments. The experience itself supersedes that which reason could admit on its own:

> These are the [non-rational] commandments by which Israel is distinguished over and above the rational. And through them the bounty of the *ʾamr ilāhī* came to Israel, though they did not know how these laws were incumbent, just as they did not know how it happened that the Glory of the Lord descended in their midst, and the fire of the Lord consumed their offerings, and how they heard the Almighty's address, and how all that happened to them took place, which intellects could not bear [believing], if it were not for eyewitness [*ʿiyān*] and personal experience [*mushāhada*], which there is no refuting. (II:48: 69)

Mushāhada thus supersedes the reasoning mind. *Mushāhada* furnishes more convincing proof than any degree of sophisticated reasoned argument.

5. *Logical Demonstration Leads Astray*

Ha-Levi goes further, however: he suggests that *mushāhada*, religious experience, not only offers a more certain form of knowledge;

mushāhada actually gives more accurate knowledge of God than does speculation, which is held to be more precise by philosophically oriented thinkers. *Mushāhada* enables one to point directly to God rather than to infer God's existence, with all the room for error that inference brings. A species of seeing brings one closer to a philosophically accurate understanding of God than does theoretical knowledge.

As we have seen, the *Ḥaver* asserts this by playing on an assonance in the Arabic words for logical demonstration (*dalāl*, *istidlāl*) and going astray (*ḍalāl*): demonstration (*al-istidlāl*) leads astray (*muḍallil*) (IV:3: 148). Logical demonstration is not only an inferior method of knowing the God; it can actually lead to error.

Ha-Levi illustrates this with a poet's feel for language. The Tetragrammaton, he points out, is a proper noun in the Bible, God's personal name. The King, however, objects to this explanation: "But how can I personalize one whom one cannot indicate,[40] one whose existence is inferred [*ustudilla*] from its effects?"[41] (IV:2: 148)

Ha-Levi here alludes to the method of inference used in the Arabic theological tradition (*kalām*), in which one demonstrates or infers something unknown or not directly perceived from something directly perceived. For example, one smells smoke and from it infers the existence or presence of a fire. The smoke, which is directly perceived,[42] in some sense points to[43] the fire,[44] which is not directly perceived.[45]

In the case of smoke and fire, we infer the presence of fire from smoke because we have many times seen one following from the other. The smoke reminds us of fire; both sign and that which the sign reminds us of are directly perceivable and knowable. This is what in Stoic logic is called a *commemorative sign*: a thing that reminds us of a fact known before.[46] The Stoics distinguish between that kind of sign and an *indicative sign*, one that deduces the existence or presence of an invisible cause from a visible effect. An indicative sign gives only a hint or indication of something that one has never directly perceived, something that may always remain somewhat of a mystery.

Although the Islamic theologians do not make this distinction explicit, it is clear that they, like the Stoics, are primarily concerned with the indicative sign. By this method, the *mutakallimūn* can infer or point to the existence of an unknown, not directly perceived God (the *madlūl*), from the evidence of God's signs (the *dal īl*) on Earth. The *mutakāllimūn* refer to this kind of proof as demonstration (*istidlāl* or *qiyās*) from the *shāhid*, the perceivable (literally: "the witness," or more generally, "the thing present") to that which is not perceivable (*ghā'ib*; literally: "the thing absent").[47]

Rather than claiming that God's existence can be demonstrated or that God can be known, the *Ḥaver* suggests that God can be indicated or pointed to (*yushar ʿilāihi*). The term *yushar*[48] is derived from the root *sh-w-r*, here in its fourth form meaning to make a sign, beckon, signal or point to; and to allude to, hint, or indicate.[49] Ha-Levi may have been interested in drawing upon the ambiguity of the term *yushar*, both its sense of alluding to or indicating (somewhat indirectly, like the Stoics's indicative sign), and its sense of pointing to, motioning, pointing out (directly, like the Stoics's commemorative sign).

The sense of pointing directly is indicated by the *Ḥaver*'s next remarks: it is, he says, as if one were to ask which of the divine forces (*elohim*) it is fitting to worship—the sun, the moon, the stars—and the answer was Lord. The connotation of the reply Lord, the *Ḥaver* explains, is that of a personal name, like Reuven or Shimʿon, if by using the names of these people one could understand their real identities (*ḥaqiqat dhawātihim*)[50]—that is, one could know and indicate who they were by using their names.

One can indicate who a person is either by pointing directly ("There's Robert," or "That's Shari") or by indicating somewhat indirectly ("Remember Robert and Shari?"). What the *Ḥaver* appears to be saying is that only someone who has encountered a person directly, who has seen or met that person, can know who is intended when that person's name is mentioned. One cannot comprehend the reality of a person by name alone unless that name is a sign reminding one of a reality previously known (i. e., through one's previous encounter with the person), or a sign alluding to a reality that will always remain somewhat of a mystery (such as the Divine).[51]

The *Ḥaver*'s response to the King's query shows Ha-Levi's critique of the philosophical method of demonstration or inference (*istidlāl*, *qiyās*):

> Ah, but [the Lord] *can* be indicated in prophetic witnessing [*mushāhada nabawiyya*] and in spiritual vision [*baṣīra*],[52] for demonstration[53] leads astray [*al-istidlāl muḍallil*], and from demonstration arises heresy and destructive ways of thought. (IV:3: 148)

The *Ḥaver* answers that there is indeed a different way of pointing to or demonstrating the existence of God, that in the case of God the method of *istidlāl* or *qiyās* is inferior. The existence of God is not proven by logical inference from the perceivable, physical world. The Biblical ancestors encounter the personal God of the Bible directly; the Lord is not a God that shows up as the final term of a syllogistic equation. It is not with the five senses and the rational mind that one can indicate or point to God, but with a sixth sense, another kind of seeing, with *mushāhada* (witness) or *baṣīra* (mystical vision, insight).

The term *baṣīra* too has an Islamic context. ʿAbd al-Razzāq in his *Dictionary of Technical Terms of the Sufis* writes:

> Insight [*baṣīra*] is the faculty of the heart—illumined by the holy light—by which [the heart] sees the true nature of things and their inner essences, like the vision of the soul, by which [the soul] sees the forms and exteriors of things.[54]

The terms *mushāhada*, *dhawq*, and *baṣīra* all signify a mode of knowing so direct that it is more akin to our ordinary experience of sense perception than to the workings of the intellect. Subverting philosophical convention, Ha-Levi argues that logical demonstration leads astray, while direct sensing is the most rigorous proof.

6. Mushāhada *as an Alternate Mode of Proof* (Dalil)

We find an additional terminological hint that *mushāhada* presents an alternate form of proof. As we have seen, in IV:3 the *Ḥaver* uses the verbal root *d-l-l* when condemning proof through logic; he asserts that logical demonstration (*istidlāl*) leads astray (*muḍallil*). However, several lines later he uses the same root to describe proof through *mushāhada*. The *Ḥaver* describes all forms of God's Glory as manifestations by which God indicates or proves to the people (*yadulluhum*—from *d-l-l*) that they are actually witnessing God and hearing the divine address:

> And the community . . . called Him Lord, insofar as His command and guidance link with the people and insofar as select, pure people link with Him, until they witness Him [*yushāhidūnahu*] by means of what is called Glory [*kavod*], Indwelling [*Shekhina*], kingdom, fire, cloud, image, likeness, the appearance of the bow, and other things by which He proved to them [*yadulluhum*] that they had been addressed by Him on High—and they called [all those] the Glory of the Lord. (IV:3: 148–49)

Visual proof, the *Ḥaver* suggests, points to or proves more directly than does inference. God finds ways to make the divine Presence manifest—ways more direct, convincing, and irrefutable than the logical cogitations of the intellect.

We find a similar use of *d-l-l* in Saʿadya Gaon's theological treatise, *The Book of Doctrines and Beliefs* (*Kitāb al-amānāt wa-l-iʿtiqādāt*).

Explaining Moses' request to see God's Glory, Sa'adya writes: "God has a light which he has created and which he reveals to the prophets by which they infer [*yastadill*—from *d-l-l*] that the word of prophecy[55] which they hear is from God."[56] According to Sa'adya, visual proof points to or proves more powerfully not only than inference, but even than auditory proof. The prophet may doubt whether the words he or she hears are really from God. God's purpose in revealing the resplendent light of the *Kavod* is to assure the prophets that the word of prophecy they hear is indeed from on High. The similarity in language between the two statements suggests that the passage in Sa'adya may well have been an inspiration for Ha-Levi.

Ha-Levi uses the root *d-l-l* to make a similar claim when the *Ḥaver* expounds upon the meaning of the divine name *Ehyeh*. The intention of the ambiguous name "I will be," says the *Ḥaver:*

> [is] to turn away the mind from thinking about the true essence, the knowledge of which is impossible. So when [Moses] asked [the Lord], "And they shall say to me, What is His name?" He answered him: "Why should they ask concerning things they are unable to grasp? . . . Say to them *Ehyeh*, which means [I will be] who I will be," the Present [Existing] One,[57] present for you whenever you seek Me. Let them search for no stronger proof[58] [*dalīl*—from *d-l-l*] than My presence among them, and name Me accordingly]. (IV:3: 150)

God's Presence alone, experienced in prophetic witness (*mushāhada*), is the only proof (*dalīl*) the Israelites need that God is real.[59]

A passage from Avicenna offers another source of support for the notion of *mushāhada* as an alternate mode of proof. It is not only the case that *mushāhada* indicates God more directly than does *qiyās*; the taste found in witness reveals a personal, affective dimension to the Divine one would not otherwise perceive. In his Glosses to the *Theology of Aristotle*, Avicenna writes:

> That [experience] is joy and light, which come from God through the Intellect; reflective thought[60] and logical analogy [*qiyās*] do not lead to it, except to confirm it. But as to its specific essence and special quality, only witnessing [*mushāhada*] indicates [*yadullu*-from *d-l-l*] that.
>
> Only someone who has prepared himself by the health of the temperament of his soul can attain that witnessing [*mushāhada*]. And one who has not tasted [*yadhūqu*][61] the sweetness may admit its delight by a kind of analogy [*qiyās*] or testimony [*shahāda*]; but one does not savor its special delight except by tasting.[62]

This passage from Avicenna recalls the epiphany of Ha-Levi's King, with which we opened our discussion:

> *The King*: Now it has become clear to me the difference between God and Lord, and I understand what [the difference is] between the God of Abraham and the God of Aristotle. The Lord, may he be blessed, one longs for with a longing of taste [*dhawq*] and witness [*mushāhada*], while we [only] incline logically [*qiyāsan*] to God. This tasting prompts one who has attained it to be consumed in love for him, and to prefer death [to being] without him, whereas that reasoning [only] demonstrates that veneration is incumbent so long as one is not harmed and does not suffer hardship on account of it.
>
> *The Ḥaver*: Whereas Abraham justly bore [all that] he suffered in Ur of the Chaldeans, in emigration, circumcision, the removal of Ishmael, and in his distressing resolution to sacrifice Isaac—for he perceived [*shāhada*] the Divine by taste [*dhawq*], not by logic. (IV:16–17: 168–69)

Ha-Levi's approach thus makes use of arguments we find in Islamic predecessors, but expands them to include collective as well as individual experience. Direct witness and taste offer both the strongest proof of God's Presence, and an emotional flavor that cannot be known in any other way, a flavor that awakens love and an intimate relationship with God.

PART 4

The Language of Prophecy

A. Prophecy as Witness (*Mushāhada*)

1. *Prophetic Witness* (Mushāhada Nabawiyya) *and Testimony* (Shahāda)

Ha-Levi repeatedly uses the verb *shahāda* (to witness) in his discussions of prophecy. *Mushāhada* thus functions as a bridge term, one which suggests a continuum between the private religious experience of those who are not prophets, the experience of prophets, and the collective revelation at Mount Sinai. Playing with the possibilities of the Arabic language, Ha-Levi takes advantage of the multiple meanings of the root *sh-h-d* to offer his own interpretation of the phenomenon of Biblical prophecy.

Ha-Levi, using an idea present in both Jewish[1] and Islamic[2] thought, suggests that in addition to the ordinary human senses prophets have an inner eye, analogous to the physical eye.[3] In contrast to Neo-Platonically inclined thinkers,[4] for whom inner vision is not clearly distinguished from other ways of knowing, Ha-Levi draws a sharp contrast between inner, spiritual vision—which is like sense perception—and intellectual knowledge. As we saw in the previous chapter, Ha-Levi describes prophecy as analogous to other kinds of sense perception, and contrasts prophetic knowing, which is direct like sense experience, with intellectual knowing, which is indirect.[5]

Notwithstanding the direct nature of prophetic witness, just as with ordinary sight there is true perception and illusion, so, too, with inner vision. In both cases communal consensus plays a role in distinguishing between the true and the illusory. The testimony over time of Israel's community of prophets is a litmus test to the truth of any one prophet's visions, just as the testimony of ordinary human beings serves as a check on the idiosyncrasies of individual sense perception.[6]

Human beings generally believe we live in a common world that most of us sense in pretty much the same way. We testify to each other that sweet is pleasant and bitter is unpleasant, that there is a difference between red and green, and so on. Those who cannot distinguish between red and green we single out as diverging from the natural state of vision; we call them "color blind." Similarly the prophets *witness* (*yushāhidūna*) a common spiritual reality about which they *testify* (*yashhadu*) to one another, and see ordinary human beings who lack this perception as blind people whom they must guide:

> One for whom this [inner] eye has been created is a clear-sighted person in truth, and he sees all [other] people as blind, and he guides them and shows them the right way. . . . And he sees a great, fearsome form which points to indisputable realities [truths]. The greatest proof of their truth is the agreement [congruence] of [the words of] all that species [of human beings] regarding these forms—I mean all the prophets. For they witness [*yushāhidūna*] things about which they testify [*yashhadu*] to one another, as we do with sensory objects. We testify about the sweetness of honey and the bitterness of colynth, and when we see someone deviating we say that he is deviating from the natural thing. [IV:3: 155]

The motif of prophets as guides to the blind was present in Jewish and Islamic thought.[7] Ha-Levi's innovation is to broaden the notion of sight, witness, and testimony. Whereas for Islamic thinkers like Ghazzālī, witness of God (*mushāhada*) is a purely private experience within the heart of the prophet or Sufi, Ha-Levi broadens prophetic witness to include communal, as well as individual experience. By broadening *mushāhada* to include collective witness, Ha-Levi makes a bridge between prophecy and non-prophetic religious experience.[8] The collective revelation at Mount Sinai, the religious experience of the seventy elders, and the prophecy of the later prophets are all mutually reinforcing testimony to the prophecy of Moses, confirming for all the people that this Law is not simply the empty claim of an individual or an elite (IV:11: 163).[9]

Whereas among Islamic thinkers there is no explicit connection drawn between *mushāhada* as witness and *shāhada* as testimony—including testimony in a religious context[10]—Ha-Levi forges this connection. Thus prophets can confirm the truth of prophecy for each other, based upon what they have experienced in prophetic witness. Ha-Levi thereby softens the impact of the metaphor of blindness, which, taken on its own, would create for him too great a gap between the experience of prophets and that of ordinary Jews. Ha-Levi wants on the one hand to respond to rationalists who find the prophets' claims to behold visions absurd. He affirms the veracity of prophetic vision by asserting that prophets have an inner eye that enables them to see what ordinary people cannot see. On the other hand, Ha-Levi wants to create a continuum between prophets and the rest of Israel. He does this by asserting that many, varied people among the nation had some experience of divine witness, if not to the degree of the prophets (IV:11: 163).

Various prophets witness a figure seated upon a throne. Each gives corroborating testimony to what the other has seen, just as the Jews at Mount Sinai each bear witness to a common experience. The fact that various prophets testify to a common spiritual reality rules out that the vision is the hallucination of an individual; the fact that these prophets live in different generations rules out the possibility of collusion in false witness (IV:3: 155).

2. *Witness of the Divine World with the Inner Eye*

The *Ḥaver* states in IV:3 that the prophets no doubt witness (*yushāhidūna*) "that divine world" with the inner eye (IV:3: 155). This, too, was a motif in Ha-Levi's milieu. The Brethren of Purity (*Ikhwān al-ṣafā'*)—a tenth-century philosophical brotherhood—had written in their Epistles that "believers, wise ones, and prophets witness [*shāhadū*] the spiritual world[11] with the eyes of their heart and the light of their intellects, just as inhabitants of this [lower] world[12] witness [*shāhadū*] things with their senses."[13] The philosopher Ibn Ṭufayl, too, used the language of *mushāhada* to describe witness of the metaphysical world,[14] showing that others in twelfth-century Spain were aware of this image.[15]

Both al-Ghazzālī and Ibn Ṭufayl set forth parables of blindness to and vision of the divine world. Ghazzālī explains that just as the eye or light of the intellect knows things that the senses would find absurd, the prophet receives another eye, which gives knowledge unavailable to the ordinary intellect. Ordinary human beings doubt the existence of prophecy only because they lack this inner eye and have not experienced its vision. The situation is like that of a person born blind who has *not* been gradually instructed about the nature of colors. If told about them suddenly, all at once, such a person would "neither understand them nor acknowledge their existence."[16]

Ibn Ṭufayl, who has obviously studied his Ghazzālī well, echoes this parable, with a significant alteration: he speaks of a blind person who *has* been gradually instructed about the nature of color. A blind person is told all about the city he lives in, including its colors.[17] When

God miraculously awakens his vision, he finds all to be just as he had learned, except that he knows it now with greater clarity and with a tremendous joy.

Ibn Ṭufayl uses this parable to suggest the difference between knowing the divine world through philosophical learning and syllogism (*qiyās*)—the original blind state—and knowing that world through direct witness (*mushāhada*), the state of being able to see. Those who know the divine world only through philosophical speculation are limited by their indirect way of knowing; they are like one born blind, who must rely for knowledge of color on the testimony of others. One who has direct mystical experience (*mushāhada* or *dhawq*) on the other hand, is like a blind person given sight, who can now see the divine world directly, in living color.[18]

Ghazzālī had used the metaphor to describe an absolute opposition between those who possess the prophetic eye and those who lack it and are thus blind to what prophets see. Ghazzālī stressed that a blind person would neither understand colors nor acknowledge their existence. Ibn Ṭufayl revises the metaphor to reflect his notion of a continuum between intellectual knowledge and the knowledge gained through *mushāhada*. For Ibn Ṭufayl, a blind person who is instructed about color would have some understanding of the phenomenon, without the clarity and joy of seeing color for oneself. Ibn Ṭufayl uses the metaphor of sense perception embodied in *mushāhada* to suggest a way of knowing that has greater clarity and joy than mere intellectual knowledge—a difference in quality perhaps, but not an absolute difference in kind.

The example of Ibn Ṭufayl shows that Ha-Levi was writing within a context: others in Spain were also trying to strike a balance between *mushāhada* and *qiyās*. Ha-Levi, however, is more similar in approach to Ghazzālī than to Ibn Ṭufayl. While Ha-Levi does not reject *qiyās* totally, he makes a decisive split between the indirect way of reason and the direct way of sense experience. Ha-Levi asserts that ordinary human beings, including philosophers, are blind to the divine world,[19] while prophets witness the divine world with their inner eye (IV: 3: 155); that demonstration leads astray and cannot give reliable knowledge of God, while God can be pointed to directly in prophetic *mushāhada* (IV:3: 148). He assumes that once Abraham has directly experienced God in *mushāhada* he would scoff at the way of *qiyās*, the path by which he had previously sought to know the Divine (IV:17: 169).

Ibn Ṭufayl, in contrast, sees immediate experience as coming at the end of a long path of intellectual preparation, at least in his own case. He explains to his student:

> I myself would not have [attained] the truth that I have arrived at, the culmination of my intellectual efforts, without pursuing the words [arguments] of Ghazzālī and Avicenna, checking them against one other . . . until finally I was able to see the truth for myself, first by way of research and speculation and now in the taste [*dhawq*] that comes in witness [*mushāhada*]. I now feel able to set down a view to be preserved in my name.[20]

Ibn Ṭufayl maintains that while theory alone is incomplete, it does have an important place on the path to direct experience.

Even this contrast between Ha-Levi and Ibn Ṭufayl is not absolute, however. In at least one passage of the *Kuzari* there is a hint that Abraham's earlier philosophical stage, which led to the composition of *Sefer Yetsirah*, may have come to fruition in his being granted a direct experience of the Divine.[21] However, later in the same passage, the *Ḥaver* reasserts that one cannot reach God by means of philosophy alone.[22] It appears that one of Ha-Levi's strategies is to offer philosophical argumentation as a kind of fallback position. While he most often argues for the absolute superiority of prophetic *mushāhada* over *qiyās*, the *Ḥaver* seems to suggest in occasional passages that philosophy and prophecy are simply two different methods whose results converge.

In IV:3, for example, the *Ḥaver* argues that the image prophets see of a figure on a throne—an image that compares God to a human being—should not be troubling to the philosophical sensibility, as philosophers, too, compare God to a human being.[23] Philosophers assert this likeness with a rational argument: that in examining God's necessary attributes—such as living, knowing, powerful, willing—we discover nothing in our direct experience (*mushāhada*) that resembles God as much as the rational soul, the perfect human. Prophets, in contrast, directly "see" the heavenly host in the form of a human being.[24] The *Ḥaver* thus suggests that philosophy and prophecy are simply two methods of arriving at the same result. We see here an additional twist; the *Ḥaver*'s argument works because it takes for granted that philosophers, too, appeal to direct experience (*mushāhada*), that Aristotelian philosophy is in fact empirically based. One might go further: perhaps the *Ḥaver* is suggesting that philosophers must resort to *mushāhada*—direct experience—because reason alone does not find anything comparable to God.

We see, then, that Ha-Levi's position is more nuanced than might appear at first glance. Ha-Levi does not completely reject the way of reason; he shows respect for the intellect and its vital role in human knowledge, including the prophet's knowledge of the divine world, as we shall now see.

3. *The Inner Eye and the Intellect: Witness* (Mushāhada) *and Inference* (Istidlāl)

While the *Ḥaver* states that the prophets witness (*yushāhidūna*) "the divine world" with the inner eye—describing what the prophets witness as an objectively existing spiritual reality—he also asserts that what they see is an image which "conforms to their own nature and to what they witness [*yushāhidūna*] corporeally" (IV:3: 155). What the prophets perceive is shaped by their nature as perceivers, who ordinarily sense physical reality.

If, for example, the prophets witness a figure seated upon a throne, they know that this is the image of a king. The sensory characteristics perceived are accurate with respect to what the senses and imagination can grasp, but the rational faculty seeks a rational essence:[25] a wise being who issues commands that are to be obeyed. The rational faculty therefore must interpret the image conveyed to it by the senses and imagination. For this reason, the *Ḥaver* states that we might think of the inner eye of the prophet as "almost" the imaginative faculty, but only "insofar as it serves the intellect" (IV:3: 155).[26]

The *Ḥaver*'s description calls to mind standard Arabic accounts of prophecy, which in turn build upon accounts of the ordinary process of perception. When the *Ḥaver* says that the prophetic inner eye may be (said to be) the imagination "insofar as it serves[27] the intellect," he in fact echoes al-Fārābī's account of the imagination's *ordinary* function, rather than Fārābī's account of its prophetic function.[28]

In al-Fārābī's theory of knowledge, the imagination functions in three ways: it preserves impressions from the senses; it combines these impressions in new ways; and it reproduces or imitates sense impressions.[29] In most people, this latter function of reproducing or imitating sense impressions takes place only during sleep, when the imagination is not kept busy receiving sensory stimuli and supplying them to the intellect. However a particularly powerful imagination can imitate sense impressions even while a person is awake.[30]

The imagination can also imitate intelligibles; the imagination can represent in sensory form the abstract ideas emanated from the Active Intellect. These images, like that of a figure on a throne, representing the idea of sovereignty, are then impressed upon the common sense and the faculty of sight. The images in the faculty of sight can in turn create impressions in the air, so that a person sees these images as if they were appearing outside the mind. Thus does al-Fārābī account for prophetic visions, which depict abstract truths in sensible images, and which the prophet sees as if they were sensory objects outside his or her own psyche.[31]

In Fārābī's account of ordinary, *nonprophetic* sense perception, the imaginative faculty receives data before the intellect does: the imagination receives sense impressions, preserves them as images, and supplies the rational faculty with these images. The rational faculty must then sift through the images, weeding out those that do not conform to what is known—for example, the image of a unicorn—and making sense of the images in accordance with reason.

In Fārābī's depiction of *imaginative prophecy*, however, the process is reversed: the human rational faculty receives data before the imagination. Intelligible "light" emanating from the Active Intellect reaches first the human rational faculty and then the imagination, which translates the intelligible idea into a sensible image. In al-Fārābī's theory, therefore, prophetic vision is simply a translation of intellectual concepts into vivid images. For Ha-Levi, in contrast, the prophet actually learns something from the visual image, which provides source material with which the intellect works.

In the *Ḥaver*'s account, the prophetic inner eye serves (that is, feeds or supplies) the rational faculty, just as the imagination serves the intellect in Fārābī's account of the ordinary process of perception. The rational faculty must interpret the images received from the inner eye just as it interprets and checks information supplied by other senses.[32] The imagination or inner eye feeds the intellect information, whether from the outer senses or from its own sensing, which the rational faculty must then interpret. Ha-Levi makes prophecy more comprehensible by suggesting that prophetic experience is not so different from ordinary perception, and the interpretation of prophecy not so different from the ordinary interpretation of reality.

4. *Tensions in Ha-Levi's Epistemology*

At the beginning of IV:3, the *Ḥaver* speaks of prophetic witness (*mushāhada*) as a more certain way of knowing than inference (*istidlāl*),[33] which leads astray (IV:3: 148). Later in IV:3, however, the *Ḥaver* says that the prophetic inner eye "sees things in their essences, without disparity, from which the intellect draws inferences [*yastadillu*][34] about the intrinsic nature of things and their heart" (IV:3: 155).[35] From the *Ḥaver*'s words at the beginning of IV:3, one would think that direct witness makes inference unnecessary; from his words in the later passage, however, we learn that prophetic witness is in fact supplemented by the intellect's process of inference.

To resolve this tension, we must examine Ha-Levi's larger theory of knowledge. In fact, we find that the *Ḥaver*'s description of prophetic knowing is parallel to his description of the ordinary process of human knowledge. Human beings find themselves immersed in matter, unable to grasp the essences of things in themselves without the mediation of sensory attributes. God thus gives human beings faculties which perceive sensible attributes; these attributes give relatively uniform sense experience to all human beings. From the attributes perceived by the senses, the human intellect draws inferences (*yastadillu*) about the essence of things.

In both the case of ordinary sensing and in prophetic awareness, then, the intellect is said to "draw inferences" (*yastadillu*) in a process which does not "lead astray"—as *istidlāl* is said to at the beginning of IV:3—but gives the person information about the essence of things.

To make sense of Ha-Levi's position on the role of inference in human knowledge, therefore, we must posit that he is using the term *istidlāl* in two different ways. The *Ḥaver* suggests that the function of the rational faculty when it draws conclusions (*yastadillu*) from the senses is similar to the immediacy of sense experience itself: a simple, natural process, far from the belabored arguments of philosophers using *qiyās* and *istidlāl*, which indeed may lead one astray from immediate experience.

Ha-Levi's view is complicated by his assertion that although the prophetic inner eye can avoid *istidlāl* on one level, it can never be completely free of *istidlāl*. The first kind of *istidlāl* creates a long series of inferences to prove the existence of God, without any direct experience of the Divine. The inner eye can directly witness God without needing this chain of inferences; it can see in an instant what the philosopher must struggle to grasp. On the other hand, any person who uses sense perception to experience the world must use intellect to interpret that sense experience. The quasi-sensory experience of the inner eye requires the use of *istidlāl* as does all sense experience.

The prophetic inner sense Ha-Levi portrays, like the outer senses, does have a more direct relationship with reality than does the rational faculty. Although it cannot sense "things-in-themselves," the inner sense gathers data about reality directly, while the intellect is dependent upon it as an intermediary. The intellect knows about the true natures of things by drawing inferences from the senses. Only sound intellect, such as is possessed by the angels, can see things-in-themselves.

Ha-Levi does not then deny the common sense use of intellect to interpret sensory reality; he even acknowledges that it is necessary for the interpretation of prophetic visions. The *Ḥaver,* in fact, describes a partnership between the intellect and the prophetic inner sense.

A second tension we find in Ha-Levi's theory is the following. In IV:3 the *Ḥaver* states that only beings that are pure intellect, like the angels, can see the essence[36] and intrinsic nature[37] of things (154), but then he goes on to say that the prophet is endowed with an inner eye that sees things in their essences (155).[38] We might thus be tempted to identify the prophetic inner eye with the "sound intellect" of the angels.[39]

However, according to the *Ḥaver,* sound intellect sees the essence of things without the need for sense perception, while the prophetic inner eye is an "internal sense" that supplies the intellect with sense data to interpret, just as other senses do. The prophetic eye is likened to the other senses, and the intellect is forced to accept and work with the evidence of the senses, whether inner or outer.[40]

Prophets therefore have access to the data of non-physical reality just as ordinary people have access to physical reality, by "sensing" it. All human beings need the rational faculty as well as the senses and the imagination in order to know.

The testimony of the prophet's inner sense perception, like that of people's ordinary senses, offers more certain proof than the method of logical inference.[41] However, even the prophet must use the rational faculty to make sense of what he or she perceives. The intellect is forced to accept the evidence of the senses, but the senses are also checked and interpreted by the intellect.

5. *The Interpretation* (Ta'wīl) *of Visions: Ha-Levi and the Geonim*

In IV:3, the *Ḥaver* grapples with the interpretive process by which the prophet makes sense of prophetic visions. He examines the psychic faculties designed by God—the senses, imagination, and reason—and asserts that just as God has designed these human faculties to apprehend the physical world, so God has designed a prophetic inner sense to apprehend divine reality.

The following cluster of questions, however, remains to be examined:

1. Does Ha-Levi carry the visual analogy so far as to assert that just as human beings witness a single physical reality, so the prophets witness the same spiritual reality?

2. Can prophetic visions be verified by others, or are these messages specific to the individual prophet?

3. When Scripture records visions in which the prophet describes a king sitting on a throne, how shall we make sense of this image? Is there an objective correlate to the image, or should we interpret such a description as a purely internal psychic vision?[42]

For his theory of the interpretation of prophetic visions, Ha-Levi is indebted to the gaonim, who in turn drew from certain Islamic thinkers.[43] The Muʿtazilite theologians—the most influential school of the Islamic rationalists—argued that the literal seeing of God is not possible. Only bodies (substances) and the accidents inherent in them can be perceived through the physical senses.[44] Since God does not have a body, God cannot be sensibly perceived, either in this world or the next. Thus al-Ashʿarī writes: "The Muʿtazilites are unanimously of the opinion that God cannot be seen by eyesight; they differ regarding the question of whether He can be seen by our hearts."[45] They explain the vision of a figure on a throne as an internal, spiritual vision.

The gaonim and other Rabbanite thinkers use comparable arguments against the possibility of actually seeing God. R. Nissim Gaon, for example, quotes a story—which he reports having received from a non-Jewish source—in which a disbeliever criticizes one of the rabbis for serving a God that he cannot see. The rabbi replies that it is only fitting that an idolator see the object of his worship, since the idol is a creation of his own hands. However, the rabbi continues, "it is impossible for me to see my God, for I am the work of His hands, and he has no end, to arrive at or to see."[46]

R. Ḥananel writes that all statements about seeing God are "as in a dream," a seeing of the heart (*ovanta de-libbā*), not a seeing of the eye, for the Creator cannot have a form.[47] According to the Muʿtazilites and the rationalistic gaonim, prophets and the pious do not encounter physical manifestations of God, for the Creator of all cannot be manifest; the visions of the prophets and the pious are rather visions in the psyche of the individual.

Saʿadya Gaon, however, takes a twofold approach, both sides of which find echoes in Ha-Levi. While in some places he explains visions as taking place internally, for the most part he speaks of God's created Glory. The created *kavod* according to Saʿadya is an objective light, more sublime than the light of the angels, which God molds into various spiritual forms when God wants to assure the prophet of the Divine Presence. At certain extraordinary times, such as the revelation at Mount Sinai, the *kavod* also becomes visible to all the people of Israel. "As for the Creator himself," Saʿadya writes, in accord with other gaonim and the Muʿtazilites, "there is no means whereby anybody might see him. Indeed, that is in the realm of the impossible."

In the *Book of Doctrines and Beliefs*, Saʿadya introduces the Glory in response to a hypothetical objection to the allegorical method: how can one explain Biblical anthropomorphisms allegorically, when the prophets themselves saw the form of a king on a throne surrounded by angels? He counters:

> Our answer to this objection is that this form was something [specially] created [*al-ṣūra makhlūqa*]. Similarly the throne and the firmament, as well as its bearers, were all of them newly produced[48] by the Creator out of fire in order that his prophet became convinced[49] that it was He that had revealed[50] his word to him.[51]

As we have seen in our discussion of *mushāhada*, elsewhere in the work he writes: "God has a light which he has created and which he reveals to the prophets by which they infer [*yastadillu*—from *d-l-l*] that the word of prophecy[52] which they hear is from God."[53] For Saʿadya then, the *kavod* functions primarily as a proof or criterion of divine revelation, an assurance to the prophet that this is indeed a prophetic vision.

It is possible that Saʿadya's doctrine of the created Glory—in particular, the spiritual forms molded from its light—served as an inspiration for the model developed by Ha-Levi. For Ha-Levi, spiritual images point to [*tadullu*—from *d-l-l*] indubitable truths:

> One for whom this [inner] eye has been created is a clear-sighted person in truth. He sees all [other] people as blind, and he guides them and shows them the right way. . . . He sees a great, fearsome form which points to [*tadullu*] realities [truths] about which there is no doubt. The greatest proof of their truth is the agreement[54] of [the words of] all that species [of human beings] regarding these forms—I mean all the prophets. [*Kuzari* IV:3: 155][55]

In Saʿadya's doctrine, the Glory or angel or cloud functions merely to assure the prophet and the people that it is actually God who is addressing them. Ha-Levi develops this idea in the direction of a symbolic language; the image not only tells the prophet from whence the communication comes, but actually instructs him more effectively than could language alone. According to both Saʿadya and Ha-Levi, visual proof can point to or prove more powerfully than can auditory proof or indirect inference. Symbols and images hit to the heart, conveying truths instantaneously in a way words cannot. A prophet can apprehend more of the Divine in one instantaneous vision than could be contained in a volume of philosophy (IV:5–6: 159–61).

In the same passage, the *Ḥaver* argues that though philosophers believe they can do without physical forms,[56] human experience shows otherwise:

> Do not believe the rationalist[57] when he claims that his thought is so well-ordered that he can arrive at all the necessary metaphysical concepts with the intellect alone, without the support[58] of anything sensible, without holding on to perception [*mushāhada*] of an image or likeness,[59] whether oral, written, visual, or imaginative. . . . Without sense which takes hold of that intellectual order with images[60] and imitations,[61] it simply would not be grasped. Thus the majesty, power, compassion, . . . of God are arranged[62] for the prophet in the greatness of that form which is created for him [*al-ṣūra al-makhlūqa lahu*] which he sees instantaneously, in one moment. . . . Such and things like it the prophet sees in one instant, and fear and love are implanted in his soul for all the days of his life. (IV:5: 160)[63]

It is the actual presence of the form that has the power to awaken love and awe in the prophet. No verbal description can match the emotional impact of a direct, visual encounter. What then is the status of the forms that the prophet sees? Saʿadya states explicitly that everything Ezekiel saw—the throne, the angels bearing the throne, the image seated upon it—each is a created form (*ṣūra makhlūqa*) newly produced, just as the word that the prophet hears is newly produced.[64]

Ha-Levi echoes Saʿadya when he suggests that visual forms are created (*makhlūqa*) for the prophet. However, the *Ḥaver* also states at the end of IV:3 that it is not known whether the angels that Isaiah and Ezekiel saw were temporary manifestations created specifically for the prophet, or permanent spiritual beings, which the philosophers identify with the separate intelligences (IV:3: 158). Moreover other passages do not make it entirely clear whether Ha-Levi holds that the image is created by God, or whether it is created by the mind of the seer. What is crucial to Ha-Levi is to establish the absolute necessity and value of images.

As in his ironic use of *taqlīd*, Ha-Levi's strategy is to turn his critics' argument on its head—here the accusation of anthropomorphism[65] and likening a creature to the Creator.[66] In fact, the *Ḥaver* argues, even philosophers use images—for example, the image of the world as a great human being, and the soul as a microcosm of the world. Philosophers themselves cannot describe spiritual realities without likening them to the physical; philosophers who claim to be able to do without images are disingenuous. The notion that one can do without images is just another pretense of the intellect.[67]

6. *Interpretation of Rabbinic* Aggadot

Ha-Levi addresses the problem of the status of images in a striking passage in III:73. Here he is discussing rabbinic *aggadot* about the Sages rather than the prophets. The passage is instructive, however, as Ha-Levi places the testimony of the Sages on a continuum with that of the prophets, connecting them through the root *sh-h-d*.

In the course of defending the veracity of rabbinic *aggadot* the *Ḥaver* says:

> And among [the rabbinic *aggadot*] are the descriptions of spiritual visions [*mushāhadāt rūḥāniyyāt*] that [the Sages] saw—[for it] is not extraordinary for such excellent ones that they see forms, among which [some are] in an imaginative mode, due to the greatness of their isolation [concentration][68] and the purification of their minds; and among which [some are] forms which have reality from outside, such as those the prophets saw. Such is the *bat qol*, which was their companion in [the time of] the Second Temple, a degree below that of *ḥazon* [prophetic vision] and *qol* [prophetic speech].
>
> Therefore, do not find far-fetched the saying of R. Ishmael, "I heard a voice [(*bat*) *qol*] cooing like a dove," and others like it, since it was already made clear from that which was seen [*mashhad*] by Moses and Elijah, which makes this conceivable. And when a reliable report [tradition][69] comes to one, it is necessary to accept it. (III:73: 144–45)

The Sages receive genuine visions (*mushāhadāt*); the *Ḥaver* here uses the plural form of *mushāhada* to describe visionary experiences, as al-Ghazzālī does when speaking of Sufi adepts.[70] Ha-Levi gives credence to the visions of the Sages by connecting them terminologically with the theophany (*mashhad*) of Moses and that of Elijah, which he also describes using the root *sh-h-d*.

In fact, he takes account of two possibilities: that the visions are seen "imaginatively," or that they have "reality from outside." Ha-Levi does not make entirely clear what he intends by this distinction.

The distinction is unclear because the *Ḥaver* asserts in IV:3 that the inner eye with which the prophet witnesses the divine world might "almost be (said to be) the imagination." In other words, the inner eye or imagination is itself the faculty by which the prophet apprehends the divine world, which does have "reality from outside."[71] Moreover Ha-Levi is clearly not dismissive of those visions witnessed "imaginatively." He ascribes these visions to purification of the mind and to *tafarrud*, a term which can have connotations both of physical seclusion and of mental withdrawal and concentration.[72] Perhaps what Ha-Levi has in mind is some sort of meditative practice that leads to visions one would not experience in an ordinary state of awareness. However, this in itself would not account for Ha-Levi's distinction between two different forms of religious experience, as what one witnesses in a meditative state could, nevertheless, have ontological reality.[73]

It is possible Ha-Levi wants to draw a contrast between what is witnessed by one individual, and what is witnessed by many individuals and is thus known to have independent existence, such as the events at Mount Sinai.[74] Both kinds of vision could be witnessed by the inner eye or imagination; the events at Mount Sinai could have been witnessed by the people with an inner, spiritual eye rather than the physical eye. The events could take place "external" to any one individual's mind, and yet in a subtle, non-physical medium such as Saʿadya's second air. Moreover, those only witnessed by a single individual could nevertheless bear a message from the Divine.[75] Another possibility is that Ha-Levi seeks to distinguish between visions produced by the psyche as a result of meditation, and those sent from the transcendent realm. Ha-Levi may hold that even a message produced by the mind of the rabbi has value, given the spiritual stature of the Sages and the process of mental purification they had undergone.

Ha-Levi's language also makes it unclear as to where he would place the heavenly voice (*bat qol*) certain rabbinic Sages were said to hear. It is possible that after creating two categories he intentionally blurs the lines between the two, in order to allow flexibility regarding any particular prophetic or rabbinic vision.[76] While it is not clear then precisely what Ha-Levi intends by distinguishing these two types of vision, it is clear from his linking of the two through the language of *mushāhada* that Ha-Levi ascribes genuine spiritual value to each.

We should note that Ha-Levi displays a similar ambiguity when speaking of prophetic visions. The *Ḥaver* first asserts that spiritual forms become visible to the physical eyesight (*baṣar*), but then goes on to suggest that the prophets witnessed them with the spiritual eye (*ʿayn ruḥāniyya*):[77]

> This place [the Land of Israel] has a special distinction. When there occurs in it [someone] receptive, who can fulfill the necessary conditions commanded

> in the Law, those forms become visible to the eye [*ʿiyānan bi-l-baṣar*] "plainly and not in dark speeches," as Moses saw the Tabernacle, and the order of sacrifices, and the land of Canaan in its parts, and the theophany [*mashhad*] [when] "the Lord passed before him" [Exodus 34:6], and the vision [*mashhad*] of Elijah in that same place. These things, which are not grasped logically [*qiyāsan*] the Greek philosophers discredit, for *qiyās* declares absurd that which it has not seen the likes of. However the prophets confirmed them, for they could not deny that which they had witnessed with the spiritual eye [*ʿayn ruḥāniyya*] with which they were graced. (IV:3: 155)

Once again, Ha-Levi is more concerned to emphasize the primacy of sense experience than to state decisively whether spiritual vision is inner or outer.

7. Mushāhada *and the Rabbinic* Pardes

Ha-Levi uses the language of *mushāhada* to describe entry into the garden (*pardes*) described in rabbinic literature as well. The *Ḥaver* quotes the story in Hebrew from the version in the Palestinian Talmud, offering his own commentary before and after in Arabic:

> Rabbi Aqiva arrived [*waṣala*] at a degree [so] near to prophecy[78] that he could conduct himself[79] in the spiritual world,[80] as it was said about him: "Four entered a garden [*pardes*]. One peered in and died; one peered in and was smitten. One peered in and cut the shoots. One entered in peace and left in peace, and that was Rabbi Aqiva."[81] And the one who died[82] was one who could not withstand witness [*mushāhada*] of that world: his constitution disintegrated [*inḥalla tarkībuhu*]. [III:65: 140]

Through use of the term *mushāhada*, the *Ḥaver* associates the *pardes* story with other experiences of the Sages such as the *bat qol*, with the visions of the prophets, and with the revelation to the nation of Israel at Mount Sinai. The *Ḥaver*'s allusion to the Sage who could not withstand witness (*mushāhada*) of the divine world is reminiscent of his comment about the people's inability to bear the divine address at Sinai: they did not possess Moses' capacity for witness (*mushāhada*) of that grand event.

The term *mushāhada* allows for a visual dimension to the experience without spelling out any specific content to the vision.[83] Rationalistic thinkers had described entrance into the *pardes* as an inner vision, an "understanding of the heart" (*ovanta de-libba*).[84] The *Ḥaver* seems to regard it as an actual vision of or journey through the spiritual world, without mentioning a specific goal, such as beholding the divine chariot or journeying through heavenly palaces. He does go on to associate the *pardes* with the world of separate intelligences:

> And the third [rabbi] denigrated actions, for he contemplated the intelligences [*al-ʿaqliyāt*] saying, "Actions are only instrumental to arriving at [*muwaṣṣila*] this spiritual level; I have already reached it [*waṣaltuhā*], so I will not worry about the actions of the Law. He was corrupted and corrupted others; he was led astray and led others astray. Rabbi Aqiva was one who could conduct himself[85] in both worlds without being harmed." (III:65: 140–41)

We see that Ha-Levi uses the term *waṣala*, like *mushāhada*, to create a link between the *pardes* narrative and other aspects of Jewish religious experience. The *Ḥaver* uses the verb here both for Rabbi Aqiva's arrival at a spiritual degree near prophecy, and for the pretense of the third rabbi, Elisha ben Abuya, to have arrived spiritually. Rabbi Aqiva reached a level near prophecy; he could conduct himself in both worlds, the physical as well as the spiritual. Elisha ben Abuya thought he had reached a spiritual level through contemplation alone. For the *Ḥaver*, contemplation is not an end in itself; true arrival (*wuṣūl*) requires action.[86]

Ha-Levi makes an additional linguistic association between entry into the *pardes* and prophetic vision. The *Ḥaver* uses an ideosyncratic Arabic phrase to describe the fate of the Sage who died—"his constitution disintegrated" (*inḥalla tarkībuhu*)."[87] Ha-Levi borrows the unusual phrase from a key passage in Saʿadya's *Amānāt*. We have had occasion to cite this passage above;[88] Saʿadya uses this phrase to decribe prophets who cannot bear the light of the Glory:

> God has a light which he creates and makes manifest to his prophets in order that they may infer [*yastadill*] from it that the word of prophecy which they hear is from God. When one of them sees this light, he says, "I have seen the Glory of the Lord." . . . However, when they beheld this light, they were unable to look at it on account of its power and brilliance. Indeed, one who looked at it—his constitution disintegrated [*inḥalla tarkībuhu*] and his spirit fled [from his body], as it says: "Lest they break through to the Lord to gaze, and many of them perish" [Exodus 19:21].[89]

Ha-Levi uses the phrase likewise in IV:3 for prophets who try to see levels of the Glory that are too subtle for their prophetic vision to bear:

> And of the Glory there is what prophetic vision[90] can bear, and after it what our vision can bear, such as the cloud, devouring fire, which are fa-

> miliar to us, and also what is more and more subtle, till it arrives at a degree which the prophet cannot grasp, and if he forces it, his constitution disintegrates [*inḥalla tarkībuhu*]. (IV:3: 158)

Ha-Levi interprets the Sages' peering into *pardes* as witness (*mushāhada*) of the divine world, and associates it terminologically with prophetic vision of God's Glory. The *Ḥaver* is agnostic about the precise ontological status of the *kavod*: whether it is a created light which God molds into the forms he shows the prophet (IV:3: 158; II:4,7: 45–46) or represents the permanent forms of the celestial world, such as the throne and the chariot (IV:3: 158). Ha-Levi emphasizies the affective, experiential dimension, the effect of the vision on the person who beholds it.[91]

In summary, Ha-Levi uses the term *mushāhada* in his account of prophecy in a variety of ways. The term dovetails with his claim that prophets possess an inner eye that can witness the divine world directly, while philosophers only learn about the Divine indirectly. He makes the further epistemological claim that prophets across the centuries testify (*yashhadu*) to a common spiritual reality that they each witness individually in their prophetic visions.

Ha-Levi builds upon the motif of sight and blindness current in his milieu. Al-Ghazzālī and Ibn Ṭufayl depicted those who have not experienced *mushāhada* as in some way blind. For Ibn Ṭufayl, this blindness is only partial; philosophy gives a useful map to the divine world, which is enhanced when one sees for oneself. Ha-Levi's position is more similar to that of Ghazzālī—an absolute opposition between those who possess the inner eye and those who do not. Yet in several passages, Ha-Levi hints that *qiyās* and *mushāhada* are two paths to the same truth. While Abraham rejects *qiyās* once he has witnessed God, the *Ḥaver* suggests that Abraham's philosophical insight may have led to this direct experience.[92] The *Ḥaver* also suggests that philosophy and prophecy use a common motif to describe God: the image of the world as a great human being, and the soul as a microcosm of the world.

Ha-Levi uses the language of *mushāhada* to draw together many types of religious experience: the revelation at Mount Sinai, prophetic visions, the *pardes* narrative of rabbinic *aggadah*, the *bat qol* of the Sages. It is clear that what interests Ha-Levi most in these narratives is not the specific ontological status of what the visionaries see, but the striking impact of direct experience. Whether a vision is produced in the psyche of the prophet or reveals a being from the permanent spiritual realm, Ha-Levi stresses that visual experience has an affective dimension which makes it more powerful than rational thought alone.

Ha-Levi does show interest in developing a sound epistemology. The *Ḥaver* explains that God has given humans mental faculties that afford some experiential knowledge of the Divine. Human beings witness forms appropriate to their natures; the imagination endows these forms with attributes it has witnessed corporeally. The fact that religious visions are perceived and interpreted by the human psyche does not explain away these experiences, but enables physical human beings to perceive something of a nonphysical, divine reality.

However, while Ha-Levi is comfortable describing the visual component of prophecy in terms of natural human capacities, he is opposed to such views with regard to the prophet's hearing of divine speech. Ha-Levi is especially adamant about the prophecy of Moses and the revelation at Mount Sinai, which he refuses to explain in natural terms, as we shall now see.

B. Prophecy as Divine Inspiration (*Waḥy, Ilhām, Ta'yīd*)

1. *Ha-Levi's Terminology for Levels of Divine Inspiration*

In addition to his treatment of prophecy using the metaphor of sense perception. Ha-Levi also speaks of prophecy as a form of divine inspiration. We recall that Ha-Levi reads back into the scene at Mount Sinai the debate about the mechanics of prophecy between philosophers and traditional monotheists. Through God's revelation at Mount Sinai, God intended to disprove the philosophical theory of prophecy, and to show that prophecy is the direct communication of God to human beings, with no intermediary Active Intellect or angel. What we will now discover is that Ha-Levi's Islamic terminology adds a dynamic, polemical dimension to his argument. There is a great debate in the Islamic world over the precise nature of prophecy and the Qurānic terms used to describe it. Understanding the history of these terms and the way they are used by Islamic thinkers will uncover the rhetorical finesse with which Ha-Levi constructs his argument.

The *Ḥaver* spells out rather accurately the philosophical account of prophecy which he believes God wants to disprove, and in its place sets forth his own idiosyncratic account of prophecy and revelation. In doing so, he uses four terms which also are used with a certain technical precision in Islamic discussions of prophecy:

a. the terms *waḥy* (revelation) and *ilhām* (inspiration), which signify respectively a higher or ultimate and a lower degree of prophetic inspiration;

b. the term *ta'yīd* (divine support, strengthening, backing, confirmation—from the second form of the root *'-y-d*, to support, strengthen, confirm), which Ha-Levi uses to signify an additional level of inspiration below that of revelation (*waḥy*);

c. the term *nubuwwa* (prophecy), which he uses to signify prophecy proper—in contrast either to lower degrees of divine inspiration such as *ilhām* and *ta'yīd*, or the higher degree of *waḥy* (revelation)—or as a loose, overarching term for prophetic phenomena in general, especially in adjectival form (e.g., *al-'amr al-ilāhī al-nabawwī*, the prophetic *'amr ilāhī*).

2. *The Debate Over* Waḥy *and* Ilhām

Islamic tradition distinguishes fundamentally between *waḥy* and *ilhām*. *Waḥy* refers to God's revelation as it is given to the prophets; God communicates to humankind as a whole through messages given to God's trusted servants. *Ilhām*, in contrast—which means literally "to make swallow" or "to make gulp down"—refers to messages given to pious friends of God (*awliyā'*; singular *walīy*) and others, messages which may be given purely for individual inspiration.[93]

Ta'yıd is a term for divine assistance—like the more common *ma'ūna* —or inspiration (like *ilhām*). It is derived from the verb *'ayyada*, which occurs three times in the Qur'ān with *rūḥ al-quds* (Holy Spirit) in regard to Jesus: "we gave Jesus, son of Mary clear arguments, and strengthened (inspired, supported) him (*'ayyadnāhu*) with the Holy Spirit."[94]

Ta'yıd is in fact a key term in Ismā'īlī thought. In Ismā'īlī terminology, the term *mu'ayyad* (passive participle of *a'-y-d*) applies to any person who receives divine inspiration (*ta'yīd*) because of his rank in the hierarchy.[95] The term is particularly prominent in the writing of al-Sijistānī—a tenth century Ismā'īlī missionary whose views on the prophetic hierarchy bear a striking resemblance to those of Ha-Levi.[96] The prophet, writes al-Sijistānī is "that pure man who is inspired with the holy spirit (*al-mu'ayyad bī-rūḥ al-quds*)."[97] *Ta'yīd* therefore appears to be yet another term which Ha-Levi has adapted from Ismā'īlī thought.[98]

The terms *waḥy* and *ilhām* were, however, in dispute in Islamic culture; as Haggai Ben-Shammai has recently argued, these terms were part of a debate which may be reflected in a controversy between Saʿadya Gaon and the Karaites as well.[99] This controversy provides a crucial backdrop to Ha-Levi's own polemical use of the terms *waḥy* and *ilhām*. While Ben-Shammai's definitions of positions in the debate are somewhat more strict than my own, I find his overall historical outline of the controversy persuasive and will sketch it here.

In the Qurʾān, in literary traditions describing the life of Muḥammed, and in the terminology of Muslim theologians, the fourth form of the root *w-ḥ-y* and its first-form verbal noun *waḥy* signify God's revelation to prophets. These terms often refer to a specific auditory and/or visual message, which the prophet reports exactly as he perceives it.[100] The recipient of *ilhām*, in contrast, does not necessarily transmit a word-for-word message or report a specific visual image from the Divine.[101]

However, while it is clear that the Qurʾān uses the root *w-ḥ-y* to signify God's direct revelation to prophets, the Qurʾān leaves some room for interpretation regarding precisely how revelation takes place. Is revelation, in the words of John Wansbrough, "the unmediated speech of God" or is it the "prophetical (angelic) report of God's speech?"[102]

Some in the Islamic world therefore began to blur the boundaries between *waḥy* and *ilhām*, often by interpreting revelation (*waḥy*) using the concept of inspiration (*ilhām*). We find a major thread in the intertwined history of these concepts in the literature of Qurʾānic exegesis. The term *ilhām*—actually its verbal form, *alhama*—appears once in the Qurʾān (Sura 96:8), where it is said that God "'caused (the soul) to swallow down' [*alhama*] her sins and her fear of God." The earliest exegetical tradition shows two streams of interpretation. Some interpreters comment that God "instructed" or "explained" to the soul what was commanded and forbidden for her. Other commentaries, perhaps of Shīʿite origin, suggest that God "created" or "implanted" these in the soul, giving the soul an intuitive sense of the rightness or wrongness of specific actions. Neither view mentions *ilhām* as a species of prophecy.

The terms *revelation* (*waḥy*) and *inspiration* (*ilhām*) came to be identified with one another through exegesis of the enigmatic Qurʾānic verse 42:51: "And it is not for man that God should speak to him except by revelation [*waḥy*], or from behind a veil, or by sending a messenger who reveals (*yūḥī*) by His command what He pleases." The Muʿtazilite commentator Zamakhsharī comments on this verse that *waḥy* is "inspiration [*ilhām*] and casting into the heart or a dream, as [God] revealed [*awḥa*] to the mother of Moses (Qurʾān 28:7) and to Abraham (peace be upon him) in the sacrificing of his son" (Qur'ān 37:102). Zamakhsharī also quotes an early commentator who writes that "*waḥy* is that which God places in David's heart by which he (David) writes the Psalms," an opinion which—while not using the term *ilhām*—defines revelation using the concept of inspiration. Another early exegete comments on the term *waḥy* in this verse: "as the Prophet saw in his dream, and He inspired him [*yulhamuhu*]."

This blending of *waḥy* and *ilhām* was taken up by a wide variety of medieval Islamic thinkers. Al-Ghazzālī, quoting this same verse, writes that the only distinction between *waḥy* and *ilhām* is the privilege in *waḥy* of witnessing (*mushāhada*) the angel who casts the knowledge into one's heart.[103] The tenth-century *Ikhwān al-ṣafā'* define revelation (*waḥy*) ambiguously as instruction about things hidden from the senses, which enters the soul without human effort or intention through dreams, through hearing a voice while awake, or through hints.[104] As for *ilhām*, the *Ikhwān,* on the one hand, view inspiration as the source of human knowledge of the arts and sciences, including philosophy. On the other hand the *Ikhwān* go so far as to attribute the composition of Scripture and the promulgation of religious Law to "receiving thoughts [*khawāṭir*] or inspiration [*ilhām*] or revelation [*waḥy*]," interchangeably:

> By means of dreams [comes] recognition of warnings and good tidings; by receiving ideas [*khawāṭir*] and inspiration [*ilhām*] and revelation [*waḥy*] [comes] recognition [which leads to] the promulgation of Laws[105] and the composition of divine books and their hidden interpretations.

Introducing the concept of *ta'yīd*, they continue:

> We have already made clear in our letter on the Laws that the promulgation of Laws and the composition of divine books is the highest level to which a human being may attain, with divine assistance [*ta'yīd*], and it is the most noble of arts to which human hands reach, such as the Law of the bearer of the Torah, the Gospel, the Psalms, and the Qur'ān.[106]

The *Ikhwān* seem to have intentionally blurred the difference between the various forms of prophecy, and it is not difficult to see why. Given their Neo-Platonic sensibility, the Brethren regard it as impossible for a prophet to hear the voice of God directly. The *Ikhwān* believe, rather, that prophets receive inspiration from the angels—whom they identify with the separate intelligences—sometimes hearing distinct words, but at other times shaping the wording of the prophetic message themselves. They write:

> The speech of angels is [by] hints and indications, while human speech is by verbal expressions and words. However as for the meanings, they are shared by all. The prophets receive revelation [*waḥy*] and information from the angels through hints and indications. . . . They bring these meanings by the tongue—which is an organ of the body which every community has—in its [own] language, and by words which each community knows.

The *Ikhwān* here use the term *waḥy* despite the fact that the prophets are said to receive only "hints and indications" from the angels, which they themselves must translate into words human beings will understand, each according to his or her own capacity.[107] Traditionalists, in contrast, insist that the word of God is literally the word which God speaks to the prophet through the angel Jibrīl, not a subtle hint or inspiration which the prophet him or herself translates into language.[108]

In the sphere of epistemology—another front in the debate—Muʿtazilites spoke out strongly against regarding *ilhām* as a valid source of knowledge. One ninth-century Muʿtazilite criticized the Shīʿites for attributing to their leader supernatural knowledge acquired through inspiration (*ilhām*), without study.[109] A ninth-century Muʿtazilite, a contemporary of Saʿadya, ridicules attempts to regard inspiration as a source of certain knowledge like logical demonstration (*istidlāl*).[110] He asks: how can one know that one has come to the right knowledge by inspiration? If it is by inspiration—the validity of inspiration is still to be proven, and you have an infinite regress; if by speculation, then one has acknowledged the need for speculation, and one no longer needs *ilhām*. The problem with *ilhām* is that inspiration in itself has no criterion that would decide whether it is true or false. As Ibn Ḥazm argues, one might say, "I have an inspiration to kill someone."[111]

The philosophical tradition also makes use of the terms *waḥy* and *ilhām*, but they reinterpret these terms in accordance with their Neo-Platonic sensibility. Al-Fārābī speaks of *waḥy* from the First Cause, through the mediation of the Active Intellect to the intellect and imagination of the prophet. This highest level of prophecy which al-Fārābī terms *waḥy* is a natural phenomenon that a person gifted with both a powerful intellect and a powerful imagination achieves at the height of his or her intellectual development. Al-Fārābī does not spell out the distinction between the two forms of prophecy. However, in practice he reserves the term *waḥy* for the prophecy of someone who has perfected his or her intellect, whereas he uses the term *nubuwwa* for the ordinary form of prophecy in which a person need only have a powerful imagination.[112]

Avicenna speaks of an imaginative form of *waḥy* in which the prophet can hear the voices of angels and see angelic forms.[113] He uses both *waḥy* and *ilhām* to describe a specifically intellectual form of prophecy, whereby one with a great capacity for conjunction with the Active Intellect is inspired (*yulham*) concerning everything that can be known.[114] For Avicenna too, prophecy is the natural development of a gifted intellect and imagination. Avicenna does not seem to preserve any remnants of the distinction between *waḥy* and *ilhām*.

3. *Reflections of the Debate in the Jewish World*

The controversy over revelation and inspiration was certainly alive within the Islamic world. As evidence for its reverberations within Judaism, Ben Shammai draws our attention to tenth-century Karaite sources and to Saʿadya's theory of prophecy.

The Karaite Qirqisānī mentions that in addition to the degrees of direct Mosaic prophecy[115] and prophecy by an angel or in a dream, "some believe that there is an additional means which is inspiration [*ilhām*] and the creation of sudden notions'"[116] but he declines to elaborate.[117] The Karaite Yefet b. ʿElī suggests that by means of the Holy Spirit (*ruaḥ ha-qodesh*), which he defines as the second of six degrees of prophecy, God inspires (*yulhimu*) the prophet with poems, prayers, and blessings. Regarding the prayer of Hannah, Yefet writes: "She said this prayer by the Holy Spirit [*ruaḥ ha-qodesh*], like 'A prayer of Moses' (Ps. 90), '[a prayer] of Habakkuk' [Hab. 3:1]. . . . The Lord saw fit to inspire her (*yulhimuhā*) with this prayer so that she could know her rank with him."[118]

Yefet here uses the language of *ilhām* to depict Hannah uttering a prayer while under the inspiration of the Holy Spirit. While Yefet does not explicitly define what he means by inspiration, his language is open to the interpretation that when Hannah or David or Habbakuk speak by the power of the Holy Spirit, it is the people themselves who shape the actual words of their prayers. Yefet's language, while not explicit, is perhaps suggestive of a view of prophecy that Saʿadya Gaon actively opposed.[119] In contrast to such ambiguous—and, in that cultural context, highly charged—language, Saʿadya insists that God reveals (*awḥā*) the text of prayers and psalms word for word, as indeed God does every word of prophecy.

Like the Muslim traditionalists, Saʿadya defines prophecy proper (*waḥy*) so as to distinguish it sharply from other sorts of inspiration. For Saʿadya, *waḥy* is the revelation of a divine message which grants certain, sensible knowledge, as the prophet reports word for word what he hears (or, if it is a visual image, exactly what he sees). Perhaps influenced by arguments against *ilhām* as a source of reliable knowledge, Saʿadya clearly seeks to protect *waḥy* from being placed on a continuum with other, less reliable forms of inspiration.[120]

In Saʿadya's view, all the books of the Bible are divinely dictated by *waḥy*. *Waḥy* is the means by which God directly addresses human beings, giving them specific visions (including those of Daniel, Job, and Eliphaz)[121] and auditory messages (the specific words that constitute Scripture). In addition, Saʿadya insists that the primary purpose of all the revealed books is commandment and prohibition. This includes even the Psalms, which he argues simply use the rhetorical form of prayer to instruct readers about divine norms of conduct.[122] Saʿadya declares that every word in the Bible is the word of God, even if it is expressed as the word of the prophet or the worshiper:

> I was compelled to begin [my commentary on Psalms] with these words, so that the reader . . . should not get confused, and attribute the word which is on the tongue of the servant to the servant rather than to his Lord; and think that "be gracious to me," "deliver me," and "save me" and similar phrases are not what God revealed [*awḥā*] to his prophet, but are rather the words of the servant. . . . It is necessary one know that all of this is from God, formulated in all forms of language used by his creatures.[123]

For Saʿadya, then, the Book of Psalms is not a book of personal prayers, but an alternative medium for instruction in commandments. Saʿadya seems to view *waḥy* as inextricably tied to the revelation of religious norms.

In summary, traditional Muslims speak of *waḥy* as God's direct revelation of messages to prophets for the benefit of humankind, and *ilhām* as God's personal communications to individuals such as pious ones. Certain groups—among them Shīʿites such as the *Ikhwān al-ṣafāʾ*—tend to blur this distinction, seeing *ilhām* as a source of supernatural knowledge for humankind, including not only the arts and sciences but even religious law. They thus raise *ilhām* to a level others reserve for *waḥy*. Philosophers also tend to blur this distinction, but in the other direction: philosophers "lower" *waḥy*. The *waḥy* spoken of by the philosophers resembles what others would call *ilhām*: a semi-natural inspiration from a source beyond the individual human intellect.

In the context not of prophecy but of epistemology, Muʿtazilites deny that individual inspiration (*ilhām*) is a valid source of knowledge. Their position is similar to the traditional view, but they formulate their position in conscious opposition to the blurring of Shīʿites and philosophers.

The Karaite Qirqisānī alludes to *ilhām* as an additional means of prophecy, but declines to describe it in detail.[124] Another Karaite thinker, Yefet b. ʿElī, suggests that the prophet utters certain prayers, poems, and blessings under the inspiration of God; there is ambiguity in his language as to who formulates the words of these utterances. Saʿadya Gaon, in contrast, flatly denies that any words in Scripture are written by the prophet himself under divine inspiration.[125] God is the Author of every word of Scripture.

4. *Examples of Ha-Levi's Use of* Taʾyīd, Ilhām, Waḥy, *and* Nubūwwa

Ha-Levi's culturally charged use of the terms *waḥy*, *ilhām*, and *taʾyīd* is most dramatic in his account of the revelation at Mount Sinai. However, with our knowledge of the controversy—between Islamic traditionalists and rationalists, between Saʿadya and the Karaites—we will also discover other interesting reverberations throughout the *Kuzari*. Let us examine these first, to prepare us for the full impact of the Sinai account.

Ha-Levi makes use of these traditional Islamic terms for prophecy to set forth his own position on levels of inspiration in Jewish tradition. He is not necessarily consistent in his hierarchical use of the terms, just as differences are found among the various Islamic thinkers. Generally speaking, Ha-Levi follows Islamic thinkers of a traditional bent. He tends to reserve the term *waḥy* for the highest level of divine inspiration, which is generally available only to prophets, but which he asserts is also made available to the whole people of Israel at Mount Sinai. The term is thus sometimes best translated "revelation."

Ha-Levi uses *ilhām* and *taʾyīd* to signify lower degrees of inspiration—including that accorded to the Sages, the heirs of legal authority with the ending of prophecy, and to pious friends of God (*awliyāʾ*, sing. *walīy*) in general. He appears to use *nubuwwa* as the Hebrew *nevuah* is used, to signify the specific phenomenon of direct divine inspiration which revealed the word of God to Moses and the later prophets, and which according to Jewish tradition ceased at a certain time in Jewish history.

1. *Taʾyıd*. Ha-Levi uses *taʾyīd* to describe a source of knowledge that has some degree of divine inspiration, support, or assistance. Ha-Levi shows that *taʾyīd* is a bridge term which can be used to describe various forms of divine and human support. For example, the *Ḥaver* asks the King:

"What is your opinion of Solomon's knowledge [ʿ*ulūm*]? Did he not discourse on all the sciences [ʿ*ulūm*] with divine, intellectual, and natural support [*ta'yīd*]? (II:66: 79).[126]

Ha-Levi does not go as far as either Saʿadya or his opponents in this passage, for he says nothing about the actual composition of specific Biblical books such as Proverbs and the Song of Songs, which were traditionally attributed to Solomon. The *Ḥaver* asserts that Solomon himself had divine assistance (*ta'yīd*), without stating that the Biblical books attributed to him were the product of *ta'yīd* as opposed to *waḥy*, or *waḥy* as opposed to *ta'yīd*. The ability of *ta'yīd* to signify various forms of support distinguishes the term *ta'yīd* from *waḥy*, which is never used for a purely human source of inspiration.[127]

The *Ḥaver* also uses *ta'yīd* (divine assistance) and its passive participle *mu'ayyad* (divinely assisted) when speaking of knowledge that is not purely rational, but is also not full-fledged prophecy, what is termed in rabbinic sources "assistance from heaven" (*sayy'ata di-shemaya*).[128] The *Ḥaver* refers to the knowledge received and passed down by Adam, and not known by the Greeks, as the divinely assisted knowledge (I:63: 17).[129] The *Ḥaver* also asserts that the work of the Masoretes—those who preserved the correct text of the Torah—is a divinely assisted science (ʿ*ilm mu'ayyad*), received from a community of favored ones or an individual who is either a prophet or an individual assisted (*mu'ayyad*) by the *'amr ilāhī* (III:32: 117). Similarly, he maintains that anyone who investigates the Mishnah honestly will realize that no human being could have composed it without divine assistance (*ta'yīd*) (III:67: 142).

In addition, the *Ḥaver* uses *ta'yīd* to refer to general divine guidance, perhaps including behavioral as well as intellectual support. The *Ḥaver* asserts that the spirit of holiness (*ruaḥ ha-qodesh*) enwraps the Nazir or the Messiah when the prophet anoints him for priesthood or kingship, or when God assists him (*yu'ayyidūhu*) or guides him[130] in any matter. *Ta'yıd* is here depicted as a kind of divine guidance by the Holy Spirit, reflecting one rabbinic use of Holy Spirit (*ruaḥ ha-qodesh*) to describe many, varied forms of religious experience, while in its stricter rabbinic sense it refers to the source of prophecy proper alone (IV:15: 168).[131]

Finally, the *Ḥaver* criticizes loose contemporary usage, whereby a person claims divine assistance as a way of bolstering his or her own ideas. The *Ḥaver* explains that a religion whose origin is God arises suddenly, in contrast to rational laws[132] whose origin is human, and which develop slowly.[133] In the latter case, when the person gains ascendancy it is said that the person is assisted by God (*mu'ayyad*) or inspired (*mulham*)

(I:81: 21–22). The phrase "it is said" is significant; we can detect in the *Ḥaver's* words a note of derision for what he sees not only as an improper use of language, but a spurious claim to divine support. Ha-Levi may have in mind here the thought of al-Fārābī, who universalizes the phenomenon of prophecy, maintaining that any law-giver is essentially a prophet. According to al-Fārābī the prophet even has the authority to formulate and change religious law of his own accord.[134] Ha-Levi may well have regarded as dangerous this co-opting of the notion of divine support to promulgate one's own law, or to abrogate religious law which is actually divine in origin.

2. *Ilhām*. Ha-Levi uses *ilhām* in a manner similar to *ta'yīd*, for personal inspiration or inspiration short of prophecy proper. Like *ta'yīd*, the term *ilhām* can serve as a bridge between divine and natural human knowledge. For example, the *Ḥaver* asserts that in the prayer "You favor human beings with knowledge" (*attah ḥonen le-adam da'at*), a person prays for intelligence (*'aql*) and inspiration (*ilhām*).The two forms of knowledge are here paired closely; there is clearly a continuum between natural and inspired knowledge. A person should ask for divine assistance ("grace us from You with knowledge, discernment, and understanding"), while recognizing that this may come through the ordinary human intellect (*'aql*), as well as the catalyst of inspiration (*ilhām*) (III:19: 108).

In V:12, in the presentation of the views of the philosophers—actually a treatise from the early thought of Avicenna—the *Ḥaver* asserts that primary truths (for example, that the whole is equal to the sum of its parts) are acquired by divine inspiration (*ilhām ilāhī*). More complex truths, however, are known by acquisition—that is, by *qiyās* and demonstrative discovery (V:12: 204).[135] Here *ilhām* seems to refer to truths implanted in the human mind by God or by nature, or at least not discovered by an active human process of acquisition. This form of knowledge once again bridges the natural and the transcendent.[136]

Like *ta'yīd*, *ilhām* can also refer to general religious guidance. In V:10, the *Ḥaver*, describing the views of the *mutakallimūn*, asserts that a person whose temperament is balanced is one who seeks advice and guidance, that God might inspire him (*yulhimuhu*) along the right path (V:10: 200).[137] In V:20, describing his own views, he asserts that a religious person seeks inspirations (*ilhāmāt*) if he is a pious friend of God (*walīy*) and miracles and wonders if he is a prophet. Here it is not clear whether the inspirations referred to are intellectual, behavioral, or some blend of the two (V:20: 220).

The *Ḥaver* speaks of *ilhām*, too, with a note of derision. We saw above that in I:81 he pairs being "divinely assisted" (*mu'ayyad min allah*) with being "inspired" (*mulham*) as a way of speaking about the founder of a rational religion. This scorn in the *Ḥaver's* tone is reminiscent of a critique of *ilhām* we saw above, advanced by a tenth-century Muʿtazilite.[138] The *Ḥaver* hints that claiming *ilhām* is just a way of inflating the authority of one's own ideas.

3. *Waḥy*. Ha-Levi uses *waḥy*, in contrast, to describe direct address from God to a prophet. For example, in II: 68, the *Ḥaver* explains that according to tradition,[139] Hebrew is the language in which God prophetically addressed (*awḥā*) Adam and Eve (II:68: 79). On a more complex level, the *Ḥaver* uses the term *waḥy* when contrasting the ordinary rational way of knowing God with supra-rational, experiential knowledge. In IV:27, the *Ḥaver* terms God's direct communication with Abraham *waḥy*; he explains that when God prophetically addressed (*awḥā*) Abraham, Abraham gave up all attempts to know God by *qiyās*. *Waḥy* communicates a knowledge inaccessible to *qiyās* alone (IV:27: 184).[140]

On the same note, in IV:27 the *Ḥaver* recounts the following anecdote (which he mistakenly attributes to Plato), in which he uses the term *waḥy* to describe God's address to a philosopher through a human oracle:

> A prophet . . . spoke in a prophetic revelation [*waḥy*] from God[141] to a philosopher who was overweening [or arrogant][142] in philosophy, saying, "You cannot reach[143] Me by this path [philosophy], but rather by those whom I have placed as an intermediary between Me and my creatures, i.e., the prophets and the true Law.[144] (IV:27: 184)

This anecdote brings to mind the contrast we have seen in our discussion of *ittiṣāl* and *qiyās*: one cannot reach God (*taṣilu*, from *w-ṣ-l*) through the philosophical method or *qiyās* alone, but only through direct contact (*waḥy* or *ittiṣāl*).

Finally, the *Ḥaver* uses *waḥy* to signify the highest level of human religious attainment. The *Ḥaver* asserts that Christians and Muslims became ascetics and hermits in order that prophetic revelation (*waḥy*) might come to them, but it did not come (II:32: 64). While asceticism does not lead to *waḥy*, observance of the *mitsvot* provides at least the necessary condition for this experience. Born Jews can achieve the degree of prophecy and receive prophetic revelation (*waḥy*) through diligent practice of the *halakhah*:[145]

> The Law which is from God confers something of the behavior[146] and form[147] of angels on human souls, a thing which cannot be attained[148] by [natural] acquisition.[149] The proof [*dalīl*] is that diligence and perseverence in the practices of this Law raise one[150] to the degree of prophetic revelation [*waḥy*], which is the human level closest to the divine [level]. (V:20: 223–24).

Here *waḥy* signifies not just a source of knowledge or a subjective experience of the Divine, but a state of being, the highest degree of religious attainment to which a human being can aspire. Passages such as this, which describe the *mitsvot* as a path to religious experience, point to a tension in Ha-Levi's thought. On the one hand, Ha-Levi wants to combat philosophical arrogance by contrasting what he sees as the poverty of the philosophical approach to God compared with the richness and power of direct experience. For this goal, he makes a sharp distinction between the knowledge attained by natural, unaided reason (*qiyās*) and knowledge attained only by inspiration. On the other hand, he does not want to go as far as Saʿadya, whose strict definition of *waḥy* might create too strong a boundary between knowledge of God available to all people and the experiential knowledge attained only by prophets. Ha-Levi clearly wants his readers to know that there are degrees of religious experience available to all Jews in his own time, just as in the ancient past.

4. *Nubuwwa*. Ha-Levi uses the term *nubuwwa* to signify the rabbinic view of prophecy as a phenomenon present among the nation of Israel in the land of Israel[151] for a certain historical period of time, after which point God removed the gift of prophecy.[152] Ha-Levi also draws attention to *nubuwwa* as a gift that comes to particular individuals. The *Ḥaver* asserts that both Abraham and Moses were eighty years old when *nubuwwa* came to them (I:83: 23), that Moses took of his *nubuwwa* and gave it to the seventy elders (IV:11: 163), and that *nubuwwa* was retained among the descendents of Abraham (II:14: 50).

Like *waḥy*, *nubuwwa* signifies for Ha-Levi the ultimate degree of religious experience, a level to which individual human beings (but, alas, only born Jews) may aspire.[153] Ha-Levi uses *nubuwwa* as a foil to *qiyās*;[154] he takes account of *nubuwwa* as a phenomenon about which many, including philosophers, were debating. He argues that God revealed the Torah at Mount Sinai lest people believe *nubuwwa* to be some form of individual inspiration (*ilhām*, *taʾyīd*), by which Moses passed off his own ideas as divinely inspired, as certain philosophers claimed (I:87: 24).[155] God also wanted to remove any suspicion that *nubuwwa* was the hoax of a small elite—the fanciful presumption of the few who claimed to possess it, rather than a genuine experience of the Divine.[156]

5. *Divine Inspiration and Legal Authority: From the Prophets to the Rabbis*

The prophets have authority by direct revelation (*waḥy*) from God. When describing the symbolism of the Temple and its service, the *Ḥaver* asserts: "From [the Ark] went forth a twofold knowledge, first, the knowledge of religious law,[157] whose bearers were the priests; secondly the knowledge of prophetic revelation [*waḥy*] which was in the hands of the prophets." (II:28: 63)

The rabbis have legal authority, both by direct inheritance of tradition from the prophets and by divine assistance and inspiration (*ta'yīd* and *ilhām*). Commenting on a series of verses in Deuteronomy 17 used by the rabbis to validate rabbinic authority[158]—the *Ḥaver* explains:

> [This refers to the time when] the Temple Service and the Sanhedrin and the groups [of Levites] which completed the organization were still intact, and the *'amr ilāhī* was connected[159] with them, without doubt, whether by prophecy [*nubuwwa*], or by divine strengthening [*ta'yīd*] and inspiration [*ilhām*], as was the case in the Second Temple. . . . And thus the law[160] of *Megillah* and *Purim* and the law of *Ḥanukkah* are binding and we can say "who has commanded us to read the *Megillah* and "to kindle the light of *Ḥanukkah*." (III:39: 122)

Direct divine inspiration did not cease, according to the *Ḥaver*, with the cessation of prophecy proper. In his defense of rabbinic tradition, the *Ḥaver* explains that the Torah's admonition, "You shall not add" to the Law refers to

> "that which I commanded you through Moses," and any "prophet from among your brethren" who fulfills the conditions of a prophet.
>
> [It] further refers to regulations laid down in common by priests and judges "from the place which your Lord shall choose." For they are supported [*mu'ayyadūna*, from *a-y-d*, root of *ta'yīd*] by the *Shekhinah*. . . . The members of the Sanhedrin, as is known by tradition,[161] had to possess a thorough acquaintance with all branches of science. Not only that, but prophecy had hardly departed from them, or rather what took its place, the *bat qol*, and things like it. (III:41: 125)

The Sanhedrin's divine inspiration in deciding law is assured, according to the *Ḥaver*, because its members receive support (*ta'yīd*) from the *Shekhinah*—if not by prophecy proper, then by the *bat qol*, the divine voice, which is a rabbinic term for a level of inspiration below that of prophecy.

The rabbis held that with the departure of the Holy Spirit (*ruaḥ ha-qodesh*) from Israel—the spirit which granted prophecy, according to rabbinic tradition—the heavenly voice or echo (*bat qol*) remained as a means of direct divine communication.[162] Ha-Levi thus draws a parallel between classical rabbinic terminology for the divine inspiration that was accorded to the Sages after the cessation of prophecy (*bat qol*), and the Arabic term he has chosen to describe such a level of divine support (*ta'yīd*).

Ha-Levi's language in this passage is perhaps deliberately ambiguous. It is not clear whether he wishes to say that prophecy had "just recently departed" from the community of the Second Temple; this would be problematic, for his language would then imply that the *bat qol*, too, had recently ceased. Perhaps, then, Ha-Levi wishes to suggest that the inspiration the Sages receive is quasi-prophetic; that prophecy had hardly ceased at all, for the *bat qol* had taken its place.

With his dislike for distinct hierarchies, it is likely that Ha-Levi is characteristically hedging on whether the Sages receive prophetic inspiration; he refers to inspiration by "the heavenly voice and things like it," without specifying what these other forms of divine communication might be. The main focus of this passage seems to be Ha-Levi's conviction—in contrast to the claims of the Karaites—that divine inspiration does indeed continue among the rabbis, that rabbinic literature itself has acknowledged this phenomenon, and that there exists a recognized vocabulary for inspiration which, if not at the level of prophecy, is nevertheless divine in origin. The *Ḥaver* also explains that while prophecy was not newly acquired (*muktasab*) during the time of the Second Temple, there still remained prophets who had acquired prophecy during the period of the First Temple. Moreover Ha-Levi apparently holds that other prophets could also draw inspiration from the *Shekhinah's* abiding in a prophetic individual, just as prophets drew inspiration from the *Shekhinah's* presence in the First Temple.[163]

The *Ḥaver* uses the vocabulary of divine inspiration to describe the Sages' extraordinary piety as well as their ability to establish law. In the following passage, he depicts a Sufi-like meditation on the participation of God in the pious person's every action. Describing God's sustaining presence in the world—an active presence Ha-Levi believes to be absolutely necessary for the world's continued functioning—the *Ḥaver* explains:

> The Creator creates limbs and gives them powers and sustains them in every moment. Imagine God's providence and guidance removed for an instant—the whole world would be destroyed. If the pious person meditates on this in all his movements, he acknowledges the Creator's participation in [his limbs' movements], for He first created them, and [now] provides them with his unceasing support [necessary] for their perfection.
>
> Then it is as if the divine Presence[164] is with him continually, and the angels virtually accompany him. If he strengthens his piety, and he abides in places worthy of the divine Presence,[165] they accompany him in reality, and he sees them with his own eyes, just next to the degree of prophecy [*nubuwwa*].
>
> Thus the best of the Sages, during the time of the Second Temple, saw a certain form and heard a heavenly voice [*bat qol*]. This is the degree of the pious,[166] and above it is that of prophets. (III:11: 99)

Even if the Holy Spirit of prophecy has left Israel, the rabbis are nevertheless of a sufficient degree of piety to merit certain gifts of the spirit, including the ability to see spiritual forms and hear the heavenly voice (*bat qol*). The Sages' accounts of heavenly visions are therefore to be accepted and not doubted.[167] Similarly, arguing that reliance on authority (*taqlīd*) is necessary for anyone who accepts the veracity of the Torah—as *taqlīd* is needed to establish the Torah's authentic text—the *Ḥaver* asserts that the *taqlīd* of the Sages is the most authoritative, as they trace their inspiration back to prophets whose divine inspiration no one would dare question.[168]

Ha-Levi appears at first glance to deviate somewhat from his terminological model when, to combat Karaite objections, the *Ḥaver* seems to endow the Sages with more direct divine authority to establish law than the terms *taʾyīd* and *ilhām* or even *nubuwwa* would imply. In explaining the Sages' establishment of the date of "putting the sickle to corn"—the beginning of counting fifty days from Passover to Shavuʿot—as the second day of Passover, Ha-Levi ascribes to the Sages at least the possibility of the highest degree of divine inspiration, *waḥy* (revelation):

> This was fixed for the second day of Passover—which does not contradict the Torah, since it originated with "the place which the Lord shall choose," on the conditions discussed before. Perhaps this was a revelation [*bi-waḥy*] from God the Exalted.[169] This is possible, and it frees us from the controversy of those who provoke controversy. (III:41: 125)

However, Ha-Levi may mean here that the Sages had an oral tradition whose original source was *waḥy*, what the rabbis call "a law of Moses from Sinai" (*halakhah le-Moshe mi-Sinai*).

Another exceptional usage of *waḥy* is found in IV:17. The *Ḥaver* says that the masses do not follow the *taqlīd* of philosophers, but rather that of the Sages, for the souls of the masses are, as it were, prophetically inspired (*wuḥiya*) with the truth—a statement he supports with the Talmudic quotation "words of truth will be recognized" (*Sota 9b*). Here it seems that he uses *waḥy* in rhetorical exaggeration to denigrate the sophisticated proof of the philosopher, which nevertheless does not fool the masses (IV:17: 169).

These two exceptional uses of *waḥy* reveal once more the parallels between Ha-Levi's arguments against the Karaites and those he uses against the philosophers. Both Karaites and philosophers claim to be above mere reliance on authority; both are actually slaves to their own sectarian *taqlīd*. Each presents its claims using the method of *qiyās*, which purports to be rationally compelling. Jewish tradition, however, possesses prophetic revelation (*waḥy*), which is even more compelling.

In summary, Ha-Levi's rendering of prophetic inspiration is less rigid than Saʿadya and the Muslim traditionalists, but more conservative than the philosophers and the Shīʿites. He uses the terms *ilham* and *ta'yīd* to describe a divine inspiration that gives the rabbis authority to legislate. Rabbinic tradition recognized in the work of the Sages the continuation of certain forms of inspiration, even after the cessation of prophecy proper. Accordingly, Ha-Levi equates rabbinic terms for such inspiration—*bat qol, sayyata di-shemaya*—with Arabic terms for inspiration (*ilhām*) and divine support (*ta'yīd*). These terms create a bridge between purely human knowledge and knowledge assisted by God, such as the Masoretic establishment of the Biblical text and the composition of the Mishnah. He also suggests that these forms of support guide the behavior of priests and prophets when they are embraced by the Holy Spirit (*ruaḥ ha-qodesh*). He connects *ta'yīd* with Solomon, although he does not state outright that Solomon composed the Biblical books attributed to him by *ta'yīd*. He also takes account of people who invent human, rational religions, calling themselves inspired (*mulham*), without true prophetic inspiration.

Like Saʿadya, he generally reserves the term *waḥy* for God's direct address to a prophet, a synonym for *nubuwwa*. *Waḥy* gives Abraham supra-rational knowledge not accessible to human *qiyās* alone. His greatest innovation is to extend the term *waḥy* to all Jews. Perhaps playfully, he suggests that the masses are inspired by *waḥy to* follow the Sages rather than the philosophers. In a more serious vein, he asserts that practicing the divine commandments can lead Jews to *waḥy*, the experiential state closest to the Divine. All born Jews have the potential for *waḥy*, a potential that is realized in the event at Mount Sinai.

6. *Three Accounts of Prophecy* (Nubuwwa)

We have noted that for medieval thinkers, receiving the Torah at Mount Sinai represents the ultimate prophetic degree, and the one most in tension with philosophical accounts of prophecy. If prophecy requires intellectual preparation, as the philosophers contend, how could the untutored masses participate in the revelation at Mount Sinai? Ha-Levi's depiction of the event of revelation must be read in light of his accounts of prophecy throughout the *Kuzari*. He offers several descriptions of the phenomenon of prophecy proper (*nubuwwa*), attributing them variously to the philosophers, the adherents of *kalām* (*al-mutakallimūn*), and to the *Ḥaver* himself.

In V:10, the *Ḥaver* presents the views of the *mutakallimūn* and offers an account that accords with traditional Islamic accounts of prophecy. Speaking of a person whose constitution of body and soul is balanced, he notes that such a person

> seeks advice and guidance, that God might inspire him [*yulhimuhu*] along the right path. This is one upon whom He will pour out a divine prophetic spirit[170] if he is worthy of prophecy [*nubuwwa*] or [a divine spirit of] inspiration [*ilhām*] if he is below that, [in which case] he is a pious friend of God and not a prophet.[171] (V:10: 200)

In V:20 the *Ḥaver* offers a similar description in the context of a discourse on his own views. The *Ḥaver* sets forth this account of prophecy and miracles—based upon Islamic models and using Arabic terminology—as a traditional Jewish approach:

> The endeavor of one who obeys God's religious laws[172] is to find favor in His eyes, and to place His desires before him. He seeks inspirations [*ilhāmāt*] if he is a pious friend of God,[173] or [seeks] miracles and wonders if he is a prophet, and if his people enjoy the divine pleasure on the basis of the conditions of time, place, and action, as set down in the Torah. (V:20: 220)

As we would expect, the *Ḥaver* offers his view of prophecy as an explicit alternative to the tenets of the philosophers. The philosophers had portrayed prophecy as the natural, humanly achieved end of a path toward human realization; God's role in revelation is at first glance unclear. Fārābī writes that a person who has perfected his or her intellect and whose soul has connected (*ittaṣalat*) with the Active Intellect

> is [the one] of whom it is fitting to say that he is granted revelation [*yuḥā ilaihi*—related to *waḥy*]. For a person is only granted revelation [*yuḥā ilaihi*]

when he has reached this level, which is that there remains no intermediary between him and the Active Intellect. . . .

And this emanation[174] which exists from the Active Intellect to the passive intellect through the mediation of the acquired intellect is revelation [*waḥy*]. For the Active Intellect emanates[175] from the being[176] of the First Cause. And because of this it is possible to say that the First Cause is the giver of revelation [*al-mūḥy*] to this person by the mediation of the Active Intellect.[177]

How different in tone this is from the *Ḥaver*'s view! Fārābī must go out of his way to inform his readers that it is possible to call the First Cause the "giver of revelation;" he implies this is merely a metaphor. The *Ḥaver*, in contrast, stresses that the prophet seeks to do the will of a personal, law-giving God. It is somewhat surprising that the *Ḥaver* depicts prophets as actively seeking miracles and wonders; this is an element that would seem out of place in rabbinic and Islamic models of prophecy, and that would constitute "striving" (*ijtihād*) in Ha-Levi's eyes. However the *Ḥaver* qualifies his assertion by stressing that in order for prophecy to take place, the conditions for prophecy set forth in the Torah must be fulfilled. Prophecy thus occurs by divine will and favor, not simply according to human effort.[178]

In V:12, in contrast, the *Ḥaver* depicts a philosophical model of prophecy, an integral part of his extended description of the views of the philosophers. This account, drawn almost literally from an early treatise of Avicenna, at first glance sounds much like the philosophical view that the *Ḥaver* claims God seeks to disprove at Sinai:[179]

In some people, the rational faculty is aided in[180] contact [*ittiṣāl*] with the universal intellect [to such an extent] that it is lifted above[181] using logical syllogism [*qiyās*] and deliberation; inspiration [*ilhām*] and revelation [*waḥy*] are rather sufficient sustenance [for it]. This special distinction[182] is called sanctification, and it is called sanctified spirit.[183] (V:12: 206)

It is instructive to compare this passage with Avicenna's exposition in the *Healing* (*Shifā'*). There Avicenna writes of the person who possesses "intuition"[184] that "it seems as though he knows everything from within himself." Given that there exist people who can find the middle term of a syllogism without effort, Avicenna deduces the possibility of a person of prophetic intellect who can find the middle terms of all syllogisms within him or herself:

Thus there might be an individual whose soul is so supported [assisted][185]by great purity and [a] great [capacity for] linking [*ittiṣāl*] with first intelligible

> principles that he blazes with intuition,[186] i.e., with the receptivity [to inspiration coming] from the Active Intellect concerning everything.
>
> Therefore the forms of all things contained in the Active Intellect are imprinted on his soul either all at once or nearly so, not that he accepts them merely on authority [*taqlīd*], but on account of their logical order which encompasses all the middle terms. For beliefs accepted on authority [*taqlīd*] concerning those things which are known only through their causes possess no rational certainty. This is a kind of prophecy [*nubuwwa*], indeed prophecy's highest form, and the one most fitted to be called divine [holy] power;[187] it is the highest human faculty.[188]

In the *Shifā'* Avicenna stresses that both in the case of ordinary knowledge and in the case of prophecy, one must seek the middle term of a syllogism. He explicitly establishes a continuum between ordinary philosophy—in which the seeking of the middle term of syllogisms is simply slower—and prophecy, in which the middle terms come all at once, without effort.[189] In a variety of formulations, Avicenna describes the effortless nature of the prophetic form of knowledge, which he terms "intuition" or "insight."[190]

In the account in V:12 that Ha-Levi borrows from Avicenna, however, there is no mention of seeking the middle term of a syllogism; the prophet seems to be lifted above *qiyās* totally. Dimitri Gutas sees this as an early formulation of Avicenna, in which he had not yet incorporated the linchpin of his mature account of prophecy—seeking the middle term through insight—which ties it to more ordinary ways of knowing.[191] Perhaps it is the sharp distinction between prophetic knowing and ordinary knowing in this early Avicennian view which made it attractive, or at least palatable, to Ha-Levi.

Given that in this account the prophet seems to be lifted above *qiyās* totally, prophecy might be said to flow directly from the universal intellect, and not from the cognitive faculties of the prophet. This is important to Ha-Levi's thinking about prophecy, as Ha-Levi wants to make it clear that prophecy is not a natural phenomenon, the highest along the continuum of human thought. Prophecy is not inspired speech or thinking, as in the thought of the *Ikhwān al-ṣafā'* and the Karaite Yefet b. 'Elī. The divine origin of prophecy cannot be explained away, as in the philosophical account of prophecy.

As we have seen, Ha-Levi deviates from this model with respect to prophetic vision—he introduces the element of the inner eye—but he refuses to describe prophetic speech in terms of natural human faculties and capacities. The origin of the Torah is God, no matter how physical divine speech might seem.

7. *The Scene at Mt. Sinai*

With this background, we are now in a good position to return to the scene at Mount Sinai. We can see what is at stake for Ha-Levi. He wants to deny (1) that the revelation that took place at Mount Sinai can be traced to a lower form of inspiration, that is, illumination (*ilhām*) or divine support (*ta'yīd*); and (2) that it took place internally in the mind, through the assistance of an angel or a universal intellect which serves as a bridge to God. The initiator of prophecy, according to Ha-Levi, is not the prophet who undergoes a process of intellectual purification, as in the thought of al-Fārābī, or who is uniquely gifted in connecting with the Active Intellect, as in Avicenna. The origin of prophecy is God.

Ha-Levi anachronistically portrays God as setting out to remove the Israelites' skepticism and doubt, engendered by the philosophical notion of prophecy as the product of an inspired human intellect. The *Ḥaver* insists it was crucial that the people know that the Torah did not originate in the mind of Moses. While Ha-Levi has shown himself comfortable with the language of inspiration and divine assistance with respect to the Sages' process of deciding law, he is adamant that the prophecy of Moses and the revelation at Mount Sinai represent a completely different phenomenon, that of *waḥy*.

With subtle irony, the *Ḥaver* depicts among the Biblical nation a group of skeptics who doubt that God could really have spoken to Moses, a group whose notion of God's transcendence is so refined that it would be marred by the attribution to God of something so corporeal as speech:

> Despite the people's belief in what Moses had brought them after those miracles, there still remained in their souls a doubt: how could God address a human being?—lest the origin of the Law be the opinion[192] or thought[193] of a human being, accompanied by inspiration [*ilhām*] and support [*ta'yīd*] from God. Address from a nonhuman being seemed far-fetched, since speech is physical. (I:87: 24)

Ha-Levi's Biblical anachronism is striking, for the Bible itself shows no hesitation in asserting that God spoke to Moses. By Ha-Levi's time, however, Biblical anthropomorphism had become a burning issue; Karaites and philosophers alike took the rabbis to task for attributing human qualities to God. The *Ḥaver* thus acknowledges that philosophers, responding to Biblical anthropomorphism, seek to diffuse the physical nature of revelation. The *Ḥaver* attributes to the philosophers the view that while inspiration or support may flow from the divine Active Intellect, prophetic speech itself issues from the mind of the prophet. We have seen such a view in the *Ikhwān al-ṣafā'*, who attribute the source of inspiration to the celestial spheres, but the words themselves to the prophet. We may also see this in the view of Yefet b. 'Elī, who attributes the source of inspiration to the Holy Spirit (*ruaḥ ha-qodesh*); it is not clear whether for Yefet the wording flows from the Holy Spirit or from the prophet. For philosophical rationalists, prophecy is not literally divine speech, but is rather the product of an inspired human mind.

Describing his own view, in contrast, the *Ḥaver* asserts that in preparation to hear the Ten Words, the people did not undergo a crash course in philosophy. Their aim was not to purify the mind to receive inspiration or assistance from the Active Intellect. Rather, they prepared themselves to receive a prophetic revelation directly from God:

> God wanted to remove this doubt from them, so he commanded them [concerning] the requirement of inner and outer [purification], and made the confirmation of it separation from women and preparation to hear the divine word. The people prepared and readied themselves for the degree of *waḥy*—or rather, to hear the address publically, all of them. (Ibid.)

Ha-Levi echoes R. Nissim Gaon here, who argues similarly that there remained among the people some who doubted the prophecy of Moses. God thus gave the nation at Sinai an experience of sensible knowledge (*yed'iat ha-hargashot*) so that they would know beyond the shadow of a doubt that these were the words of the living God.[194] Also like R. Nissim, Ha-Levi contrasts the sensory experience of the Jews at Mount Sinai with indirect knowledge by proof. In this passage, however, he is most concerned to refute the philosophical view of prophecy as mental inspiration (*ilhām*). The *Ḥaver* thus distinguishes explicitly between the prophetic revelation (*waḥy*) that took place at Mount Sinai and the philosophical account of prophecy. He describes in detail the philosophical view which the event at Sinai conclusively disproved for the Israelites who experienced it:

> The people heard with distinctness[195] the words of the Ten Commandments. . . . And these Ten Words the masses did not transmit from isolated individuals, nor from a prophet, but from God. However they did not have the power of Moses for *mushāhada* of that great thing.[196]
>
> And the people believed from that day that Moses [peace be upon him] was addressed by a word whose origin was God. Moses did not first have a thought or an opinion—lest prophecy be, as the philosophers con-

> tend, from a soul which has purified its thoughts and connected [*tatta ṣilu*] with the Active Intellect, which is called Holy Spirit[197] or Gabriel, and been inspired [*yulhamu*—related to *ilhām*]. Or perhaps it occurred to him imaginatively—in that moment in sleep, or between sleep and waking—that an individual had spoken to him, and that he heard his spoken word in an imaginative mode in his soul, not with his ears, or that he saw in an imaginative mode, not with his eyes, and then said that God had spoken to him.
>
> These views were disproved in that great vision [*mashhad*] and the divine writing which followed the divine address, when He wrote those Ten Words on two tables from a subtle substance and handed them over to Moses. And they saw that it was divine writing as they heard that it was divine address. (I:87: 24–25)

The *Ḥaver*'s description of the philosophical view corresponds in broad strokes to the views of intellectual and imaginative prophecy in the thought of philosophers such as al-Fārābī and Avicenna. For al-Fārābī a process of learning and purification of thought is necessary for the philosopher's ultimate union with the Active Intellect. The philosopher must acquire primary intelligibles from the Active Intellect, deduce complex knowledge through syllogistic reasoning, and thereby perfect his or her own intellect.

It is true that for al-Fārābī the Active Intellect initially supplies the mind with its primary truths, and continually supplies the "light" by which the potential intellect passes into actuality.[198] However, it is only when the intellect has completely purified itself of sensible dross and reached a level Fārābī terms "acquired intellect" that he or she can make ultimate contact (*ittiṣāl*) with the Active Intellect and achieve revelation (*waḥy*) and immortality. It may be this process of intellectual purification that Ha-Levi has in mind when speaking of the prophet cleansing his thoughts, uniting with the Active Intellect, and being inspired. Moreover Fārābī—like the *Ḥaver*'s foil, the philosophical skeptic—explicitly likens the Active Intellect to the angel of revelation, Gabriel, and to the holy or trustworthy spirit.[199]

The imaginative aspect of prophecy is also clearly recognizable from the theories of both al-Fārābī and Avicenna.[200] Al-Fārābī and Avicenna both attribute this form of prophecy to an imagination especially sensitive to impressions upon it, whether in sleep or—in someone whose imagination is particularly active—in waking. They differ only in that Avicenna ascribes the source of these prophetic impressions to an emanation from the souls of the celestial spheres, while al-Fārābī attributes them to an emanation from the Active Intellect.

8. Ha-Levi's Approach to the Sinai Revelation

With our understanding of the Islamic background and Ha-Levi's terminology, we can now appreciate the complexity of his view. Ha-Levi wants to deny the philosophical account of prophecy, which seems to make prophecy an individual achievement of human realization—an impersonal, spontaneous, natural ability attained by the prophet, as opposed to a gift from the sovereign will of a personal God. Most importantly, the philosophical account threatens to make the words of prophecy human words rather than divine words. The *Ikhwān al-ṣafā'* take this position explicitly; Sa'adya is clearly disturbed by such a view. It is true that al-Fārābī and Avicenna do not state explicitly that the prophet is the source of prophetic language. However, they do describe prophecy as a natural phenomenon, the product of human faculties illumined by the Active Intellect.

The *Ḥaver* expresses in I:87 the most feared result of this position: if prophecy is the natural product of a fully developed human mind, then Moses, and not God, could mistakenly be said to be the author of the Torah. Elsewhere, the *Ḥaver* states clearly his conviction that the words of the Torah come directly from God, and not Moses:

> Our laws were laid down[201] in the Torah from the divine address[202] to Moses [which] he handed to the masses assembled in the desert. There was no need to cite the support of other individuals, chapter by chapter, verse by verse.[203] Everything [was given] in explicit detail[204] by God. (I:99:33)

Even the words that issue directly from the prophet's mouth are not of human origin: "The speech of prophets at the time the Holy Spirit[205] enwraps them, is in every word directed from the *'amr ilāhī;* the prophet cannot alter a word (V:20: 221).[206]

It is true that both al-Fārābī and Avicenna acknowledge that the source of *waḥy* or *ilhām* is ultimately the Active Intellect—a divine emanation—and not the prophet's own mind. However, for the philosophers, this is true of all human knowledge. In the Neo-Platonic scheme the lines between revelation, inspiration, and ordinary knowledge are blurred, for there is a continuum between the human mind and the divine mind.

If such philosophical views of prophecy were applied to the Bible, one could maintain that the events of revelation at Mount Sinai did not take place "objectively" but were creations of the human imagination, and the Torah the product of an inspired human mind. The event at Mt. Sinai could be reduced to a group hallucination, the receiving of the

Torah to a natural process of learning by realized human beings, rather than the revealed words of a living God.

Ha-Levi thus stresses the public, objective, external nature of the revelation at Mt. Sinai: that it is accompanied by lightning and thunder, that the people see Moses walk into a cloud, and see the cloud on the mountain for days. Ha-Levi skillfully uses the language of witness to reinforce his description of the event at Mount Sinai as *waḥy*—the direct revelation of an active divine agent—rather than a more vague internal form of inspiration such as *ilhām* or *ta'yīd*. In Ha-Levi's use of the root *sh-h-d* and the terms *mashhad* (pl. *mashāhid*) (a vision or scene of a religious event) and *mushāhada* (witnessing), one sees Ha-Levi's desire to stress the objective nature of revelation: that these were not just individual, internal visions, but public displays or scenes, religious events which a great multitude witnessed together and to which they could therefore give valid testimony.[207]

However, one should also note that although he uses the vocabulary of vision, not all of the manifestations the people witness are visual; some are auditory, for example the thunder that accompanies the lightning. The Torah itself mixes the senses in its account of the events at Mt. Sinai, telling us that the people "saw the sounds." Such a phenomenon bespeaks another state of consciousness; synesthesia is known cross culturally to be characteristic of altered states of awareness. Of course the Ten Words themselves are presumably received aurally, rather than visually. We find in Ha-Levi an echoing, although in reverse, of the Torah's language of synesthesia.[208] The Torah states that the people "saw the sounds"; the *Ḥaver* asserts that they were prepared to *hear* the divine address publically and did hear some of the Ten Words, but they did not have a capacity equal to Moses for the *witness* (*mushāhada*) of that great thing.[209] The root *sh-h-d* thus serves Ha-Levi here in its broadest sense of testimony, indicating a witnessing that is not confined to the visual but is an all-encompassing experience, including all the senses—indeed every facet of a person's being.[210]

The people do experience a direct revelation from God; they are prepared for the level of prophetic revelation (*waḥy*), not the lower level of inspiration (*ilhām*) or divine assistance (*ta'yīd*). Moreover they clearly have some capacity for *mushāhada*, otherwise they would not witness any divine manifestations at all. In essence then, the nation receives the Ten Words directly from God, in prophetic witness. However on account of their fear of the Divine, they cannot sustain the experience or the altered state, as Moses could, to receive all the words of revelation. Ha-Levi thus follows rabbinic tradition according to which the people become afraid after hearing the first two of the Ten Words. Expressing this rabbinic idea using his Arabic terminology, Ha-Levi writes: "And these Ten Words the masses did not hand down[211] from individual people, nor from a prophet, but rather from God. However they did not have the capacity for the witness [*mushāhada*] of that great thing" (I:87: 24).[212]

Ha-Levi's repeated use of the root *sh-h-d* in this passage suggests that he wants to draw upon the root's mystical associations. Ha-Levi's text evokes the Sufi sense of *mushāhada*, the state of witnessing the Divine with the inner eye of one's heart, a motif which appears repeatedly in Ha-Levi's poetry. At the same time, the text alludes to the philosophical notion we have seen in Avicenna, that *mushāhada* is an unmediated, experiential form of knowing. Yet, because of its connotations of objective witness and testimony, Ha-Levi can also use the root to prove that the event at Sinai was a direct manifestation of divine power, and thus to bolster his assertion that there is direct divine causality in the world (I:88–89: 25–26). The conviction that God acts directly in the world—with no need for intermediary causes—is apparently one of the fruits of prophetic experience according to Ha-Levi.

The *Ḥaver* thus emphasizes that he does not need to establish an elaborate theory of how revelation and prophecy take place. All who directly experience the Divine know that what they are witnessing is no product of the human imagination.

9. *Revelation as God's Created Speech*

In I:89 the *Ḥaver* confesses:

> We do not know how the intention[213] became corporealized so that it became a word[214] which struck our ear, nor do we know how He created something from that which was nonexistent or from that which was available to him from among existing things. (I:89: 26)

Like Philo and Sa'adya Gaon before him, Ha-Levi is led to the notion of revelation as God's created speech by two factors: the problem of how an immaterial God can speak when words seem to be physical entities, and the exegetical difficulties of the statement in Exodus 20:15 that "all the people saw the sounds." R. Aqiva explains the verse as a description of synesthesia; the people both saw and heard that which was visible.[215] Sa'adya develops from this the notion that when the Torah says "God spoke," it literally means that "God created a word which is conveyed through the air to the hearing of the prophet or the people."[216] Philo, too, derives from the Biblical statement that "all the people saw the sounds" (Exodus 20:15) the notion of a "newly created voice" that the people could both hear and see.[217]

Ha-Levi, however, is less interested in the metaphysics of the issue than is Philo and certainly than Sa'adya, who develops the theory of a "second air" in which the divine speech is created.[218] He thus has the *Ḥaver* characteristically hedge his explanation in I:91:[219]

> The *Ḥaver*: I do not assert authoritatively that the thing was like this description, and perhaps it was in a way more difficult to comprehend than I could imagine. Nevertheless, the result of this was that whoever witnessed [*shāhada*] those theophanies [*mashāhid*] had conviction that the thing was from the Creator, without an intermediary.
>
> It is to be compared to the first act of creation. The belief in the law connected with those theophanies [*mashāhid*] is as firmly established in the mind as the belief in the creation of the world, and that He created it in the same manner in which, as is known, He created the two tablets, the manna, and other things. Thus disappear from the soul of the believer the doubts of the philosophers and materialists. (I:91: 26–27)

It is clear from I:87–91 that the focus of Ha-Levi's attention is not whether the scene (*mashhad*) at Mt. Sinai is ultimately to be traced to the outer, physical eye or to the inner, spiritual eye; or whether the manifestations witnessed are themselves physical, spiritual, or some intermediate between the two. The *Ḥaver* makes very clear what concerns him ultimately: that "whoever witnessed [*shāhada*] those scenes [*mashāhid*] had conviction that the thing was from the Creator, without an intermediary;"[220] and that "the belief in the Law connected with those theophanies [*mashāhid*] is as firmly established in the mind as the belief in the creation of the world." Direct witness (*mushāhada*) provides certainty, a direct, personal relationship to God, and firm conviction in the divine origin of the Law.

Our examination of Ha-Levi's account of the Sinai revelation suggests that for Ha-Levi the experience of prophetic witnessing (*mushāhada*) is not simply visual, but has broader experiential overtones. We will see how these overtones come to the fore in Ha-Levi's depiction of the story of Abraham.

PART 5

The Language of Intimacy (*Uns*), Longing (*Shawq*) and Love (*ʿIshq*)

1. The Language of Love in Ha-Levi's Poetry

We have seen in our discussion of *ittiṣāl* that Ha-Levi regards the human connection with God as a true relationship between two parties; Ha-Levi is more interested in the experiential dimension to the language of *ittiṣāl* than he is in any suggestion of ontological union. This does not necessarily imply that the idea of mystical union was offensive to him. However, in Ha-Levi's view it is precisely the element of mutuality that is the key to the divine-human relationship. Ha-Levi's vision of *ittiṣāl* suggests the Jewish covenantal ideal: a concrete, mutual relationship of love, commitment, and loyalty.

We find in Ha-Levi's poetry expression of the intensity of the poet's search for such a relationship with God, the pathos of his longing to be met by the divine beloved:

> O Lord, before Thee is my whole desire—
> Yea, though I cannot bring it to my lips.
> Thy favour I would ask a moment and then die—
> Ah, would that mine entreaty might be granted!
> That I might render up the remnant of my spirit to Thine hand,
> Then should I sleep, and sweet my sleep would be.
> When far from Thee, I die while yet in life;
> But if I cling to Thee I live, though I should die.[1]

In the last two lines we find an expression of Ha-Levi's view of the afterlife. True connection with God is available in this life, and guarantees life in the world to come, just as the *Ḥaver* asserts in the *Kuzari*:

> For one whose soul is attached [*ittaṣalat nafsuhu*] to the *ʾamr ilāhī* while he is [still] busy with the accidents of the body, it stands to reason that he will join [*yattaṣilu*] [the *ʾamr ilāhī*] when he withdraws and leaves this unclean vessel. (III:20: 110)
>
> The promises of all these laws are included under one principle: the expectation of drawing near to God and his angels. One who has reached [*waṣala*] this level need not fear death; our Law has demonstrated this plainly (I:109: 36–37).

What we find further in the poem is confirmation that Ha-Levi made an association between the Arabic *ittiṣāl* and the Hebrew *devequt:*[2]

> When I am far from Thee, I die while yet in life;
> But if I cling [*edbaq*] to Thee I live,
> though I should die.

We witness here the poet's experience of being far from God and being drawn near. In the next stanza, Ha-Levi expresses his conviction that it is through service of God that human beings are able to draw close—even to reach and cling—to God. Indeed, we hear an echo of the Khazar King's search for the true way to worship the Divine:

> Only I know not how to come before Thee,
> Nor what should be my service nor my Law.
> Show me, O Lord, Thy ways!
> And turn me back from bondage of my folly.[3]

In other poems we hear the answer to this quest to "show me Thy ways." It is through the *mitsvot*, the Jewish framework for service of God, that the Divine can be met in human experience. We find this expressed most clearly in Ha-Levi's poems about the experience of prayer; through prayer, the poet attests, God becomes an ever-present companion:

> With all my heart—O Truth—and all my might
> I love You, with my limbs and with my mind.
> Your Name is with me: Can I walk alone?
> With it for lover, how can I be lorn?
> With it for lamp, how can my light go dim?
> How can I slip with it the stick by which I stand?
> They mock who do not understand: The shame
> I bear because I bear Your name is pride to me
> Source of my life, I bless You while I live;
> My Song, I sing to You while yet I breathe.[4]

As Raymond Scheindlin has pointed out, the opening lines of this poem recall the language of the *Shema*ʿ, a central Biblical call to the love of God:

> Hear, O Israel, the Lord is our God, the Lord alone
> You shall love the Lord your God with all your
> heart, with all your soul, and with all your might.
> And these words which I command you this day shall be on
>   your heart.
> You shall speak of them when you sit in your house,
> when you walk upon the way,
> When you lie down and when you rise up.

Scheindlin notes that in Ha-Levi's poem, the narrator in one sense expresses the collective experience of Israel, who suffer for God's name. At the same time, he expresses a very personal sense of God's presence, not just as a desire, but as an actual fact. In the *Shema*ʿ, the believer is enjoined to love God and to speak of God always. In this poem, the poet declares that the *Shema*ʿ's injunction has become a fact: God's Name is with him as an ever-present source of sustenance.[5] Through prayer, the poet asserts, he sings to God and blesses the Source of his life; in response, his way is illumined by the lamp of God. Note too that the poet's love for God is a passionate and embodied love. He worships God with his very limbs, and not with his mind alone. Like Abraham, he is willing to suffer for the God he knows not merely by logic, but by taste.

Ha-Levi most dramatically expresses his sense of the nearness of God—despite God's awesome transcendence—in one of his most famous devotional poems:

> Lord, where shall I find Thee?
> High and hidden is Thy place;
>   And where shall I not find Thee?
> The world is full of Thy glory.[6]

There are many paradoxes expressed in this poem: God is present everywhere, but cannot be contained anywhere; God is found within our hearts, but is the Creator of the external world. The Lord is transcendent and remote from all creatures, and yet is closer to them than their own body and soul.[7] In contrast to the world-denying dualism of the ascetics, the poet affirms the inherent goodness of the world. God is fully present, indeed the whole world is full of God's glory. We find a striking parallel to this poem in the first gate of Baḥya's *Duties of the Heart*. Baḥya expresses the paradox in the name of "one of the pious" [*ba'ḍ al-ṣāliḥin*]—which usually refers to a non-Jewish source—who prayed:"My God, where can I find Thee? Nay, where can I not find thee? Hidden and invisible art Thou; Yet the universe is filled with Thee."[8]

It is in moments of prayer, in calling out to God, that the poet experiences the miracle of God's nearness. The poet is not only the seeker, but also the sought, not only a lover of God, but also God's beloved:

> I have sought Thy nearness,
> With all my heart have I called Thee
> And going out to meet Thee
> I found Thee coming toward me.

As Bernard Septimus has noted, Ha-Levi draws here upon a midrashic account of the event at Mount Sinai. The Bibical text tells us that Moses brought the people out to meet God. The rabbis point out that the term *to meet* (*liqrat*) carries a sense of motion toward someone who is himself coming forward; the people go out to meet a God who is himself coming forth to meet them. Hence, "the *Shekhinah* went out to meet them as a groom goes out to meet a bride."[9] For Ha-Levi, the personal aspect of relationship with God is not one-sided: the seeker is actually met by God, who is also in search of the seeker. The relationship is one of genuine mutuality; God needs human beings just as human beings need God.

The notion of the inner eye or the eye of the heart, which we explored above, finds expression in Ha-Levi's poetry as well. Yehudah Ratzaby and Raymond Scheindlin have shown the influence of Sufi poetry on Ha-Levi's liturgical poems.[10] Among the Sufi themes we find in Ha-Levi's poetry is that while the physical eye fails, the heart has the privilege of beholding God:

> To behold Him [*la-ḥazoto*] the eye fails,
> But from my flesh[11] He is revealed to my heart.[12]

And in another poem:

> The Creator, who brought forth everything
> from nothing,
> Is revealed to the heart,
> but not to the eye.[13]

2. *The Sufi Language of Intimacy*

In the *Kuzari* Ha-Levi expresses these Sufi ideas in Arabic terms; Ha-Levi finds in the Sufi lexicon Arabic words to express the love, longing, and intimacy that characterize the relationship of a Jew with the Divine. The *Ḥaver* asserts that the Jewish experience of God is one of direct witness (*mushāhada*) and that the experience of witnessing God leads to a natural response of passionate love, worship, and obedience. In one passage, he even speaks of *ittiṣāl* in a way that suggests the Sufi notion of union with the divine beloved.

The *Ḥaver* explains in IV:15 that the meaning of the Bible's generic term for God (*Elohim*) can be known by logic; *qiyās* can prove that there must be a God who orders and governs the world. The personal name Lord, in contrast, represents that God known to Israel through direct witness,[14] not through reason:

> As for the meaning of Lord, it cannot be grasped[15] logically,[16] but rather experientially [by witness],[17] by that prophetic vision by which a person gets to the point where he almost separates himself from his species and becomes attached to [*yattaṣilu bi*][18] an angelic species.[19] (IV:15: 167–68)

The *Ḥaver* cites several Biblical expressions that illustrate this process by which a prophet transcends the human, by which there befalls him another spirit: "you will become another man,"[20] "and God gave him another heart"[21] "and a spirit enwrapped [*lavsha*] Amasai,"[22] "the hand of the Lord was upon me,"[23] "uphold me with your free spirit."[24] All of these expressions, the *Ḥaver* asserts, "are allusions to the spirit of holiness [*ruaḥ ha-qodesh*] that enwraps [is on intimate terms with, *mulābisa*] the prophet at the time of his prophesying" (IV:15: 168).

Ha-Levi's Hebrew and Arabic vocabulary are of note here. The Hebrew root *l-b-sh*, like its Arabic cognate *l-b-s*, signifies enclothing. The Biblical phrase "A spirit enclothed [*lavsha*] Amasai," which the *Ḥaver* quotes, thus invokes the image of the prophet Amasai's being enwrapped by the spirit. In the Arabic, however, Ha-Levi uses the active participle of the third form, whose primary sense is to be in close association or on intimate terms with; we find a similar use in Ghazzālī, who writes that "intimate experience [*mulābasa*] of [the prophetic] state is tasting [*dhawq*]."[25]

Ha-Levi thus takes advantage of the literary possibilities of Judaeo-Arabic culture. By juxtaposing the Hebrew *lavsha* and the Arabic *mulābisa*, Ha-Levi draws upon two images for the relationship of the Holy Spirit with the prophet: one of a garment in close physical contact with the prophet's body, and one of the spirit of holiness in close association with the human spirit. Both suggest the intimacy of the relationship between God and the prophet, particularly when he or she is being prophetically inspired.[26]

The prophet, graced with the Holy Spirit, is freed from the doubts which plagued him or her when searching for God through *qiyās*. What replaces doubt is passionate love, service, and the bliss of *ittiṣāl*. The prophet becomes

> a servant of God,[27] passionately in love[28] with the object of his worship,[29] almost annihilating himself out of his love,[30] due to the greatness of the bliss[31] of union [*ittiṣāl*] he feels, and the pain and suffering in being apart from Him. (IV:15:168)[32]

The passionate lover we find here is well known in Arabic poetry of both sacred and secular love; we often see him on the verge of death when separated from the bliss of union with his beloved.[33] Sufi writers, like the *Ḥaver* here, weave together imagery of passionate love, worship, and obedience even unto death, as in the following verse of an early Islamic poet:

> If you would say, "Die!"
> I would die in perfect obedience
> And would say to the one who calls me to death:
> "Welcome, welcome!"[34]

The connection between love and obedience is likewise expressed in the following verses quoted by Ghazzālī:

> You are disobedient to God and pretend to love Him
> That is, by my life! a very novel action:
> If your love were sincere, you would obey Him,
> For the lover is obedient to him whom he loves.[35]

Love inspires the ultimate obedience and surrender, as another poem quoted by Ghazzālī illustrates:

> I want union [*wuṣūl*] with him, and he wants
> separation from me;
> Therefore I give up what I want for what he wants.[36]

Ha-Levi's "worshiping servant, passionately in love with the object of his worship, ready to annihilate himself out of his love,"[37] is thus the hero of Sufi literature; Ha-Levi's language in IV:15 echoes the ideals of Islamic pietism. The phrase "bliss of union" (*ladhdhat al-ittiṣāl*) also has Sufi resonance; Sufi mystics use the root *l-dh-dh*—signifying joy, sweetness, delight or bliss—to suggest the subjective experience, the pleasurable sensation of "tasting" union with the divine beloved.[38]

As we have seen, however, these terms can encompass a broad range of meaning;[39] Ha-Levi's language of union does not mean that he regards *ittiṣāl* as ontological oneness or *unio mystica*, as do the most radical Sufis. On the other hand, his pairing of the term *ittiṣāl* with *ladhdha* does add an ecstatic, passionate dimension to the divine-human relationship, transforming the covenantal bond we see elsewhere in the *Kuzari.*

Strikingly, the *Ḥaver* goes on to contrast the blissful experience of union with the Divine to the intellectual refinement of the pseudo-philosophers:

> This forms a contrast to those who dabble in philosophy,[40] who see in the worship of God nothing but extreme refinement, extolling Him in truth above all other beings—just as the sun is placed on a higher level than other visible things—and [who see] in the denial of God nothing more than the baseness of a soul content with a lie. (IV:15: 168)

In drawing such a stark contrast, the *Ḥaver* ignores the fact that philosophers, too, use the term *ittiṣāl* to extoll the joy of contact with the Divine. However, while philosophers describe this as intellectual contact with the divine intelligence,[41] the *Ḥaver* points here to *ittiṣāl* with a distinctly Sufi, non-philosophical flavor and discredits the philosophical path to God as indirect, uncertain, and uncommitted. The *Ḥaver* argues that a person would be willing to die rather than be deprived of One with whom he or she has experienced the bliss of union, whereas he denies one would perish at the thought of being without the results of a syllogism.[42]

The *Ḥaver*'s prime concern is thus the commitment, love, and obedience awakened when one knows God through direct experience. Union with an abstract intellect, he argues, cannot have the emotional impact of union with a Person to whom one is devoted. Direct knowledge of God is transformative and not merely cognitive. Conversely, the King points out that according to Aristotle, God himself has no knowledge of individuals. Without such personal knowledge—human knowledge of God, and God's knowledge of individual human beings—a relationship of loyalty and service makes no sense. For Ha-Levi, *ittiṣāl* as union with a personal God and *ittiṣāl* as covenant with God go hand in hand.

3. *Love, Longing, and the God of Abraham*

The King's epiphany in IV:16 echoes this sentiment, and is in many ways the heart of the *Kuzari* as a whole. The *Ḥaver* identifies the generic God of the Bible with the God of Aristotle and the Lord with the God of Abraham:

> The Lord one yearns for tasting [*dhawqan*] and directly witnessing [*mushāhadatan*],[43] whereas to God we incline through syllogistic reasoning [*qiyās*]. And this tasting prompts one who grasps it to be consumed in love for him, and to prefer death [to being] without him, whereas that reasoning [only] demonstrates that veneration is incumbent so long as one is not harmed and does not suffer pain. (IV:16: 168–69)

For the *Ḥaver*, it is not only actual taste and witness of God that characterize Jews' relationship with the Divine, but the yearning (*shawq*) to partake of such a relationship. Ha-Levi chooses a key Sufi term to express this idea: *shawq*, like *mushāhada*, is one of the spiritual states one attains on the Sufi path by the grace of God.[44] Ha-Levi suggests here that the human longing to be close to God—a longing he expresses so poignantly in his poetry—is in fact the core of Jewish faith.[45] The Biblical ancestors devoted their lives to a God whom they could not bear to live without. The *Ḥaver*'s language here is reminiscent of a verse quoted by Ghazzālī:

> The day of separation is longer than the day of
> Resurrection,
> And death is more beautiful than the pain of being
> separated.[46]

Ha-Levi also makes full use of the resonance of *mushāhada* in this passage. A witness (*shāhid*) can offer accurate testimony (*shahāda*); one who has witnessed God can give the only indubitable testimony to God's existence—or better yet, presence. The language of witness is also key to the Arabic love poetry of the Middle Ages. The love-sick individual willing to die for the divine beloved is a witness/martyr (*shahīd*) to God.[47]

The *Ḥaver* expands on the King's theme of such ultimate witness by relating it to the story of Abraham. Whereas philosophers would not suffer for a mere idea, Abraham rightly suffered through his various trials. As we saw earlier, the *Ḥaver* describes Abraham's painful but transformative experiences using Sufi terms:

> Rightly Abraham bore what he bore . . . in his distressing resolution to sacrifice Isaac, when he witnessed [*shāhada*] the Divine by tasting [*dhawqan*], not by logic [*qiyāsan*]. He saw that not the smallest detail of his [doings] could escape God. He saw that He rewarded him instantly for his good, and that He guided him [*yahdihi*] on the right path to such an extent that he did not move a step forward or backward without His permission. (IV:17: 169)

The *Ḥaver*'s reference to the binding of Isaac illustrates most clearly the breadth of Ha-Levi's use of the term *witness*. Abraham's experience of witnessing through taste (*shāhada . . . dhawqan*) was indeed a theophany. Ha-Levi does not necessarily use the term *mushāhada* to indicate that Abraham "saw" the angel who addressed him. Rather, by using the Sufi terms *witness* and *taste*, Ha-Levi suggests that whatever Abraham's experience was, it had nothing whatsoever to do with logic; Abraham found God in the intensity of this key moment in his life.

It is striking, too, how the nuance of religious experience has been broadened in this passage, through use of the familiar Islamic root *h-d-y* for divine guidance. Abraham's religious experience included whatever direct witness he had of the Divine, but also his realization that the events of his life showed immediate reward and punishment:

> He saw that there was nothing of the details of his [doings] that was hidden, and he saw that [God] rewarded him instantly and guided him on his right course to the point where he did not make a move forwards or backwards without [God's] permission. (IV:17: 169)

Similarly, the priest or the prophet's guidance by the Holy Spirit could extend to general guidance beyond specifically prophetic or priestly functions (IV:15: 168). God likewise promises the people of Israel they will be guided as a nation: "you will witness [*sa-tushāhidūna*] that an order higher than the natural order guides your order." The Jews will become aware of God's constant providential care, hidden or visible, in both nature and history (I:109: 36).

Ha-Levi in fact seems to connect these two forms of religious experience: witnessing God through taste, and awareness of divine guidance. Abraham did not engage in theological proof; he became convinced—not through mental reflection but through direct experience—that the presence of God was guiding him. Through his experience of God by taste, Abraham saw that his footsteps were guided.

The *Ḥaver* then goes on to make a logical leap not taken, for example, by the Arabic thinker Ibn Ṭufayl. One who has tasted the Lord directly would scoff at the intellectual path he or she had once taken to know the Divine:

> So then how could he not belittle his former syllogistic reasoning [*qiyāsāt*]? As the Sages explain the verse "He brought [Abraham] outside" [Gen. 15:5] [as meaning] "give up your study of the stars!" [*Shabbat* 156a]. That is to say, he commanded him to relinquish his speculative study of the stars and other things, and to take upon himself obedience [*ṭāʿa*] to Him whom he had perceived by taste [*dhawqan*],[48] as it is said, "Taste and see that the Lord is good" [Psalm 34:9].[49]

For Ha-Levi it is axiomatic that the appropriate response to direct experience is to become obedient to God. Direct, sensory, personal knowledge—in contrast to knowledge through *qiyās*—awakens emotions that foster loyalty.[50]

We see, too, that Ha-Levi has built the entire passage around exegesis of a psalm which combines language of taste and seeing. It is often said that Hebrew thought builds on the sense of hearing, as opposed to the Greeks' emphasis on sight—the most common example given is the injunction "Hear O Israel!" (*shemaʿ Yisrael*). Ha-Levi finds one verse in the Bible supporting his conviction that taste and sight, as the most direct and irrefutable of the senses, are the metaphors most apt for religious experience. Whereas one can hear another person's syllogistic proof and assent to it, it is only for oneself that one can taste or see—and it is only seeing for oneself that awakens true love for God.

The *Ḥaver* links this seeing specifically with Israel and asserts it is lacking in other nations. The Lord is the God of Israel because only Israel possesses the ability to taste and see God.[51] The *Ḥaver* affirms that every person who follows the divine Law

> follows the people of this seeing.[52] Their souls take pleasure in reliance on their authoritative traditions [*taqlīd*], in [spite of] the simplicity of their parables—a pleasure they do not take in reliance on the authoritative traditions [*taqlīd*] of the philosophers, in [spite of] the delicacy of their tales, and the excellent arrangement of their compositions, and the brilliance of their demonstrations.[53] Nevertheless, the masses do not follow them, for their souls are inspired [*wuḥiya*] with the truth, as it is said, "The words of truth are recognizable." (Sota 9b) (IV:17: 169)

We saw in our discussion of *qiyās* that the *Ḥaver* uses the term *taqlīd* ironically, insisting that reliance on someone who has had a direct experience of God is more certain than relying on the indirect, wavering human intellect. This is ironic because the way of *qiyās* had been touted as the way of the elite, with *taqlīd* consigned to the uneducated masses. Ha-Levi deflates the pretension of the intellectual elite, envisioning in its place a spiritual elite based on the capacity for direct religious experience.

The *Ḥaver* points out that philosophers do not discover philosophical truths *ex nihilo*, but rely on Aristotelian tradition, putting as much faith in the words of Aristotle as the religious masses do in the words of the Sages. The philosophers, then—with all their pretense to the originality of *qiyās*—simply practice another form of *taqlīd*.[54] The masses, however, by a native intuition which the *Ḥaver* describes as a form of revelation (*waḥy*), are inspired to rely for religious truth on the Sages, not the philosophers.

In a curious way then, Ha-Levi places the masses above the philosophers. The intellectual elite are distracted by the pseudo-sophistication of logical proof (*burhān*). The masses, on the other hand, sense that truths which are missed in the niceties of *qiyās* can be found in the simple wisdom of the Sages. The masses enjoy a kind of religious intuition—which he calls *waḥy*—simply in knowing upon whom to rely for truth. For Ha-Levi, such pure-hearted reliance (*taqlīd*), in contrast to the dry syllogisms of the philosophers, expresses true love for God.

4. *Intimacy* (Uns) *for Ha-Levi's Age*

Did Ha-Levi, then, believe that all that was left for Jews in his time was *taqlīd*? Did Jews in his day not have the possibility of intimacy with their Lord? The *Ḥaver* does suggest in III:1 that the intimacy with God enjoyed by Abraham and the prophets is lacking in his age; exile and the absence of the *Shekhinah* prevent attempts at the contemplative life from reaching fruition.[55] Biblical figures such as Enoch and Elijah who spent time in seclusion did not suffer from loneliness; they retired from the company of humans to the company of angels.[56] Indeed, in a striking use of Sufi terms, the *Ḥaver* asserts that solitude and seclusion[57] became their very fellowship (*uns*). It is rather in human company that such prophets would feel lonely,[58] for they miss contemplation (*mushāhada*) of the angelic realm (III:1: 90).[59] However, ascetics in his contemporary age, unlike the prophets of old, do not make contact (*yattaṣil*) with the divine light, which would offer them the intimate fellowship (*ya'nasu ilaiha*—related to *uns*) it did the prophets of old (III:1: 136).

Intimacy or fellowship (*uns*) is another Sufi stage on the path, along with longing (*shawq*) and passionate love (*ʿishq*). Intimacy removes the fear of loneliness. A classical Sufi text tells the story of a Sufi master who placed his disciple in a very lonely corner and forgot him for a week. When he returned and asked his student to forgive him, the student replied, "Do not worry; God has taken away the fear of loneliness from His friend."[60]

While in this story intimacy (*uns*) leaves no room for *waḥsha* ("feeling frightened by loneliness"), the latter term can also be used for the feeling of estrangement from all creation which can accompany intimacy with God.[61] It is precisely this paradox that Ha-Levi expresses in III:1. While the contemplative prophets of old could be fulfilled in the presence of angels and lonely in human community, those who attempt asceticism today will experience the loneliness of human isolation.

Thus the best hope for intimacy with God today is in community. While Ha-Levi as poet does express an acute mystical longing, much of this longing for contemplation is expressed in the realm of liturgical poetry. As in the *Kuzari*, Ha-Levi the poet suggests that God is met most intimately through Jewish communal prayer. On the other hand, Ha-Levi's poetry does express an impulse toward withdrawal for communion with God that cannot be easily squared with certain passages of the *Kuzari*.[62]

However, we find resolution of this tension in the *Kuzari* in the figure of Abraham. Abraham's passionate love for God is expressed through painful human trials; the loneliness he experiences is not that of the solitary ascetic, but that of the engaged man of faith, taking those actions in the world required by God. This is the model of intimate relationship and passionate love that Ha-Levi esteems. Using Sufi terms, Ha-Levi transforms the Sufi ideal of ascetic isolation to reflect a Jewish ideal: a path of love for God that can hazard the travails of this world.

Conclusions

1. General Remarks: Ha-Levi's Transformation of Terminology

What, then, has our exploration of Ha-Levi's terminology shown us about the *Kuzari*? We have seen that Ha-Levi is keenly sensitive to nuances of language; he is a master of Arabic prose and uses the sounds and rhythms of the Arabic language to underscore key themes. Ha-Levi is clearly aware of the power of the Arabic terms he chooses, and uses them with ironic twists to draw in his Judaeo-Arabic readers.

Like Maimonides in his *Eight Chapters on Ethics* (*Shemonah Peraqim*), Ha-Levi may be addressing Jews drawn to Sufi spirituality and asceticism. We have seen that he never mentions the Sufis by name, that the Sufi is the absent interlocutor in the dialogue, whose presence is evoked only through characteristic terms and themes. These terms and themes are at the heart of the dialogue, however.

While the *Ḥaver* mentions his Karaite and philosophical opponents by name, he alludes to Sufism only indirectly. Perhaps this indicates that Ha-Levi does not see the Sufi as an opponent. Ha-Levi's religious sensibility has much in common with certain aspects of Sufi spirituality; his devotional poems show the influence of Sufi poetry.[1] The fact that the Sufi is absent as an opponent shows to what extent Ha-Levi has internalized and identified with certain Sufi spiritual ideals. Ha-Levi appropriates Sufi terminology to describe Jewish religious experience, while denying certain ideas associated with the mystical path—for example, the notion that asceticism and isolation are a component of the true spiritual life. His approach is thus very different from that of Baḥya ibn Paqūda, who adopted not just the literary form of a Sufi manual, but also ascetic ideals of the Sufi path.

Scholars have long noted that Ha-Levi stands out in the history of Jewish philosophy for his emphasis on concrete experience and the particulars of Jewish history over universal categories of logic. Our study has revealed a new dimension to Ha-Levi's project: he is a phenomenologist of religion, creatively adapting the new Arabic vocabulary of religious experience to the Jewish context.

Ha-Levi does this in several striking ways. He uses the term *mushāhada* for both the individual religious experience of Abraham and the collective revelation at Mount Sinai; similarly, he uses the term *ittiṣāl* to describe both God's connection with individuals from Adam to the prophets and God's collective covenant with the Jewish people. Ha-Levi thus invests Jewish communal experience with the privileged status which individual religious experience had come to hold in the medieval world. At the same time, he creates a new focus on the experiential dimension within Judaism. The goal of his project is thus twofold. By using Islamic vocabulary to describe Jewish religious experience, he implicitly translates the language of classical Judaism into a universal, experiential language with contemporary appeal. This translation is also critical in nature; it involves a transvaluation of the Sufi experience.

We have seen that while Baḥya adopts both the language of Sufism and its ascetic ideals, Ha-Levi shows an ambivalent relationship to the Sufi terminology he adopts. While he is clearly influenced by certain dimensions of Sufi spirituality, he is also critical of the ascetic excesses to which some are drawn on the Sufi path. He suggests that the basic impulse of the Jew attracted to Sufi asceticism is valid, as is the basic impulse of the philosopher, the Karaite, and even the practitioner of the occult. All seek to draw near to the Divine; and, indeed, how we are to draw near to the Divine in this life is the *Kuzari*'s central concern. For Ha-Levi, however, it is not simply that the Karaite, the occultist, the philosopher, and the Jew attracted to Sufi asceticism have chosen the wrong means of reaching God; they have misunderstood the nature of the journey.

Ha-Levi suggests each of these seekers err because they conduct their search through human *qiyās* and striving (*ijtihād*); they believe that the path to God is one human beings themselves can map out. Ha-Levi finds a fundamental flaw in this approach. Only God, and not human beings can show us the way to the Divine, and God has done so through revelation. The event at Mount Sinai is a self-disclosure of the Divine, a revelation of the awesome reality of God's presence. That reality—directly witnessed by the entire Jewish nation—grounds the authority of God's commandments.

Ha-Levi is sensitive both to the intensity of individual contact with God and to the centrality of community for Jewish religious experience. He portrays degrees of contact (*ittiṣāl*) with the Divine, insisting that God's providential guidance of Jewish history in itself creates a powerful connection in which every member of the nation participates. Jewish communal life is an essential vehicle for religious experience; Jews find

God's presence not as isolated seekers, but in community. The mitsvot constitute a bond (*ṣila* from *w-ṣ-l*) between Jews and God. The three daily times of prayer and Shabbat, in particular, are set aside for *ittiṣāl* with the Divine, to serve God in joy, not contrition—a joy that may even lead to singing and dancing.

Ha-Levi therefore fundamentally inverts the image of *ittiṣāl* in the Islamic world. Union with the divine realm is not reached by a disembodied intellect, as the philosophers would have it, nor by the isolated ascetic, as some Sufis would claim. Nor need one wait for the afterlife to achieve *ittiṣāl*. Connection with God is experienced by Jews first of all in this world through the communal life of *mitsvot*. This "taste of the world to come" will naturally continue and come to full fruition in the afterlife.

The ultimate degree of religious experience for Ha-Levi, as for most medieval Jewish thinkers, is prophecy (*nubuwwa* or *nevuah*); the prophet alone is privileged to receive direct divine communication (*waḥy*). At Mount Sinai, however, all the nation of Israel experienced *waḥy*, if only briefly. Ha-Levi even suggests that diligent practice of the *mitsvot* can lead to the degree of *waḥy*, "the human level closest to the divine [level]" (V:20: 223–224).

In contrast, Ha-Levi is suspicious of any humanly invented path to reach God. All are prone to a common error: they seek to obtain by human striving that which is essentially a divine gift. Ha-Levi wants to make clear, however, that true connection with God is available to all Israel, and that the divine Law—far from presenting a barrier to contact with God—is an essential prerequisite for such communion. Ha-Levi thus inverts the antinomianism of certain radical Sufis.

Ha-Levi finds the Sufi term *mushāhada,* and all its derivatives, a rich resource for the expression of a distinctly Jewish religious ideal. Sufis had used the term *mushāhada* to describe witness of God within an individual's heart. Philosophers, too, used the term to describe direct perception of the Truth. Whereas logical analogy (*qiyās*) is by its very nature indirect, witness (*mushāhada*) and taste (*dhawq*) are immediate and irrefutable.

One who has witnessed (*shāhada*) God can offer reliable testimony (*shahāda*). Ha-Levi takes this notion one step further: the nation of Israel as a whole witness the reality of God. The idea that Israel is a witness to God is present in the Biblical book of Isaiah, in rabbinic midrash,[2] and in gaonic thought. However, Ha-Levi brings a new texture to the idea by creatively appropriating the potent language of Sufi spirituality. Direct witness of God (*mushāhada*) is the province not of the Sufis, he suggests, but of the nation of Israel. Throughout Jewish history, elders, prophets, and Sages have testified to powerful encounters with the Divine—one need only call to mind the theophanies (*mashāhid,* sing. *mashhad*) experienced by Moses and Elijah, or the visions (*mushāhadāt*) of pious scholars such as R. Aqiva and R. Ishmael.

Ha-Levi's central paradigms for religious experience, however, are the event at Mount Sinai and the life of Abraham. The event at Mount Sinai disproves the philosophical model of prophecy, which places prophecy on a continuum with other modes of knowledge. The origin of the Torah, the *Ḥaver* asserts, is not individual inspiration (*ilhām*) or divine assistance (*ta'yīd*) which philosophers claim to receive from the Active Intellect (1:87). Rather, the origin of the Torah is God. Philosophically untutored, the nation of Israel received the Torah as *waḥy*, a direct revelation of the divine word. All who were witness (*shāhada*) to the grand theophanies (*mashāhid*) at Sinai knew this to be a revelation from the Eternal—direct and unmediated.

Ha-Levi describes Abraham's encounter with God in similar terms: once Abraham had directly witnessed (*shāhada*) the Divine, he abandoned the indirect way of *qiyās* to become an obedient servant of the Lord. Ha-Levi uses the language and imagery of Sufi love poetry to convey the intensity of Abraham's encounter with the One for whom he would give his life—even the life of his beloved son. Ha-Levi does not stray from the rabbinic biography of Abraham, however, to paint Abraham as a solitary mystic or ascetic. Rather, Abraham enters into the covenant of circumcision—a sign of the ongoing, historical connection (*ittiṣāl*) between God and his descendents, the Jewish people. Intimate connection with God, suggests Ha-Levi, need not take one away from community. This represents a fundamental rethinking of the Sufi ideals of *ittiṣāl* and *mushāhada*. Ha-Levi's linguistic innovation was thus revolutionary. Using the terms *ittiṣāl* and *mushāhada* for both individual and collective communion, Ha-Levi creates a new model of religious experience.

2. *Ha-Levi's Rhetorical Strategies*

Ha-Levi employs several favorite rhetorical strategies cutting across terminological lines. Among them, we find the following:

1. Ha-Levi Plays Off One Opponent against Another

In the opening dialogue, Ha-Levi plays off Sufi and philosophical notions of union (*ittiṣāl*) against each other, and against what he sees as a more direct, concrete, and powerful religious experience: that found in the relationship between the Biblical God and the people of Israel. Elsewhere, he sets the philosopher against the pious Christian or Muslim (I:110:38). The *Ḥaver* argues that the philosophers' notion that one can achieve immortality by accumulating knowledge is as absurd as the religious notion that one can save one's soul by a mere verbal confession of faith.[3]

In the same vein, Ha-Levi plays off the philosopher and the Sufi against the Orthodox Muslim (I:109: 36–38). Here the *Ḥaver* upholds many of the Sufi and philosophical values associated with *ittiṣāl* and juxtaposes them with the Orthodox conception of an afterlife. Choosing the term *maw'id*—a variant of *wa'd*, which Orthodox Muslims use for the promise of the afterlife—the *Ḥaver* argues that connection with God (*ittiṣāl*) is itself the greatest promise (*maw'id*). However, he describes here a form of *ittiṣāl* colored with themes from classical Jewish thought—an *ittiṣāl* that is communal, this-worldly, and achieved through the life of *mitsvot*.

2. *Ha-Levi Also Plays One Term against Another*

Whereas for Sufis the virtue of submissiveness (*khushū'*) is associated with *ittiṣāl*, the *Ḥaver* contrasts the two (III:5: 94). He also plays the ascetic view of *ittiṣāl* held by both philosophers and Sufis against the virtue of moderation (*i'tidāl*), an alternative philosophical ideal. Rejecting a dualistic, Neo-Platonic ideal of asceticism, the *Ḥaver* instead embraces the Aristotelian doctrine of the mean. He argues that, like Platonic and Aristotelian philosophy, the Torah commands moderation (*i'tidāl*) and justice (*'adl*), not extreme self-denial (II:50: 69).[4]

3. *Ha-Levi Artfully Turns the Tables on His Opponents*

a. Ha-Levi turns the Christian argument from history on its head. Against his Christian critics, the *Ḥaver* argues that they cannot have it both ways: if they extoll the spiritual virtue of suffering and lowliness, they cannot point to the Jews' degraded status as a sign of God's displeasure (I:113: 38–39).

b. The *Ḥaver* also turns the tables on those who would criticize Judaism for a lack of philosophical sophistication. In fact, he argues, the philosophers only turn to logical argument (*qiyās*) because they lack the more fruitful gift which the Sages have: divine assistance and authentic tradition (I:65: 17; V:14: 212).

c. Ha-Levi reverses the Karaite charge that the rabbis add to Biblical law through rabbinic legislation. The *Ḥaver* argues that it is the Karaites who add to the Torah by using their own human *qiyās* to derive law rather than relying on the tradition of the Sages (III:40–41: 124).

d. Ha-Levi also reverses the potent charge that religious law stands in the way of union with God (*ittiṣāl*). In his creative reinterpretation of *ittiṣāl*, he suggests that *mitsvot* are not only not antithetical to religious experience, they are in fact essential to the achievement of *ittiṣāl* (II:34: 65; III:23: 112).

e. In an incisive response to those attracted to Sufi ideals of asceticism, the *Ḥaver* suggests that the human impulse to ascetic denial is actually a form of egoistic self-assertion (*ijtihād*). The Law itself presents a greater challenge: the life of moderation, responding to God equally with fear or awe (*yir'ah*), love (*ahavah*), and joy (*simḥah*) (II:50: 70). Moderation requires a person to give each of these responses its due, just as one must give each human faculty its due, so that one may be "a prince obeyed by his senses" (III:5: 92).

f. Responding to the charge that Judaism is an unspiritual, this-worldly religion, lacking in promises of the afterlife, Ha-Levi contrasts Jewish this-worldly fulfillment with the afterlife portrayed in the Qurʾān. Jewish fulfillment in this world, he suggests, is in fact more spiritual than the Islamic afterlife. Moreover, *ittiṣāl* in this life will continue in the world to come (I:104–9: 35–38).

3. *Ha-Levi's Relationship to Judaeo-Arabic Predecessors*

a. R. Saʿadya Gaon

We have found that Ha-Levi was not writing in a vacuum, that he both appropriates and alters concepts from his Judaeo-Arabic predecessors. In several instances, Ha-Levi directly borrows from Saʿadya Gaon, both in language and ideas. In a variety of contexts, Ha-Levi echoes a key passage from Saʿadya's *Book of Doctrines and Beliefs* which describes the purpose of God's self-revelation through the Glory. Saʿadya asserts that God creates the light known as Glory (*kavod*) so that prophets might infer (*yastadillu*—from *d-l-l*, to show or prove) that they are actually hearing the word of God. Similarly, the *Ḥaver* asserts that God appears to the prophetic elite (*ṣafwa*), who witness God by what is known as Glory or the *Shekhinah* in order that he might prove to them (*li-yadullahum*—from *d-l-l*) that they had indeed been addressed by God (IV:3: 149).[5]

Ha-Levi is thus indebted to Saʿadya for a significant element in his theory of revelation. Both thinkers suggest that visual experience is more powerful than auditory experience; one who sees God's Glory is convinced that the word which he hears is in fact divine. Ha-Levi, however, takes the idea further than Saʿadya. He argues that the images prophets see are more than a means of proof; they function as a vital symbol system, teaching the prophet through a visual, emotional language more powerful than words alone (IV:5–6: 159–60). Furthermore, Ha-Levi weds Saʿadya's theory of the *kavod* with his Sufi language of religious experience. The *Ḥaver* asserts that while God connects (*yattaṣilu*) with all Jews, the prophets experience a more powerful degree of *ittiṣāl* in which they witness (*yushāhidūna*) God by means of the Glory (I:3: 149).

Ha-Levi also echoes Saʿadya's language when he suggests that the visual forms which the prophet sees are created specifically for the prophet. Saʿadya had written that the Glory, cloud, and throne are each a created form (*ṣūra makhlūqa*), newly produced (*muḥdathun*), as is the speech heard by the prophet. The *Ḥaver* says similarly that divine attributes such as God's majesty and power and the compassion of God become visible to the prophet in a great form created just for him (*al-ṣūra al-makhlūqa lahu*), which he sees instantaneously (IV:5: 160). The *Ḥaver* also states, however, that it is not known whether the angels that Isaiah and Ezekiel saw were temporary manifestations created specifically for the prophet, or permanent spiritual beings, which the philosophers identify with the separate intelligences (IV:3: 158). Moreover, other passages do not make it entirely clear whether Ha-Levi holds that the image is created by God, or whether it is created by the mind of the seer.

This suggests that Ha-Levi himself may have been agnostic with respect to certain theosophical descriptions he expresses through the *Ḥaver*. Concerned most of all with the integrity of spiritual life, he offers his readers alternative philosophical options with one goal: to help them accept the reality of prophetic visions. His focus is not ultimately on the ontological status of the Glory or its spiritual forms, but on the fact that these images inspire awe, love, and reverence in the religious believer.

Similarly, Ha-Levi, like Philo and Saʿadya before him, draws on the notion of God's created speech to explain the revelation at Mount Sinai. Ha-Levi's *Ḥaver*, however, is hesitant to endorse the precise metaphysics of this explanation. What is important to him is the simple fact of direct revelation, which the experience at Sinai made indubitable.[6] While Ha-Levi seems to find Saʿadya's metaphysical explanations useful, he is far from asserting them as dogma.

It is true that Sa'adya's purpose is avowedly apologetic; he asserts that he has written his book of theology to rescue fellow Jews from the sea of confusion. Sa'adya, however, shows more conviction in his *kalām* arguments than does Ha-Levi;[7] he exudes optimism about his project of rationalizing the faith and rescuing the befuddled by means of rational proof:

> If both the scholar and the learner follow this path in reading this book, the certainty of him who feels certain will increase; the doubt of him that is in doubt will vanish. The believer who blindly relies on tradition [*taqlīd*] will turn into one basing his belief on speculation [*naẓar*] and understanding; those who put forth erroneous arguments will be silenced. Those who are obstinate and defy evidence will be ashamed; and the righteous and upright will rejoice. . . .
>
> In this way the innermost thoughts of a man will be purified and brought into conformity with his outward behaviour; his prayer will be sincere, as there will be enshrined in his heart an inner voice rebuking and summoning him to right conduct, as the prophet says, "Thy words have I laid up in my heart, that I might not sin against Thee" (Psalm 119:11).
>
> Their faith will show itself in their dealing with each other; jealousy between them in matters of this world will diminish. All will turn towards the Master of wisdom and not to anything else. He will be for them salvation, mercy and happiness, as God [be He praised and sanctified] has said, "Look unto Me and be ye saved, all the ends of the earth, for I am God, and there is none else" (Isaiah 45:22).
>
> All this will result from the disappearance of doubts and the removal of errors. The knowledge of God and his Law will spread in the world like the spreading of water in all parts of the sea, as is said, "For the earth shall be full of the knowledge of the Lord, as the waters cover the sea" (Isaiah 11:9).[8]

Sa'adya shows not a trace of ambivalence about the value of logical argument; he boldly proclaims the spiritual rewards of rationalizing the faith. Ha-Levi's stance in this matter is at first glance quite different. However, while his words on *kalām* are biting,[9] Ha-Levi's own use of rational argument is not completely different from that of the *kalām* theologians, Sa'adya among them.[10] As Leo Strauss points out, the very form of dialogue detracts from the absolute nature of any one interlocutor's statement.[11] Beyond this, Ha-Levi often has his protaganist the *Ḥaver* hedge his assertions, or offer them as one of several possibilities. Only select tenets are non-negotiable for Ha-Levi: foremost, the reality of direct revelation and the self-validating nature of prophetic experience. These convictions give integrity to one's personal religious life.

Ha-Levi weds Saʿadya's ideas with Sufi language in another aspect of his prophetology. He describes the rabbinic story of the four who enter a garden (*pardes*) as a vision of the divine realm. The one who died could not bear witnessing (*mushāhada*) that world, and his constitution disintegrated (*inḥalla tarkībuhu*). Ha-Levi uses this same odd Arabic phrase to describe prophets who strain to see a level of the Glory which they are not prepared to grasp: their constitution disintegrates (*inḥalla tarkībuhu*).[12] This notion and language in fact have their origin in Saʿadya's *Book of Doctrines and Beliefs*. In the key passage on the Glory discussed above, Saʿadya asserts that only when they see God's Glory do prophets become certain that God is speaking to them. However, he then goes on to qualify this assertion. The light of the Glory is actually too brilliant for prophets other than Moses to behold; the prophet who dares gaze upon it—his constitution disintegrates (*inḥalla tarkībuhu*).

Ha-Levi thus shares with Saʿadya the notion that there are various degrees of divine light as well as degrees of spiritual ability to witness this light. Both thinkers suggest that some levels of the Glory can only be seen by the angels, and that Moses is superior to the rest of Israel in his ability to behold exalted levels of the Glory.[13]

What is new in Ha-Levi is the link between these ideas and the language of *mushāhada*. The *Ḥaver* asserts that the people did not have Moses' ability to witness the grand event at Mount Sinai, just as Ben Zoma lacked the ability of Rabbi Aqiva to witness the vision of the *pardes*. It is true that conceptually, the notion of witness was already present in the writings of Saʿadya and other gaonim. R. Nissim Gaon, for example, argues that the nation of Israel knows the reality of God by sensible perception, whereas the other nations engage in proof; he even quotes Isaiah's statement that the people of Israel are witnesses to God. Ha-Levi weds these notions with Sufi terminology, and—most importantly—places experience at the heart of things. Ha-Levi transforms gaonic ideas by investing them with a new experiential dimension that would speak powerfully to his contemporaries.[14]

We find an additional possible borrowing from Saʿadya in Ha-Levi's parable of the travelers to India who arrive at (*waṣala ʿilā*) the palace of the King (I:109). We recall that Saʿadya had used the phrase "clinging in obedience" (*lāzimīna ṭāʿa*) to translate certain instances in which the Bible speaks of people clinging (*deveqim*) to God.[15] Ha-Levi softens the language of union that he uses in this parable by echoing Saʿadya's conservative rendering of *devequt* as obedient service. The *Ḥaver* suggests that later generations of Jews took upon themselves obedience (*iltazama ṭāʿa*) to the Divine in order to make connection (*li-yattaṣila*) with the King, knowing that connection (*ittiṣāl*) is bliss (*saʿāda*).

As we saw in the previous chapter, we have some evidence from Ha-Levi's poetry that he associated the Biblical language of clinging to God (*devequt*) with the Arabic notion of union or connection (*ittiṣāl*)—an association that many Judaeo-Arabic thinkers and translators were making. Here, however, by echoing Saʿadya's conservative rendering of *devequt*, Ha-Levi's language suggests that the way to connection with God is through obedience or worship; arriving at God in a Jewish context does not take one out of the domain of halakhic service. While Avicenna, for example, describes Sufi arrival (*wuṣūl*) as unitive absorption in the one Truth that is God,[16] Ha-Levi describes arrival as respectful obedience, rather than direct clinging. It is true that manuals of Sufi piety themselves enjoin acts of obedience (*ṭāʿa*). The more radical Sufis, however, would have seen these as characterizing the path *to ittiṣāl* or *wuṣūl*, whereas Ha-Levi suggests that obedient worship characterizes the life *of* connection and arrival with God.

Ha-Levi thus borrows key terms, themes, and Judaeo-Arabic associations from Saʿadya Gaon. While the two thinkers' overall attitude toward the value of rational argument may diverge somewhat, Ha-Levi and Saʿadya show important similarities in religious temperament.

b. Baḥya ibn Paqūda

Ha-Levi's relationship to Baḥya ibn Paqūda is not as clear as his relation to Saʿadya. We found no direct borrowings from Baḥya in the *Kuzari*, although we noted one striking parallel in Ha-Levi's poetry.[17] While Baḥya was highly influenced by the ascetic strain of Sufism, Ha-Levi's references to contemporary ascetism—in passages filled with Sufi language—are overwhelmingly negative.[18] Baḥya structures his work like a Sufi manual, with a step-by-step program for the spiritual life; Ha-Levi, in contrast, resists any systematic approach to spirituality outside the Torah's commandments.

Somewhat surprisingly, Baḥya—the pious unworldly ascetic—is more appreciative of the value of philosophical and theological proofs than is Ha-Levi.[19] Baḥya borrows from *kalām* discourse proofs for the existence of God and for creation; however he embellishes these *kalām* proofs with Sufi ideals, particularly with respect to the absolute unity of God (*tawḥīd*).[20] One might say that Baḥya lived at a time before the entrenchment of radical Aristotelian philosophy, one in which philosophy and theology could serve as humble handmaidens to the life of faith.[21] In fact, Baḥya stresses the religious obligation to rationalize one's belief, sharply denouncing *taqlīd* as a shirking of the duty to discover the truth for oneself.[22] Ha-Levi, in contrast, sees philosophical investigation as having reached arrogant proportions and holds up simple *taqlīd* as an ideal. He asserts through the voice of the King—perhaps ironically—that investigation is incumbent only on those who have unfortunately fallen into the pit of argument and dispute (V:1: 191).

Baḥya describes people who rely on the knowledge of others in *taqlīd* as a company of people who are blind, each following the blind person in front of him. Only the prophet can see—a most unfortunate situation for all except the prophet. Baḥya's metaphor of vision here, however, is mental; "seeing" is not distinguished from intellectual knowledge. Baḥya holds that every person is required to prove for himself the truths of faith; those who follow blindly are lacking intellectual vision. For Ha-Levi, in contrast, those who approach the Divine through the intellect are themselves, as it were, blind. The prophet alone can truly see the divine realm; those who do not possess the prophetic faculty have no choice but to rely in *taqlīd* upon those who do. All of Israel, however, have at least the potential for this prophetic vision, awakened at Mount Sinai. Ha-Levi thus softens the gap between prophets and other Jews by suggesting that through the life of *mitsvot*, Jews can achieve the degree of prophetic revelation (*waḥy*)—a degree which, as Jews, they possess in potentia. *Waḥy* does not require rationalizing the faith, but rather observing the commandments.

Baḥya and Ha-Levi, then, immersed in some of the same currents of thought, offer very different responses. Baḥya adopts both the form and vocabulary of Sufi manuals of piety; we do not find in Baḥya the transformation of Sufi terminology that we find in Ha-Levi. Baḥya's statement that the soul yearns to connect (*li-tattaṣila*) with the divine light,[23] for example, is a standard Neo-Platonic and Sufi motif. His views on *taqlīd* and the necessity of discovering truths for oneself are shared by Sufis, philosophers, and *kalām* theologians.

Baḥya is therefore fundamentally in harmony with the intellectual trends of his day. While he seeks to bring out the pietistic, interior element in Judaism, he does not do so at the expense of other values held by the intellectual elite. Ha-Levi's adoption of Arabic, and specifically Sufi terminology is more subtle and subversive. What Baḥya and Ha-Levi share is a common vocabulary and a concern for the integrity of spiritual life. The religious sensibilities of the two thinkers are, however, fundamentally quite different.

3. *Ha-Levi's Relationship to Islamic Predecessors*

a. Al-Fārābī, Avicenna, and Ibn Bājja

Ha-Levi's use of contemporary Islamic thought is equally subtle and varied. Herbert Davidson, Shlomo Pines, and others observed that the doctrine laid out by the philosopher in I:1 corresponds to the doctrine of the Spanish philosopher Ibn Bājjah, while that in V:12 is a treatise copied word for word from Avicenna. The *Ḥaver*'s description of the philosophical theory of prophecy in I:87 corresponds in broad strokes to the theories of al-Fārābī, Avicenna, and Ibn Bājja.

Our study has placed Ha-Levi's use of philosophical material in a broader context. Ha-Levi has not simply rejected philosophical views, but appropriated a vocabulary common to both Sufis and philosophers for his own purposes. In I:87, for example, the *Ḥaver* explains that the revelation at Mount Sinai disproved the philosophical theory that prophecy occurs through lesser degrees of inspiration such as *ilhām* and *ta'yīd*. We now have a broader framework for understanding this statement. The *Ḥaver* tells us, in fact, that the Sanhedrin themselves are guided in their judging by *ilhām* and *ta'yīd*; they also come upon their scientific knowledge through these forms of inspiration. *Ilhām* and *ta'yīd* are rejected, however, as ways of describing the revelation at Mount Sinai and the origin of the Torah. The Torah did not originate in the mind of Moses; prophecy is not simply mental assistance that the prophet receives from the divine Active Intellect. While these forms of internal support do not explain the origin of the Torah, Ha-Levi does not completely reject their existence and validity.[24] *Ilhām* and *ta'yīd* not only explain the assistance the Sanhedrin receives in deciding law—prophets, too, receive inspirations (*ilhāmāt*), just as they perform wonders and miracles through the aid of God.

The event at Mount Sinai, in contrast, represents a higher degree of inspiration altogether, which Ha-Levi terms "revelation" (*waḥy*). Here Ha-Levi again follows Sa'adya, who reserves the term *waḥy* for revelation of the books of the Bible, insisting that every word of sacred Scripture is divinely dictated. Sa'adya appears to be polemicizing against Karaite opponents, who attribute the psalms and perhaps other prayers and poems to inspiration (*ilhām*) rather than word-for-word revelation (*waḥy*).

Ha-Levi reflects the debate over *waḥy* and *ilhām*, but shifts opponents. His concern is philosophers such as Al-Fārābī and Avicenna, who describe prophecy in naturalistic terms as inspiration, and thus blur the boundaries between ordinary thinking, inspiration (*ilhām*), and revelation (*waḥy*).[25] Ha-Levi is also concerned to combat philosophical skepticism, to preserve the divine origin of the Torah, and to uphold the uniqueness of the revelation at Mount Sinai. Ha-Levi's relationship to these philosophers is not, however, wholly negative. He does incorporate a treatise of Avicennian thought in Part Five of the *Kuzari*. At times, he offers philosophical argument as a kind of fallback position. The *Ḥaver* goes to great lengths in IV:3 to justify the reality of prophetic visions through a sound epistemology. Ha-Levi apparently views philosophy as a tool which, like *kalām*, has great dangers and is often misused, but which is not without value in bolstering faith.

b. al-Ghazzālī

As I noted in the Introduction, David Kaufmann emphasized the similarities between Ha-Levi and al-Ghazzālī, giving some the impression that Ha-Levi had essentially translated the ideas of Ghazzālī into a Jewish framework.[26] More recent scholars have sought to qualify this characterization, among them David Baneth in his insightful examination of the two thinkers. Let us explore what our study has revealed about the relationship between Ha-Levi and Ghazzālī.

Our research does affirm certain of Kaufmann's assertions, including the possible literary relationship between the two thinkers—but with some qualification. For example, Kaufmann traced to Ghazzālī a metaphor in *Kuzari* III:37, in which the King compares the Karaites—admired for their diligent striving (*ijtihād*) in matters of religious law—to wanderers in the wilderness, who must ever be prepared for battle. In contrast, followers of the rabbis can rest, body and soul, upon their humble mats of *taqlīd*.

The passage in Ghazzālī that Kaufmann cites is not an exact parallel.[27] Ghazzālī writes that *kalām* theologians are like guards hired to protect pilgrims on the *ḥajj* against bands of marauders. If the brigands would cease their oppression, he asserts, there would be no need for guards. Just so, theology is needed to protect the hearts of the faithful masses from the innovations of heretics. If the innovators would cease spewing out their nonsense—the vehemence is Ghazzālī's—there would be no need for theology.

The greatest error of the theologians, Ghazzālī continues, is that they exaggerate the scope of their territory; they claim to have insight into the nature of God, divine attributes, the afterlife, and other matters which belong to the science of revelation (*ʿilm al-mukāshafa*) proper. Let the theologians rather confine themselves to the matter of dialectics, and not mistakenly consider themselves among the learned (*'ulamā'*).[28]

We can see that while there are points of contact between the two metaphors, there are also significant differences. Ghazzālī's metaphor is directed against the theologians; he describes *kalām* dialectics as mere weapons of protection to guard the hearts of the faithful, with no intrinsic value. This, indeed, was a standard critique of *kalām*—that it was a weapon of debate, of religious polemics, and could not be relied upon as valid proof (*burhān*).

Ha-Levi's metaphor in III:37, in contrast, is framed in the context of law, rather than theology. Because Karaites approach Biblical law with individual *qiyās*, they do not arrive at one common *halakhah* as do those who rely upon rabbinic tradition. The Karaites therefore must be ever prepared to defend their legal reasoning against new arguments they meet each day. Ghazzālī portrays *kalām* dialectic as a weapon against theological innovation; the *Ḥaver* describes Karaite legal *qiyās* as a weapon of protection to fend off shifting arguments in *halakhah*.

We should remember, however, that while Ha-Levi's argument against the Karaites is here framed within a legal context, the *Ḥaver* also refers to the Karaites explicitly in his attack on *kalām* in V:1–2 and in V:15–16. Further, we have seen a clear rhetorical pattern with regard to the term *qiyās*; Ha-Levi uses the negative associations he establishes for *qiyās* in one sphere to taint other spheres. We may therefore surmise that Ha-Levi intends his attack on Karaite legal *qiyās* in III:37 to extend to theological *qiyās* as well, for which the Karaites were also well known.

Kaufmann's enthusiastic assertion of direct literary borrowing must therefore be qualified somewhat. The common metaphor to which Kaufmann pointed has shifted from the sphere of theology to that of law, and we find no direct linguistic links between the two passages. Ha-Levi and Ghazzālī do, however, show a very similar attitude toward dialectical argument, particularly if we take Ha-Levi's critique of Karaite *qiyās* in Book Three together with his attacks on *kalām* in Book Five.

And indeed, we find a terminological connection between Books Three and Five which strengthens Kaufmann's case. Ha-Levi's critique of *qiyās* in Book Three is linked to his attack on *kalām* in Book Five through the concept of *taqlīd*. *Kalām* theologians argue that peace of mind (*sukūn al-nafs*) can be found only by proving the truths of faith for oneself, not by relying in *taqlīd* on the arguments of others. In III:37–38 Ha-Levi inverts this argument. To the contrary, it is those who rely upon their own *qiyās* who can never find rest, for they must ever be prepared to battle those who challenge their views. Reliance (*taqlīd*) on the rabbis brings true rest to the soul. In fact, if the Karaites are ever found agreeing with one another, it is only because they, too, have resorted to *taqlīd* on one of their founders. They might just as well rely on those who are in fact reliable, the rabbis.

The *Ḥaver* argues similarly in V:14 and in IV:23 that philosophers only agree with one another if they follow the *taqlīd* of the same philosophical school. The masses, however, prefer *taqlīd* on the rabbis to *taqlīd* on the philosophers; they are not fooled by the superficial elegance of the philosophers' proofs. Here, too, he uses the concept of peace of mind (*sukūn al-nafs*); the masses find peace of mind with the Sages, not with the philosophers, as intellectuals may have led them to expect (IV:17: 169).[29]

The tie between *taqlīd* and *kalām* in Book Five links this attack to the earlier passages. The King asserts in V:1 that *taqlīd* is only appropriate for one with pleasantness of soul (*ṭīb al-nafs*); for someone who has already fallen into doubts, conjectures, and philosophical debates, investigation is necessary. We recall that the *Ḥaver* responds with pathos:

> But who among us has a calm soul, which is not deceived by these passing views—the views of natural scientists, astrologers, makers of talismans, magicians, materialists, philosophers and others. One does not [today] arrive at faith except after one has passed through many stages of heresy [*zandaqa*]. Life is short and the labor long. Only unique individuals have faith by nature, and these opinions are all repugnant to them; their souls immediately note the point of their offensiveness. And I hope that you may be among those singular ones. [However] if it be thus, and I cannot avoid [acceeding to your request], I will not travel the way of the Karaites who ascended to metaphysics without levels. (V:2: 191)

Ha-Levi's tone with respect to *kalām* is more biting in V:16. The *Ḥaver* asserts that *kalām* has little value; the practitioner of *kalām* only fools his listeners into thinking he is superior to the simple, pious believer. The tragic irony is that the theologian, like the Karaite, pretentiously extends his intellect in vain search of that which the Jew possesses by tradition. The *Ḥaver* even suggests that the Jew is endowed by nature with a gift for spirituality. Like the natural poet, the Jew needs only hints to awaken a latent understanding (V:16: 213).

In both Book Five and Book Three, then, Ha-Levi contrasts the superficial attraction of legal and theological *ijtihād* with the simplicity of *taqlīd*. In III:37, the *Ḥaver* argues that people are fooled by the greater striving (*ijtihād*) of the Karaites and mistake the calm of the rabbis for laziness. In V:16, he argues likewise that people are fooled by the theologian's "luster of knowledge" and mistakenly think the theologian superior to the simple believer. The thread between Ha-Levi's attacks on legal and theological *qiyās* thus strengthens the parallel to Ghazzālī. Ha-Levi may well have been aware of Ghazzālī's metaphor of *qiyās* as a weapon of battle in the sphere of *kalām*, and applied it to the field of law as well.

Ha-Levi's attack on philosophy in V:14 is also quite reminiscent of Ghazzālī. Like Ghazzālī, the *Ḥaver* asserts that many had been fooled by the philosophers. Since philosophers achieved certainty in mathematics and logic, people thought their statements in metaphysics had the status of apodictic proof (*burhān*) as well (V:14: 208–9).[30]

We find an equally strong literary link in another sphere. As Kaufmann pointed out, both Ha-Levi and Ghazzālī make use of the Sufi image of the "inner eye."[31] In his spiritual autobiography *Al-munqidh min al-ḍalāl*, Ghazzālī describes a stage after the intellect in which another eye is opened, which sees both the hidden and the future. He compares those who are skeptical about this power of vision and the realities it sees to a person born blind who has no understanding of color. Similarly, a person who had never experienced the dream state would doubt the fantastic visions people claim to have had there. Ghazzālī writes:

> Just as the intellect is one human stage in which a person receives an eye by which he sees various species of intelligibles from which the senses are far removed, the prophetic power [*al-nubuwwa*] is an expression signifying a stage in which man receives an eye possessed of a light, and in its light the unknown and other phenomena not normally perceived [*yudraku*] by the intellect become visible.
>
> Doubt about prophecy touches either its possibility, its existence, or its belonging to a specific individual. The proof [*dalīl*] of its possibility is its existence [*wujūd*]. And the proof [*dalīl*] of its existence is the existence in the world of knowledge which could not conceivably be obtained by the intellect alone, such as the knowledge of medicine and of astronomy. For whoever examines such knowledge knows of necessity that it can be obtained only by a Divine inspiration [*ilhām*] and special help [*tawfīq*] from God Most High, and that there is no empirical way to it. . . . The properties of prophecy beyond those just mentioned can be perceived only by taste [*dhawq*] as a result of following the way of Sufism [*sulūk tarīq al-taṣawwuf*].[32]

Almost every statement in this passage finds a parallel in Ha-Levi. Like Ghazzālī, the *Ḥaver* in IV:3 describes the gift of prophecy as an inner eye that sees what the intellect cannot perceive. The prophet regards others who do not possess this eye as blind people whom he or she must guide (IV:3: 155). Ha-Levi is adamant, moreover, that prophetic vision is self-validating. Greek philosophers rejected prophecy only because *qiyās* rejects whatever it has not seen. The prophets, however, could not deny what they witnessed with the inner eye (IV:3: 157).

Ghazzālī asserts similarly that the proof of prophecy is simply its existence. While prophecy is self-validating, however, its existence is proved by the existence of knowledge that could not be attained except through divine inspiration. Ha-Levi likewise argues that prophecy brings scientific and metaphysical knowledge that human *qiyās* on its own could not obtain.[33] Like Ha-Levi, Ghazzālī argues that the properties of prophecy can only be known by taste (*dhawq*); Ha-Levi, too, characterizes the unique prophetic way of knowing God as *dhawq* (IV:16–17: 168–69).

Consider, moreover, the following formulation, in Ghazzālī's *Mishkāt al-anwār* (*The Niche for Lights*):

> Why should it be impossible that beyond reason there should be a further plane on which there appear things which do not appear on the plane of intelligence, just as it is possible for the intelligence itself to be a plane above the discriminating faculty and the senses, and for revelations of wonders and marvels to be made to it beyond the reach of senses and the discriminating faculty? Beware of making the ultimate perfection stop at yourself! Consider the intuitive sense [*dhawq*] for poetry, if you would have an example of everyday experience taken from those special gifts which particularize some people.[34]

Here Ghazzālī compares the additional source of knowledge to the intuitive sense (*dhawq*: literally "taste") for poetry, just as the *Ḥaver* in V:16 compares pure faith to a poetic gift.[35] The *Ḥaver* points out that in contrast to those who quantify meter through the study of prosody, natural poets sense (*yadhūqu*: literally "taste") the correct meter. Similarly, the person of innate faith senses the Divine, while the theologian—who arrogantly constructs proofs for the existence of God—is in fact as awkward in religion as is the student of prosody in poetry (V:16: 213). And just as the *Ḥaver* pokes fun at the uninspired pedantry of those inept at poetry, so Ghazzālī writes of someone lacking *dhawq*: "Even were all the masters of music in the world to call a conference with a view of making him understand the meaning of this musical sense [*dhawq*], they would be quite powerless to do so."[36]

Ha-Levi and Ghazzālī thus agree that prophets possess an intuitive gift for seeing or sensing the Divine which ordinary human beings do not. Is such a talent innate or can it it developed? Ghazzālī suggests that the inner eye may be developed by traveling the path of Sufism.[37] Indeed, anyone who has not traveled the path and had an experience of *dhawq* knows nothing of prophecy except the name.[38] Ha-Levi, too, indicates that the capacity for prophecy may be developed, through practice of the commandments (V:20: 223; 1:103: 35). The nation of Israel is naturally endowed with a potential for prophecy that must be realized; like the natural poet, they need only hints to bring out the hidden sparks of faith.

It is true that we do not find in Ha-Levi the openly enthusiastic embrace of Sufism we find in Ghazzālī. Nevertheless, the two thinkers share a religious sensibility in many ways. Both are serious and respectful students of Aristotelian philosophy, who criticize it using similar arguments. Both reject *kalām,* and do so for similar reasons. For both Ha-Levi and Ghazzālī, reason has its place, but must be superseded by direct tasting of the Divine (*dhawq*). Both use the metaphor of the inner eye to make prophetic experience comprehensible in scientific terms. Influenced by similar intellectual and spiritual currents—Sufism, neo-Platonism, and an incipient revolt against rationalism—Ha-Levi and Ghazzālī weave these elements together in a strikingly similar fashion.

A final parallel that should be mentioned is the two thinkers' attitudes towards the commandments of their respective religions. Both were apparently concerned about the potential for anti-nomianism in pursuit of the mystical or ascetic life. Ghazzālī—like Qushayri, another moderate Sufi-inclined thinker—was disturbed by anti-nomian trends within Sufism, and insisted on the necessity of the commandments in drawing near to God.[39] This concern finds a close parallel in Ha-Levi, as noted by Hava Lazarus-Yafeh, who quotes Ha-Levi to elucidate Ghazzālī: "It is therefore impossible to overestimate the tremendous importance of the commandments [for Ghazzālī] since, in the words of Judah Halevi, man does not attain to *al'Amr al-'Ilāhi* except by divine command; that is, by deeds that God has commanded."[40]

4. *Concluding Remarks*

My aim in this study has been to understand Ha-Levi's thought more fully by situating his language and arguments in their Islamic context. Ha-Levi shows a complex, dialectical relationship to the spiritual and intellectual streams of his day: Sufism, philosophy, Karaism, *kalām*. He has woven together diverse strands of medieval Islamic culture in a unique and unprecedented way. This study has shown that Ha-Levi's relationship to Islamic thought is indeed multi-dimensional.

This multi-dimensional fabric includes doctrines that challenge the reader; Ha-Levi never shies away from the provocative elements of his theories. To comprehend his thought fully, we must hold the conflicting elements of his views in tension, not diminishing the importance or function of any aspect of the debate. Perhaps this is the ultimate reason Ha-Levi chose the medium of dialogue: not to hide his true views, but to reveal the complexity of truth.[41]

Our literary-philological analysis has revealed that the *Kuzari* is a work of philosophical poetry, in which Ha-Levi expands and re-shapes language to express his spiritual vision. Deeply indebted to the experiential language of Sufism, he depicts a Judaism of rich individual and communal religious experience. His spiritual stance is at once militantly Jewish and intensely personal. He cannot be easily placed in a conceptual box; Ha-Levi is neither a Jewish Sufi, an Aristotelian philosopher, a *mutakallim*, nor a dogmatic anti-rationalist. Ha-Levi's transformation of Sufi vocabulary reveals a unique dimension to the artistry and spiritual texture of the *Kuzari*. Through it, he points to the religious experience he senses at the heart of Judaism.

Abbreviations

All references to the *Kuzari* are from *Kitāb al-radd waʿl-dalīl fīʿl-dīn al-dhalīl* (*al-kitāb al-khazarī*), edited by David H. Baneth and Haggai Ben-Shammai. The following abbreviations have been used for other works cited in the text (see bibliography for full details).

"*Madīna*"	Al-Fārābī, *Mabādi' ārā' ahl al-madāna al-fādila*, translated by R. Walzer as *Al-Fārābī on the Perfect State*. Published by F. Dieterici as *Der Musterstaat von AlFārābī*.
"*Halevi ve-al-Ghazzālī*"	D.W. Baneth, "*Yehuda Ha-Levi ve-al-Ghazzālī*," translated by G. Hirschler.
"A Polemical Element"	Haggai Ben-Shammai, "On a Polemical Element in R. Saʿadya Gaon's Theory of Prophecy."
"Active Intellect"	Herbert Davidson, "Alfarabi and Avicenna on Active Intellect."
"Cuzari"	Herbert Davidson, "The Active Intellect in the Cuzari."
Intellect	Herbert Davidson, *Alfarabi, Avicenna and Averroes, on Intellect.*
"Mysticism"	Israel Efros, "Some Aspects of Yehuda Halevi's Mysticism."
Studies	Israel Efros, *Studies in Medieval Jewish Philosophy.*
Gauthier	*Ḥayy ben Yaqdhān: Roman philosophique dʿIbn Thofaïl*, translated by L. Gauthier.
Goodman	*Ibn Tufayl's Ḥayy Ibn Yaqẓān*, translated by L. Goodman.
"Arguments"	Alfred Ivry, "The Philosophical and Religious Arguments in Rabbi Yehuda Halevy's Thought."

Lazarus-Yafeh, *Studies*	Hava Lazarus Yafeh, *Studies in al-Ghazālī.*
Leaman, "Imagination"	Oliver Leaman, "Maimonides, Imagination, and the Objectivity of Prophecy."
McCarthy	Al-Ghazzālī's *al-Munqidh min al-ḍalāl*, translated by R. J. McCarthy, S.J. as *Freedom and Fulfillment.*
Rahman, *Prophecy*	Fazlur Rahman, *Prophecy in Islam: Philosophy and Orthodoxy.*
Rosenblatt	Sa'adia Gaon: *The Book of Beliefs and Opinions*, translated by Samuel Rosenblatt.
Silman, *Filosof*	Yochanan Silman, *Ben Philosoph le-navi: hitpatḥut haguto shel Rabi Yehudah Ha-Levi be-Sefer ha-Kuzari. Philosopher and Prophet: Judah Halevi, the Kuzari, and the Development of His Thought*, translated by L. Schramm
Watt	Al-Ghazzālī's *al-Munqidh min al-ḍalāl*, translated by Montgomery Watt as *The Faith and Practice of Al-Ghazzālī.*
Wolfson, "Prophecy"	H. A. Wolfson, "Maimonides and Hallevi on Prophecy."
Wolfson, "Merkavah Traditions"	Elliot Wolfson, "Merkavah Traditions in Philosophical Garb: Judah Halevi Reconsidered."
JQR	*Jewish Quarterly Review*
IOS	*Israel Oriental Studies*
PAAJR	*Proceedings of the American Academy of Jewish Research*
REI	*Révue des études islamiques*
REJ	*Révue des études juives*
JAOS	*Journal of American Oriental Society*
EI	*Encyclopaedia of Islam*
EI2	*Encyclopaedia of Islam, 2nd Edition*
EJ	*Encyclopaedia Judaica*
HUCA	*Hebrew Union College Annual*

Notes

Introduction

1. So called because it is built around the story of the *Khazar* king. For a sketch of Ha-Levi's life, see S. D. Goitein, *A Mediterranean Society*, vol. 5 (Berkeley, 1988), 448–68; Ḥayyim Schirmann, "The Life of Judah Halevi," *Studies in the History of Hebrew Poetry and Drama* (Jerusalem, 1979) (Hebrew) I:250–318; idem, "Completions to the Life of Judah Halevi" (Hebrew), ibid. I:319–41. Schirmann includes a bibliography of Goitein's studies on the life of Ha-Levi, p. 341. On Ha-Levi's standing among Spanish Jewry, see Goitein, ibid. 289, 448.

2. The Cairo Genizah was a storehouse of letters and manuscripts found in the attic of the Ezra Synagogue; the Genizah was re-discovered mainly by Solomon Schecter in 1896 and researched by many scholars, including S. D. Goitein. Its vast materials range from Second Temple texts to signed documents such as the letters of Ha-Levi. On the genesis of the *Kuzari*, see Goitein, "Autographs of Yehuda Hallevi," *Tarbiz* 25 (1955–56): 393–412; idem, "The Biography of Rabbi Judah Ha-Levi in Light of the Cairo Genizah Documents," *PAAJR* 28 (1959): 41–56; D. H. Baneth, "Some Remarks on the Autographs of Yehuda Hallevi and the Genesis of the *Kuzari*," *Tarbiz* 26 (1956–57): 297–303. But see now Y. T. Langermann, "Science and the *Kazari*," *Science in Context* 10,3 (1997), 501. Langermann questions whether the "heretic" mentioned by Ha-Levi was necessarily a Karaite.

3. The term *rabbinic Judaism* refers to the religion of the rabbis or Sages (*Ḥakhamim*) whose teachings are recorded in the Mishnah and Talmud in the first five centuries of the Common Era. The Karaites challenged the central claim of rabbinic Judaism—the claim that rabbinic law possesses divine authority. In rejecting rabbinic oral tradition, the Karaites claimed to be pure Biblicists; their Hebrew name, *Qara'im*, means "readers," i.e., readers of Scripture. Like all "fundamentalists," however, the Karaites developed their own authoritative tradition of Scriptural interpretation, which they held up as a counterclaim to rabbinic tradition. For

the history of the Karaites, see Daniel J. Lasker, "Islamic Influences on Karaite Origins," in *Studies in Islamic and Judaic Traditions*, vol. 2, ed. W. M. Brinner and S. D. Ricks (Atlanta, 1989), 23–47; idem, "Karaism in Twelfth-Century Spain," in *Jewish Thought and Philosophy*, vol. 1, 179–95; Zvi Ankori, *Karaites in Byzantium* (New York, 1959); idem, "Karaites and Karaism," *EJ*, 777–80.

4. *Kitāb al-radd wa'l-dalīl fī'l-dīn al-dhalīl.* In the letter of Ha-Levi to his friend Ḥalfon b. Netanel in which Ha-Levi suggests that the book began in response to questions from a Karaite scholar, he refers to the work as *The Book of the Kuzari* or *The Kuzari Book* (*Ha-sefer ha-kuzari*). Goitein and Baneth both believe that this is a reference to a first edition of the work that was mainly concerned with Karaism, some form of which we find now in Book Three. Goitein, "Autographs," 402 and n.33; Baneth, "Autographs," 297–99.

5. See Gerson Cohen, *Abraham Ibn Daud: The Book of Tradition* (*Sefer ha-qabbalah*) (Philadelphia, 1967), 296–300; Yitzḥak Baer, *A History of the Jews in Christian Spain,* vol. 1, tr. L. Schoffman (Philadelphia, 1961), 67–77.

6. This correspondence is reprinted in *Letters of Jews Through the Ages*, vol. 1, ed. Franz Kobler (Philadelphia, 1952), 97–115.

7. Ha-Levi uses the term *'amal*, which signifies action in the broadest sense. While the King is very diligent in the worship (*ta'abbud*) and practices (*a'māl*) of the Khazar religion, his behavior (*'amal*) as a whole is not pleasing to God.

8. I have rendered the Arabic term *al-Ḥabar* in its familiar Hebrew translation: *ha-Ḥaver*. *Ḥabar* is an Arabic term for a non-Muslim cleric or a rabbinic scholar; *Ḥaver* is a Mishnaic Hebrew term for a Jewish scholar. I have chosen the familiar Hebrew term *Ḥaver* to capture what I believe to be Ha-Levi's intent—to connote a rabbinic scholar and teacher, an authoritative spokesperson for rabbinic Judaism.

9. On the rise of Sufism, see Annemarie Schimmel, *Mystical Dimensions of Islam* (Chapel Hill, 1975), 3–97; Margaret Smith, *The Way of the Mystics: The Early Christian Mystics and the Rise of the Sufis* (London, 1976), 125–257; David Ariel, "'The Eastern Dawn of Wisdom': The Problem of the Relation between Islamic and Jewish Mysticism," in *Approaches to Judaism in Medieval Times*, vol. 2, ed. D. Blumenthal (Chico, 1985), 151–54.

10. See for example, *Sufis of Andalusia: The Rūḥ al-quds and al-Durrat al-fākhirah of Ibn Arabi*, tr. R. W. J. Austin (London, 1971). Ibn 'Arabī—himself a celebrated Sufi teacher—compiled these biographical sketches to show that there continued to exist living Sufi masters in 12th to 13th century Muslim Spain. The work is an important source for our knowledge of the history of Sufism in the Muslim West. See also Paul Fenton, *'Obadyāh b. Abraham b. Moses Maimonides' The Treatise of the Pool* (*al-Maqāla al-ḥawḍiyya*) (London, 1981), 1–2.

11. The history of scholarship on Baḥya's sources is reviewed in the "Translator's Introduction," to Baḥya's *Book of Direction to the Duties of the Heart*, tr. Menahem Mansoor (London, 1973), 18–39 and in the article of Amos Goldreich, "Possible Arabic Sources for the Distinction between 'Duties of the Heart' and

'Duties of the Limbs'" (Hebrew), *Te'udah* 6 (1988): 179–208, see esp. 184–87; cf. A. S. Yahuda, *al-Hidāja 'ilā farā'iḍ al-qulūb* (Leiden, E. J. Brill, 1912), 63–64; Baneth, "*Maqor meshuttaf le-Rav Baḥya bar Yosef u-le-al-Ghazzālī*," *Sefer Magnes* (Jerusalem), 23–30.

12. Amos Goldreich has argued cogently for this possible influence; he traces the title of Baḥya's book to al-Muḥāsibī's *Masā'il fī a'māl al-qulūb wa'l-jawāriḥ* (*Questions Concerning the Actions of the Heart and the Limbs*); Goldreich also found in this work of Muḥāsibī a parallel to a key statement in Baḥya. See Goldreich, ibid., 193–96, 179–83.

13. This text was first published by Franz Rosenthal as "A Judeo-Arabic Work under Sufic Influence," *HUCA* 15 (1940): 433–84. More recently, it has been identified by Paul Fenton as the work of David b. Joshua b. Abraham Maimonides, the great-grandson of Moses Maimonides, and published by Fenton under its Arabic title *al-Murshīd 'ila al-tafarrūd* (Jerusalem, 1987), tr. in *Deux traites mystique juive* (Lagrasse, 1987). For other Judaeo-Arabic works in the Geniza, see Fenton, *Treatise of the Pool*, 5; Goitein, "A Jewish Addict to Sufism in the Time of Nagid David II Maimonides," *JQR* 44, 38.

14. I am indebted to Professor Twersky for sharing this observation of Wolfson's.

15. Ha-Levi was an inspiration for such diverse circles as thirteenth-century Kabbalists, fourteenth- and fifteenth-century antirationalists, and eighteenth-century Ḥasidim. The standard traditional edition of the *Kuzari* includes commentaries of the Italian Renaissance thinker Yehuda Moscato (*Qol Yehudah*) and the eighteenth-century Haskalah figure Israel of Zamosc (*Otsar Neḥmad*). In the nineteenth and twentieth centuries, Samuel David Luzzato, Franz Rosenzweig, and Abraham Isaac Kook were all indebted to Ha-Levi. A full history of Ha-Levi's influence on Jewish thought has yet to be written. For one recent study, see Dov Schwartz, "The Revival of *Sefer ha-Kuzari* in Jewish Philosophy (The Thought of a Circle of Interpreters of the *Kuzari* in Provence in the Beginning of the Fifteenth Century)" (Hebrew) in *Studies in Medieval Jewish History and Literature, vol. 3* (Cambridge, Mass., forthcoming).

16. See David Kaufmann, *Geschichte der Attributenlehre in der judischen Religionsphilosophie von Saadia bis Maimmuni* (Gotha, 1877) 119–40, 202 n.180, 203, n.181; idem, "R. Yehuda Ha-Levi," in Fishman ed., *Rabbi Yehudah Ha-Levi* (Jerusalem, 1940–41) (Hebrew), 184–85.

17. See Ghazzālī, *Al-Munqidh min al-ḍalāl* (Damascus, 1939), 146; tr. R. J. McCarthy, *Freedom and Fulfillment* (Boston, 1980), 102; tr. W. M. Watt, *The Faith and Practice of Al-Ghazali* (London, 1953), 70.

18. See for example Kaufmann, *Attributenlehre*, 231 n.221; David Neumark, *Judah Halevi's Philosophy in Its Principles* (Cincinnati, 1908); Baneth, "*R. Yehudah Halevi ve-al-Ghazzālī*," *Kenesset:* 7, 312–29; Julius Guttmann, "Religion and Knowledge in Medieval Thought and the Modern Period" (Hebrew), in idem, *Religion and Knowledge* (Jerusalem, 1955), 21–23.

19. Goldziher himself acknowledged that Ha-Levi was not systematically precise in the mode of other emanationist Neo-Platonic thinkers. Goldziher anticipated Pines in tracing the conceptual roots of Ha-Levi's term to the Ismāʿīlī doctrine of a series of divinely elected prophets. See Goldziher, "*Le ʾAmr ilāhī (ha-'inyan ha-'elohi) chez Juda Halevi*," *REJ* 50 (1905): 32–41, 34.

20. Julius Guttmann, "*Religion und Wissenschaft im mittelalterlichen und im modernen Denken*," *Hochschüle für die Wissenschaft des Judentums* (Berlin, 1922), 153–55, 166–73. Hebrew tr., see above, n.17; Baneth, "*Halevi ve-al-Ghazzālī*," 312ff.

21. For example, Efros asserts that Ha-Levi recognizes two states of prophecy: one that he characterizes as *ilhām* and one that he characterizes as *waḥy*. While Efros presents this distinction as if Ha-Levi uses it consistently, several of the passages he adduces do not fit neatly into his scheme, and some do not use these terms. Efros, "Some Aspects of Yehudah Ha-Levi's Mysticism," in idem, *Studies in Medieval Jewish Philosophy* (New York, 1974), 148–50 and notes; see below, Part 4, section B.

22. H. A. Wolfson, "Hallevi and Maimonides on Prophecy," in idem, *Studies in Religious Philosophy*, ed. I. Twersky and G. Williams (Cambridge, 1973–79), 68–85. Wolfson also suggests as a source the work of the first-century Alexandrian Jew Philo. Ibid., 86–95; idem, *Repercussions of the Kalām in Jewish Philosophy* (Cambridge, Mass., 1979), 102–8.

23. See Leo Strauss, "The Law of Reason in the *Kuzari*," in *Persecution and the Art of Writing* (Glencoe, 1952; Chicago, 1988), 95–141; Eliezer Schweid, "The Literary Structure of the First Book of the *Kuzari*" (Hebrew), *Tarbiz* 30 (1961); idem, *Taʿam ve-haqashah* (Ramat Gan, 1970); Isaak Heinemann, "*Helekh ha-raʿyonot shel hatḥalat sefer ha-Kuzari*," in *Rabi Yehudah Halevi: kovets meḥkarim ve-haʿarakhot*, ed. I. Zemorah (Tel Aviv, 1950); idem, "*Ha-filosof ha-meshorer: be'ur le-mivḥar piyyutim shel rabbi yehudah ha-levi*," in ibid., 166–235.

24. Herbert Davidson, "The Active Intellect in the Cuzari and Hallevi's Theory of Causality," *REJ* 131 (1973): 381–95; idem, *Alfarabi, Avicenna, and Averroes, on Intellect* (Oxford, 1992), 180–95.

25. Shlomo Pines, "Shīʿite Terms and Conceptions in Judah Halevi's *Kuzari*," *Jerusalem Studies in Arabic and Islam* 2 (1980): 167–92, 215–17, 218 n.290.

26. Judah b. Samuel Halevi, *Kitāb al-radd wa'l-dalīl fī'l-dīn al-dhalīl (al-kitāb al-khazari)*, ed. David H. Baneth and Haggai Ben-Shammai (Jerusalem, 1977). All page references will be to this edition of the text. R. Joseph Qafih has come out with a new Hebrew translation with facing Judaeo-Arabic text, whose page numbers correspond closely with the Baneth/Ben-Shammai edition: *Sefer ha-Kuzari: maqor ve-targum* (Kiryat Ono, 1997). Charles Touati has also published an excellent new French translation, *Le Kuzari: Apologie de la religion meprisée* (Paris, 1994). Barry Kogan is completing a new English translation, based on the manuscript left by L. V. Berman at his untimely death. Parts of Berman's translation appear in Colette Sirat's *History of Jewish Philosophy in the Middle Ages* (Cambridge, 1985).

27. Yochanan Silman, *Ben filosof le-navi': Hitpatḥut haguto shel rabbi Yehudah ha-Levi be-sefer ha-Kuzari* (Ramat Gan, 1985), tr. L. Schramm, *Philosopher and Prophet: Judah Halevi, the Kuzari, and the Evolution of His Thought* (Albany, 1995). For Silman's central thesis, see Silman, "*Yiḥudo shel ha-ma'amar ha-shelishi ba-sefer ha-Kuzari, Eshel Be'er-Sheva* vol. 1 (Be'er Sheva, 1976): 94–119; idem, *Filosof*, 109–10; (English) 116–18; for a review of the scholarly debate, see Michael Berger, "Toward a New Understanding of Judah Halevi's *Kuzari*," *Journal of Religion* 72 (2)(1992): 211–14. For some of my differences from Silman, see p.12.

28. See Daniel Lasker, "Judah Halevi and Karaism," in *From Ancient Israel to Modern Judaism Essays in Honor of Marvin Fox*, ed. N. M. Sarna et al. (Atlanta, 1989), vol. 3, 118–19.

29. Cf. Schweid, "Literary Structure," 259–60.

30. Strauss, "Law of Reason," 101 n.17; 103–12; see also Aryeh Motzkin, "On Ha-Levi's *Kuzari* as a Platonic dialogue," *Interpretation* 9.1 (1980), 120, n.5, 114, 118–20.

31. For a masterful study of Socrates' process of *elenchus*, see Kenneth Seeskin, *Dialogue and Discovery: A Study in Socratic Method* (Albany, 1987).

32. Let us examine these passages. In III:17, the *Ḥaver* examines the first three blessings of the silent prayer (*'Amidah*) and asserts that the third blessing which describes the holiness of God points to the philosophers' "negative" description of God: the philosophers assert God's utter transcendence of all physical attributes. This blessing, however, is necessarily preceded by the blessings describing God's involvement in the lives of the Biblical ancestors and God's mighty deeds, which together show that God is in fact connected with the affairs of this world, governing and guiding as Lord and Sovereign:

> And after the affirmation of the blessings "ancestors" (*Avot*) and "mighty deeds" (*gevurot*) which suggest that He is connected (*yata'allaqa*) with this material world (the worshipper) declares him too high (*yunazzihuhu*) and holy (*yuqaddisuhu*) and exalted (*yurafi'uhu*) for it to be fitting to connect him (*yata 'allaquhu*) with any material attributes, in the blessing "The Holiness of God," (which reads) "You are Holy."
>
> And in this blessing he conceives (*yataṣawwara*) (him) as the philosophers describe him, as free from anthropomorphism (*tanzīh*) and holy (*taqdīs*), after declaring his Lordship (*rubūbiyyatihi*) and sovereignty (*mulkihi*) in the blessings "Ancestors" and "Mighty Deeds," by which we affirm that we have a king and legislator. (III:17:106)

The *Ḥaver* makes clear, Silman argues, that the third blessing is not meant to negate the first two. The two aspects of God—transcendence and immanence—appear together in the same prayer. Silman argues that in his early thought Ha-Levi saw these two ways of knowing and describing God as complementary; it is only later that he conceives of them as mutually exclusive. (Silman, *Filosof*, 112–14, 162–63; English, 120–23, 183–86).

However, if we look at IV:3—which Silman ascribes to the later period in Ha-Levi's thought—we see that the *Ḥaver* decribes the paradox of transcendence and immanence in almost identical language. Here the *Ḥaver* explains the divine name "Holy One:"

> Holy [*Qadosh*] is an expression for that which is free from all anthropomorphism [*tanzīh*] and too exalted [*tarfīʿ*] for any attribute of created things to be appropriate, even if he is called that only metaphorically.
>
> And thus Isaiah heard, "Holy, holy, holy," without end, meaning that God is too high [*munazzah*], too exalted [*muraffaʿa*] too holy [*muqaddasa*] and too pure [*mubarraʾa*] for any impurity of the people in whose midst his light dwells [*ḥalla*] to touch him. "Holy" is a term for the spiritual, which is never corporealized and to which no corporeal thing can cling [or: which no corporeal thing can resemble].
>
> However God is called "Holy One of Israel" as an expression for the *ʾamr ʿilāhī* which is connected to him [Israel] [*al-muttaṣil bi-hi*] and then to all his descendents, a connection of governance and guidance, not a connection of clinging and touching. And [thus] not everyone who wants to has permission to say, "My God" and "My Holy One," except metaphorically, by way of imitation [*taqlīd*]. In truth, only a prophet or a *walīy* can say that, one to whom the *ʾamr ʿilāhī* is connected [*yattaṣilu bi-hi*]. (IV:3:151)

We see once again the two poles Silman points to in III:17: God is transcendent and free of all attributes (*tanzīh*) as the philosophers assert, but God is also connected to the affairs of human beings in the material world. The *Ḥaver* expresses this paradox by juxtaposing the name "Holy One," which suggests the absolute transcendence of God, with the name "Holy One of Israel," which asserts that God is nevertheless connected (*muttaṣil*) with Israel (Jacob) and all his descendents—not physically, but through providential guidance.

Silman asserts that in his late thought, Ha-Levi conceives of God as radically transcendent and unknowable, whereas in his early thought, he conceives of God as essentially intellect and thus knowable. However, we have seen that III:17 and IV:3 describe the paradox of God's transcendence and immanence almost identically.

33. Ibid., 174; English, 199.

34. For Silman's central thesis, see Silman, *Yiḥudo shel ha-ma'amar ha-shelishi ba-Sefer ha-Kuzari, Eshel Beʿer-Shevaʿ* vol. I (Beʿer-Shevaʿ, 1976): 94–119; idem, *Filosof*, 109–10; (English) 116–18; for a review of the scholarly debate, see Michael Berger, "Toward a New Understanding of Judah Halevi's *Kuzari*," *Journal of Religion*, 72 (2) (1992), 211–14.

35. For two recent excellent summaries, see Barry Kogan, "Judah Halevi," in *History of Islamic Philosophy*, ed. M. Fakhry (London, 1996), 710–24; Lenn Goodman, "Judah Halevi," in *History of Jewish Philosophy*, ed. D. Frank and O. Leaman (London, 1997).

36. One element of fiction is clear. Even if he had before him the correspondence between Joseph and Ḥasdai Ibn Shaprut, he could not have known the actual

arguments that convinced King Bulan to convert. Rather, Ha-Levi chose this historical setting as a context for his own exposition of the Jewish faith.

37. See Abraham Ibn Ezra's long commentary to Exodus 20:2, where he responds to Ha-Levi's query as to why God addressed Israel thus. Ha-Levi does not quote Exodus 20:2 verbatim, but interprets it in Arabic: *anā allah ma'abuduka* (I:25: 11).

38. See below, 29ff.

39. On the relationship between the conversion story in Book Two and Book One, see Daniel J. Lasker, "Proselyte Judaism, Christianity, and Islam in the Thought of Judah Halevi, *JQR* 81: 1–2, 75–78; Robert Eisen, "The Problem of the King's Dream and Non-Jewish Prophecy in Judah Halevi's *Kuzari*," *Jewish Thought and Philosophy*, vol. 3, 240–41; Silman, *Filosof*, 111–12 nn.1, 2; (English) 120 n.1.

40. I follow here the felicitous French translation of Touati, *Le Kuzari: Apologie de la religion méprisée*, 42.

41. While paragraph one speaks of a pious person (*muta'abbid*), paragraphs two and three describe the good person (*khayyir*).

42. Strauss remarks that here "the account of the philosophic teaching is introduced as an account of the *kalām*," and that in V:14, the *Ḥaver* describes the various philosophical sects (those of Pythagoras, Empedocles, Plato, and Aristotle), as sects of *mutakallimūn*. For Strauss, this failure to distinguish between philosophy and theology is a symptom of difficulties in Halevi's presentation of philosophy. Strauss, ibid., 110 n.44. For Wolfson's view, see below, 175, n 43.

Part 1

1. For primary texts, see al-Fārābī, *Mab'ādi' ārā' ahl al-madīna al-fāḍila*, tr. R. Walzer, as *Al-Fārābī on the Perfect State* (Oxford, 1985), 240–47; idem, *al-Siyāsa al-madaniyya*, ed. F. Najjar (Beirut, 1964), 79–80; idem, *Risāla fi'l 'aql*, ed. M. Bouyges (1938), 22; Ibn Sina, *Shifā': De anima*, ed. F. Rahman (London: Oxford University Press, 1959), 245–48; tr. Rahman, *Avicenna's Psychology* (Oxford, 1952), 90–93; idem, *Kitāb al-ishārāt wa-l-tanbīhāt*, ed. J. Forget (Leiden, 1892), 129; idem, "*Commentary on Aristotle*, De Anima," in *Ārisṭu 'inda al-'arab*, ed. A. Badawi (Cairo, 1947), 100–101; idem, *Mubāḥathāt*, ibid., 230–31; idem, *Glosses on the Theology of Aristotle* (*Sharh kitāb uthūlūjiya al-mansūb 'ilā Arisṭu li-'ibn Sīnā*), ibid., 73; Ibn Bajja, *Kalām fī ittiṣāl al-'aql bi'l-insān*, tr. M. Asin Palacios as "Tratado de Avempace sobre la Union del Intelecto con el Hombre," *Al-Andalus* 7 (1942): 1–47.

2. For secondary literature, see Alexander Altmann, "Ibn Bajja on Man's Ultimate Felicity," in idem, *Studies in Religious Philosophy and Mysticism* (Ithaca, 1969), 47–48ff.; Alfred Ivry, "Averroes on the Possibility of Intellection and Conjunction," *JAOS* 86, 2 (April-June, 1966): 76–85; idem, "Moses of Narbonne's 'Treatise on the Perfection of the Soul,' A Methodological and Conceptual Analysis," *JQR*: 271–97; Herbert Davidson, *Intellect*, 48–58, 65–73, 83–94, 103–5,

180–209, 320–40; idem, "Active Intellect," *Viator*, 142, 152–54, 166–72; David Blumenthal, "Maimonides' Intellectualist Mysticism and the Superiority of the Prophecy of Moses," in *Approaches to Judaism in Medieval Times*, vol. 1 (Chico, Calif., 1984), 27–28, ad loc.

3. In medieval Aristotelian thought, the celestial world consisted of nine spheres, each governed by an emanated divine intelligence. Medieval thinkers such as al-Fārābī also posited a tenth intelligence, which they identified with the "active intellect" spoken of by Aristotle in *De Anima*. This Active Intellect was held to govern our world in the sphere under the moon and to bring potential human thought into actuality. Most philosophers believed that the Active Intellect was the celestial limit beyond which the human mind could not reach. The goal of spiritual life was therefore union with the tenth divine intellect. See Herbert Davidson, "Cuzari," *REJ*, 352ff., idem, "Active Intellect," *Viator*, 109, 134ff.; idem, *Intellect*, 3–4, 44ff.

4. *qunū*ʿ, *khudū*ʿ, *khushū*ʿ

5. He is called called *al-kāmil*, a term with both Sufi and philosophical resonance. See below, p. 30. See also Nicholson, "The Perfect Man," in *Studies in Islamic Mysticism* (Cambridge, 1921), 77–148; Schimmel, *Mystical Dimensions*, s.v. "Perfect Man."

6. Schimmel, ibid., 144; al-Ghazzālī, *Al-Munqidh*, 133; Watt, *Faith and Practice*, 61; McCarthy, *Freedom and Fulfillment*, 95.

7. Pines suggests that the doctrine of the philosopher depicted in I:1 conforms most closely to that of Ibn Bājja, although both he and Davidson point out similarities with the doctrines of al-Fārābī as well. Pines, "Shīʿite Terms," 211–15, 219; idem, "The Limitations of Human Knowledge According to Al-Fārābī, ibn Bajja, and Maimonides," *Studies in Medieval Jewish History and Literature*, ed. I. Twersky (Cambridge, Mass., 1979), 82–109; Davidson, *Intellect*, 185–87; idem, "Cuzari," *REJ*, 361–68; Altmann, "Ibn Bājja," 73–107.

8. See for example, Nicholson, "*Ittiḥād*," *EI2*; Moshe Idel, *Kabbalah: New Perspectives* (New Haven, 1988), 38–42.

9. Cf. A. Altmann and S. M. Stern, *Isaac Israeli: A Neoplatonic Philosopher of the Early Tenth Century* (London, 1958), 184 and n.1.

10. Plotinus, *Enneads* IV.8.1, tr. A.H. Armstrong (Cambridge, Mass., 1984), Vol. 4: 397.

11. *The Theology of Aristotle* was actually a loose translation of three books from Plotinus' *Enneads*. See *Kitāb uthūlūjiya Aristatalis* (*The Theology of Aristotle*), ed. F. Dieterici (Leipzig, 1883), 8; Translation in A. Altmann and S. M. Stern, *Isaac Israeli: A Neoplatonic Philosopher of the early Tenth Century* (London: Oxford, 1958), 191. Also in English translation of the *Theology* by G. Lewis in *Plotini Opera*, ed. P. Henry and H-R. Schwyzer (Paris, 1959), 69.

12. *ʿāqil . . . maʿqūl*

13. *Theology of Aristotle*, ed. Dieterici 21; also in *Plotinus apud Arabes*, ed. A. Badawi (Cairo, 1955), 35. Tr. in Davidson, "Active Intellect," *Viator*, 132.

The full passage reads: "When the soul leaves this world and enters that upper world, she makes her way to the intellect and cleaves to it (*iltazamathu*), and having cleaved to it unites with it [*tuwaḥḥidat bi-hi*] without loss of her self. On the contrary, she becomes more distinct and purer and clearer, because she and the intellect are then one thing and two, like two species. If the soul is in this state, she does not admit change in any way at all, but is unchanging in her world, for she knows herself and knows that she knows herself, with a single knowledge, with no division between them. And she becomes like that only because she becomes herself the thinker and the object of thought, and she becomes so only through the intensity of her conjunction [*shaddat al-ittiṣāl*] and union [*tawaḥḥud*] with intellect, so that it is as if she and it were one." Full translation by G. Lewis in *Plotini Opera*, ed. P. Henry and H-R. Schwyzer (Paris, 1959), 69.

14. Avicenna indeed echoes the language of this passage, which speaks of the intensity of *ittiṣāl* (*shaddat al-ittiṣāl*) with Intellect. In the *Shifā'*, Avicenna writes: "Thus there might be an individual whose soul is so supported (assisted) by great purity and intensity of *ittiṣāl* (*shaddat al-ittiṣāl*) with first intelligible principles that he blazes with intuition, i.e. with the receptivity (to inspiration coming) from the Active Intelligence concerning everything." Avicenna, *Shifā'*: *De Anima,* published as Avicenna's *De Anima,* ed. F. Rahman, 249–50. And see below, pp. 137–38. On the ecstatic element in Plotinus, see Philip Merlan, *Mysticism, Monopsychism, Metaconsciousness: Problems of the Soul in the Neo-Aristotelian and Neoplatonic Traditions* (The Hague, 1963), pp. 79–82.

15. Ibn Sīnā, *Ishārāt*, chapters 9 and 10; tr. A-M. Goichon, *Livre des directives et remarques* (Paris, 1951), ibid; tr. S. C. Inati, *Remarks and Admonitions*, tr. S. C. Inati (Toronto, 1984), ibid.

16. For a different view, see Hava Lazarus-Yafeh, *Studies in Al-Ghazzālī* (Jerusalem, 1975), 264–68. Professor Lazarus-Yafeh argues that Ghazzālī found in Sufism a way to defuse attraction to the foreign ideas of Neo-Platonism.

17. See *Munqidh*, 133; Watt, 61; McCarthy, 95.

18. We should note Ghazzālī's extensive use of Sufi terminology here; in addition to the root *w-ṣ-l*, Ghazzālī alludes to the Sufi notions of taste (*dhawq*), mystical state (*ḥāl*), annihilation (*fanā'*) and permanent abiding (*baqā'*). *Mishkāt al-anwār*, ed. A. Afīfī (Cairo, 1964) 56 (92); W. H. T. Gairdner, *Al-Ghazzālī's Mishkāt Al-Anwār* ("*The Niche for Lights*") (English) (Lahore, 1952), 158.

19. It is true that Baḥya furnishes *kalām* proofs to demonstrate the unity of the Divine (*tawḥīd*). Yet Baḥya is not simply a *mutakallim*. A strong Neo-Platonic and Sufi sensibility emerge as well, as he brings forth the paradox of God's utter transcendence and yet absolute nearness. Baḥya in fact quotes an anonymous verse that will reappear in the poetry of Ha-Levi: "My God, where can I find You, or rather where can I not find You? You have hidden Yourself so as not to be seen, while the whole is full of You!" Baḥya ibn Paqūda, *Al-Hidāja 'ilā farā'iḍ al-qulūb*, ed. A. S. Yahuda (Leiden, 1912), 82; *Torah Ḥovot ha-Levavot*, ed. J. Qafih, 85; tr. M. Mansoor, *The Book of Direction to the Duties of the Heart*, 143.

20. Baḥya, *Al-Hidāya*, ed. Yahuda, 379; Qafih, 410; Mansoor, 427. Ibn Tibbon translates *tattaṣil* as *teddabeq*. See *Duties of the Heart*, tr. Y. Ibn Tibbon, M. Hyamson (New York, 1962), 342.

21. Or: the most balanced (upright) of ways (*aʿdal al- ṭurūq*). On justice and moderation (*iʿtidāl*), see below p. 46.

22. Ha-Levi evokes this image once again in III:11: 99. In this passage, the *Ḥaver* depicts a Sufi-like meditation on the participation of God in the pious person's every action. The Sufi resonance of this motif—the notion that God acts through the limbs of the fully perfected human being—can be heard in the language of Ghazzālī: "All movements [*ḥarakāt*] and all restings [*sakanāt*] [of the Sufis], whether external or internal, are illuminated from the light of the lamp of prophecy [*nubuwwa*]; and beyond the light of prophecy, there is no other light on the face of the earth which may be the source of illumination." *Munqidh*, 132; McCarthy, 94; Watt, 60.

The Sufis based themselves on the following *ḥadīth qudsī* (a tradition in which God speaks): "My servant ceases not to draw nigh unto Me by works of devotion, until I love him, and when I love him I am the eye by which he sees and the ear by which he hears. When he approaches a span I approach a cubit, and when he comes walking I come running." Abū Naṣr al-Sarrāj, *Kitāb al-lumaʿ*, ed. Nicholson (Leiden, 1914), 59; cited by Schimmel, *Mystical Dimensions*, 133.

A similar motif occurs in III:51 of *Guide of the Perplexed*, in which Maimonides depicts Moses and the patriarchs as acting with their limbs only, while their intellects are engaged in the contemplation of God. Barry Kogan and David Shatz note the similarity to this passage in *Kuzari* 1:1. See Shatz, "Worship, Corporeality, and Human Perfection: A Reading of *Guide of the Perplexed* III:51–54," in *The Thought of Moses Maimonides: Philosophical and Legal Studies*, ed. I. Robinson, L. Kaplan, J. Bauer (Lewiston, New York, 1990), 126 n.47.

23. *Munqidh*, 140; Watt, 66; McCarthy, 99. It may also be that the philosophers were forced to define and explain prophecy through the Active Intellect in response to Sufi claims that it was the Sufi path alone that led to, and could fully comprehend, prophecy. The Islamic philosophers sought to describe a theory of knowledge that would encompass philosophy, prophecy, and religious experience. See Fazlur Rahman, *Prophecy in Islam: Philosophy and Orthodoxy* (London, 1958). On Ha-Levi's use of the term *dhawq*, see Efros, "Mysticism," 147–48 and nn.23–24.

24. *maṭlūb*

25. Or: knowledge of the hidden (*ʿilm ghayb*).

26. Ha-Levi turns the philosopher's ironic tone against the philosopher by using the term *maṭlūb*—by which Sufis referred to the divine beloved—to refer to a much more modest object of union, the Active Intellect of the philosophers. On the King's dream, see Robert Eisen, "The Problem of the King's Dream and Non-Jewish Prophecy in Judah Halevi's *Kuzari*," *Jewish Thought and Philosophy*, vol. 3, 231–47.

27. The King also protests that he would expect tales of miracles and wonders (*muʿjizāt wa-karamāt*) among the philosophers. These, too, are included in philosophical accounts of prophecy. See Rahman, *Prophecy*, 45–52; Aviezer Ravitsky, "The Anthropological Theory of Miracles," in *Studies in Medieval Jewish History*

and Literature, vol. 2, ed. I. Twersky (Cambridge, Mass., 1984), 231–72. On the term *ʾamr ilāhī* and my translation, see below, pp. 29–30.

28. On the *sirr*, see Schimmel, *Mystical Dimensions*, 192.

29. *la taskunu al-nufūs.*

30. *wa-bi-l-ḥarā* or *bi-l-aḥrā.* See also I:6: 8–9; Baneth/Ben-Shammai, *Kuzari*, 9 n.18; Reinhart Dozy, *Supplément aux dictionaires arabes* (Leiden, 1967), vol. 1, 280; Yefet b. ʿElī, *Commentary on the Book of Daniel,* ed. D. S. Margoliouth (Oxford, 1889), 7 and no. 12; (English) 2, 91; Seymour Feldman, "Review Essay: Judah Halevi's *The Kuzari* in French" (Review of Charles Touati, trans. *Le Kuzari: Apologie de la religion méprisée*) *AJS Review* 21:1 (1996): 121–22.

31. Or: how did this great thing become firmly established in your souls (*fa-kayfa tamakanna fi-nufūsikum*).

32. *ʿināya*, the standard Arabic philosophical term for providence.

33. *Naṭiqīna*, literally "speaking beings."

34. Ha-Levi uses the standard Islamic coupling of prophets (*anbiyā'*) and pious friends of God (*walīy: awliyā'*).

35. *ḥulūl.* The term *ḥulūl* has a technical sense of "incarnation": the complete indwelling of God in a human being. It is the Islamic Arabic term for the Christian incarnation. Ha-Levi here uses the term *ḥulūl* in a general, nontechnical sense of indwelling. He then does go on to use it in the sense of incarnation when he speaks of the Messiah. As a term for incarnation, *ḥulūl* was also a heresy leveled against Sufis and others. See Carl W. Ernst, *Words of Ecstasy in Sufism* (Albany, 1981), 118–23; Lois Anita Giffen, *Theory of Profane Love among the Arabs: The Development of the Genre* (New York, 1971). On the problem of *ḥulūl,* see my forthcoming study "A Dwelling Place for the *Shekhinah*," *JQR* 90 (1–2), July–Oct. 1999.

36. *ḥulūlahu.* Here both shades of the verb *ḥalla* are interwoven—a nontechnical sense of alighting, resting, or dwelling, and the technical Arabic sense of incarnation. The Christian has thus contextualized this *ḥulūl* in the larger history of God's connection with the Jewish people; there are precedents for this "indwelling" of God. Ha-Levi uses this term repeatedly to describe God's presence among the Jewish people. There is also one other passage in which *ḥalla* comes a bit closer to the Christian sense of incarnation. The *Ḥaver* explains that prophecy ceased with the destruction of the First Temple, except for rare individuals: "[Newly] acquired prophecy ceased with the departure of the *Shekhinah*, and only came at extraordinary times or on account of a great force, such as that of Abraham, Moses, the expected Messiah, Elijah and their equals. For they in themselves were a dwelling place [*maḥall*] for the *Shekhinah*, and their very presence helped those present to acquire the degree of prophecy" (III:65: 137). On the verb *ḥalla* and this passage in Ha-Levi, see my forthcoming article "A Dwelling Place for the *Shekhinah*," *JQR* 90 (1–2), July–Oct. 1999.

37.Pines points out, however, that while later philosophers speak of individuals' quests to unite their human intellect with the divine Active Intellect, early philosophers such as Ibn Sīnā described this process in the reverse: the Active Intellect conjoins with (*yattaṣilu bi*) the human intellect. Pines, "Shīʿite Terms," 177 n.76.

38. Ibid., 177.

39. Ibid.

40. For example, Pines cites a passage in the treatise *Kitāb al-radd 'ala'l-rawāfiḍ aṣḥāb al-ghuluww* (attributed to al-Qāsim b. Ibrāhīm, a Zaydi theologian) in which we find *ṣafwa* denoting "choice" or "election," and the divine *'amr* bestowing this choice. Ha-Levi uses the term *ṣafwa* strictly to refer to those who are selected, and never to the fact of selection, as in this text. Ibid., 167–70.

41. For example, in the *Risāla al-Jām'ia* (part 2, fourth *risala,* p. 147), we find *ittiṣāl* in an elaborate Neo-Platonic framework like that described in the Letters of the Brethren of Purity (*Ikhwān al-ṣafā'*). Here we see the divine *'amr* coming down through a series of emanations to the prophets. Ibid., 176.

42. This is of course also true for incarnation, referred to by the Christian in I:4.

43. Note, for example, Ha-Levi's playful use of the term *'amr* in I:109: "you will see that an *'amr* higher than the natural *'amr* guides your *'amr*" (I:109: 36).

Ha-Levi's literary sensitivity to the term *'amr* comes to the fore in I:97–98 as well. The *Ḥaver* argues that the sin of the golden calf consisted not in building an image per se, but in attributting an *'amr ilāhī* to something chosen and created themselves, without a command of God (*'amr allah*) (I:97: 31). This, says the King, confirms the angel's message in his dream: one can only reach the *'amr ilāhī* through a command of God, an *'amr ilāhī* (I:98: 32).

44. As Barry Kogan expressed it, the *'amr ilāhī* is "Halevi's multivalent term for diverse aspects of divine immanence." Kogan, "Judah Halevi," in *History of Islamic Philosophy*, ed. M. Fakhry 721. On the *'amr ilāhī*, cf. Goldziher, "Le *'Amr ilāhī*," 32–41; Efros, "Mysticism," 145–46; Wolfson, "Prophecy," 68–85; Davidson, "Cuzari," *REJ,* 381–95; Howard Kreisel, *Theories of Prophecy in Medieval Jewish Philosophy* (Ann Arbor, 1981), 93–114; Silman, *Filosof,* 115–19, 172–77; (English) 124–29, 196–203.

45. See now Touati, who made the same choice, for similar reasons. He translates *'amr ilāhī* as *le divin*. Touati, *Le Kuzari*, xiii.

46. There is a passionate, ecstatic strain to Ha-Levi's thought which figures prominently in IV:15–17 of the *Kuzari* and finds eloquent expression in his poetry. The relationship of these two strands in Ha-Levi's poetry—the individual quest for union with the Divine, and the historical, God-initiated relationship with the nation of Israel—are a subject for further research.

47. *Al- 'ārif.*

48. *dūna ta'alīm, bal bi-ahwān fikra.* We see traces in Ha-Levi of the medieval philosophical debate over Sufi *ittiṣāl*, and particularly over Sufi claims to achieve access to universal knowledge without a long process of philosophical study. Ibn Bājja refers explicitly to the Sufi claim that "the attainment of ultimate happiness may come about without learning (*bi-lā ta'allum*), but through devotion and constant remembrance of God (*dhikr*)." He criticizes the Sufis on this point; insofar as they seek to bypass the intellect, they have settled for an illusory goal.

Avicenna, like the Sufis, believes it possible to receive all potential knowledge in the immediate experience of *ittiṣāl*; although for the Sufis *ittiṣāl* is union with God, while for Avicenna *ittiṣāl* represents conjunction with the Active Intellect. Al-Fārābī, in contrast, is skeptical about such claims and insists that the prophet must engage in philosophical study in order to receive intelligibles from the Active Intellect.

See Ibn Bājja, *Tadbīr al-mutawaḥḥid* (*Governance of the Solitary*) *in Ibn Bājjah, Opera Metaphysica*, ed. M. Fakhry (Beirut: Dār al-Nahār), 55–56; cf. 68–69. Translation by Steven Harvey, "The Place of the Philosopher in the City According to Ibn Bājjah," in *The Political Aspects of Islamic Philosophy: Essays in Honor of Muhsin S. Mahdi,* ed. C. Butterworth (Cambridge, Mass.: Harvard, 1992). See also Lenn Goodman, "Ibn Bajjah," in *History of Islamic Philosophy*, ed. M. Fakhry, 302; Davidson, *Intellect*, 58–65, 116–123; idem, "Cuzari," *REJ*, 362–66;" idem, "Active Intellect," Viator, 122, 134–170, 175–78. On the perfect human being, see above, p. 22.

49. Or: Capacity, faculty (*quwwa*). Ibn Ṭufayl, another twelfth-century Spanish thinker writing in Arabic, speaks of the capacity for "witnessing" the Divine (*mushāhada*) as something he can term a faculty [*quwwa*] only by way of metaphor. Both he and Ha-Levi suggest that the capacity for connection with the Divine lies beyond the realm of the intellect, but each is hesitant to locate it within a specific faculty of soul. *Hujwīrī*, an eleventh-century Persian Sufi thinker, writes similarly: "God causes man to know him with a knowledge that is not linked to any faculty."

See *Ḥayy ben Yaqdhān: Roman philosophique d'Ibn Thofail*, ed. L. Gauthier (Beirut, 1936) 6, 9; *Ibn Ṭufayl's Ḥayy Ibn Yaqzān*, tr. L. Goodman (Los Angeles, 1983), 96, 97, 173n. 17; R. A. Nicholson, *The Kashf al-Maḥjūb, the Oldest Persian Treatise on Sufism by ʿAli b. 'Uthmān al-Jullabi al-Hujwīrī* (London, 1911), 271.

50. Compare his description of the excellent person (*al-khayyir*): "He calls upon his community as a leader who is obeyed calls upon his army, to help him make connection [*ittiṣāl*] with the degree which is above it [intellect], I mean the divine degree [*rutba*], which is above the degree of intellect" (III:5: 93).

51. For philosophical portraits of Adam, cf. Maimonides, *Guide* I:2; Nahmanides on Genesis 2:9; Bezalel Safran, "Rabbi Azriel and Nahmanides: Two Views of the Fall of Man," in *Rabbi Moses Nahmanides* (*Ramban*)*: Explorations in His Religious and Literary Virtuosity*, ed. I. Twersky (Cambridge, 1983), 86–87.

52. On the question of mystical union within Judaism, see Moshe Idel, "Abraham Abulafia and *Unio Mystica*," in *Studies in Ecstatic Kabbalah* (Albany, 1988), 1–31; idem, *Kabbalah*, 35ff.; Gershom Scholem, *Major Trends in Jewish Mysticism* (New York, 1961), 122–23, 55–56, 5–9; idem, "*Devekut* or Communion with God," in *The Messianic Idea in Judaism* (London, 1971), 203–4; idem, *Kabbalah* (Jerusalem, 1974), 174–76.

53. Or: quintessence, prime, choicest part (*lubāb*)

54. *muttaṣilan*

55. Or: according to (ʿ*ala*)

56. *wa-hāulā'i 'āla ittiṣālihim lubāb adam wa-ṣāfwatuhu*

57. The particle *fa-* often has a consequential sense.

58. Or: upon (*fī*) a group: *fa-ṣārat al-'ilāhīyya fī jamā'a*

59. *niyya khāliṣa*

60. *ḥaqqun lahu 'an yaṭma'a*

61. I sincerely wish I could, with Hirschfeld, translate *dūna* as "among" rather than "to the exclusion of" the other nations, but the Arabic does not permit it.

62. Elsewhere the *Ḥaver* speaks of striving for prophecy and achieving it or nearly achieving it (I:103: 35). Ha-Levi in several passages hints at a process of developing one's spiritual gifts through the *mitsvot* (e.g., V:20, Fourth Principle: 223), but is inconsistent about levels of development. At times prophecy is spoken of as the peak of religious experience, whereas elsewhere he speaks of praying *for ittiṣāl* at the degree of prophecy (III:20: 109–10), suggesting that *ittiṣāl* itself is the ultimate goal of religious life.

63. There is abundant aggadic literature filling in the biography of Abraham. Abraham is praised for being the first to recognize God, whether as a child or as an adult. Rabbinic literature tells the well-known story of the patriarch's iconoclasm: he smashed his father's idols and risked his life in the fiery furnace of Nimrod. Abraham underwent ten trials of faith, among which is circumcision; he is tried because of his righteousness, and his triumph preserves the entire world. For sources, see Israel Ta-Shema "Abraham," *EJ*; Louis Ginzberg, *Legends of the Jews* (Philadelphia, 1942–47), vol. 1, 185ff.; vol. 5, 297ff.

64. A classic rabbinic statement of this process is found in the Babylonian Talmud, *Shabbat* 104a, *Yoma* 38b: "If one comes to defile himself, the doors are opened to him, but if he comes to purify himself, he is helped."

65. *wajaba*. Or: when he became distinguished and his *ittiṣāl* with the *'amr il-lahi* became necessary.

66. Translation assisted by that of L. V. Berman in Colette Sirat, *A History of Jewish Philosophy in the Middle Ages* (Cambridge, 1985), 125.

67. Or: theophany (*mashhad*). See Genesis 15:7–21.

68. *al-siyāsa*

69. Or: (so) that the *'amr ilāhī* might connect.

70. *khāṣṣatan*. Even-Shemuel and Touati translate "as an individual;" Touati suggests that unlike Christianity and Islam, Judaism does not proselytize among other nations. Ibn Tibbon renders *khāṣṣatan* as *bi-frat*, in particular (*ki-frat*, as an individual?); Qafih translates *be-meyuḥad*, in particular, and suggests that Ha-Levi refers to someone who undergoes a complete conversion, as opposed to someone who merely renounces idol worship but remains a Gentile.

The verb *yanal* can be traced to the root *n-w-l* or *n-y-l*. The form attested here appears to derive from *n-y-l*, which signifies to attain or obtain (the object of one's aim or desire). Lane defines the verb noun *nayl* as what one obtains or acquires (of the bounty of another). Lane, Supplement, 3039–40. On the significance of *khāṣṣatan*, see below, p. 37.

71. lit: obtains some of our good.

As Qafih notes, Ha-Levi may be echoing Numbers 10:29: "And Moses said to Ḥobab son of Reuel the Midianite, Moses' father in law, 'We are setting out for the place of which the Lord has said, "I will give it to you." Come with us and we will be good to you (*hetavnu lakh*) as the Lord has promised to be good to Israel (lit: spoken good to Israel; *dibber tov 'al yisra'el*).'" In his Arabic translation of the Torah, Sa'adya renders the phrase "we will do good to you" (*nuḥsinu ileka*) as "God has promised good to Israel" (*wa'ada 'ilā Isrā'īl bi-khayrin*). The *Ḥaver* says that one who joins Israel "will obtain some of our good" (*yanāl min kayrinā*).

The rabbis identify Ḥobab with Jethro, Moses' father in law, whom they consider a proselyte.

72. Baneth, for example, remarks that Ha-Levi's doctrine of a special religious faculty possessed by the Jewish people bears an unmistakable resemblance to modern racial theories. See Baneth, "*Halevi ve-al-Ghazzālī*," 322–23; tr. G. Hirschler in *Studies in Jewish Thought: An Anthology of German Jewish Scholarship*, ed. A. Jospe (Detroit), 192; cf. Salo Baron, "Yehudah Halevi: An Answer to an Historic Challenge," *Jewish Social Studies*, 271. Both scholars, however, go on to qualify their assertions somewhat.

73. This shift was anticipated in the Christian's speech in Ha-Levi's opening dialogue (1:4) The Christian's words—which link providential *ittiṣāl* to God's special relationship with Israel—find expression in III:11: 100 as well.

74. See Marvin J. Pope, *The Song of Songs: A New Translation with Introduction and Commentary* (New York, 1977), pp. 89–112; Bernard Septimus, "*Divre ḥazal be-shirat sefarad*," *Tarbiz* 53 (1984), 611.

Note, too, the midrashic statement that maidservants at the Red Sea beheld what Isaiah and Ezekiel did not behold. Ha-Levi alludes to this midrash in 1:95: 27, where the *Ḥaver* asserts that the *'amr ilāhī* rested upon the entire nation, and even rested upon the women, some of whom became prophetesses. See *Mekhilta de-Rabbi Ishmael*, ed. Horovitz-Rabin, 126.

75. Notice Ha-Levi's deft allusion to Islamic traditions, with which he expected his Jewish readers to be familiar. This version of the *ḥadīth* is from *Saḥīḥ Muslim* (Cairo, 1930's, reprinted in Beirut, five volumes), *Kitāb al-Musājid*, vol. 1, 370–71. For other versions, see A. J. Wensinck, *Concordance et Indices de la Tradition Musulmane*, vol. 1, 194–95, 513; vol. 3, 20; vol. 6, 26. I am grateful to Professors William Graham, Sarah Stroumsa, and Wheeler Thackston who aided me in tracking down the *ḥadīth*.

76. Goldzhizer, *Muslim Studies* (Chicago, 1967–71), 243–44.

77. Or: creation as a whole (*buithtu/ursiltu 'ilā al-khalq kāfatan*). See Farid al-Dīn 'Attār, *Manṭiq al-ṭayr* (Tehran, 1342), 281, 279.

78. This passage may echo a debate among Jews in the medieval Islamic world over whether the Torah obligates non-Jews. The discussion in the tenth and eleventh centuries is reflected in Samuel ben Ḥofni Gaon's *Treatise on the Commandments,* Questions Two and Three. See David Sklare, *Samuel ben Ḥofni Gaon and his Cultural World: Texts and Studies* (Leiden, 1996), 157, 259–81.

We find a terminological key to Ha-Levi's view in his repetition in 1:27 of the Arabic root *s-w-y*, to be equal. The English translations of Heinemann and Hirschfeld render the second sentence: "If the law were binding on us (only) because God created us, the white and the black *would be equal* (*lastawā*) since He created them all."

These translations obscure an important point in the passage; they omit the crucial Arabic particle *fī-hi* (in it): "the red and the black would indeed share equally in it [*lastawā fī-hi*]," i.e. in the law. This phrase sheds light on the *Ḥaver*'s earlier statement that "whoever from among the nations joins us, in particular, shares in our good, although they are not quite the same as (or equal to) us [*lam yastawi maʿnā*]." He clearly means that they do not share equally in the law—a logical answer to the question of whether the law is incumbent only on Jews (1:26: 12).

79. The adverb *khāṣṣatan*, then, can refer both to the action of joining and the group joined. Whoever takes the specific step to join this nation in particular will share in its good fortune. Responding to the historic claim that Islam and Christianity are superior because they offer a revelation which is universal, Ha-Levi holds up the Jewish revelation as historically particular—a law to which one is tied by a particular history, or which one must take deliberate steps to join.

80. Menachem Kellner writes, "Fairness to Halevi demands that we take note of the special circumstances surrounding the adoption of his position, and that we not accuse him of nor blame him for twentieth-century racism. Halevi flourished in a place and time in which conflicting national and religious groupings each advanced its own claims to nobility and belittled the character of its opponents. Christian Spaniards affirmed their superiority over Jews and Muslims; Muslims affirmed their superiority over Jews and Christians; Muslim Arabs affirmed their superiority over non-Arab Muslims; Halevi affirmed the superiority of the Jews over the Spaniards, Arabs, and North Africans." Menachem Kellner, *Maimonides on Judaism and the Jewish People* (Albany, 1991), 110 n.16.

81. Pines suggests that this character is a composite of two figures; it is not clear whether he is Iraqi or Iranian. See Pines, 189–90, n.168b.

82. It is true that in the context of the debate, this passage is itself a parody. However, the fact that these ideas were being parodied indicates that they were well known in that cultural milieu.

On Ha-Levi's adaptation of climatological theory, and its use in ʿArabīyya/Shuʿūbiyya polemics, see Alexander Altmann, "The Climatological Factor in Yehuda Ha-Levi's Theory of Prophecy (Hebrew)," *Melilah* 1 (1944) : 1–17; Nehemia Aloni, "The *Kuzari*: an Anti-Arabiyyah Polemic (Hebrew)," *Eshel Beʿer Shevaʿ*, 2: 119–44. On Shuʿūbiyya ideology, see *The Shuʿūbiyyaa in Al-Andalus: the Risāla of Ibn Garcia and Five Refutations*, tr. James T. Monroe (Berkeley, 1970).

83. See Wolfson, "Prophecy," 103.

84. Cf. 1:102: The King: Why was guidance [on the true path] not given to all? That is what wisdom deems proper.

1: 103: The Ḥaver: And would it not have been best for all animals to be rational beings? You have apparently forgotten what we said previously about the succession of

Adam's descendents, and the continuity of the resting of the prophetic *ʾamr ilāhī* on one person, who was the heart of his brothers and the select of his father, receiving that light, while the rest were like husks, not receiving it. [This continued] until the sons of Jacob, select and heart, distinguished among human beings by a divine distinction which made them almost another species and angelic essence, all of them seeking the level of prophecy and most of them attaining it.

85. *khayyir.*

86. Ibn Sina, *Ishārāt*, 204; Goichon, *Directives*, 495–97; also quoted in Ibn Ṭufayl, *Ḥayy*, Gauthier, 7; Goodman, 97.

87. *ṣalāḥ*

88. *khulūs al-khālis*

89. Or: falseness, pride (*zaif*)

90. *bi-khulūṣinā wa-bi-ṣalāḥina*

91. On the one hand, the Jewish nation exists to serve as a bridge between God and the world. On the other hand, Ha-Levi introduces an element of tension by suggesting that the world as a whole was arranged for the sake of this divine-human relationship. See continuation of the passage, II:44: 67–68.

92. The virtue of pure-heartedness is described most often with the fourth form of the root *kh-l-s; ikhlās* is dedication to the exclusive worship of God, and the participle *muklhis*, describing one who devotes himself to God, appears frequently in the Qurʾān. The first form, we find here, also carries the dual sense of purity and salvation. Jurjānī's *Book of Definitions*, for example, notes that "one who is pious [*al-ṣāliḥ*] is pure and free [*khalīs*] of all imperfection [*fasad*]." Jurjānī, *Kitāb al-Taʾrifāt*, ed. G. Flugel (Leipzig, 1845), "*ṣalīḥ*." The fifth gate of Baḥya's *Hidāya* is titled *Ikhlās al-ʿamal*, wholehearted devotion of action.

93. *tadbīr*

94. The *Ḥaver* indicates the special relationship of the prophets and the pious in other ways as well. Later in IV:3 he tells the King that only one with whom *ʾamr ilāhī* has made *ittiṣāl* can really use the phrases "my God" or "my Holy One" (IV:3: 151).

95. Jewish thinkers throughout the Middle Ages struggled with the tension between the concept of prophecy as the end of a significant discipline of preparation, and the experience of the entire nation at Mount Sinai. See, for example, Maimonides, *Guide* II:35; Albo, *Iqqarim* III:11.

96. *niyya khālisa*

97. Presumably, to observe God's commandments, or to imitate God's ways of acting in the world. Saʿadya renders Deut. 4:4, "you who cling [*deveqim*] to the Lord your God are all alive today," in Arabic as "you who cling to *the obedience* of the Lord your God [*antum al-lāzimīna ṭāʿat Allah rabbakum*]" (cf. *Targum Onqelos*: "you who cling to the fear of the Lord your God [*attun de-eddeveqtun be-daḥleta de-Hashem elahakon*]). Similarly, Saʿadya renders Deut. 13:5—"You shall walk after the Lord your God, you shall fear him, and keep his commmandments,

and obey his voice; him [alone] shall you serve and to him shall you cling [*u-vo tidbaqun*]"—in Arabic as "you shall follow God your Lord and accept his command [*wa-amrahu taqbalu*] and worship him alone and cling *to his obedience* [*fa- ṭāʿatahu fa-lzamūhā*]" [*Targum Onqelos*: "and draw close *to his fear u-le-daḥleteh titqarevun*"]. And Deuteronomy 30:20—"To love the Lord your God, to listen to his voice, and to cling to him [*u-le-dovqa-vo*]"—Saʿadya translates "to love the Lord your God, to accept his command [*taqbalu amrahu*] and cling *to his obedience* [*wa-talzamu ṭāʿatahu*] (*Onqelos*: "and draw close *to his fear* [*u-le-etqarava le-daḥleteh*]").

On the other hand, Deuteronomy 11:22—"If you shall diligently keep all these commandments which I command you, to do them, to love the Lord your God, to walk in all his ways, and to cling to him (*u-le-dovqa-vo*)"—Saʿadya translates, "if you observe all these commandments that I am commanding you and do them, to love God your Lord and follow in all his ways and cling *to him*" [*wa-talzamuhu*]," rendering *u-le-dovqa-vo* as "to cling to him," rather than "to cling to his obedience" as in Deut. 30:20. However, this may be because the verse itself makes clear that it is enjoining "walking in God's ways." (*Targum Onqelos*, on the other hand, consistently renders the phrase as "you shall draw close *to his fear* [*u-le-etqarava le-daḥleteh*]," just as in Deut. 30:20.)

98. The complete title of the third gate of the *Hidāya* is "On the Duty to Take on Obedience to God on High" (*fī wujūb iltizām ṭāʿat Allah jalla wa-ʿazza*). As we have seen, however, Baḥya uses the term *ittiṣāl* itself to signify the soul's unitive attachment to the light of God, a usage Ha-Levi avoids.

99. *saʿāda*. In a religious context: eternal bliss.

100. *ʾawāmir* (sing: *ʾamr*) *wa-ʿuhūd*

101. *ruṣul*

102. Ghazzālī, in his *Munqidh*, uses *ṭarīq* as a more general term for the various ways, and uses *ṭarīq* or *ṭarīqa* to specify the Sufi way. For example: "When I had finished with all those kinds of lore, I brought my mind to bear on the way [*ṭarīq*] of the Sufis. I knew that their particular Way [*ṭarīqa*] is consummated [realized] only by knowledge and by activity [by the union of theory and practice]." Tr. McCarthy, 89, 68; Watt, 54, 27; *Munqidh*, 79 (*ṭarīq al-ṣūfīya*), 122.

103. causative form of *w-ṣ-l*

104. *saʿāda*. In Arabic philosophy, *saʿada* is a term with eschatological connotations of ultimate, eternal bliss. Arabic translators used the term to translate Aristotle's *eudaimonia*.

105. *Devequt* was in fact the Hebrew term most often used to translate the Arabic terms *ittiṣāl* or *wuṣūl*.

106. See Avicenna, *Ishārāt*, 204; Goichon, 496–97; Ibn Ṭufayl, *Ḥayy*, Gauthier, 7; Goodman, 97.

107. *ittiṣāl tadbīr wa-sīyāsa, lā ittiṣāl luṣūq wa-mumāssa*

108. The latter was more precisely known as *ittiḥād*. Moshe Idel notes that rabbinic interpretation of the Biblical injunction to cling to God ranges from the

cautiousness of the school of R. Ishmael—who interprets clinging to God as marrying one's daughter to a Talmudic scholar—to the boldness of R. Aqiva, who is credited with the following bit of exegesis: "But you that did cling unto the Lord your God [are surely alive today]" (Deut. 4:4)—literally, "clinging" [*devuqim mamash*] (*Sanhedrin* 64a). Idel suggests that while the masses were called upon to participate in clinging to God only indirectly, the elite were enjoined to a more direct clinging, ranging from adhering to God's ways in *imitatio dei* to "a real contact between two entities, more than mere attachment of the devotee to God."

The *amora* Rav interprets the above verse in Deuteronomy as suggesting "two palm dates that cling to one another" (*ke-shtei temarot ha-devuqot zu be-zu*) (Sanhedrin 64a); another image used is the contact of a bracelet with a woman's arm. Thus while the Talmudic rabbis are known for their emphasis on God's awesome transcendence, and for their caution regarding the possibility of human beings attaining union with God, we can also find a "distinctly mystical understanding" of *devequt* among the rabbis. Ha-Levi inherits and displays both tendencies: warnings against the literal understanding of clinging for the masses, with more direct and unitive language reserved for the elite, the prophets and pious. Idel, *Kabbalah*, 38–39. See also below, p. 152, n.26.

109. This broadens the concept of religious experience. Cf. Larry Shinn, *Two Sacred Worlds: Experience and Structure in the World's Religions* (Nashville, 1977), 25–29; and below, p. 50.

110. See below, pp. 151–153ff.

111.This ascetic strain did not eclipse traditional views, but did bring to greater prominence a latent option in Islam. It is true that the new ideal of withdrawal, expressed by Ibn Bājja in *The Regime of the Solitary* (*Tadbīr al-mutawaḥḥid*), is not the dominant view among the *falāsifa*; there are even many Sufis who hold that one should not withdraw from society. Nevertheless, asceticism was clearly a live option that troubled Ha-Levi. He mentions it explicitly in connection with the philosophers, and implicitly—through his terminology—in relation to the Sufis. Cf. Fenton, *Treatise of the Pool*, 54 n.3; Jane Idleman Smith and Yvonne Yazbeck Haddad, *The Islamic Understanding of Death and Resurrection* (Albany, 1981), 19.

112. See below, n.120.

113. *tazahhud*, *zuhd*, *zihāda*. Cf. II:46: 68; III:1: 91.

114. *khushū'*, *khudū'*, *tadhallul*. Cf. II:46: 68; I:115: 39; III:1: 91; III:5: 94; I:1: 5; I:103: 35.

115. *tafarrud*, *inqiṭa'*, *waḥda*, *khalwa*. III:1: 90–91; IV:22: 171

116. *zahadū fī'l-dunyā* V:14: 213

117. *i'tazala wa-tazahhada* (IV:18: 170)

118. For example, in *The Philosophy of Plato*, Al-Fārābī writes: "[Plato] started by investigating what true justice is [*al-'adl, ma huwa fī-l-ḥaqīqa*], how it ought to be, and how it ought to be applied. As he was conducting this investigation, he found he had to investigate the justice generally accepted and applied in cities

(*al-ʿadl al-mashhūr wa-l-mustaʿmal fī-l-mudun.*" Al-Fārābī, *Falsafat Aflatūn*, ed. F. Rosenthal and R. Walzer (London, 1943), 19–20; *The Philosophy of Plato and Aristotle*, tr. M. Mahdi, 64–65.

119. *tataʿabbaddunā bi-l-tazahhud*

120. Compare Maimonides' response to Sufism in, *Shemonah Peraqim*, chapter 4 in *Haqdamot ha-Rambam la-Mishnah*, ed. Y. Sheilat (Jerusalem, 1994), 383 (Arabic), 238 (Hebrew); *Ethical Writings of Maimonides*, ed. R. Weiss and C. Butterworth (New York, 1975), 71. Cf. *Mishneh Torah, Hilkhot Deʿot* 3:1, 6:1. For Maimonides' attitude toward asceticism, see Isadore Twersky, *Introduction to the Code of Maimonides* (New Haven, 1980), 459–68.

121. I:1: 5; II:49: 69.

122. Built into Jewish observance are regular times for prayer as well as the weekly rest of Shabbat, which provides an opportunity for introspection (III:5: 94).

123. Note that it is specifically revelational, and not rational *mitsvot*, that are said to lead to *ittiṣāl*.

124. Or: designated

125. *Waʿd* and *mīʿād* are more common, but Ha-Levi uses *mawʿid*, pl. *mawāʿid*. On Islamic eschatology, see Smith and Haddad, *The Islamic Understanding of Death and Resurrection.*

126. *la yukhlifu*. See *Sūra* 39:20: "As a promise of God—God will not go back on the promise" (*waʿda llāhi lā yukhlifu llāhu l-mīʿād*). Cf. *Sūra* 13:31, 3:9, 3:194, 34:30.

127. *khilāfahu*, but should probably read *ikhlāfuhu*, "rescinding."

128. *la yukhāfa khilāfahu*

129. See Shinn, *Two Sacred Worlds*, 32.

130. *Mekhilta de Rabbi Ishmael* on Exodus 15:3, 20:2.

131. *yataṣarrafūn*: made their way about. See below, pp. 117 n.79, 118 n.85.

132. *khayyir*

133. For a different interpretation of this passage, see Yehudah Even-Shemuel, tr., *The Kosari of R. Yehudah Halevi* (Hebrew) (Tel Aviv, 1972), I:109, p. 41, 255; Silman, *Filosof*, 162 and n.3, 157; (English) 185, 177.

134. *tafarrud, waḥda*, and *khalwa*

135. *bene ha-nevi'im.*

136. *ya'nas ilaihi*, related to *uns*, "companionship"

137. *uns*

138. *tadhallul bi-l-khushūʿ wa-khudūʿ*

139. *tadhallul al-amrad*

140. *inqiṭāʿ bi-l-zahāda*

141. *Iltidhadh* is the verbal noun of the eighth form of *l-dh-dh*; *tadhallul* is the verbal noun of the fifth form of *dh-l-l*. Arabic speakers would notice the similarity in the roots of these two verbs, despite the difference in their forms.

142. On the tension between solitude and community in Judaism, see Moshe Idel, *Ecstatic Kabbalah*, 103–4.

143. *dhilla*

144. *maskana*

145. For thus said He who high aloft
Forever dwells, whose name is holy:
I dwell on high, in holiness;
Yet with the contrite (*daka*) and the lowly in spirit
(*shefal ruaḥ*)—
Reviving the spirits of the lowly,
Reviving the hearts of the contrite.
(Isaiah 57:15; tr., Jewish Publication Society *Tanakh*)

Part 2

1. See Noel Coulson, *A History of Islamic Law* (Edinburgh, 1964), 60; Joseph Schacht, *The Origins of Muhammadan Jurisprudence*, 4th ed. (Oxford, 1967), 99, 127–28; idem, *An Introduction to Islamic Law* (Oxford, 1964), 37, 69–73.

2. These groups were also known as those who use legal reasoning (*aṣḥāb al-ra'y*) and those who use Tradition (*aṣḥāb al-ḥadīth*). *Ra'y* in Islamic jurisprudence is similar both linguistically and conceptually to *re'aya* in Jewish law. Both systems of law ultimately moved toward restricting individual judgement in order to attain consensus. On *ra'y* and *qiyās*, see Ignaz Goldziher, *The Ẓāhirīs: Their Doctrine and their History*, tr. W. Behn (Leiden, 1971), 3–4; Judith Wegner, "Islamic and Talmudic Jurisprudence: The Four Roots of Islamic Law and Their Talmudic Counterparts," in *The American Journal of Legal History* 26 (1982): 44–45; Schacht, *Introduction*, 34–35; idem, *Origins*, 129–30; Coulson, *History*, 42–43; 61.

3. See for example, Schacht, *Introduction*, 69ff., Coulson, *History*, 81.

4. See Wael B. Hallaq, "Was the Gate of Ijtihād Closed?" in *International Journal of Middle East Studies* 16 (1984): 3–41, 3–4ff. Hallaq notes on page 3 that W. M. Watt seemed already to be aware of inaccuracies in the standard view, but did not yet propose an alternative model. Cf. Watt, "The Closing of the Door of Igtihād," *Orientalia Hispanica* I (Leiden, 1974), 676, 678.

5. Ghazzālī, for example, believed that everyone who had the power of reasoning was obligated to rationalize his religious faith and even to act in religious matters according to his independent judgment. In his critique of the Shī'ite notion of the infallible Imām upon whom one must rely, Ghazzālī writes: "For instance, if a man is in doubt about the *qiblah* [the direction in which Mecca lies, in which a Muslim must face in saying his prayers], the only course open to him is to pray according to his independent judgment [*ijtihād*]. If he were to go to the city of the Imām to obtain a knowledge of the *qiblah*, the time of prayer would be past. As a matter of fact prayer fulfills the law even when directed to what is wrongly supposed

to be the *qiblah*. There is the saying that the man who is mistaken in independent judgment [*ijtihād*] receives a reward, but the man who is correct [receives] a twofold reward; and that is the case in all questions left to independent judgment." The saying to which Ghazzālī alludes is a well-known *ḥadīth* (see al-Bukhari, *I'tiṣām* 13, 20, 21), which is also often quoted in the beginning of Jewish responsa in medieval times. See *Munqidh*, 112–15; Watt, 46–48; McCarthy, 84–85; Lazarus-Yafeh, *Studies* 501; Schacht, *Introduction*, 71–73.

6. Coulson, *History*, 53–57; Goldziher, *The Ẓāhirīs*, 20–25; Schacht, *Introduction*, 48; idem, *Origins*, 256–59. This conventional view is also disputed by Hallaq, ibid., 587–605.

7. Muḥammad ibn ʿAbd al-Karim-al-Shahrastānī, *al-Milal wa-al-niḥal*, ed. W. Cureton (London, 1846), 154. Tr. Goldziher, *The Ẓāhirīs*, 6.

8. Ibn Ḥazm, however, replaced *qiyās* with the "implicit sense" (*mafhūm*) of the text. The term *ẓāhiri* derives from the term *ẓāhir*, the "outward," literal sense of the text, in contrast to its inward, hidden meaning (*bāṭin*). Shaʿbī is attributed with the famous rejection of *ra'y*: "*Ra'y* is like a carcass; it is used as food in an extreme emergency only." Goldziher, *The Ẓāhirīs*, 7 and n.1; Edward E. Salisbury, "Contributions from Original Sources to Our Knowledge of the Science of Muslim Tradition," *JAOS* n.116.

9. Originally, the term *sūlūjismūs* was employed. See al-Fārābī, "Treatise on the Canons of the Art of Poetry," tr. A. Arberry, "Fārābī's Canons of Poetry," *Revista degli Studi Orientali* 17 (1937): 268 (Arabic), 274 (English).

10. *qiyās al-ghā'ib ʿala-l-shāhid*. Joseph Van Ess, "The Logical Structure of Islamic Theology," in *Logic in Classical Islamic Culture*, ed. G. E. von Grunebaum (Wiesbaden, 1970), 21–50, 33. See below, 75, 90, 98.

11. See above, p. 2 n.2.

12. See Lasker, "Judah Halevi and Karaism," 122; idem, "Islamic Influences on Karaite Origins," 31–32; idem, "Karaism in Twelfth-Century Spain," 179–95; Shmuel Poznanski, "*Anan et ses écrits*," *REJ* 44 (1902): 182, n.3; Zvi Ankori, *Karaites in Byzantium*, 217, 223, n.38; idem, "Karaites and Karaism," *EJ* 777–80; Zucker, "Fragments from Rav Saʿadya Gaon's Commentary to the Pentateuch from Mss," *Sura* 2 (1955–56) (Hebrew), 330–31 and n.47; Naphtali Wieder, *The Judean Scrolls and Karaism* (London, 1962), 62–63, 76–77, 77 n.2.

13. Moshe Zucker, ibid.; idem, "*Qeṭaʿim mi-Kitāb taḥṣīl al-sharāʿi al-samʿiyya li-Rav Saʿadya Gaon*," *Tarbiz* 41 (1971–72), 383ff.

14. *Naql* is a standard Islamic term for true tradition. As we saw above, *ra'y* is a term for individual legal opinion, the personal reasoning of individual legal scholars. Shafīʿi, however, narrowed the scope of individual opinion accepted as a root of law to that based on the method of analogy (*qiyās*) alone. See above, nn.2, 6; Zucker, "*Qeṭaʿim*," 375–76.

15. The rabbis' principles of Biblical interpretation (*middot*) function in the way *qiyās* does in Islamic law. See Zucker, *Qeṭaʿim*, 378, 376 n.17; Jay Harris, *How*

Do We Know This? Midrash and the Fragmentation of Modern Judaism (New York, 1994), 76–80.

16. Zucker, "*Qeṭa'im*," 393. See especially the fragment from the beginning of Sa'adya's commentary on Leviticus published by Zucker, Cambridge ms. T-S 50.159, ibid., 375–76. Zucker notes interesting Islamic parallels to this argument in the works of al-Shafī'i, Ghazzālī, and the Mu'tazilite 'Abd al-Jabbar. Ghazzālī may thus parallel Ha-Levi by framing a critique of *qiyās* in both legal and philosophical domains. However, Ha-Levi's critique extends beyond these two spheres as well. Ibid., 379–80.

17. Sa'adya's arguments show that he was familiar with Islamic definitions of the various forms of *qiyās* (ibid., 322–24, 327). Zucker even finds a close Islamic parallel for Sa'adya's anti-Karaite argument that one cannot derive through *qiyās* the branches of religious law from the roots revealed in Scripture. Zucker argues that not only is the Karaite-Rabbanite debate over *qiyās* parallel to the Islamic debate between the Party of Tradition and the Party of Reason, but that Sa'adya and the Islamic Traditionist Ibn Ḥazm in fact drew their arguments from a common source: Dāwūd al-Ẓāhirī. For Islamic parallels, see Ibn Qutayba, *Kitāb ta'wīl mukhtalif al-ḥadīth* (Cairo, 1326), 70; cited by Zucker, "Fragments," 327 and n.46, and by Schacht, *Origins*, 129, 331.

18. III:39, III:41, III:43, III:47, III:49, III:53, III:65, III:67; Moshe Zucker, *Perushe Rav Sa'adia Gaon le-Vereshit* (Jerusalem, 1984), 16 (Arabic), 187–88 (Hebrew).

19. III:39, III:41.

20. Ya'qūb al-Qirqisānī, *Kitāb al-anwār wa-l-marāqib*, ed. L. Nemoy (New York, 1939), II:10, 11, 98–99; A. S. Halkin, "*Mi-petiḥat Rav Sa'adya Gaon le-ferush ha-Torah*" in *Sefer ha-yovel li-khevod Levi Ginzberg* (New York, 1945) 132 n.19; Zucker, "*Qeṭa'im*," 374.

21. Yefet uses the term *madhāhib*, plural of *madhhab*, a school, ideology, doctrine or teaching; also the technical term given to the major schools of Islamic law.

22. *istikhrāj*—the tenth form verbal noun of *kharaja*, "to go out," hence, "taking out, drawing forth, deduction, inference."

23. Yefet b. 'Elī, Commentary to Exodus 21, British Museum Manuscript 2468, p. 7; see Zucker, "*Qeṭa'im*," 374–75.

24. In the introduction to his Torah commentary, Sa'adya lists seven arguments for the necessity of oral law. These seven arguments have a common root: the Torah did not spell out the details of *mitsvot* required to fulfill them, or in some cases did not mention them at all. Halkin, "*Mi-petiḥat Rav Sa'adya Gaon*," 134, 143–47; Harris, *How Do We Know This?* 76.

25. See Harris, 78; Zucker, "*Qeṭa'im*," 378.

26. *tafsīr halakhot*

27. *tafsīr pasuq*

28. *Taqlīd* is necessary (*wājib*); on *taqlīd*, see below, 64–65.

29. *Ijtihād*. See below, pp. 65–68.

30. Ha-Levi uses the the standard Islamic term for sound tradition (*naql*) to describe both cases. Either the rabbis possess a specific tradition (*naql*) on the exegesis of the verse and they are simply using the method of *asmakhta*, or they possess by tradition (*naqlan*) methodological secrets for interpreting verses using the thirteen hermeneutical principles. From Ha-Levi's language it is possible, but less likely, that the methodological secrets the rabbis possess are other than an application of the thirteen principles (III:73: 143).

31. III:23: 112–14; III:7: 95–96.

32. III:38: 120–21. On Karaite *taqlīd*, see below pp. 64–65.

33. Al-Qirqisānī, *Kitāb al-anwār* I:3, I:10, 22, 51 (Arabic); tr. L. Nemoy, "Al-Qirqisānī's Account of the Jewish Sects and Christianity," *HUCA* 7 (1930): 340, 381; tr. B. Shiesa and W. Lockwood, "Ya'qub al-Qirqisānī on Jewish Sects and Christianity: A Translation of *Kitāb al-anwār* Book I and Two Introductory Essays," in *Judentum und Umwelt* (Frankfurt am Main, 1984), vol. 10, pp. 113, 143, 144 (English); Naphtali Wieder, *The Judean Scrolls and Karaism*, 213 n.3.

34. *yataʿaqqalu*

35. *yataḥakkamu*

36. Ha-Levi here echoes a Karaite critique of Saʿadya's. In his rhymed work *Esa Meshali*, Saʿadya argues that because they rely upon their own exegesis of Scripture, Karaites have no certainty or stability in their system of law. "Verily they give their lives for one of the laws; if only they had lived, it would, in time, have changed." Saʿadya extends this critique to normative rabbinic *halakhah*: if *midrash halakhah* genuinely created law, rabbinic law could fall victim to the anarchy that plagues the Karaites. Hence Saʿadya insists that rabbinic *midrash* is pure *asmakhta*, that the rabbis are faithful transmitters of tradition, rather than creators of legislation. See Saʿadya, *Esa meshali: sefer milḥemet ha-rishon neged ha-Qara'im*, ed. B. Lewin (Jerusalem, 1942), 32, lines 9–10; Harris, *How Do We Know This?* 178.

37. R. J. McCarthy translates *taqlīd* as "servile conformism" and explains: "The word contains the basic notion of putting a rope on an animal's neck; then, to put on a necklace; then, to copy, imitate, ape; then, to follow someone blindly and to accept a thing without hesitation or question." McCarthy, *Freedom and Fulfillment* 116 n.4; Lazarus-Yafeh, *Studies* 488.

38. For R. Hai's responsum, see B. Lewin, *Otsar ha-Geonim: Rosh Ha-Shanah*, 60–61. A portion of this responsum has recently been translated into English by Tsvi Groner; see Groner, *The Legal Methodology of Hai Gaon* (Chico, Calif., 1985), 16–17.

39. *mu'ayyadan bi-'amrin ilāhiyyin*. For the concept of divine assistance (*ta'yīd*), see below, pp. 121, 127–29.

40. *maʿna*

41. III:32: 117; III:35: 117; III:50: 131.

42. *arā'ahum*. Sing: *ra'y*. *Yajtahidūna* is related to *ijtihād*.

43. related to *qiyās*

44. *taḥakkum*

45. *manqūlan*, related to *naql*, sound tradition

46. III:37: 120. David Kaufmann traced this motif to a passage in Ghazzālī. Ghazzālī writes that theology (*kalām*) is necessary to defend the faith against heretical attacks, just as pilgrims to Mecca need bodyguards to protect themselves against robbers. If the marauding robbers would give up their attacks, the pilgrims would no longer need escorts; just so, if heretics would give up their disputes, the science of *kalām* would be unnecessary. Ghazzālī goes on to say that *kalām* does not know anything about the truths of God and metaphysics in themselves. Kaufmann cites this motif as proof that Ha-Levi read Ghazzālī's *Iḥyā' 'ulūm al-dīn*. Ghazzālī, *Iḥyā' 'ulūm al-dīn* (Bulaq, 1872–73), I:22; *The Book of Knowledge*, tr. N. A. Faris (Lahore, 1962), 54–55; Kaufmann, "R. Yehudah Ha-Levi," in Fishman, 184 n.112; idem, *Attributenlehre*, 137 n.53. For an evaluation of Kaufmann's thesis, see below, 75–78, 171–174.

47. *ijtihād fi-wājib* III:32: 117.

48. *ṣidq*

49. III:47: 127. There are certain Islamic parallels for the positive use of *ijtihād*; even in conservative legal circles, scholars are praised for their *ijtihād* in transmitting tradition faithfully.

50. III:73: 144, 146.

51. III:49: 130–31.

52. *dhawq . . . qiyās*. The *Ḥaver* here uses the terms *dhawq* (ṭaste) and *qiyās* as parallels, whereas elsewhere he uses them as opposites (see Part 3). Here *qiyās* seems to mean something akin to personal opinion. For instances in which he uses the term *qiyās* to mean "common sense," see below, p. 71.

53. *madhāhib*, a technical term for the major schools of Islamic law. Ha-Levi here echoes an internal Karaite critique of the tenth century Karaite Qirqisānī. See Qirqisānī, *Kitāb al-anwār*, I: 2, I:19, pp. 14, 63; Nemoy, "Al-Qirqisānī's Account," 330, 396.

54. *al-manqūl*—related to *naql*

55. *al-maktūb*—that which is written

56. Literally: the analogies (*qiyāsāt*) used in the established tradition (*al-qiyāsāt al-musta'mala bi-l-qanūn al-manqūl*). It is clear that Ha-Levi is here using *qiyās* as an overarching term for rabbinic modes of interpretation, not confined to analogy (*heqesh*); Sa'adya does the same. See Halkin, "*Mi-petiḥat Rav Sa'adya Gaon,*" 132 n.19.

57. *al-qiyāsāt al musta'mala bi-l-qanūn*

58. Compare Ibn Khaldun's statement that in contrast to the philosophical sciences, which use intellect (*'aql*), in the traditional sciences—under which he includes both theology (*kalām*) and jurisprudence (*fiqh*)—"there is no place for the intellect

(*ʿaql*) . . . save that the intellect may be used in connection with them to relate the branches (*furūʿ*) of their problems with the roots (*usūl*)." Ibn Khaldun, *Muqāddimah*, vol. II, 385, lines 11–12. Quoted by Wolfson, *Kalām*, 5–6.

59. See Yaʿaqov Gartner, "*Hashpaʿatam shel avale tsion ʿal minhage tishʿa be-av bi-tequfat ha-geonim*," *Annual of Bar-Ilan University: Studies in Judaica and Humanities* 20–21 (1983): 128–44; see also Moshe Zucker, "*Teguvot li-tenuʿat avale Tsion ha-Qar'iyim be-sifrut ha-rabbanit*," in *Sefer ha-yovel li-Rabbi Hanokh Albeck* (Jerusalem, 1963), 378–401. On Karaite asceticism, see Naphtali Wieder, *The Judean Scrolls and Karaism*, 97–103.

60. Schweid, "Literary Structure," 257–72; *Taʿam va-haqasha*, 37–79.

61. See Lasker, "Judah Halevi and Karaism," 123–24.

62. III:7: 95; IV:13: 164; I:65: 17; V:14: 212. Kaufmann notes that Ha-Levi almost feels sorry for the philosophers who torment themselves and yet do not find that which could be theirs without effort. See Kaufmann, *Attributenlehre*, 122.

63. Cf. Lasker, "Judah Halevi and Karaism," 123 n.57.

64. *mujarrad fikra*: lit, thought alone. Ghazzālī, on the other hand, apparently believed he could provide not just a dialectical argument, but adequate philosophical proof that the world was created in time. Cf. Baneth, "*Halevi ve-al-Ghazzālī*," 317 (English, 186).

65. "Creation of the world [from nought] [*ḥudūth*] is known by authentic tradition [*naql*] from Adam, Noah, and Moses by prophecy, which is more trustworthy [*aṣdaqu*] than *qiyās*." I:67.

66. Cf. Lasker, ibid., 123. On *naql*, see above, pp. 59–62; below, 211 n.116.

67. For example, the nature of God, the angels, and human immortality.

68. *mashhad*. See below, pp. 94, 115, 117.

69. Or: vision (*baṣar*). Lit: "which has a vision clearer than *qiyās*" (*li-l-nubuwwa baṣar ājla min al-qiyās*).

70. Compare Ghazzālī's comments on philosophers' explanation for the revolution of the spheres: "They are fantasies that achieve nothing; the secrets of the universe [*asrār malakūt al-samawāt*] will never be uncovered by such fantasies. God informs his prophets and pious friends [*awliyā'*] of them by way of inspiration [*ilhām*], not by way of demonstration [*istidlāl*]." Al-Ghazzāli in M. Bouyges, ed., *Al-Gazel: Tahāfot al-Falasifāt* (Beirut, 1927), Problem 15, 252; S. A. Kamali, tr. *Al-Ghazālī's Tahāfut al-Falāsifāt* (Incoherence of the Philosophers) (Lahore, 1958), 170–71. Cited by Kaufmann, *Attributenlehre*, 132.

71. *yaltazimu ṭāʿa*. See above, 42–44.

72. Compare Ghazzālī's autobiographical account in *al-Munqidh*.

73. Ha-Levi alludes to the midrash on his experience at Ur of the Chaldeans. See below, pp. 90, 93, 152, 154–156.

74. This is the view of al-Ghazzālī, as we have noted above, 201, n.5. Among Jews, Baḥya ibn Paqūda's view of *taqlīd* is very similar to that of al-Ghazzālī: he

holds that rationalizing the faith is incumbent upon everyone of sound mind. Baḥya compares the person who relies upon tradition to a person who is blind, led by someone who can see. He then uses the image of a company of blind people, all led by one person who can see, to describe a person who learns from others who themselves only learned by *taqlīd*. If the leader should fail to watch over those in his or her charge, or should any among the company stumble or fall, the company as a whole would fall down. Baḥya's intent, therefore, is to show the danger of *taqlīd*: if one does not come to an understanding for oneself, one can easily stumble or be led astray by counter-arguments from heretics. Note that his sense of "seeing" for oneself in this parable is intellectual rather than experiential.

Sufis also denounced *taqlīd*, as did certain orthodox thinkers. Among Sufis, al-Qushayri quotes Abū Muḥammad al-Jarīrī: "One who has not grasped the knowledge of unification [*tawḥīd*] by proofs—his foot of arrogant pride has slipped into the abyss of destruction. That is to say, one who relies on *taqlīd* and does not contemplate proofs of *tawḥīd* has fallen off the paths of salvation and fallen down into the clutches of perdition." Al-Qushayri, *Risāla*, Introduction, 3; Baḥya, *Al-Hidāja*, ed. Yahuda, 15ff., 39–40; ed. Qafih, 25ff., 49. Georges Vajda, *La theologie ascetique de Baḥya ibn Paqūda*, 18 and n.1. For Ghazzālī on *taqlīd*, see Ghazzālī, *Iḥyā' 'ulūm al-dīn* (Cairo, 1356/57) IV:1, p. 2081, 2121; *Mizān al-'amal* (Cairo, 1328), 212ff.; Lazarus-Yafeh, *Studies*, 488ff.; 361; 59, 197–99, 448–50, 488–502; W. Montgomery Watt, *Muslim Intellectual: A Study of al-Ghazālī* (Edinburgh, 1963), 164–65. On *taqlīd* in general, see Toshihiko Izutsu, *The Concept of Belief in Islamic Theology* (Tokyo, 1965), 119ff.; Joseph van Ess, *Die Erkenntnislehre des 'Aḍudaddīn al-Icī: Ubersetzung und Kommentar des 1. Buches seiner Mawāqif* (Wiesbaden, 1966), 44ff.

75. This observation is made also by Ghazzālī: "And how many people have I seen believing in sheer heresy only because of their blind following of ['*Taqlīdan li'*] Plato and Aristotle and a group of philosophers of good fame. Their motive in doing so is to be accepted in the circles of the philosophers and not be included among those who are supposed to be less intelligent than the philosophers." Ghazzālī, *Faḍā'iḥ al-bāṭiniyya wa-faḍā'il al-mustaẓhiriyya*, ed. A. Badawi (Cairo, 1964), 35, tr. Lazarus-Yafeh, *Studies*, 493.

And in the *Tahāfut*: "They [the philosophers] are heretics who have nothing to rely upon for their heresies but tradition blindly accepted from hearsay and habit, like the blindly accepted traditions of Jews and Christians, who are born and grow up in a religion different from that of Islam, as their fathers and forefathers did." Ghazzālī, *Tahāfut al-falāsifa*, ed. M. Bouges (Beirut, 1927), 4; tr. Lazarus-Yafeh, *Studies*, 448.

76. IV:17: 169; V:14: 212; IV:25: 183–84.

77. *faylasufan 'āliman 'ābidan*

78. *shawqan li-llahi*

79. Ha-Levi uses almost identical terms to describe the God-loving prophet in IV:15–16; he is said to become "a servant of God ['*ābid*], passionately in love ['*āshiq*] with the object of his worship [*ma'būdihi*]. . ." and to discover that "the Lord one yearns for with a yearning [*shawq*] one tastes [*dhawqan*] and directly experiences

[witnesses] [*mushāhadatan*]" [*yutashawwaqa shawqan dhawqan wa-mushāhadatan*] (IV:15–16: 168).

80. *'amr ilāhī*. See below, 84–87.

81. Or: are aware.

82. *ittiṣālika bihi*

83. The *Ḥaver* asserts in IV:3 that demonstration enabled the dualists to posit two eternal causes. Kaufmann traces this notion to the fifth disputation in Ghazzālī's *Tahāfut al-falāsifa*, in which Ghazzāli shows philosophers that their proofs do not even contain the means for refuting dualism. Kaufmann, *Attributenlehre*, p. 131; Ghazzālī, *Tahāfut*, ed. Bouyges, 143–62; tr. S. A. Kamālī, 96–108.

84. See Kaufmann, "*Yehuda Halewi und Ghazzālī*," in *Geschichte des Attributenlehre*, p. 119.

85. On this issue, see Maimonides, *Guide* I:62–64; Wolfson, *Philo* I:19, 210; II:120, 121; Shlomo Pines, "*Celui qui est*," in *Celui qui est: interpretations juives et chrétiennes d'Éxode 3,14*, ed. A. de Libera and E. Zum Brunn (Paris, 1986), 15–24. See also below, p. 101.

86. Or show.

87. I:67: 18; I:89: 25.

88. On the tension between direct experience and tradition, cf. Silman, *Filosof*, 163 n.6; (English) 86 n.5.

89. The *Ḥaver* explains: "Then Cain and Abel knew Him after their *taqlīd* on their father, in prophetic *mushāhada*, then Noah. Then Abraham, Isaac, and Jacob, until Moses and those prophets who came after him. They called him Lord by [in] their *mushāhada*." (IV:3: 148–49)

This passage is quite difficult to translate. Did Cain and Abel themselves have a direct experience, after relying on their father? Or did they simply rely on their father, who knew God through *mushāhada*? I have translated literally, but I understand the passage according to the first interpretation, and so could translate: "Then Cain and Abel knew him in prophetic *mushāhada* only after their reliance on their father."

90. V:14: 208–9; IV:25: 183. See Baneth, "*Yehudah ha-Levi ve-al-Ghazzālī*," 315–16; (English) 185–86.

91. IV:17: 169; V:14: 212; IV:25: 183–84.

92. It is true that in contrast to characteristic medieval philosophers such as Sa'adya or Maimonides, Ha-Levi does not believe it necessary to show the correspondence between faith and reason, between the principles of Judaism and scientific metaphysics. Nevertheless, the *Ḥaver* declares in no uncertain terms that the Torah and reason are in accord. The difference between Ha-Levi and Maimonides is that for Maimonides there is a religious obligation to prove for oneself the accord between faith and reason, an obligation Ha-Levi's *Ḥaver* denies (V:1: 191; V:16: 213).

As Davidson and Wolfson have shown, the typical medieval philosopher considered it a religious obligation not only to believe in the existence of God but to verify God's existence through rational proof. Even the obligation to love God required study of physics and metaphysics in order to cultivate appreciation of God's world. Maimonides codified these ideas in his code of Jewish law, the *Mishneh Torah*. Maimonides stresses the importance of a systematic study of physics and metaphysics in order to increase one's knowedge, awe, and love of the Divine. It is precisely this kind of religious rationalism that is foreign to Ha-Levi.

Maimonides' purpose is to reconcile religion and philosophy for those whose faith may have been shaken by Aristotelianism. Sa'adya lived before the full impact of Aristotelian philosophy had been felt, and thus saw philosophy as a tool to bolster faith. Ha-Levi, in contrast to both, seeks to show that Jewish tradition is self-supporting and does not need the bolstering of philosophy. See Isadore Twersky, "Some Non-Halakhic Aspects of the *Mishneh Torah*" in *Jewish Medieval and Renaissance Studies* (Cambridge, 1967), 95–118; Herbert Davidson, "The Study of Philosophy as a Religious Obligation," in Goitein, ed., *Religion in a Religious Age* (Cambridge, 1974); Wolfson, "What Is New in Philo?" in *Philo*, 439–60; idem, "The Double Faith Theory in Saadia, Averroes, and St. Thomas, and Its Origin in Aristotle and the Stoics," in *Studies* I, 583–618; Heschel, "The Quest for Certainty in Sa'adia's Philosophy," *JQR* 33 (1942–43), 265–313; Efros, "Sa'adya's Theory of Knowledge," *Studies in Medieval Jewish Philosophy*, 7–36.

93. *'iyānan, burhānan*

94. I:67: 18; I:89: 25.

95. For the problem of mistaken experience, see below, p. 216 n.33; pp. 103–105.

96. *'iyān, mushāhada*

97. Cf. I:87–91: 24–27.

98. In perhaps the ultimate irony, the *Ḥaver* asserts that Aristotle decided on the eternity of the world through his intellect because he lacked a tradition accepted upon *taqlīd*. (I:65: 17–18).

99. *al-ghā'ib*

100. *al-shāhid*

101. IV:2–3: 148; see above, 202 n.10; below, 90, 98.

102. Wolfson notes that the term *kalām*—which literally means "speech" or "word"—is used to translate the Greek term *logos* (word, reason, or argument), but also to designate any special branch of learning. The participle *mutakallim* (pl. *mutakallimūn*) signifies the master or exponent of that special branch of learning. Thus Ha-Levi in V:14 refers to "people belonging to the same school of *mutakallimūn* . . . such as the school of Pythagorus, the school of Empedocles, the school of Aristotle . . ." (p. 212). In that passage he is clearly referring to thinkers in a broad sense, and not theologians in the more specialized, Islamic sense of the term. (Contrast Strauss, above, Introduction, p. 19, n.42.)

The term *kalām* also took on the technical Islamic sense of the discussion of articles of faith (theology) in contrast to discussion of matters of law (*fiqh*), and *mutakallimūn* were those whose specialty was theological discussion. Ha-Levi uses the terms *kalām* and *mutakallimūn* in the latter, technical sense in V:1 and V:15–16.

In V:15 he speaks of the "*uṣūliyyīn*, who are called by the Karaites 'practitioners of the science of *kalām* [*aṣḥāb 'ilm al-kalām*]'" (213). And in V:1, the King asks to be instructed about "the principles [*uṣūl*] and beliefs [*'aqā'id*] according to the method of the *mutakallimūn* who are involved in dialectics [or: dispute *jadaliyyīn*]," 191. See Wolfson, *The Philosophy of the Kalām*, 1–8.

103. Modern scholars such as Van Ess and Wolfson tend to agree. They characterize the method of *kālam* as fundamentally apologetic and polemical, noting that it does not offer apodictic proofs, but merely rebuts the arguments of opponents as they arise. Maimonides dismisses *kalām* for the same reasons. See Ibn Khaldūn, *Al-Muqāddima*, volume 3, 155 and 34; *Prolegomenes d'Ebn-Khaldoun, Texte Arabe par E. Quatremere* (Paris, 1858), volume 3, 123; volume 3, 27. Cited by Van Ess, "The Logical Structure of Islamic Theology," 24; for other classical definitions of *kalām* with the same tenor, see *Die Erkentnisslehre des Aḍudaddin al-Ici*, 39 and 52ff., and the words of Van Ess, "The Logical Structure of Islamic Theology," 24–25; Maimonides, *Guide* I:71 and the observations of Shlomo Pines, "Translator's Introduction: The Philosophic Sources of the *Guide of the Perplexed*," *Guide* volume 1, lxxxiii–lxxxvi.

104. V:1–2; 191; V:16: 213.

105. Literally: according to the method of the theologians (*mutakallimūn*) who are dialecticians (*jadaliyyīn*) (*'ala ṭarīqa al-mutakallimīn al-jadaliyyīn*).

106. *ṭīb al-nafs*. See nns 115–116; my dissertation, 121 n.185.

107. *baḥth*

108. *'ilm*

109. *zandaqa*

110. Wolfson maintains that Ha-Levi is not here arguing against studying metaphysics without the necessary preliminary discussion of physical concepts, as Maimonides cautions. Rather, Wolfson argues, the *Ḥaver* asserts that he will describe metaphysics with levels, i.e., with "graded ranks of beings, such as he himself describes later in his exposition of the Neoplatonized Aristotelian system of emanation." Wolfson's reading is plausible, but I am not convinced it is necessary to read the passage in this way. See Wolfson, *The Philosophy of the Kalām*, 87–88.

111. *yadhūqu*: literally, "taste." On Ghazzālī, see Efros, "Mysticism," 178.

112. *ishāra*. On teaching by hints, compare Maimonides' introductory letter to his student in the *Guide*: *Dalālat al-Ḥā'irīn*, 1; Even-Shemuel, *Moreh ha-Nevukhim*, 3; Pines, *Guide*, 3.

113. *akhyār*, plural of *khayyir* (cf. III:1)

114. See Ghazzālī, *Iḥyā' 'ulūm al-dīn* III:1, p. 1368:9–15. Cited by Lazarus-Yafeh, *Studies*, 489 n.2.

115. See Van Ess, *Die Erkentnisslehre des 'Adudaddīn al-Icī* 46, 75ff. Thus the *Ḥaver* tells the King: "I communicated these principles to you lest the philosophers confuse you, and you might think that if you follow them, your soul would find rest in satisfactory proof [*la-araḥat nafsuka bi-l-burhān al-shāfī*]" (IV:25: 183).

116. Translators from Ibn Tibbon on have translated both *naql* and *taqlīd* as *mesorah*, *qabbalah* or "tradition," confusing two distinct concepts which are not interchangeable. In Islamic parlance, *naql* is true, sound tradition, and always has a positive connotation. *Taqlīd* is unquestioning reliance, and is most often looked upon as a necessary evil for the simple-minded.

In IV:17, the *Ḥaver* proclaims: "All who follow the divine law [*al-nāmūs al-ilāhī*] follow the people of this seeing. Their souls find pleasantness [*ta ṭuayyaba*] in *taqlīd* upon them, [despite] the simplicity of their speech and the coarseness of their examples, a pleasantness they do not find in *taqlīd* on the philosophers, [despite] the fineness of their examples, and the fine order of their compositions, and the proof [*burhān*] that appears to them. Nevertheless the masses do not follow them. Their souls are inspired [*wuḥiya*] with the truth, as it says, 'Words of truth are recognized'" (Sota 9b) (IV:17: 170).

And at the end of the *Ḥaver*'s exposition of the principles of rabbinic Judaism in Book Three, the King expresses his satisfaction thus: "You have given me pleasantness of soul [*ṭayyabta nafsī*] and strengthened my belief in sound tradition [*naql*]" (III:74: 146).

117. See Goldziher, "Asceticism and Sufism," in *Studies in Islamic Law and Theology*, tr. A. and R. Hamori (Princeton, 1981); Schimmel, *Mystical Dimensions*, 109–30.

118. See Allan Lazaroff, "Baḥya's Asceticism against Its Rabbinic and Islamic Background," *JJS*, 11–38; Vajda, *La théologie ascetique.*

119. *ʿubbād wa-zuhhad*

120. *taʿaqqul*

121. (or playing the judge): *taḥakkum*

122. *taḥduthu lahu rūḥaniyya*

123. *tashawwuq*, a Sufi term.

124. Perhaps Ha-Levi was also uncomfortable with the spiritual path laid out by Baḥya, who arranged *al-Hidāya* in a series of ten gates through which the soul travels in its journey towards God. Baḥya in fact seems to have followed the degrees of piety laid out by the Sufi teacher al-Makkī. Amos Goldreich observes that Baḥya may have seen the duties of the heart as an autonomous system of inner duties parallel to the 613 commandments. In contrast, *Kuzari* I:103, for example, describes Jacob's sons as ascending in purity and holiness, but not through a systematic path.

Strictly speaking, Sufi thinkers distinguished between spiritual stages or stations (*maqāmāt*), which could be mapped out and attained by the disciple, and mystical states (*aḥwāl*, sing. *ḥāl*), which could only be granted by the grace of God. On Sufi stages and states, see Abū Naṣr al-Sarrāj *Kitāb al-luma' fī'l-taṣawwuf*, ed. R. A. Nicholson (Leiden, 1914), 42; Nasr, "The Spiritual States in Sufism," 68–83; Goldreich, "Possible Arabic Sources," 193–96, 179–83; Abū Ṭālib al-Makkī, *Qūt al-qulūb fī muʿāmalāt al-maḥbūb* (Cairo, 1892–93); Vajda, *La théologie ascetique de Baḥya Ibn Paqūda*, 23; Mansoor, *The Book of Direction to the Duties of the Heart*, 31–32.

125. I:79: 20–21;, III:23: 112–15; III:53: 132–35.

126. I:79: 20–21;, III:23: 112–15; III:53: 132–35.

127. I:98:32; II:46: 68; III:23: 112; III:53: 135.

128. *itqarana*

129. *niyya khālisa*

130. Or: depends upon

131. Or: completion

132. Or: acceptance

133. *al-nāfiʿu bi-dhātihi*

134. *al-munfaʿa bi-dhātihi*

135. For the notion of prophets as physicians, dispensing medicine in the form of religious commandments, see Ghazzālī, *Munqidh*, 146, 161; Watt, 70, 82; McCarthy, 101–2, 111–12; *Iḥyā' ʿulūm al-dīn* IV:1, p. 2145. Cf. Bazat-Tahera Quṭbuddīn, "Healing the Soul: Perspectives of Medieval Muslim Writers," *Harvard Middle Eastern and Islamic Review* 2 (1995), 2:62–87.

136. *aṣḥāb al-rūḥaniyyāt*; *ba'ale ha-ruḥaniyyim*. See Shlomo Pines, "On the Term *Ruḥaniyyut* and Its Origin, and on Judah Ha-Levi's Doctrine" (Hebrew) *Tarbiz* 57 (1988), 511–34.

137. *'ulamā' mutaḥakkimīna*

138. Or: prophecied to (*nubbi'a*)

139. *al-ʿamal al-sharʿiyya*

140. lit: your having connected (*ittiṣālika*)

141. *taʿaqqul*

142. *al-naql al-saḥiḥ*

143. *niyya khālisa*

144. See above, n. 136.

145. *aṣḥāb al-ruhaniyyāt*

146. Or: acceptance (*riḍa*)

147. Pines, *Ruḥaniyyut*, 528–30.

148. *taʿaqqul*

149. *aʿmalihim al-qiyāsiyyāt*

150. Or choice (*ikhtiyār*)

151. See for example Psalm 115:4ff.; Psalm 135:15ff.; Isaiah 40:18–20; 42:17; 44:9–20; Jeremiah 2:28, 10:1–162.

152. Pines, "*Ruḥaniyyut*," 529.

153. I agree with Pines that Ha-Levi's overall attitude toward idolatry is more forgiving than that of other medieval Jewish thinkers, in particular Maimonides. For example, the *Ḥaver* exonerates the Israelites somewhat for worshiping the golden calf, arguing that they did not intend disloyalty to the God who had brought them out of Egypt; their sin, rather, lay in worshiping a form whose worship had not been

commanded, whereas "there was nothing strange in the forms of the cherubs, which (God) himself had commanded" (I:97: 32).

154. Ibid., 532.

155. For the issue of *ṭa'ame ha-mitsvot* in the history of Jewish thought, see Isaak Heinemann, *Ṭa'ame ha-mitsvot be-sifrut Yisrael* (Jerusalem, 1956–57).

Part 3

1. We have noted that this inductive form of proof was known as *qiyās al-ghā'ib 'ala-l-shāhid*: an argument from that which is hidden, not given to perception (*al-ghā'ib*)—especially God and the divine attributes—to that which is present or perceptible (*al-shāhid*). See Van Ess, "Logical Structure," 33; Wolfson, *Kalām*; above 58, 75; below 98.

2. *See Genesis Rabbah* 38, *Tanna deve Eliyyahu* 6.

3. *Sefer Yetsirah*—in Scholem's words, "the earliest extant Hebrew text of systematic, speculative thought"—was attributed to Abraham because of its closing: the author depicts Abraham as the first person to study and practice its ideas. In several manuscripts the work is subtitled "Alphabet of Our Father Abraham" (*Otiyyot de-Avraham Avinu*). Scholem, *Kabbalah*, 23–30; idem, *On the Kabbalah and Its Symbolism*, tr. R. Manheim (New York, 1965), 165–73.

4. Moses Ibn Ezra, for example, speaks of repenting for his life as a poet; poetry and philosophy were both seen to be secular studies, which serious scholars gave up after their youth. Moses Ibn Ezra, *Kitāb al-Muḥāḍara w'al-Mudhākara*, tr. into Hebrew as *Shirat Israel* by Ben-Tsion Halper (Leipzig, 1923–24), 85ff., 89, and Halper's introduction, 13. Ed.; Gerson Cohen, *The Book of Tradition (Sefer Haqabbalah) by Abraham Ibn Daud*, 102–3; 296–99.

5. "*En mazal le-yisrael.*" *Shabbat* 156a; *Nedarim* 32a. R. Yehudah quotes the Babylonian *amora* Rav, who interprets the verse in this way. The Palestinian Amora R. Yoḥanan, on the other hand, in proving that Israel is above astral influence cites the words of Jeremiah 10:2: "Thus says the Lord, 'Learn not the way of the nations, and be not dismayed at the signs of heaven, for the nations are dismayed at them.'" *Shabbat* 156a.

6. 'Abd al-Razzāq is a theosophical Sufi of the Ibn 'Arabī school. 'Abd al-Razzāq al-Qashāni, *Istilāhāt al-Sufiya* (Dictionary of the Technical Terms of the ṣufies), ed. A. Sprenger (Calcutta, 1845), 162. On *dhawq*, see Efros, "Some Aspects of Yehuda Halevi's Mysticism," 147–48 and nn.23–24. Efros mentions the *mushāhada-dhawq* connection, but not the exegetical link Ha-Levi makes with Psalm 34. Efros notes that *mushāhada* signifies "the general experience of beholding God, of which *dhawq* is the first taste." On *dhawq*, see also Warren Zev Harvey, "Judah Halevi's Synesthetic Theory of Prophecy amd a Note on the Zohar" (in Hebrew), *Jerusalem Studies in Jewish Thought 13* (1996) (Rivkah Schatz-Uffenheimer Memorial Volume), 151–52.

7. R. J. McCarthy draws an intuitive connection between Ghazzālī's use of *dhawq* and Psalm 34:8. He notes that the true meaning of the Biblical verse may be best conveyed in Dahood's translation—not as "taste and see that the Lord is good," but as "taste and drink deeply" for the Lord "is sweet." (Professor Wolfhart Heinrichs pointed out to me that this translation assumes that the verb *re'u* derives from the root *r-w-h*, "to be saturated, drink one's fill," rather than from *r-'-h*, "to see.") McCarthy writes: "The Hebrew verb is *ṭa'amu* (taste, relish, savor)—like the Arabic *ṭa'ima*. I think, then, that *dhawq* is not simply a kind of cognition, but an immediate experience accompanied by savoring, or relishing, and enjoyment, i.e., what I like to call a fruitional (fruitive) experience."

Hava Lazarus-Yafeh shows a development in Ghazzālī's thinking as he gropes for an appropriate metaphor for religious experience, moving from scent to taste. See 'Abd al-Razzāq al-Qashānī, *Istilāhāt al-ṣūfiyya*, 162; Translation here is my own. Efros, "Mysticism," 147–48 and nn.23–24; McCarthy, *Freedom and Fulfillment*, 133, n.162; Lazarus-Yafeh, Studies, 341–42, nn.70 and 71; 298–99, 194.

8. See the interesting remarks on visual experience by Silman, "The Visual Experience in the *Kuzari*," *Yearbook for Religious Anthropology: Ocular Desire* (Berlin, 1994), 117–26.

9. Isaiah 43:10, 12. Poznanski, "*Megillat Setarim*," 177–84. R. Nissim quotes Job 42:5: "I had heard of You by the hearing of the ear; but now my eye sees You," and comments: "Before, I knew your ways (*darkhe midotekha*) through hearsay and proofs, but now your knowledge is confirmed for me by the senses, such as sight." Poznanski, 177.

10. This profession of faith has its origin in Qur'ān III:18: "God bears witness (*shāhada*) that there is no god but He—and also do the angels and those possessed of knowledge—maintainer of justice; there is no god but He, the mighty, the wise."

11. While the term *shahīd* is used in the Qur'ān in the sense of ordinary theological witness, the technical sense of *shahīd* as witness unto death for the sake of the faith is a post-Qur'ānic development. At the same time the notion grew that the greater *jihād* or striving for the sake of the faith was not to be found on the outer battleground but in the inner field of one's own soul, in the struggle with one's passions. Thus grew the notion in Islam of the ascetic martyr, the person who experiences passionate love but restrains his passion and dies chaste. The tradition about martyrs of love appears first in Abū Bakr Muḥammad b. Dāwūd al-Iṣfahānī (868–910): "The Messenger of God—on him be blessing and peace—said: He who loves and remains chaste and conceals his secret and dies, dies a martyr" (*Kitāb al-Zahra, 66*).

We find another use of the root *sh-h-d* in the poetry of both sacred and secular love—the beloved is termed a *shāhid* (not to be confused with the martyr, *shahīd*); his beauty is held to be a physical testimony to the beauty of the Divine. To put it differently, the boy is a "thing present" (*shāhid*) which points to the "thing absent" (*ghā'ib*); the youth's beauty gives the contemplator some sense of the beauty of the Divine. Joseph Norment Bell, *Love Theory in Later Hanbalite Islam* (Albany, 1979), 140; Annemarie Schimmel, *Mystical Dimensions*, 76, 291; idem, *As through a Veil:*

Mystical Poetry in Islam (New York, 1982), 30; Lois Anita Giffen, *Profane Love*, 99–105.

12. *Mishnah Berakhot* 9:5; *BT Berakhot* 54a, 61b.

13. *dhawqan, lā qiyāsan*

14. Annemarie Schimmel intuits that there lies a deeper connection between witness and martyrdom than a mere coincidence of terminology. Quoting a Turkish poet, she asks rhetorically, "Is the poet, perhaps, declaring that death is the only legitimate way to express the secret of loving union? And does he aver that the ultimate experience is communicable through the silent language of martyrdom, for in the martyr [*shahīd*] God has His true witness [*shāhid*]?" Schimmel, *Mystical Dimensions*, 76.

15. *Mekhilta* on Exodus 20:16, *Pesikta Rabbati* 22, *Yalqut Shim'oni* 2: 447, 981; *Shir ha-Shirim Rabbah* 1:2–4, *Midrash Tehillim*, Psalm 88.

16. Midrashic literature too contrasts the people, who each heard the voice of God according to his or her capacity (*koaḥ*), with Moses who heard the voice as it was. See *Mishnat Rabbi Eliezer* 6:106; *Exodus Rabbah* 5:9.

17. See also below, 139–144, 108–109, 136–138.

18. Or: scene.

19. R. Nissim Gaon too had argued that the revelation at Mount Sinai was given to establish the truth of Moses' prophecy for those who doubted that God speaks to human beings. See *Megillat Setarim*, 178.

20. Cf. Ghazzālī, who asserts that the first tastes of prophecy take place at the beginning of the Sufi path; anyone who has not had a taste of this experience has no real idea of the meaning of prophecy. *Munqidh*, 134; McCarthy, 95; Watt, 61.

21. See above, p. 193, n.49.

22. Or: theophanies.

23. On Sufi stages and states, see above, p. 211, n.124. Later Sufi-influenced Jewish thinkers such as Abraham b. Maimonides and 'Ovadiah b. Abraham Maimonides depict their movement of Jewish pietism as a systematic path whose ultimate goal is the attainment of prophecy. Moses Maimonides, too, seems to suggest that prophecy can be cultivated by a moral and intellectual discipline. See Maimonides, *Mishneh Torah, Hilkhot yesode ha-Torah* 7:1: *mi-yad ruaḥ ha-qodesh shorah 'alav*; *Shemonah Peraqim*, Introduction, Sheilat, 375 (Arabic); 227–28 (Hebrew); Weiss-Butterworth, 60–61. Fenton, *Treatise of the Pool*, 8–11 and n.38–46.

24. Gauthier, *Ḥayy* 1–20 (French), 1–18; Goodman, 95–103.

25. Ghazzālī's epigram rhymes in the Arabic: *arbāb al-aḥwāl, lā asḥāb al-aqwāl.*

26. *bi-ṭarīq al-'ilmi*

27. Ghazzālī, *Munqidh*, 126; McCarthy, 90; Watt 55.

28. Gauthier, *Ḥayy* 18 (Arabic), 16 (French); Goodman, 102. Explaining the parable of the blind man who is given sight, Ibn Ṭufayl writes: "There is rarely found one who is of penetrating insight [*baṣīra*], whose vision [*baṣar*] is open,

without needing philosophical speculation [*naẓar*].” See below, 105–106. Gauthier, 9 (Arabic), 7 (French); Goodman, 98.

29. Gauthier, 7 (Arabic), 6 (French); Goodman, 87.

30. Ibn Sina, *Ishārāt*, ed. Forget, 56. Translation my own. See also the translation of Inati, *Remarks and Admonitions.*

31. Ibid., 213. Cf. Ghazzālī, *Iḥyā' ʿulūm al-dīn* (Cairo, 1910), part 4, p. 2946, line 5: “It is possible that there is also another, weaker *mushāhada*, a prophetic *mushāhada*, by which I mean *mushāhada* in dreams, which is among the lights of prophecy.”

32. A-M. Goichon, *Lexique de la langue philosophique d'ibn Sīnā* (*Avicenne*) (Paris, 1938), 165. Translation my own; emphasis the author's.

33. Avicenna pairs propositions whose assent we derive from the senses—those which offer information about the external world, such as the existence of the sun—with subjective propositions, direct perception of our inner states. On the question of whether medieval thinkers such as Avicenna took seriously the possibility of sensory error and illusion, see below, 103–105, which also explores whether what prophets witness in their visions constitutes an objective reality; cf. Silman, “Visual Experience,” 124. Saʿadya, *Kitāb al-mukhtār fī'l-amānāt wa'l-iʿtiqādāt*, tr. J. Qafih (Jerusalem: 1970), 17; *Saadia Gaon: The Book of Beliefs and Opinions*, tr. S. Rosenblatt (New Haven, 1948), 19–20.

34. Louis Gardet, *La Pensée réligieuse d'Avicenne* (Paris, 1951), p. 176. Translation from French my own.

35. *al-ladhdha al-ʿaqliyya*

36. *kunh aḥwāl*, plural of *ḥāl*, technical term for Sufi mystical state.

37. *al-mubāshara*

38. *bi-muyassar;* literally: made easy, within easy reach. Ibn Sīnā, *Sharh kitāb uthūlūjiya al-mansūb ʿilā Arisṭū li-'ibn Sīnā* (Glosses on the Theology of Aristotle) in *Arisṭū ʿind al-ʿArab*, ed. A. Badawi (Cairo, 1947), 44. Translation my own.

39. Ghazzālī speaks similarly of the difference between studying the causes and condition of drunkenness and actually experiencing the state of intoxication. *Munqidh*, 124–25; Watt, 55; McCarthy, 90.

40. *La yushar ilaihi*; *yushar* is related to *isharāt*, hints.

41. *athār*

42. the *dalīl*

43. *yadullu*

44. the *madlūl*

45. Saʿadya brings this *kalām* proof in his *Amānāt*. See Qafih, 18–19; Rosenblatt, 21.

46. See Van Ess, “Logical Structure,” 33.

47. *Istidlāl bi-l-shāhid ʿala l-ghā'ib or qiyās al-ghā'ib ʿala l-shāhid*. Van Ess, ibid., 34–35.

48. *ramaz* in Ibn Tibbon's translation.

49. Avicenna uses the same form of this verb (the fourth form, in its nominal form *ishāra*) in the title of his famous "Eastern" work in which he discusses Sufism, *al-Ishārāt wa-l-tanbīhāt*. *Ishārāt* is often translated as "directions" or "directives," viz., *The Book of Directives and Hints* (A-M. Goichon, tr. *Livre des directives et remarques*).

50. Literally: "reality of their being(s)." The expression *ḥaqiqat dhawātihim* is itself multivalent; each word is both a philosophical and mystical term for truth or essence. *Al-ḥaqq* is the truth or the true; *dhawāt* is the plural of *dhāt*, which signifies essence or being. The phrase could thus plausibly refer to discovering some essential truth about God conveyed by God's personal name Lord.

51. The *Ḥaver* introduces the subject of *mushāhada* specifically in answer to the question of how God can have a personal name when God cannot be pointed to or indicated—i.e., in answer to the question of how a transcendent God can be known.

The *Ḥaver*'s answer is that God can be "seen" in prophetic witness (*mushāhada nabawiyya*) and spiritual vision or insight (*baṣīra*). One who meets God in prophetic *mushāhada* knows the Divine in such a way that calling God by a personal name is entirely fitting. The *Ḥaver*'s words thus suggest the distinction between impersonal knowledge and personal knowledge, expressed in French by the terms *savoir* (to know a fact) and *connâitre* (to know a person or thing). *Mushāhada* offers personal, experiential knowledge, the sense in which we know someone because we have met that person and experienced his or her presence. To know or to see a person is an experience that is direct and unmediated, one that cannot occur vicariously—and this for Ha-Levi is the mode of prophetic knowing.

52. Or: in (*bi*) prophetic witness and in spiritual vision

53. Or: inference.

54. He goes on: "This is the faculty which philosophers call speculative or reflective [*al-quwwa . . . al-ʿāqila al-naẓariyya*]. However, when it is illumined by the holy light and its veil is withdrawn by the guidance of the Truth, philosophers call it the holy faculty." Jurjānī quotes this definition of *baṣīra* in his dictionary, and gives a similar definition for *dhawq*: "Taste [*al-dhawq*] in the knowledge [or knowing] [*maʿrifa*] of God is an expression for a knowing light [*nūr ʿirfānī*] which the Truth in his Revelation throws out into the hearts of his Companions, by which they distinguish between the true [*al-ḥaqq*] and the false, without their reporting [*yanqūlū*] it from a book or other [source]."

David Kaufmann called attention to the Sufi character of the terms in this passage (IV:3) in Ha-Levi, and mentions ʿAbd al-Razzāq. ʿAbd al-Razzāq, *Iṣṭilāḥāt*, ed. Sprenger, 16, "*baṣīra*." Translation given here is my own. Jurjānī, *Definitiones*, 47, 112; Kaufmann, *Attributenlehre*, 177 n.135. On the heart (*qalb*) as the center of spiritual knowledge (*maʿrifa*) and vision (*baṣīra*), see Louis Massignon, *Essai sur les origines du lexique technique de la mystique musulmane* (Paris, 1922), 172, 263; Wolfson, "Merkavah Traditions," 219 and n.125.

55. *kalām al-nubuwwa*

56. The continuation of Sa'adya's passage gives additional indication that Ha-Levi may have had it in mind. Sa'adya writes of the prophets: "When one of them sees this light, he says, 'I have seen the Glory of the Lord.' Often, however, he would say simply: 'I have seen God,' by way of ellipsis." Similarly, in IV:3 after the *Ḥaver* describes all the manifestations included under the rubric "Glory," Ibn Tibbon's Hebrew translation reads: "And they called that Glory of the Lord, and sometimes they called it Lord. And sometimes they called the ark Lord."

Some Arabic manuscripts leave out "and sometimes they called it Lord," and Baneth-Ben-Shammai suggest that the addition may be a scribal error. Even without the addition, Ha-Levi notes the ellipsis present in calling the ark of the Lord "Lord." If Ha-Levi did have the Sa'adya passage in mind, this argues for the additional phrase on calling the Glory "Lord" as authentic. See Baneth and Ben-Shammai, *Kitāb al-radd wa'l-dalīl*, 149, n.8; *Amānāt*, Qafih, 110–11; Rosenblatt, 130.

Elsewhere in the *Amānāt*, Sa'adya writes: "It is a form nobler even than [that of] the angels, magnificent in character, resplendent with light which is called the Glory [*Kavod*] of the Lord. It is this form, too, that one of the prophets described as follows: 'I beheld till thrones were placed, and one that was ancient of days did sit [Dan 7:9], and that the Sages characterized as Abiding [*Shekhinah*].'" *Amanāt*, 103–4; Rosenblatt, 121. Cf. below, 113, 118.

57. *al-khādir*

58. Or: indication

59. Philo presents a similar notion: we can only know that God is, not what God is. See Philo, *On Rewards and Punishments* 39; cf. Silman, *Filosof*, 158 (Hebrew), 178 (English). Compare this statement of Ghazzālī's in the *Munqidh*: "Doubt about prophecy touches either its possibility or its existence and its occurence, or its attainment by a specific individual. The proof [*dalīl*] of its possibility is its existence [*wujūd*]." Ghazzālī, *Munqidh*, 139; Watt, 65; McCarthy, 98.

60. *fikra*

61. related to *dhawq*

62. *taṭ'īm*. Avicenna, *Sharh Kitāb uthūlūjiya al-mansūb 'ilā Arisṭū li-ibn Sīnā* (*Glosses on the Theology of Aristotle*), *Arisṭū 'inda al-'Arab*, ed. A. Badawi (Cairo, 1947), 56.

Part 4

1. The Talmudic tractate *Ḥagigah* 14b describes the vision of the chariot (*merkavah*) as an "understanding of the heart" (*ovanta de-libba*). R. Ḥananel, a thinker of the gaonic period, uses the same phrase to characterize the visions of prophets: "The Holy One, blessed be he, makes his Glory visible to those who fear him and his pious ones through an understanding of the heart [*be-ovanta de-libba*] in the image of a man sitting, as it is written, 'I saw the Lord seated upon His throne' [I Kings 22:19]. . . . It is clear to us that the vision spoken of here is a vision of the

heart [*re'iyat ha-lev*] not a vision of the eye [*re'iyat ha-'ayin*]." [*Commentary to BT Berakhot 6a.*] R. Ḥananel likewise describes the vision of the four who entered *Pardes* as an understanding of the heart: "They did not ascend to heaven but they contemplated and saw by means of an understanding of the heart [*bi-ovanta de-libba*]." (Commentary to BT Ḥagigah 14b).

R. Nathan of Rome interprets R. Hai Gaon's description of the visionaries of the chariot similarly: "They do not ascend on high, but they see and envision in the chambers of their heart like a man who sees and envisions something clearly with his eyes, and they hear and speak with an eye that sees by means of the holy spirit (or: by means of a seeing eye, by the holy spirit [*be-'eyn ha-sokheh be-ruaḥ ha-qodesh*])." Here R. Nathan borrows a phrase used in Leviticus Rabbah 1:3 with reference to prophecy: "prophets who see by the Holy Spirit" [*nevi'im she-sokhim be-ruaḥ ha-qodesh*]. See *'Arukh Completum*, ed. A. Kohut (Vienna, 1926), 1:14, s.v. *avney shayish ṭahor*; Idel, *Kabbalah*, 88–91; Scholem, *Major Trends*, 49; Elliot Wolfson, "Merkavah Traditions in Philosophic Garb: Judah Halevi Reconsidered," *PAAJR* (1990–91), 215ff.

2. The metaphor of the inner eye is common in Sufi thought, which often speaks of the seeing of the heart (*ru'yat al-qalb*). See Abū Ṭālib al-Makkī, *Qūt al-qulūb* (Cairo, 1310) I, 235; cited by A. J. Wensinck, "On the Relation between Ghazālī's Cosmology and His Mysticism," *Mededeelingen der Koninklijke Akademie van Wetenschappen, Afdeeling Letterkunde*, Deel 75, Serie A, No. 6 (Amsterdam, 1933), 9; Ghazzālī, *Munqidh*, 138–40; McCarthy, 97–99; Watt, 64–66; Lazarus-Yafeh, *Studies*, 295–306.

3. Medieval philosophical texts spoke of internal senses, faculties residing within the brain and operating without bodily organs. Today we regard such phenomena—for example imagination, memory, estimation—as mental functions. Ha-Levi twice lists the various internal senses (III:5, V:12). In V:12—a passage drawn from Avicenna—he also describes how these internal senses function.

In the extended passage on prophecy in IV:3, however, the *Ḥaver* uses the term *internal sense* in a non-technical way. Ha-Levi is seeking a means to describe what goes on in the phenomenon of prophecy. Based on his knowledge of Arabic sources, he attributes it to a "sixth sense," which in IV:3 he describes alternately as: the inner sense (*al-ḥass al-bātin*), an inner eye (*'ayn bāṭina*), a vision (*baṣar*) clearer than logic (*qiyās*), and the spiritual eye (*al-'ayn al-ruḥāniyya*) by which the prophets were made superior (*fuḍḍilu*). He also explains that this inner eye "might almost be said to be" the imaginative faculty (*al-quwwa al-mutakhayyila*) insofar as it serves (supplies) the intellect. See Harry Wolfson, "The Internal Senses in Latin, Arabic, and Hebrew Philosophic Texts," *Studies* I, 250–52; Alfred Ivry, "The Philosophical and Religious Arguments in Rabbi Yehuda Halevi's Thought" (Hebrew) in *Thought and Action: Essays in Memory of Simon Rawidowicz on the Twenty-Fifth Anniversary of His Death*, ed. A. Greenbaum and A. Ivry (Tel Aviv, 1983), 28 and nn.13 and 14; Davidson, "Cuzari," *REJ*, 367 and n.4. See below, pp. 108–111.

4. Hebrew poets such as Moses and Abraham Ibn Ezra commonly speak about the eye of the intellect (*'eyn ha-sekhel*), using the phrase interchangably with eye of the heart (*'eyn ha-lev*). Cf. the words of the *Ikhwān al-ṣafā'*, below p. 105;

Yehudah Ratzaby, "Borrowed Elements in the Poems of Yehuda Halevi from Arabic Poetry and Philosophy" (Hebrew), *Molad* 5 (1975), 173; Wolfson, "Merkavah Traditions," 207 and n.90; 221 and n.134.

5. We have seen that R. Nissim Gaon argued similarly that the event at Mount Sinai gave Israel direct, irrefutable, sensible knowledge (*yed'iat ha-hargashot*) in contrast to knowledge by proofs (*yed'iat ha-re'ayot*) upon which he argues the other nations must rely. Poznanski, "*Megillat Setarim*," 178–80.

6. For a modern theologian who offers a similar argument with respect to communities of revelation, see H. R. Niebuhr, *The Meaning of Revelation* (New York, 1941).

7. Ghazzālī, for example, writes: "In general, then, the prophets [peace be upon them] are the healers of the maladies of hearts. Reason is simply useful to inform us of this; to testify to prophecy that [prophecy} is correct; and to itself that it is unable to reach what can be reached by the eye of prophecy; and to take us by our hands and turn us over to the prophets, [just] as blind men are handed over to guides and as troubled sick men are handed over to compassionate physicians. Thus far may the intellect proceed, but it is precluded from going beyond that, except to understand what the physician prescribes for it." Ghazzālī, *Munqidh*, 146; Watt, 70; McCarthy, 102; cf. Baḥya, *Al-Hidāja* I:2, ed. Yahuda, 39–40; Qafih, 49; Monsoor, 113.

8. Similarly, Ghazzālī sees *mushāhada* and *dhawq* as a bridge between the religious experience of Sufis at the beginning of their path and that of prophets. Lazarus-Yafeh notes the danger traditionalists would see in such a doctrine, which erases the distinction between prophets and others. Ha-Levi, however, extends this bridge to include not only the pious (*awliyā'*), but the entire people of Israel who stood at Mount Sinai. *Munqidh*, 134; Watt, 61; McCarthy, 95; Lazarus-Yafeh, *Studies*, 304–5.

9. A recurring theme in the *Kuzari* is that of mutually corroborating testimony. Ha-Levi draws from the Islamic legal tradition the concept of *tawātur*, the chain of tradition—ideally, that which is passed down by several independent chains of transmission, which taken together offer mutually corroborating testimony. Because independent chains of tradition give the same report, collusion and error are ruled out. Ha-Levi draws upon this concept with respect to prophetic visions as well as the transmission of law. Cf. IV:3: 157; I:25: 12; V:14: 213. On *tawātur*, see Aron Zysow, *The Economy of Certainty: An Introduction to the Typology of Islamic Legal Theory* (Ann Arbor: University Microfilms, 1984), 11ff.

10. For example, the Islamic confession of faith is known as the *shahāda*, and a religious martyr is known as a witness (*shahīd*) to God. See above, 92–93.

11. Or: the world to come (*al-ākhira*)

12. *al-dunyā*

13. *Rasā'il Ikhwān al-ṣafā'* (Cairo, 1928), IV:141.

14. He contrasts the natural world (*'ālam al-ṭabi'a*) with the metaphysical (world) (*mā ba'da al-ṭabi'a*).

15. Note that the *Ikhwān al-ṣafā'* draw upon Neo-Platonic ideas; they do not distinguish the inner eye from the eye of the intellect which sees non-physical truths. While at times Ghazzālī, too, identifies the heart with the intellect or a power within the intellect, in other passages he draws upon the Sufi image of a knowing of the heart that is superior to intellectual knowledge. Ibn Ṭufayl stands somewhere between the two traditions. He recognizes that the kind of knowing Avicenna speaks of when describing the Sufis transcends purely intellectual knowledge, and asserts that his notion of *mushāhada* echoes this Sufi conception. Ha-Levi, like Ghazzālī, draws a sharp contrast between prophetic knowledge—which for him is like sense experience—and intellectual knowledge. See Baneth, "*Halevi ve al-Ghazzālī,*" 316 n.4; Julius Guttmann, "Religion and Knowledge," 21–23; Ibn Ṭufayl, *Ḥayy*, Gauthier, 5–7; Goodman, 96–97; Wolfson, "Merkavah Traditions," 223–24 and nn.140–41.

16. Ghazzālī, *Munqidh*, 138; translation, McCarthy 97; Watt, 64. David Kaufmann traced Ha-Levi's notion of the inner eye to this passage in Ghazzālī. Kaufmann, *Attributenlehre*, 202 n.180. Ghazzālī suggests that the dream state offers another analogy; its claims would seem absurd to a person who had never dreamed.

17. For example, that gray is a sad color, red a lively color. These examples were suggested to me by Professor Everett Rowson.

18. Originally, the blind person is given enough information to make his way around the city; his knowledge is *functional knowledge*. However it is indirect knowledge, knowledge based upon hearsay or blind trust (*taqlīd*). When given sight, it becomes direct, experiential knowledge.

Ibn Ṭufayl compares the difference between theoretical understanding and actual experience to that between seeing the world in black and white and seeing the world in color. However, he believes that just as it is crucial that one experience for oneself, so it is crucial that one come to an intellectual understanding for oneself; otherwise one is simply relying blindly on someone else's understanding, with no understanding of one's own—i.e., one is left in the situation of *taqlīd*. Ibn Ṭufayl's position here is thus similar to Baḥya's (See above, p. 206, n.74). One might compare this to the difference between receiving the answer to a complicated mathematical problem and personally going through the process of arriving at the solution.

Ibn Ṭufayl offers an interesting argument against *taqlīd*: if one believes something on blind faith, one cannot develop it further. A person who has been given the solution to a mathematical proof can do no further investigation into the matter for him or herself. Ibn Ṭufayl, *Ḥayy*, Gauthier, 18–20; Goodman, 102–3.

19. Ha-Levi makes an exception for the collective experience of Mount Sinai (I:87–91: 24–27), and does describe a continuum in the capacity for *mushāhada* (IV:11: 163). The *Ḥaver* also absolves the philosophers for their use of *qiyās*, noting that they only resorted to *qiyās* because of the absence of prophecy and divine light (V:14: 212).

20. Gauthier, 18; Goodman, 102. Translation aided by Goodman.

21. The King: "Why should the letters H W Y or an angel or a sphere or other things be required if we believe in the divine will and creation?"

The *Ḥaver*: "Well spoken, O King of the Khazars, to God [be attributed your excellence] [*aḥsanta ya malik al-Khazar, wa-li-llahi anta*]! This is the truth, the real faith, and the abandoning of everything superfluous. Perhaps this was Abraham's insight [*naẓar*] when he verified [divine] sovereignty and oneness, before God revealed [himself] [*yuḥa*] to him. When God revealed [himself] [*awḥa*] to him, he abandoned all his logical arguments [*qiyāsāt*] and turned to seek the favor of God (IV:26–27: 184–85).

22. In a quote mistakenly attributed to Plato. A prophet received a prophetic revelation (*waḥy*), which he related to a philosopher: "You cannot reach me [*taṣilu*] by this path [*ṭarīq*], but by those I have set as an intermediary between myself and my creatures, that is, the prophets and the true law" (IV:27: 184).

23. As Altmann points out, Karaites and Muslims of a rationalistic bent charged Rabbanite Jews with gross anthropomorphism, in these very terms; they accused the Rabbanites of *tashbīh*, or the "likening" of God to a human being. See Altmann, "Moses Narboni's 'Epistle on *Shi'ur Qomah*" in idem, *Studies*, 181.

24. For, the *Ḥaver* asserts, "prophets have a vision [*baṣar*] clearer than *qiyās*. And that vision perceives the supernal host clearly [directly] [*'iyānan*], and sees the heavenly inhabitants—the spiritual beings that are near [to God] and others—in the form of a person [*adam*]. There is an allusion to them in his saying, 'Let us make humanity in our image, according to our likeness [Gen. 1:26]'" (IV:3: 156).

Moshe Idel suggests that Ha-Levi is drawing here on a notion from the *Shi'ur Qomah* literature, which describes the angels as collectively comprising a giant human form. Idel also points out a problem in Ha-Levi's argument: while prophetic vision is more direct, what is seen is not God himself, but those who serve as God's primary instruments and thus can only figuratively be pointed to as God. The philosophers, in contrast, use analogies which are indirect, but do nevertheless arrive at a description of the Divine itself.

Idel's point is well taken, and sheds a somewhat different light on Ha-Levi's view of prophetic visions. The *Ḥaver* explains that God cannot be pointed to directly, for God is not encompassed by place. To speak about God, therefore, we use metonym; we point to God through things associated with him. The closest representations we have for God are things that follow God's will directly, with no intermediary—the heavens, the ark of the covenant, the pillar of cloud and fire, even prophets and scholars.

> In this context the *Ḥaver* refers to the vision of Ex. 34: the spiritual form [*al-ṣūra al-ruḥāniyya*] which the elite saw, "and under his feet was a saphire pavement" and which was called "the God of Israel." And likewise, one points to the ark of the covenant and says that it is the Lord of all the earth, on account of the appearance of miracles when it is present and their absence when it is not, just as we say that the eye sees, even though that which sees is really other than [the eye], namely, the soul. (IV:3: 152)

The *Ḥaver* suggests that the spiritual form which the nobles saw is called the God of Israel by association, just as we call the ark of the covenant "Lord of all the earth" because it is associated with God's miracles. The *Ḥaver*'s words suggest that we sometimes point to physical images such as the ark, the pillar of cloud, or the spiritual form, and speak of them as divine through an association which is to be understood figuratively, not literally. Thus Ha-Levi's view of prophetic visions may not be as far from the view of the rationalists as is often assumed. See also above, p. 218, n.56. See Idel, "The World of Angels in Human Form" (Hebrew), in *Studies in Philosophy, Mysticism, and Ethical Literature presented to Isaiah Tishby on His Seventy-Fifth Birthday* (Jerusalem, 1986), 17 and n.64. Cf. below, 119 n.91.

25. *dhāt*

26. *yushiku ʿan takuna tilka al-ʿayn hiya al-quwwa al-mutakhayyila mahmā khadamat al-quwwat al-ʿaqliyya.* On this passage, see now Warren Zev Harvey, "Judah Halevi's Synesthetic Theory of Prophecy and a Note on the Zohar," 143n5.

27. *khadama*

28. *Al-Fārābī on the Perfect State: Abū Naṣr al-Fārābī's Mabādi' ārā' ahl al-madīna al-fāḍila*, tr. R. Walzer (Oxford, 1985), 210 (my translation aided by Walzer's); Walzer, "Al-Fārābī's Theory of Prophecy and Divination," in idem, *Greek into Arabic: Essays on Islamic Philosophy* (Oxford, 1962), 206–19, 211.

29. Fārābī writes: "The faculty of imagination is intermediate between the [faculty of] sense and the rational [faculty]. . . . It is [also] kept busy in serving [*khadama*] the rational faculty and in supporting [supplying] the appetitive faculty."

The imagination can also, according to al-Fārābī, work on its own, independently of the material supplied by the senses and stored in the memory; it can translate metaphysical truths into sensory images through "imitation." Al-Fārābī, *al-Madīna al-fāḍila*, ed. F. Dieterici as *Der Musterstaat von Alfarabi* (Leiden, 1900), 47–48; and Walzer, *Al-Fārābī on the Perfect State*, 210–13.

30. Al-Fārābī, *Madīna*, ed. Dieterici, 51–52; Walzer, 220–23.

31. Al-Fārābī, ibid., Dieterici, 51–53; Walzer, 220–23; for Maimonides' account of this phenomenon, see Oliver Leaman, "Maimonides, Imagination, and the Objectivity of Prophecy," *Religion* 18 (1988): 73.

32. Cf. Silman, *Filosof*, 156; (English) 175–76.

33. Or: drawing conclusions (*istidlāl*—from the tenth form of *d-l-l*)

34. Also from the tenth form of *d-l-l*

35. See Ivry, "Arguments," 28.

36. Or: quiddity (lit: "whatness") *mahiyya*

37. *maʿna*

38. *bi-aʿyānihā.*

39. This is apparently the reading of Aryeh Motzkin, who writes: "Those who rely on the faculty of imagination [and have trust in the experiences that emanate from the imaginary faculty] are as blind people, who must be steered and guided. Who is to guide them and steer them? He who sees well, who has a powerful intellect, he who has attained the active intellect."

This characterization, however, picks up only one side of the *Ḥaver*'s typology—that which describes the prophet's eye as seeing the essence of things—and ignores the fact that in the same passage, the *Ḥaver* describes the prophetic "inner eye" as "almost the imagination, insofar as it serves the intellect," and as witnessing great, fearsome forms. Ha-Levi does entice the philosophical reader with the description of an inner eye that sees the essence of things, like the Neo-Platonic "eye of the intellect," but he contradicts this assertion in the very same passage. Motzkin, "On Halevi's *Kuzari* as a Platonic Dialogue," *Interpretation* 9.1 (1980): 116–17.

40. This is not a radical or anti-philosophical position; as we have noted, it is in keeping with Aristotle's empiricism.

41. Cf. Saʿadya, who upholds the veracity of sense perception as a source of knowledge. See *Amānāt*, Introduction, ed. Qafih, 14–23; Rosenblatt, 16–26; Efros, "Saʿadya's Theory of Knowledge," 8–11.

42. For useful discussions of this issue, see Leaman, "Prophecy"; Marc Saperstein, *Decoding the Rabbis: A Thirteenth-Century Commentary on the Aggadah* (Cambridge, Mass., 1980), 13; Wolfson, "Merkavah." For Ha-Levi on visions and the visual in general see Colette Sirat, *Les théories des visions surnaturelles dans la pensée juive du Moyen Age* (Leiden, 1969), 83–88; Yochanan Silman, "The Visual Experience in the *Kuzari*," 117–26.

43. Islamic thinkers had confronted the problem of anthropomorphism when they encountered Greek rationalism in the eighth through the tenth centuries. While these scholars were engaged in translating, interpreting, and digesting Greek philosophical texts, they also attempted to make sense of Qur'ānic accounts of visions of God in light of Greek philosophy. Jewish rationalists in the period of the gaonim—both Rabbanite and Karaite—drew from the work of these Islamic philosophers and theologians.

44. The Karaite Josef al-Baṣir uses this characteristic Muʿtazilite argument. See Altmann, "Saʿadya's Theory of Revelation: Its Origin and Background," in *Saadya Studies*, ed. E. I. J. Rosenthal (Manchester, 1943), 8.

45. Ibid., 9–10; A. J. Wensinck, *The Muslim Creed* (Cambridge, 1932), 64.

46. R. Nissim compares this to the fact that God can have no place, for he is the creator of all place. He explains that this story was mentioned among "their *haggadot*," which Poznanski interprets to mean Arabic tales. Poznanski could not find the source of this legend; he posits that perhaps R. Nissim learned it orally from a Muslim sage. See Poznanski, "*Megillat Setarim*," 186–87.

47. The gaonim speak of a "seeing of the heart" similar to that of Sufis and Sufi-influenced thinkers such as Ghazzālī. The inner eye (*ʿayn bāṭin*, *Kuzari* IV:3: 155) and the eye of the heart (*ʿeyn ha-lev*), which he speaks of in his poetry, probably derive from both gaonic and Sufi sources. See above, notes 1 and 2.

48. *maḥdutun*

49. *li-yasiḥḥa ʿinda nabīyihi*

50. *awḥā*

51. *Amānāt*, Qafih, 103–4; Rosenblatt, 120–21.

52. *kalām al-nubuwwa*

53. *Amānāt*, Qafih, 110; Rosenblatt, 130. See also Judah b. Barzilai, *Perush Sefer Yetsirah*. ed. S. Halberstam (Breslau, 1885), 20–21; Sirat, *Visions surnaturelles*, 17–33.

54. Or: congruence

55. We see here a similarility in both language—the use of d-l-l—and in conception. In our discussion of *mushāhada* we noted that Ha-Levi also echoes this passage closely in another statement of the *Ḥaver*'s, in which he says that the select "witness [God] [*yushāhidūna*] by means of what is called Glory [*kavod*], *Shekhina* . . . and other things by which he proved to them [*yadullahum*] that they had been addressed by him on High." (IV:3: 149). We also saw additional evidence of Ha-Levi's borrowing from this passage in Sa'adya. See above, 101 and n.56; below, 118.

56. *tajsīm*

57. Or: pseudo intellectual (*al-muta'aqqila*)

58. *isnād*

59. *mithāl*

60. *mithālāt*

61. *ḥikāyāt*

62. *tantaẓimu*

63. The *Ḥaver* offers this explanation in response to the king's rhetorical question: isn't it possible to arrive at knowledge of all God's attributes intellectually, without engaging in anthropomorphism (*tajsīm*)? In his reply, the *Ḥaver* ironically shifts the negative connotation of *tajsīm*, showing that his philosophical critics themselves have need for *tajsīm* to describe God.

Although the *Ḥaver* does not use the word *qiyās* in this particular passage, he uses the terms *likeness* (*mithāl*) and *imitation* (*ḥikāya*), which are close to the primary sense of the term *qiyās*, analogy. In contrast to philosophical *qiyās*—the Aristotelian syllogism—the *qiyās* of the theologians is considered by the philosophers to be just a form of imitation (*tamthīl*) of the physical. However in this passage, the *Ḥaver* suggests that the philosophers themselves cannot speak of God without *tamthīl*.

64. *muḥdathun* Ibid., Qafih, 103; Rosenblatt, 121. Sa'adya says specifically that the spirit and word referred to by David—"The spirit of the Lord spoke by me and His word was upon my tongue" (II Sam. 23:2)—are things "specially created by God, constituting the detailed speech revealed [*awḥā*] by God to his prophet." Ibid., Qafih, 92; Rosenblatt, 105; see below, pp. 125 – 126.

65. *tajsīm*

66. *tashbīh*

67. It may be useful to compare Ha-Levi's position on the role of images or imitations (*ḥikāyat*) with the view of al-Fārābī. As we have seen above, al-Fārābī explains that, in addition to the imagination's role in ordinary perception, it has the

function of reproductive imitation (*muḥakāt*). That is, the imagination can copy sensations or rational concepts; it can imitate the concept of a sovereign being by producing the image of a splendid king. If the person's imagination is extremely powerful, the light from the Active Intellect that produces this image in the imagination can even produce the image before his or her physical eyes.

In al-Fārābī's description it seems that the mind of the prophet creates the image; the imagination translates an abstract idea emanated by the Active Intellect into a sensible image. Ha-Levi's language, however, is ambiguous; the *Ḥaver* says "there is arranged or ordered" (*tantaẓimu*) for the prophet God's majesty, omnipotence and other attributes in an instantaneous image. This ambiguous phrase could suggest that, as for al-Fārābī, the prophet's mind arranges the abstract concept of a king into a visual image. However, the *Ḥaver* also asserts that the form is created specifically for the prophet. It is not clear whether the form is created in his mind, or in the spiritual realm, whether it is created by God, or by the prophet's own cognitive faculties.

In contrast to al-Fārābī, Ha-Levi does not mention a role for the Active Intellect in the production of images. However, he seems to leave open several possibilities: (1) that the form is newly created by God for the prophet (IV:5: 160, IV:3, 158; Saʿadya's view); (2) that the form is a permanent celestial being (IV:3, 158; the Karaite view, and that of classical *merkavah* literature); (3) that the form is created by the mind of the prophet (IV: 5: 160; the view of al-Fārābī). Note also the view of II:4–7: 45–46 that the spiritual forms arise from the action of the divine light upon a subtle spiritual substance. See Wolfson, "Prophecy," 87–95; Altmann, "Saʿadya's Theory of Revelation," 5 (original); 141 (reprint); Daniel J. Lasker, "The Philosophy of Judah Hadassi the Karaite," in *Shlomo Pines Jubilee Volume* Part 1, *Jerusalem Studies in Jewish Thought* 7, 1988, 487ff.; idem "Judah Halevi and Karaism, 115 and n.17. See above, pp. 108–109 and notes.

68. *tafarrud*

69. *al-khabar al-ṣādiq*

70. Ghazzālī writes: "From the beginning of the Way [*ṭarīqa*] the revelations and witnessings [*mushāhadāt*] begin, until [even] when they are awake, they witness [*yushāhidūna*] angels and the spirits of the prophets, and hear voices [coming] from them, and acquire useful lessons from them. Then their state [*ḥāl*] ascends from witness [*mushāhada*] [sing.] of forms and likenesses [*amthāl*] to degrees for which the boundary [scope] of words is too confining."

We see then that the term *mushāhada* is used in two ways: (1) in the plural (*mushāhadāt*) for discrete experiences or for the witnessing of forms, for visions that have content; (2) in the singular (*mushāhada*) for a contemplative experience, which may include witness of forms, or may simply be an awareness of the divine presence, often within the heart of the seeker. Ghazzālī alludes to the second kind of *mushāhada* when he writes that Sufis ascend to "degrees for which the scope of words is too confining." Ghazzālī, *Munqidh*, 133; Watt, 61; McCarthy, 94–95. This is the only passage in the *Kuzari* in which I have found *mushāhada* in the plural.

71. Cf. Ibn Ṭufayl, who states that that by which one witnesses (*yushāhidu*) the metaphysical world can only metaphorically be termed a faculty. Gauthier, 6; Goodman, 96. See above, 193 n.49.

72. Moshe Idel points to the Sufi background of *hitbodedut* as both physical seclusion and mental concentration. Idel, *Ecstatic Kabbalah*, 106–7.

73. Elliot Wolfson, for example, asserts that "the object of prophecy is a real entity, albeit spiritual in nature"; it is "an objectively verifiable datum, although the means of verification may exceed the bounds of the normal processes of sense or intellection." See Wolfson, "Merkavah Traditions," 206.

74. This appears to be Herbert Davidson's reading of Ha-Levi. See Davidson, "Cuzari, 389 and n.10; Wolfson, "Merkavah Traditions," 206 n.86.

75. In Islamic thought, a private message for an individual is called *ilhām* (inspiration), in contrast to that which bears a message for others as well, which is known as *waḥy* (revelation). Maimonides makes a similar distinction between prophecy in which the prophet learns something for his or her own edification, and that in which the prophet receives a message to communicate to others. See Wolfson, "Prophecy," 64 n.20; Maimonides, *Mishneh Torah*: *Hilkhot Yesode ha-Torah* 7:7; *Guide* II:37. Cf. below, 121ff.

76. Cf. Marc Saperstein, *Decoding the Rabbis*, 13.

77. For the distinction between *baṣar* as physical vision and *baṣīra* as spiritual vision or insight, see Lazarus-Yafeh, *Studies*, 295–96, 340–41, n.64 and 65.

78. *nubuwwa*

79. *yataṣarraf*. Or: move about freely, make his way about. See above, p. 50 on I:109, and below, p. 118 on III:65: 140.

Here, perhaps "make use of," which follows a rabbinic locution in BT *Ḥagigah* 15b. The Holy One tells the ministering angels who want to push away R. Aqiva: "Let this elder be, for he is worthy to make use of (*le-hishtamesh be*) my Glory."

80. *ʿalām al-ruḥāniyyīn*. See Shlomo Pines, "On the term *Ruḥaniyyat* and Its Origin and on Judah Halevi's Doctrine" (Hebrew), *Tarbiz* 57 (1988): 525.

81. *Yerushalmi, Ḥagigah* 77b.

82. "Ben Zoma looked [*hetsits*] and died." Yerushalmi, *Ḥagigah* 77b. The Babylonian Talmud and the London manuscript of the Tosefta read "Ben Azzai." See Halperin, *The Merkavah in Rabbinic Literature*, 66–67, 86–87; Ephraim Urbach, "*Ha-mesorot ʿal torat ha-sod bi-tequfat ha-tannaim*," *Studies in Mysticism and Religion Presented to Gershom Scholem* (Jerusalem, 1969), 1–28, 12ff.

83. As we noted above (note 70) the term *mushāhada* can describe both formless, contemplative awareness of God's presence and an experience with visual content.

84. R. Ḥananel writes of the four who enter *pardes*: "they did not ascend to heaven but they contemplated and saw by means of an understanding of the heart [*ovanta de libba*]." (See above, n.1.) R. Hai Gaon identifies the *pardes* narrative explicitly with vision of the *merkavah*: "Regarding these contemplations (of the

merkavah) the *tanna* taught, 'Four entered *pardes*'—those palaces were alluded to by the term *pardes*, and they were designated by this name. . . . For God . . . shows to the righteous, in their interior, the visions of his palaces and the position of his angels."

R. Nathan of Rome, a younger contemporary, maintains that R. Hai is describing an inner vision. R. Hai, he writes, intended to suggest that those contemplating the *merkavah* "do not ascend on high, but they see and envision in the chambers of their heart like a man who sees and envisions something clearly with his eyes, and they hear and tell and speak with an eye that sees by means of the Holy Spirit."

R. Hai's famous responsum has been much discussed by scholars in this century. Scholem believes R. Hai is describing contemplation of the *merkavah* as an actual ascent to heaven, and he translates R. Hai's account accordingly: ". . . he perceives the interior and the chambers, as if he saw the seven palaces with his own eyes, and it is as though he entered one palace after the other and saw what is there."

Idel, however, argues that Nathan of Rome's interpretation is essentially correct, that R. Hai is speaking of an inner journey rather than a celestial ascent. The chambers perceived, therefore, are chambers in the heart of the visionary him–or herself: ". . . he perceives within himself and in the chambers [of his heart] as if he saw the seven palaces with his own eyes, and it is as though he entered one palace after another and saw what is there." Idel maintains that R. Hai misinterpreted what was originally an ecstatic experience as an inner vision; he suggests this would be congruent with R. Hai's view of prophetic vision of God's Glory as an "understanding of the heart."

See *Otsar ha-Geonim*, ed. B. Lewin on *Ḥagigah* (Jerusalem, 1932), *Teshuvot*, pp. 14–15; *'Arukh ha-Shalem*, ed. Kohut, 1:14, s. v. *avenay shayish ṭahor*; Idel, *Kabbalah,* 90–91 and nn.102, 104; Scholem, *Major Trends*, 49–50; David J. Halperin, "A New Edition of the Heikhalot Literature," *JAOS* 104, no. 3 (1984): 544, 547, 550–51; idem, *The Merkavah in Rabbinic Literature* (New Haven, 1980), 3, 89, 177.

85. *yataṣarraf*. Or: move about freely, make his way about. See above, p. 50 on I:109, and p. 117 on III:65: 140.

86. We are reminded of the *Ḥaver*'s parable of seeing the king of India; final arrival (*wuṣūl*) includes not just seeing (*ru'ya*) the king, but keeping his commandments and covenants. See I:109: 37–38 and above, 42–44.

Like *mushāhada*, the term Ha-Levi chooses for Elisha b. Abuya's act of contemplation (*ashrafa*) contains a visual component. However, the fact that he contemplates the separate intelligences, and believes contemplation exempts him from action, highlights the intellectual nature of his pursuit.

Mention of the separate intelligences reminds us of the *Ḥaver*'s agnostic statement about angels: "Perhaps they are the spiritual entities [*rūḥāniyyūn*] of which the philosophers speak. We have neither to accept nor reject [their position]" (IV:3: 158). Ha-Levi is agnostic about the precise ontological status of what one witnesses in the spiritual world. His emphasis is the subjective dimension, and he draws equally upon philosophical and aggadic motifs to make his point: that direct witness is more powerful than logic.

87. *inḥalla* means to dissolve, disintegrate; *tarkīb* is a structure, construction, physique or constitution.

88. See above, 101, 103.

89. Sa'adya Gaon, *Amānāt* II:12, Qafih, 110–11; Rosenblatt, 130; Rosenblatt translates: "Indeed whoever looked upon it incurred the disintegration of his entire makeup [*inḥalla tarkībuhu*]."

For an interesting comparison, see Maimonides, *Guide* I:5. Maimonides in general interprets verses about vision as signifying intellectual vision. However, he asserts that it is permissible to understand the Glory as light—as the Targum seems to—although to do so reveals an incomplete understanding. This is presumably because for Maimonides, light occupies a middle ground between that which is manifestly physical and that which is wholly incorporeal. See *Dalālat al-ḥā'irīn*, I:5 end, 20; Even-Shemuel, 27; Pines, 31. On this point, see now Howard Kreisel, "Judah Halevi's Influence on Maimonides," in *Maimonidean Studies II*, ed. A. Hyman (New York, 1991) 110–12.

90. *baṣar nabawī*

91. Ha-Levi emphasizes the importance of spiritual forms for awakening love and awe in believers. As Idel remarks, the *Ḥaver* stresses this is true not only for the masses, but even for prophets. Idel points out that the *Shi'ur Qomah* literature may have suggested to Ha-Levi the image of the angelic world in the form of a human being. He also notes that Ha-Levi believed that the value of this vision—not only for the masses, but for the prophets as well—is the awe it inspires in the human soul. See Idel, "The World of Angels in Human Form," 15–19; Altmann, "Moses' Narboni's Epistle on *Shi'ur Qoma*," 183–88 and "Sa'adya's Theory of Revelation," 5 (original); 141 (reprint); Daniel J. Lasker, "The Philosophy of Judah Hadassi the Karaite," in *Shlomo Pines Jubilee Volume* Part I, *Jerusalem Studies in Jewish Thought* 7, 1988, 487ff.; idem "Judah Halevi and Karaism, 115 and n.17. For a somewhat different view, see Wolfson, "Merkavah Traditions," 190–91; 197–99; idem, *Through a Speculum That Shines: Vision and Imagination in Medieval Jewish Mysticism* (Princeton, 1994), 163–73. See also above, p. 222 n.24.

92. *waḥy*. See below, pp. 121ff, 130–131.

93. See Wolfson, "Prophecy," 64 n.20.

94. See Qur'ān 2:87, 2:253, 5:110; Ismail K. Poonawala, "Ismā'īlī *ta'wīl* of the Qur'ān," in *Approaches to the History of the Interpretation of the Qur'ān*, ed. Andrew Rippin (Oxford: Clarendon, 1988), 203–5, 207 and note 16; Paul Walker, *Early Philosophical Shiism: The Ismaili Neoplatonism of Abū Ya'qūb al-Sijistānī* (Cambridge, 1993), 117 and n.24.

95. Pines, "Shī'ite Terms," 182 and n.123.

96. Walker, Ibid., 115–18; Poonawala, Ibid., 203–5, 207; Pines, "Shī'ite Terms," 180–89.

97. Abū Yaq'ūb al-Sijistānī, *Ithbāt al-nubūwa*, ed. A. Tāmir (Beirut: Catholic Press, 1966), 119, 121; Walker, 117 and n.22; cf. Poonawala, 203.

98. The term appears frequently in the Epistles of *Ikhwan al-ṣafā'*, and is found also in the *Risāla al-Jāmi'a*, a related text whose Ismā'īlī leanings are even clearer. In the latter work, we read of Adam that "the lights of the Intellest ['*aql*] were united [*ittaḥadat*] with him, as well as the graces of the Soul [*nafs*], the inspiration [*ta'yīd*] of the Creator, may He be exalted and honored, and His commandment and prohibition." See Pines, 175, 171.

The *Ikhwān al-ṣafā'* write that various angels in the celestial hierarchy are "those who bear revelation [*waḥy*] and assistance [*ta'yīd*] to those who are below them, and are those who bring the messages of their Lord to the prophets." *Rasā'il Ikhwān al-ṣafā'* (Beirut, 1957) volume 4, 84, letter 46; volume 4, 224–25, and Yves Marqet, "*Révélation et vision véridique chez les Ikhwān al-ṣafā',*" *REI* (1964), 28–32. (See also Volume 4, 136 on the parable of the tree).

An additional source in which we find the term is the *Risāla al-manāmiyya*, a treatise on dreams attributed to Avicenna. There we find the following: "There is a noble force (*quwwa*) which has supervision (providence) ('*ināya*) over human interests. . . . The Arabs call it the "angels" and the divine strengthening (or inspiration) (*al-ta'yīd al-ilāhī*) . . . if there were a man safeguarded, helped, and taught by this force in the fullest measure, that man would be a prophet receiving prophetic inspiration (*yuḥā ilaihi*)." See Pines, "The Arabic Recension of Parva Naturalia and the Philosphical Doctrine concerning Veridical Dreams according to *al-Risāla al-manāmiyya* and Other Sources" *IOS* 4 (1974), 117. See also below, p. 137 and n.185, for the term *mu'ayyada* in Avicenna.

99. See Haggai Ben-Shammai, "On a Polemical Element in R. Sa'adya Gaon's Theory of Prophecy," *Jerusalem Studies in Jewish Thought,* volume 7 (*Jubilee Volume Dedicated to Shlomo Pines*, 1971–72, part 1), 127–46.

100. Ben-Shammai asserts categorically that in these sources *waḥy* signifies an audio-visual revelation, with the famous exception of Qur'ān 16:68, in which the bees are said to receive revelation. Commentators tend to interpret this verse using the term *ilhām*, explaining it as a kind of instinct: "And my Lord revealed [*awḥā*] to the bee: Make hives in the mountains and in the trees and in what they build . . ."

It is not clear to me, however, that *waḥy* as a rule signifies audio-visual revelation, and that all attempts to interpret it using the more diffuse term *ilhām* are deviations. It appears rather that the term *waḥy* itself, even in the Qur'ān and the literature of Qu'rān commentary, was open to various interpretations. Wensinck, "*Waḥy*," *EI2*; Ben-Shammai, ibid., 129–30; Wansbrough, *Qur'ānic Studies: Sources and Methods of Scriptural Interpretation* (Oxford, 1977), 34, 58ff, 33–37.

101. The medieval theologian Jurjānī acknowledges that a prophet, too, may receive *ilhām*, but distinguishes *ilhām* as that which is received in the heart, whereas *waḥy* signifies the external presence of an angel. He writes: "The prophet is one who receives a revelation [*ūḥiya ilaihi*] through an angel, or is inspired [*ulhimu*] in his heart, or is informed in a true dream; the messenger [*rasūl*] is distinguished by the special revelation [*waḥy*] which is superior to the revelation of the prophet. For the apostle is one to whom Gabriel is revealed [or reveals] [*ūḥiya* or *awḥā*]; he is distinguished in bringing down [*tanzīl*] a Book from God." See

Jurjānī, *Definitiones*, ed. Flugel, 258–59; cf. Louis Gardet, *Dieu et la destinée de l'homme* (Paris, 1967), 154.

102. John Wansbrough, *Qurānic Studies: Sources and Methods of Scriptural Interptrtation* (Oxford, 1977), 34.

103. Cf. the statement of Jurjānī, n.5. For Ghazzālī on *ilhām*, see above, 166 n.11. Cf. Al-Ṭabari, *Jāmiʿ al-bayān ʿan Ta'wīl al-Qur'ān* (Cairo, 1954), volume 30, 210–11; Zamaksharī on Qur'ān 42:51; partially translated in Helmut Gatje, *The Qur'ān and Its Exegesis* (London, 1971), 45–6. Al-Ghazzālī, *Iḥyā' ʿulūm al-dīn*, 1376–77; Ben-Shammai, ibid., 133–36.

104. They, too, quote Qur'ān 42:51; see preceeding note. *Rasā'il Ikhwān al-ṣafā'* (Beirut, 1957), volume 4, 84.

105. *nawāmis*

106. *Rasā'il Ikhwān al-ṣafā'* (Beirut, 1957) volume 4, p. 84, letter 46.

107. They continue: "Those who hear the words or read the revelations in their books are varied in the levels of their intellects . . . the common folk understand from those expressions one meaning, while the elite understand another, more subtle meaning. And this is healthy for all." *Rasā'il Ikhwān al-ṣafā'*, IV:122; Ben-Shammai, ibid., 135; Marquet, *Ikhwan al-ṣafā'*, 501–8; idem, "*Révélation et Vision Véridique,*" 28–9.

Compare al-Sijistānī's interpertation of the same Qur'ānic verse: "*Waḥyan* (by revelation) means *ta'yīd* from the Intellect; *min wara' ḥijābin* (from behind a veil) means *ta'yīd* from the Intellect through the Soul, the latter being a veil between the Intellect and the Nature; and *aw yursila rasūlan* (or that He should send a messenger) means that, when the *nāṭiq* (divine speaker/prophet) attains his rank (i.e. receives the call), he is obliged to translate what has been brought down to his heart by the Trusted Spirit into his own tongue in order to convey it to his people." Al-Sijistānī, *Ithbāt al-nubūwa*, 149; translation in Poonawala, 204.

108. Another question is whether Jibrīl translates the heavenly prototype of the Qur'ān (*umm al-kitāb*), written in some divine language, into Arabic and then relates it to the Prophet. See Wansbrough, *Qur'ānic Studies*, 33–37, 58–63; Ibn Qutayba, *Ta'wīl mushkil al-Qur'ān,* 2d ed. (Cairo, 1973), 106:4–112:10; J.R.T.M. Peters, *God's Created Speech* (Leiden, 1976).

109. Abu al-Husayn al-Khayyat, *Kitāb al-intiṣār* (Cairo, 1925), 104:2–4.

110. ʿAbd al-Jabbar, *al-Mughnī* volume 12, 343:17–346; Wansbrough, *Qur'ānic Studies*, 33–37; Ben-Shammai, ibid., 134; Van Ess, *Erkenntnislehre*, 120–22.

111. Van Ess, ibid., 121. It is likely that the Muʿtazilite polemic against *ilhām* as a source of knowledge was directed against the *Ikhwān* or those who held to their view, those who regarded inspiration as a source of philosophical and scientific, and not just religious, knowledge. Ben-Shammai, ibid., 136.

112. al-Fārābī, *Madīna*, Dieterici, 51–52, 58–59; Walzer, 223–25, 243–45; idem, *al-Siyāsa al-madaniyya*, ed. F. Najjār (Beirut, 1964), 79–80; idem, *Fuṣūl*

al-madanī, tr. D. Dunlop (Cambridge, 1961), par. 89. Davidson, *Intellect*, 58–62; idem, "Active Intellect," *Viator*, 144–47; Leo Strauss, "The Philosophical Grounding of the Law," 92–95; Fazlur Rahman, *Prophecy*, 30–31, 37–38; Jeffrey Macy, "Prophecy in al-Fārābī and Maimonides: The Imaginative and Rational Faculties," in *Maimonides and Philosophy*, ed. S. Pines and Y. Yovel (Dordrecht, 1986), 185–92.

113. Avicenna, *Shifā': Ilāhiyyāt*, ed. G. Anawati and S. Zayed (Cairo 1960), 435–36; Avicenna, *Najāt* (Cairo, 1938), 299. See Davidson, *Intellect*, 120; idem, "Active Intellect," *Viator*, 177, Rahman, *Prophecy*, 33ff.; Strauss, "The Philosophical Grounding of the Law," 95. Both Rahman and Davidson maintain that for Avicenna, "the projection of visions takes place within the faculties of the soul, not in the external world as Alfārābī wrote." Davidson, "Active Intellect," *Viator*, 177 n.424; Rahman, 38.

114. Avicenna, *Shifā' De Anima*, ed. Rahman, 249–50; idem, *al-Najāt* (Cairo, 1938), 167–68; *Avicenna's Psychology*, tr. Rahman (London, 1952) (English), 36–37; Landauer, "Die Psychologie des *Ibn Sīnā*," 364–65; Davidson, "Active Intellect," *Viator*, 160–78; idem, *Intellect*, 83–126; Rahman, *Prophecy*, 31–36.

115. *Peh el-peh*, lit. "mouth to mouth," from Num. 12:6–8: "Hear my words: When a prophet of the Lord arises among you, I make myself known to him in a vision, I speak with him in a dream. Not so with my servant Moses; he is trusted throughout my household. With him I speak mouth to mouth [*peh el peh*], plainly and not in riddles, and he beholds the likeness of the Lord."

116. *al-ikhṭar bi-l-bāl.*

117. Ben-Shammai, noting Van Ess's discussion of the negative evaluation of *ilhām* on the part of the early Muʿtazilites, speculates that this may have motivated Qirqisānī to shy away from discussing *ilhām* in any detail, given his Muʿtazilite tendencies. Al-Qirqisānī, *Kitāb al-ānwār*, 177:3–5; Ben-Shammai, *Shitot ha-maḥshava ha-datit shel Abū Yūsuf Yaʿaqūb al-Qirqisānī ve-Yefet ben ʿElī* (Jerusalem, 1977); idem, "Polemical Element, 136–37; Van Ess, *'Aḍuddadīn*, 123.

118. Ben-Shammai, *Qirqisānī ve-Yefet Ben ʿElī*, 270–71; tr. from Uriel Simon, *Four Approaches to the Book of Psalms*, tr. L. Schramm (Albany, 1991), 81.

Yefet depicts a similar form of inspiration in his comment on the story of the seventy elders in Numbers 11:25: "[The Torah's] words 'And they prophesied and did no more' [signify] the prophecy that they prophecied when the Spirit of Wisdom [*ruaḥ ha-ḥokhmah*] rested upon them. The Torah does not explain what they prophesied; it is possible that they said song and praise by the Holy Spirit [*shir ve-shevaḥ be-ruaḥ ha-qodesh*]. [The Torah's] words 'and they did no more' teaches that the spirit of prophecy [*ruaḥ ha-nevuah*] did not rest upon them except for that time alone."

Ben-Shammai comments on this passage: "The Holy Spirit is not a sort of speech or vision that the prophet hears or sees and transmits to his audience; it is an inspiration that causes the possessor of the Holy Spirit to do certain things, to act in a certain way, or to say certain things, chiefly words of songs and praise." He believes Yefet's pairing of the Holy Spirit with *ilhām* is deliberate and far reaching:

Yefet intends to suggest that while Hannah speaks under the inspiration of the Holy Spirit, it is she herself who shapes the words of her prayer.

Ben-Shammai adduces much textual evidence to support his notion that Yefet is suggesting an equation between the Holy Spirit and *ilhām*. Ben-Shammai's textual evidence is highly suggestive, although I am not certain it is conclusive. That is, the notion of divine inspiration is a slippery one; it is not always clear what the Sages themselves intend when they speak of David or other Biblical figures being inspired by the Holy Spirit. The term *Holy Spirit* is used in rabbinic literature in many different senses, some of which refer to prophecy, some to a more diffuse form of divine guidance.

If the rabbis did make a clear distinction, it was between literal dictation—Mosaic prophecy—and inspiration by the Holy Spirit, that accorded to other prophets. We find in rabbinic literature a sense that the background and personality of particular prophets does shape their individual messages. For example, we find the notion that Isaiah and Ezekiel see the same divine realm; however, given Isaiah's aristocratic background, the heavenly court is not a surprise to him, while Ezekiel, as a villager, is awe struck and so describes it in great detail. Underlying such a statement is the assumption that the prophet is not a passive instrument receiving dictation. The prophetic message in some way reflects who the prophet is; the message is to some perceptible degree filtered through the human personality. On the Holy Spirit, see below p. 133 n.162. For discussions of prophecy and inspiration, see James Kugel, ed., *Poetry and Prophecy* (Ithaca, 1990). For Ben-Shammai's textual evidence that Yefet is equating prophecy and *ilhām*, see Ben-Shammai, *Qirqisānī ve-Yefet ben ʿElī* volume I, pp. 251–73, including notes and passages cited in appendices (volume 2). I translate several of these passages into English in my dissertation, pp. 361–62.

119. The notion of David or Hannah's uttering prayers under the inspiration of the Holy Spirit is not in itself radical, nor does it necessitate non-literal inspiration. *Ilhām*, on the other hand, had clearly become a charged term in the Islamic world. What is problematic in Yefet's statement about Hannah is his equation of Holy Spirit with *ilhām*, not the fact that Hannah uttered the prayer under the influence of the Holy Spirit.

120. For Muʿtazilite arguments against *ilhām*, see above, 124. This motivation, it seems to me, is clear in Ha-Levi as well. For example, Ha-Levi writes: "The speech of prophets at the time the Holy Spirit [*ruaḥ ha-qodesh*] enwraps them is in every word directed from the *ʾamr ilāhī;* the prophet cannot alter a word" (*Kuzari* V:20: 221).

This statement in Ha-Levi calls to mind Muḥammad's words regarding the recitation (Qurʾān) he received: "It is not for me to change it of my own accord [*min tilqāʾ nafsih*] I only follow what is revealed to me [*ūḥiya ʿilāyya*]." It is interesting to note that the *Ikhwān al-ṣafāʾ*, while holding that the prophet himself shapes the words of prophecy, insist that the prophet does not inject anything of his own ideas or opinions into the revelation he transmits. See *Rasāʾil Ikhwān al-ṣafāʾ* volume 4, 136.

121. See Saʿadya's commentary to Daniel 7:15, *Daniel im Targum u-ferush Rabenu Saʿadya Ben Yosef Fayyumi u-ferush Tanḥum ha-Yerushalmi*, tr. J. Qafih (Jerusalem, 1980–81), p. 138:4; and his commentary to Job 4:13, *Iyov ʿim Targum u-ferush ha-Gaon Rabenu Saʿadya ben Yosef Fiyyumi*, tr. J. Qafih (Jerusalem, 1972–3), 47. In his commentary on Genesis, too, Saʿadya refers to God's revelation to Job using the verb *awḥa*. See *Perushe Rav Saʿadya Gaon li-vereshit*, tr. M. Zucker (New York, 1984), 121 (Arabic), 370 (Hebrew).

122. See *Tehilim ʿim tirgum u-ferush ha-Gaon Saʿadya ben Yosef Fayyumi*, tr. J. Qafih (Jerusalem, 1965–66), 23, 24, 21; Moshe Sokolow, "Saadiah Gaon's Prolegomenon to Psalms", *PAAJR* 51 (1984): 146, 143; Moshe Zucker, "Notes on Saadiah's Introduction to Psalms," *Leshonenu* 33 (1969), 224.

123. See *Tehilim*, tr. Qafih, 35 (long introduction); 53 (short introduction). Among other reasons, Saʿadya is countering those Karaites who saw the Book of Psalms as prayers that David himself wrote under divine inspiration, and which Jews could therefore use at any time as their personal prayers. Saʿadya restricts permissible prayer to those prayers prescribed at set times of the day by rabbinic authorities.

While Simon sees this polemic against the Karaite use of psalms for prayer as Saʿadya's primary motive in his long introduction to Psalms, Ben-Shammai argues that the polemic over prayer must be understood within the context of the wider issue of revealed Scripture as *waḥy*, divinely dictated text. See Uriel Simon, *Four Approaches to the Book of Psalms* (Hebrew) (Ramat Gan, 1982), 18–24; (English), tr. Schramm, 5–12; Sokolow, "Saadiah Gaon's Prolegomenon to Psalms," 148 n.75; Ben-Shammai, "On a Polemical Element," 131; idem, Review of Uriel Simon, *Four Approaches to the Book of Psalms* in *Kiryat Sefer* 58, 400–406. For a fuller discussion of the Karaite view of inspiration, see my dissertation, Appendix B.

124. One might regard this blurring of boundaries either as a raising of *ilhām* to the level of prophetic revelation, like the Shīʿites, or as a lowering of *waḥy* to the level of inspiration, like the philosophers.

125. Even, apparently, *ruaḥ ha-qodesh*. See my dissertation, 471–72; Ben Shammai, "On a Polemical Element," 128ff.

126. Compare I:42: "The king: This degree [of the prophets] is divine and angelic, if it exists, and it is of the nature of the Divine [*ʾamr ilāhī*], not the intellectual [*ʾamr ʿaqli*], the human [*ʾamr insaniyy*], or the natural [physical] [*ʾamr ṭabiʿi*]" (I:42: 13)

127. The philosophers adapt the term *waḥy* to describe the highest level of human intellectual attainment precisely because the term signifies inspiration whose source is in some sense divine. The philosophers, however, do not preserve the substantive distinction between *waḥy* and other forms of inspiration which exists in traditional Islamic usage.

128. Or *sayy'ata min shemaya*, as in the following passage from the Babylonian Talmud, *Megillah* 6b: "R. Isaac said: If a person says to you, I have labored and not found, do not believe him. If he says, I have not labored but still have found, do not believe him. If he says, I have labored and found, you may believe him. This is true with respect to words of Torah, but with respect to business, all depends on the

assistance of heaven [*sayy'ata hu min shemaya*]. And even for words of Torah this is true only of penetrating to the meaning, but for remembering what one has learned, all depends on the assistance of heaven [*sayy'ata min shemaya hi*]."

129. *al-ʿilm al-mu'ayyad bi-ʾamr ilāhī*

130. *yurshiduhu*

131. In this passage Ha-Levi appears to blur the boundaries somewhat between prophecy or *waḥy* proper and other forms of inspiration, for he also asserts that the Holy Spirit enwraps the prophet at the time of prophecy, as well as the priest who inquires of the *urim ve-tummim*. However by mentioning divine guidance of the Nazir and Messiah separately from prophecy, he may be pointing to various degrees of inspiration by the Holy Spirit, as in the looser rabbinic use of the term *ruaḥ ha-qodesh*. More systematically inclined thinkers, for example Yefet b. ʿElī and Maimonides, spell out a hierarchy of degrees of prophecy, which they maintain more consistently.

132. *al-nawāmis al-ʿaqliyya*

133. On this passage, see the interesting study of Daniel Lasker, "Proselyte Judaism, Christianity, and Islam in the Thought of Judah Halevi," *JQR 81*, 1–2 (July–Oct. 1990): 75–92; cf. Robert Eisen, "The Problem of the King's Dream and Non-Jewish Prophecy in Judah Halevi's *Kuzari*," *Jewish Thought and Philosophy*, vol. 3, 240–41.

134. *min tilqā' nafsih*. Al-Fārābī gives as the legitimate reason for such change that the original law was fully appropriate in its own time, whereas a changed historical context demands new legislation. See al-Fārābī, *Kitāb al-milla*, ed. M. Mahdi (Beirut, 1967), 49–50.

135. *istinbāṭ burhānī*, 204. Published by S. Landauer, "Die Psychologie des Ibn Sina," *ZDMG* 29 (1876): 364–65. See also Dimitri Gutas, *Avicenna and the Aristotelian Tradition* (Leiden, 1988), 161, 171 (159–81); Davidson, *Intellect*, 88.

136. Compare Ghazzālī: "The proof [*dalīl*] of [prophecy's] existence is the existence in the world of knowledge which could not conceivably be obtained by the intellect alone, such as the knowledge of medicine and of astronomy. For whoever examines such knowledge knows of necessity that it can be obtained only by a divine inspiration [*ilhām*] and special help [*tawfīq*] from God Most High, and that there is no empirical way to it." *Munqidh*, 139–40; Watt, 65; McCarthy, 98.

137. *Ilhām* is here paired with the root *r-sh-d* (here in its tenth form "to seek guidance" (*mustarashada*), which is paired with *taʾyīd* in the example of the Nazir and the Messiah; God is said to assist him (*yu'ayyiduhu*) and guide him (*yurshiduhu*). The root *r-sh-d* (like *h-d-y*), which signifies general guidance, is found frequently in traditional Islamic texts.

138. See above, p. 124.

139. *naql*

140. Perhaps Ha-Levi intends to suggest that something personal of the Divine—not mere words or concepts—is revealed in *waḥy*. See above p. 217, nn.50, 51.

141. *ʿan Allah*

142. Or: misled, deceived, or beguiled by; or negligent, unprepared (*mughtarra bi*)

143. *taṣilu*, from *w-ṣ-l*

144. *al-nāmus al-ḥaqq*

145. The *Ḥaver* asserts that only born Jews can achieve the level of prophecy and receive prophetic revelation (*waḥy*); converts can reach the level of the pious (*awliyā'*) but not the prophets (*anbiyā'*) (I:115: 39–40).

146. *sayr*

147. *haya*

148. *yudrak*

149. *iktisāb*

150. Or: awaken, inspire one (*yunhiḍu*)

151. Or regarding the Land, for Ha-Levi

152. The *Ḥaver* asserts, for example, that the ark was with Israel as long as *nubuwwa* lasted (I:87); *nubuwwa* stayed with Israel forty years during the period of the Second Temple (III:65); the Mishnah was redacted 530 years after the cessation of *nubuwwa* (III:67); Jews are distinguished (*khaṣṣa*) as the people (worthy) of *nubuwwa* (*ahl al-nubuwwa*) (I:115); Jewish fulfillment lies in *ittiṣāl* with the *ʾamr ilāhī* by *nubuwwa* and what approaches it (I:109); the Biblical ancestors were well known for *nubuwwa* (IV:15); Jews in the land of Israel were a people prepared for *nubuwwa* (III:1); the Land of Israel is the land of *nubuwwa*; the light of *nubuwwa* was in the Temple; the *ʾamr ilāhī* was with the Sanhedrin, whether by *nubuwwa*, *ilhām*, or *taʾyīd* (III:39).

153. The *Ḥaver* asserts that all the sons of Jacob sought the level of *nubuwwa* (*darajat al-nubuwwa*), and most of them achieved it (I:103); when the *Shekhinah* was present in the Land, all who prepared for *nubuwwa* achieved it (II:14); *nubuwwa* is rare among individuals, all the more so among groups (IV:15); the excellent person (*fāḍil*) reaches the highest degree next to the angels, and can rightly aspire to *nubuwwa* (III:22); R. Ishmael reached a degree near *nubuwwa* (III:65); some of the Sages saw the *Shekhinah* in the degree just less than *nubuwwa* (III:11); if one prays in the degree of *nubuwwa* one can experience *ittiṣāl* in this life and earn it for the world to come (III:20); the heads of the tribes as well as the seventy elders were fit (*ṣalaḥū*) for *nubuwwa* (I:95); R. Aqiva reached a degree so near *nubuwwa* that he was able to conduct himself in the spiritual world (III:65).

154. Philosophers turned to *qiyās* because of their lack of *nubuwwa* and divine light (V:14); *nubuwwa* has a more penetrating eye than *qiyās* (IV:3).

155. The *Ḥaver* here reiterates his words in I:81 regarding the difference between a rational religion and one founded by God. In a rational religion, a person who rises to leadership is said to be divinely inspired. God wanted the people to know that the Torah was not originally an idea in the mind of Moses to which God gave support, assistance or inspiration.

156. IV:11. In addition, Ha-Levi uses the term *nubuwwa* to signify the Biblical writings, in contrast to the words of the rabbinic Sages: for example, the *Ḥaver* asserts that *nubuwwa* contains some mention of the doctrine of resurrection, although the words of the Sages (*kalām al-aḥbār*) are more explicit (I:115). Ha-Levi also uses *nubuwwa* to signify the source of true tradition (*naql*); accurate astrological calculations, for example, are known by *nubuwwa* (II:64).

157. *ʿilm al-sharīʿa*

158. *Sanhedrin* 86bff.

159. *yattaṣilu*

160. *sharīʿa*

161. *naql*

162. "When the last of the prophets, Haggai, Zechariah, and Malakhi, died, the Holy Spirit departed from Israel, but they still availed themselves of the *bat qol* ["heavenly voice" or "echo"]" (*BT Yoma 9b*).

Rabbinic statements—perhaps rhetorical in nature—can also be found suggesting that some of the Sages themselves were accorded a certain degree of prophetic inspiration. For example, according to the Amora R. Avdimi of Haifa, "Since the destruction of the Temple, prophecy was taken away from the prophets and given to the Sages" (*BT, Bava Batra 12a*). Many of the phenomena associated with the Holy Spirit continued among the early rabbis, including wonder working, intercessionary prayers, divination, and receiving messages through dreams.

There is also debate about when the Holy Spirit (*ruaḥ ha-qodesh*) ceased from Israel. In addition to the statement in *Yoma 9b* that it ceased with the death of the last prophets, we find opinions both that it dated from the destruction of the First Temple and from the destruction of the Second Temple (*Yoma 21b*). See Ephraim Urbach, "*Matai paskah ha-nevuah*?" *Tarbiz* 17, 1–11; idem, *The Sages: Their Concepts and Beliefs*, tr. I. Abrahams (Jerusalem, 1965), 576ff. and passim; Joshua Abelson, *The Immanence of God in Rabbinical Literature* (London, 1912); Arthur Marmorstein, "The Holy Spirit in Rabbinic Legend," in *Studies in Jewish Theology; the Arthur Marmorstein Memorial Volume*, ed. J. Rabbinowitz and M. S. Lew (London, 1950); Herbert Parzen, "*The Ruaḥ ha-Kodesh* in Tannaitic Literature," *Jewish Quarterly Review* 1929–30, New Series 20, 51ff. Nahum Glatzer, "A Study of the Talmudic Interpretation of Prophecy," *Review of Religion* 10 (1946), 195ff.; Rivka G. Horwitz, "*Ruaḥ ha-Kodesh*," *EJ*.

163. "Prophecy accompanied the people of the Second Temple for forty years, on account of the elders who were assisted (*al-mu'ayyadīn*) by the power of the *Shekhinah* which was present in the First Temple. [Newly] acquired prophecy ceased with the departure of the *Shekhinah*, and only came at extraordinary times or on account of a great force, such as that of Abraham, Moses, the expected Messiah, Elijah, and their equals. For they in themselves were an abiding place of the *Shekhinah* (*hum bi-dhawātihim maḥall al-shekhinah*) and their very presence helped those present to acquire the degree of prophecy" (*Kuzari* III:65). On this passage, see above, p. 191 n.36. The *Ḥaver* also asserts in II:14 that during the period of the First

Temple, when the *Shekhinah* was present in Jerusalem, all those among the select (*ṣafwa*) who were prepared for prophecy achieved it. See also *Qol Yehudah* and *Otsar Nehmad*, II:14, III:39, III:41, III:65.

164. *sakīna*

165. *Shekhinah*

166. *al-awliyā'*

167. Note the similar language of Ghazzālī with respect to pious Sufis: "All movements [*ḥarakat*] and all restings [*sakanāt*] of the Sufis whether external or internal, are illuminated from the light of the lamp of prophecy [*nubuwwa*]; and there is no other light on the face of the earth which may be the source of illumination." *Al-Munqidh*, 132; Watt, 60; McCarthy, 94.

168. "Prophecy accompanied [those of] the Second Temple almost forty years; Jeremiah in his prophecying [*nubuwwa*] extolled the people of the Second Temple for their saintliness and their learning and their piety. If we are not to rely [*nuqallid*] on these, on whom are we to rely [*nuqallid*]?" (III:39: 123).

169. *min Allah ta'allah*

170. *rūḥ ilāhī nabawī*

171. *walīy, lā nabīy*

172. *al-mutashar'i bi-shar'iat Allah*

173. *walīy*

174. *ifāḍa*

175. *fā'iḍ*

176. *wujūd*

177. Al-Fārābī, *al-Siyāsa al-madaniyya*, ed. F. Najjār (Beirut, 1964), 79–80.

178. It is interesting that the *Ḥaver* speaks here of inspirations (*ilhāmāt*), without mentioning revelation (*waḥy*).

179. Published by S. Landauer, "Die Psychologie des Ibn Sina," *ZDMG* 29 (1876): 335–418, chapter 9; compare Gutas, *Avicenna and the Aristotelian Tradition*, 161; Davidson, *Alfarabi*, 81 n.30.

180. *tus'adu*. The text upon which this was apparently modeled, published by Landauer reads "is prepared [predisposed] for" [*yasta'iddu*] rather than [*tus'adu*] "is aided in." See below, n.14.

181. Or: freed from

182. Or: specific property

183. Compare this with the text published by Landauer—an early work of Avicenna—upon which this passage was apparently based: "In some people, keenness of mind [*yaqẓa*] and contact with the universal intellect [*al-ittiṣāl bi-l-'aql al-kulli*] may so predispose [*yasta'iddu*] the rational faculty as to free it from having recourse to syllogism [*qiyās*] and reasoning [*rawiya*] in order to acquire knowledge ['*inda al-ta'arruf*]; inspiration [*ilhām*] and revelation [*waḥy*], rather, are sufficient sustenance for it. This specific property of the rational faculty is called sanctification [*taqdīs*], in

accordance with which it is then called sanctified spirit (*rūḥ muqaddas*). None shall gain the enjoyment of this rank except prophets and messengers of God." Landauer, 364–65.

184. *hads*

185. *mu'ayyada*, related to *ta'yīd*. See above, pp. 121, 127–129.

186. *hads*

187. Or: faculty (*quwwa qudsiyya*)

188. Avicenna, *Shifā': De Anima*, published as *Avicenna's De Anima*, ed. F. Rahman, 249–50.

189. In the ordinary process of knowledge, the cogitative faculty (*mufakkira*) must search through the images of the imagination for the middle term, while the prophet simply makes contact with the Active Intellect and comes upon it immediately. In Avicenna's theory of intellect, the human intellect must link (*yattaṣilu*) with the Active Intellect each time it has an actual thought. Thoughts, therefore, are never contained totally within the human soul; the ordinary person, the philosopher and the prophet must all turn to the Active Intellect for actual knowledge. The distinction between ordinary knowledge, philosophy, and (intellectual) prophecy is therefore blurred. Avicenna, like al- Fārābī, also describes an imaginative form of prophecy.

190. *hads*. "Learning occurs in two ways: one is by way of intuition [*hads*], which consists of the middle term occurring to the mind without search and thus being obtained, along with the conclusion [of a syllogism]. The second is through contrived means [*hīla*] and [after] search. Intuition [*hads*] is a divine overflow [*fayḍ*] and an intellectual contact [*ittiṣāl*] taking place without any act of acquisition [*kasb*] at all. Some people may reach a stage [of consummate intuition] that they almost have no need of reflection in most of what they learn, and possess the sacred faculty of the soul." Avicenna, *Kitāb al-mubāḥathāt*, in *Arisṭū ʿind al-ʿArab*, 231; Davidson, "Active Intellect," 167. For two comprehensive examinations of Avicenna's theory of intuition or insight (*hads*), see Davidson, *Alfarabi*, 95–102; Gutas, *Avicenna*, 159–76.

191. Gutas, ibid., especially 170–72.

192. *ray'*

193. *fikra*

194. See Poznanski, *Megillat Setarim*, 181–82, 178–80.

195. *faṣīḥan*

196. *'amr*

197. *al-rūḥ al-qiddīs*. He uses the Arabic term here, as used by Islamic philosophers in their theories of prophecy.

198. The light metaphor, which Fārābī borrows from Aristotle, compares the awakening of knowledge in the passive or material intellect to the awakening of vision. Colors require light to be seen; intelligible objects similarly require an overflow from outside to become intelligible to the mind, which Fārābī compares to light. *Al-madīna al-fāḍila*, ed. Walzer, 198–203.

199. Al- Fārābī writes, "Of the Active Intellect, it must be said that it is the reliable spirit (*al-rūḥ al-amīn*) and the Holy Spirit (*al-rūḥ al-qudus*). . . ." Quoted from ms. Leiden, or. 1002/3, fol. 221, by Wensinck, "On the Relation Between Ghāzālī's Cosmology and his Mysticism," 188; cf. Efros, "Mysticism," 153 n.52.

200. Ha-Levi uses two technical terms for the imaginative and estimative faculties of the soul, *khayal* and *wahm*, which are among the "internal senses" he lays out in detail in several passages of the *Kuzari*. Like his use of inner eye and internal sense in IV:3, Ha-Levi may be using the terms in a less precise, nontechnical sense here.

201. *manṣūṣan*

202. *mukhātaba*

203. *isnād afrād, sūra sūra, wa-aya aya*

204. *bi-bayyān*

205. *ruaḥ ha-qodesh*

206. Of course, the philosophers, too, use such traditional religious language. Avicenna, for example speaks of the capacity for prophecy as sanctified spirit (*ruḥ muqaddas*) and describes the prophet's mind as a holy intellect or divine power (*quwwa qudsiyya*). However the philosophers radically reinterpret these traditional terms. We recall that for Avicenna all human knowledge requires linking with the Active Intellect. What, then, distinguishes ordinary knowledge from "prophetic" knowledge for Avicenna, other than the speed with which it is acquired? Not withstanding Avicenna's religious language, the "holy intellect" of the prophet is simply more adept at discovering the middle terms of syllogisms.

207. Interestingly, Ha-Levi uses the verb *ra'a* (to see) rather than *shāhada* (to witness) when speaking of the people's witness of natural events (the lightning and thunder) and of Moses entering the cloud, although he repeatedly uses *shāhada*, *mashhad*, and *mushāhada* when speaking of the experience as a whole.

208. For an extended sense of the concept of synesthesia, see Warren Zev Harvey, "Judah Halevi's Synesthetic Theory of Prophecy and a Note on the *Zohar*," 147–58, 151–52.

209. "And the people prepared themselves for the degree of prophetic revelation [*waḥy*], even to hear the divine address explicitly [*jahran*], all of them. . . . And these Ten Words the masses did not hand down from individual people, nor from a prophet, but rather from God. However they did not have the capacity for the witness [*mushāhada*] of that great thing" (I:87: 24). Hirshfield's text reads *shāhadan*, rather than *jahran*, which would make this point even stronger: "The people prepared themselves for the degree of prophetic revelation [*waḥy*], even to *hear* the divine address *witnessing* [*shāhadan*]." Ha-Levi does use such adverbial phrases with respect to Abraham: "The meaning of Lord is not grasped analogically [*qiyāsan*], but by witnessing [*mushāhadatan*]" (IV:15). Similarly in IV:17: "when Abraham witnessed [*shāhada*] what he witnessed of the divine *ʾamr* by tasting [*dhawqan*], not analogically [*qiyāsan*]."

210. Cf. Kreisel, *Prophecy*, 96ff.; Silman, "Visual Experience," 122–23.

211. *yanqūlūha*, related to *naql*, true tradition

212. This point echoes Saʿadya's notion that the difference between Moses and other prophets is that Moses was able to behold the *Kavod* and the angels for a longer period of time than could others. Saʿadya, *Amānāt*, ed. Qafih, 111.

213. *maʿna*

214. *kalām*

215. *Mekhilta*, Exodus 20:15.

216. *Amānāt* II:12, Qafih, 109; Rosenblatt, 128. Saʿadya develops this in a more explicitly metaphysical direction, which Ha-Levi does not pick up. Commenting upon the *ruaḥ elohim ḥayyim* (divine living spirit or wind) of *Sefer Yetsirah* IV:1, he posits a subtle "second air" in which are created both the visual forms of the *Kavod* and the created Word of God. From this second air, the word proceeds to the "visible air," and then to the ears of the prophet and the people at Mount Sinai. See my dissertation, 471–72.

217. Philo, *The Decalogue* 32–35. H. A. Wolfson points out the similarity between Philo's account and that of Ha-Levi, and does not rule out literary influence; he asserts that there did exist a condensed Arabic version of Philo's *The Decalogue* before the time of Ha-Levi. Wolfson, "Prophecy," 104–6.

218. Saʿadya asserts that the visual manifestations of the *Kavod* are created in the second air as well.

219. Cf. the *Ḥaver* on the sacrifices, II:26: 63.

220. Note the King's statement in I:8: "For hardly [is it the case] that souls [can] accept this great thing, that the Creator of this world and the next world and the heavens and the heavenly bodies makes contact [*yattaṣilu*] with this dirty piece of mud, I mean a human being, and that God talks to him, and fulfills his requests, and does his will" (I:8: 9).

Part 5

1. *Diwān des Abū-l-Haṣan Jehuda ha-Levi*, ed. H. Brody (Berlin, 1894–1930) 3:266; *Selected Poems of Yehudah Halevi*, tr. N. Salaman (Philadelphia, 1928), 87, number 48; see also Hayyim Schirmann, *Ha-shirah ha-ʿivrit be-sefarad u-ve-provans* (*Hebrew Poetry in Spain and Provence*) (Jerusalem and Tel Aviv, 1960–61) II, 521–23, no. 228.

2. On this association, see my dissertation, Appendix A, "*Ittiṣāl* and *Devequt*," 452–61.

3. See note 1 above.

4. Tr. Raymond Scheindlin, *The Gazelle: Medieval Hebrew Poems on God, Israel, and the Soul* (Philadelphia, 1991), 131; Schirmann, *Ha-shirah ha-ʿivrit* I:465, number 188; Dov Jarden, *Shire ha-qodesh le-Rabi Yehuda Ha-Levi*, 4 volumes (Jerusalem, 1978–85) 4:1172.

5. Scheindlin, *Gazelle*, 133–34. For a different interpretation of the significance of God's Name in this poem, see Elliot Wolfson, "Merkavah Traditions," 237–41.

6. *Diwān*, ed. Brody, 3:150–51; *Selected Poems*, tr. Salaman, p. 134, no. 73; Schirmann, *Ha-shirah ha-'ivrit* II, 524–25, no. 231.

7. Cf. Isaak Heinemann, "*Ha-pilosof ha-meshorer*," 176–83; Aharon Komem, "*Ben shirah le-nevuah*," *Molad* 25 (1969), 688–89; Ya'aqov Levinger, "*Ahavah ke-bitui la-ḥavayyah ha-datit etsel Rabi Yehudah ha-Levi*," in *Mishnato ha-hagutit shel Rabi Yehudah ha-Levi* (Jerusalem), 218–20; Silman, *Filosof*, 167–71 (Hebrew), 191–96 (English); Kaufmann, ibid.

8. While David Kaufmann cautiously suggested that Baḥya and Ha-Levi were drawing upon a common Arabic source, Aharon Mirsky shows how very close is the language of the two texts, and explains a plausible path of transformation from the Arabic lines in Baḥya to the Hebrew poem of Ha-Levi. Baḥya, *Ḥidāya*, Yahuda, 82; Qafih, 85; Mansoor, 143; Kaufmann, *Meḥqarim ba-sifrut ha-'ivrit shel yemey ha-benayyim*, tr. I. Eldad (Jerusalem, 1962), 68 and n.154; Aharon Mirsky, *Mi-Ḥovot ha-Levavot 'ad shire ha-levavot* (Jerusalem, 1992), 54–55.

9. Bernard Septimus, "*Divre Ḥazal be-shirat sefarad*," *Tarbiz* 53 (1984), 611.

10. Yehudah Ratzaby, "Borrowed Elements," 173; Raymond Scheindlin, "Ibn Gabirol's Religious Poetry and Sūfī Poetry," *Sefarad* LIV (1994), 125–29.

11. Elliot Wolfson points out that this is a play on Job 19:26, "but I would behold God while still in my flesh" (*u-mi-besari eḥezeh Eloha*). Wolfson, "Merkavah," 229 n.159.

12. *Diwān* 3:6 (poem no. 5). Tr. Elliot Wolfson, ibid., 229.

13. *Dīwān* 4, 189 (poem 87). Tr. Elliot Wolfson, ibid., 229.

14. Note Philo's understanding of Israel as one who sees God (perhaps from a Hebrew etymology, *ish ra'a El*). See Ellen Birnbaum, *The Place of Judaism in Philo's Thought: Israel, Jews, and Proselytes* (Atlanta, 1996), 67–90.

15. *yudraku*

16. *qiyāsan*

17. *la yudraku qiyāsan lakin mushāhadatan*

18. Or: joins, unites; makes contact with; conjoins with, attaches himself to. Ha-Levi's use of the verb *yattaṣilu* here is open to at least two interpretations. On the one hand, his language is suggestive of an intellectual or spiritual ascent, by which a person of prophetic vision disengages himself from that which is human in order to ascend to the angelic realm and make contact with the angels and the higher visions available to them. However one could also read Ha-Levi's language of attachment here as a matter of classification rather than as a phenomenological description. When a person grasps the meaning of the Tetragrammaton directly by prophetic witness, he or she can no longer be classified strictly as a member of the human species; the person has now joined the species of angels, insofar as he or she has exhibited this angelic faculty.

19. The *Ḥaver*'s language here brings to mind his answer to the King's query in IV:2 as to how one can individualize or personalize one to whom one cannot point, whose existence can only be inferred from traces. The *Ḥaver* explains that on the contrary, God can be alluded to or pointed to directly in prophetic witnessing (*bi'l-mushāhada al-nabawwiyya*) and spiritual vision (*bi'l-baṣīra*) (IV:2: 148).

20. I Samuel 10:6, regarding Saul.

21. I Samuel 10:9, regarding Saul.

22. I Chronicles 12:18.

23. Ezekiel 37:1. Even-Shemuel corrects the text to quote "And the spirit of the Lord came upon them," from II Chronicles 12:18, noting that the subject of the passage is the Holy Spirit, as expressed in the latter quote by the term *spirit*. Even-Shemuel, *Sefer ha-Kuzari*, 288.

24. Psalms 51:14.

25. Ghazzālī, *Munqidh*, 134; McCarthy, 95; Watt, 61.

26. There exist such images for intimate relationship with the Divine in rabbinic literature as well. See above, p. 199, n.108. Moshe Idel has pointed out that the first Biblical use of the root *d-b-q* occurs in the story of the Garden of Eden. After Eve is created from Adam's side, the text tells us "thus a man leaves his father and mother and clings [*davaq*] to his wife, and they become one flesh." Idel notes that this clinging suggests an actual union and interpenetration; he speculates that the verb was chosen by Jewish mystics precisely because it could convey such intimate contact, or even total union (*unio mystica*). Idel thus suggests that when the Book of Deuteronomy uses the root *d-b-q* to enjoin clinging to God, the term retains at least some hint of a very intimate connection. He asserts further that when we find in rabbinic literature the motif of Israel's clinging to God as two dates cling to one another, the rabbis are developing an image of intimate union inherent in the root's Biblical usage. Moshe Idel, lecture on "*Devequt*," Harvard Divinity School, spring 1993.

27. *ʿābid*

28. *ʿāshiq*

29. *maʿbūdihi*. An *ʿābid* is a worshiper or adorer of God; the *maʿabūd* is the object of worship, the worshiped or adored Deity.

30. Or: on the verge of perishing out of his love (*mustahlikan fi-ḥubbihi*). *Mustahlikan* is used in this poetry to mean self-annihilation.

31. *ladhdha*

32. Or: a worshiper, a passionate lover of his Adored One (*ʿābid ʿāshiq li-maʿbūdihi*) ready to perish (*mustahlikan*) out of his love (*ḥubb*), given how great is the bliss of union (*lidhat al-ittiṣāl*) and the loss and suffering in remoteness from him.

33. At a certain point, the boundary between sacred and secular love poetry became blurred. Any love poem might be quoted and understood in a religious sense, and poets often played with the ambiguity. This trend—which Raymond Scheindlin has called the "intentional overlapping of secular and sacred love, this pretended confusion of the boundaries"—was present in medieval Jewish poetry as well. See

Scheindlin, *Gazelle*, 39–41; A. R. Nykl, *Hispano-Arabic Poetry and Its Relations with the Old Provencal Troubadours* (Geneva, 1974), 52; Lois Anita Giffen, *Profane Love*, 99–115; Schimmel, *Mystical Dimensions*, 76; idem, *As Through a Veil*, 30; Joseph Norment Bell, *Love Theory*.

34. Aḥmad Abū Nuʿaim al-Iṣfahānī, *Ḥilyat al-awliyāʾ wa ṭabaqāt al-aṣfiyāʾ*, 10 volumes (Cairo, 1932–37) 10:310; Tr. Schimmel, *As Through a Veil*, 30; idem, *Mystical Dimensions*, 135.

35. The verse is attributed by Ghazzālī to Ibn Mubarak; by others, to Rābiʿa. Ghazzālī, *Iḥyāʾ ʿulūm al-dīn,* IV:319; tr. Schimmel, *As Through a Veil*, 29; al-Ghazzālī, *Livre de L'Amour*, tr. *M. L. Siauve* (Paris, 1986), 171; J. N. Bell, *Love Theory*, 180.

36. Ghazzālī, *Iḥyāʾ ʿulūm al-dīn,* IV:319. tr. Schimmel, *As Through a Veil*, 29; idem, *Mystical Dimensions*, 135; Ghazzālī, *Livre de L'Amour*, ed. Siauve, 170.

37. *ʿāshiq li-maʿbūdihi, mustahlikan fi-ḥubbihi*

38. For example, describing the experience of a Sufi adept, Avicenna writes: "Then when his training and willpower reach a certain point, glimmerings of the light of Truth will flicker before him, delightful [*ladhdha*], like lightning, flashing and going out." Avicenna, *Ishārāt*, tr. Goichon, 493; quoted by Ibn Ṭufayl, *Ḥayy*, Gauthier, 6; Goodman, 96.

39. For example, in addition to its Sufi sense, we find in Avicenna a philosophical use of *l-dh-dh* to describe the bliss of perfect conjunction with the Active Intellect: "When [a person] is delivered [liberated] from the body and the accidents of the body, it becomes possible for him to be conjoined [*yattaṣilu*] in a perfect conjunction [*ittiṣāl*] with the Active Intellect. There he will encounter the intellectual beauty and eternal delight [*ladhdha*]." Avicenna, *De Anima*, 248.

Maimonides, too describes the tremendous delight (*al-ladhdha al-ʿaẓīm*) of intellectual apprehension, which is greater than any bodily pleasure. One who dies in this state of apprehension remains permanently in that state of intense joy. *Guide* III:51; Joel, 462, line 25; 463, line 12; 459, line 6; Even-Shemuel, 488–89, 483; Pines, 627–28, 623. Cf. Warren Zev Harvey, "Crescas versus Maimonides on Knowledge and Pleasure," in *A Straight Path: Studies in Honor of Arthur Hyman*, ed. Ruth Link-Salinger (Washington, 1987), 119.

40. *al-mutafalsifīna*

41. As in the passage from Avicenna above, note 0. The *Ḥaver* himself asserts that the Greek philosophers had the ability to immerse themselves in the delight (*ladhidha*) of intellectual pursuits, whereas today knowledge has dimmed and we have lost that ability (III:1: 91).

42. He apparently ignores the case of Socrates, who was willing to die for his philosophical commitments.

43. *yutashawwaq shawqan dhawqan wa-mushāhadatan.* Baneth/Ben-Shammai suggest that the noun *shawq* (longing)—which functions here as a cognate accusative—may be a gloss, as it is not translated by Ibn Tibbon. The sentence literally

reads: the Lord is yearned for with a yearning (*shawqan*) of tasting and witnessing. The phrase is difficult to translate. Tasting and witnessing here are adverbs; it is the yearning that one viscerally experiences. However, it would seem that Ha-Levi wants to say that the seeker yearns to taste and witness the Lord, as the Psalm suggests. My translation, if somewhat awkward, is an attempt to allow for both senses, while being true to Ha-Levi's Arabic.

44. Abū Naṣr al-Sarrāj lists ten states (*aḥwāl*) of the soul: constant attention (*murāqaba*), proximity (*qurb*), love (*maḥabba*), fear (*khawf*), hope (*rajā'*), spiritual yearning (*shawq*), familiarity (*uns*), tranquility (*iṭmi'nān*), contemplation (*mushāhada*), and certainty (*yaqīn*). *Shawq* is also one of the terms discussed and defined in the theory of profane love. See Sarraj, *Kitāb al-luma'*, ed. Nicholson, 42; S. H. Nasr, "The Spiritual States in Sufism," 76; Schimmel, *Mystical Dimensions*, 132; Lois Giffen, *Theory of Profane Love*, 93.

45. Cf. the *Ḥaver*'s statement in I:109: 36: "The promises [*mawā'id*] of all these laws are included under one principle: the hope [expectation] of drawing near to God and his angels." Even-Shemuel reads this passage as referring to the promises of the other religions (Christianity and Islam), but I am not convinced by such a reading.

46. Al-Ghazzālī, *Iḥyā' 'ulūm al-dīn*, IV:336; tr. Schimmel, *As Through a Veil*, 24.

47. See above, 93 n.11.

48. *yaltazimu ṭā'a man adraqu dhawqan*

49. *ṭa'amu u-re'u ki tov Hashem*

50. As we have noted, the phrase *yaltazimu ṭā'a* harkens back to Sa'adya's Arabic translation of several passages in the book of Deuteronomy which use the language of clinging (*d-b-q*) to God. Sa'adya softened the Biblical language by using the phrase "clinging in obedience," (*lāzimīna ṭā'a*). Here the Arabic phrase *iltazama ṭā'a*—in the context of language of direct experience (*dhawq*)—might remind Ha-Levi's readers of certain tensions in the interpretation of *devequt*. See above, 42–44.

51. This notion is found in Philo, who offers an etymology of the name "Israel" as "one who sees God." See, for example, Philo, *On Rewards and Punishments* 44; *On Dreams* 2.173; *On Abraham* 57; *The Embassy to Gaius* 4. Ellen Birnbaum discusses this idea extensively in her illuminating study of Philo. See Birnbaum, *The Place of Judaism in Philo's Thought: Israel, Jews, and Proselytes* (Atlanta, 1996). It is interesting that Ha-Levi uses a new verb term, *naẓar*, as this is one used by philosophers, as well, to refer to philosophical speculation, contemplation, discernment, or insight.

52. *baṣar*

53. *burhān*

54. This notion has a precedent in al-Ghazzālī. See above, 207 n.5.

55. The *Ḥaver* suggests that the level of philosophical wisdom has degenerated as well. The ancient Greek philosophers practiced asceticism and seclusion profitably because of their powers of intellectual concentration (III:1: 90–91).

56. *suḥbat al-malā'ika*

57. *waḥda wa-khalwa*, two Sufi terms.

58. *yastawḥish*. The forms we have in manuscripts are all incorrect. Given the context, and the usual juxtaposition of *uns* and *waḥsha* (as in the example from Ghazzālī cited below), *yastawḥish*—feeling loneliness, pained by separation—makes most sense here. (Baneth-Ben-Shammai have *yatsawḥish*, which has no meaning in Arabic and is due to a copyist's reversal of letters. On the next line, the verb appears correctly as *yastawḥish*.)

59. *malakūt al-samā'*

60. 'Abdur Raḥmān Jāmī, *Nafaḥāt al-uns min ḥaḍarāt al-quds*, ed. Mahdi Tauḥīdīpur (Tehran, 1957), 94, cited by Schimmel, *Mystical Dimensions*, 132.

61. Schimmel, *Mystical Dimensions*, 132; see Ghazzālī, *Iḥyā' 'ulūm al-din*, IV:291.

62. As in the following striking verses, translated gracefully by Raymond Scheindlin:

> If only I could see Him in a dream.
> I'd sleep at ease, not caring if I died.
> If I could see His face within my heart,
> My eyes would never turn their gaze outside.

Aharon Komem has traced the theme of dreaming and sleep in Ha-Levi's poetry, as the states of the soul most conducive to intense religious experience. He notes Ha-Levi's paradoxical use of the image of sleep: it can express the laziness of the soul mired in the delights of the temporal, or its opposite, the soul running towards communion with her Creator. Komem points out that in both secular and sacred poetry, Ha-Levi expresses a longing to remain in sleep so as to prolong dream visions, a preference for prophetic vision over everyday reality. He suggests that Ha-Levi's emigration to the East, in contrast, expresses a desire to realize on the historical stage that which he had experienced in dream-visions—in particular, the event at Mount Sinai.

This latter pole is expressed in an exchange between the King and the *Ḥaver* in Book One:

> The *Ḥaver*: What do you think of someone who experienced those grand, divine theophanies [*man yushāhidu al-mashāhid al -'aẓīma al-malakutiyy*]?
>
> The King: No doubt he would long for his soul to separate from her senses and remain delighting [*tabqā maladhdatuhu*] in that light. Such a person would long for death.
>
> The *Ḥaver*: But *our* promises are *ittiṣāl* with the *'amr ilāhī* by prophecy and what approaches it, and the *ittiṣāl* of the *'amr ilāhī* with us by providence and wonders and miracles. (I:107–9: 35–36)

Both impulses were no doubt present in Ha-Levi. Komem interprets Ha-Levi's emigration to the Land of Israel as a turning away from the inwardness of meeting God in dreams and visions, a dramatic statement of the necessity of meeting God through action. Note Ha-Levi's striking phrase in the *Kuzari*: "Observance of the

Sabbath is in itself an acknowledgment of [divine] sovereignty, but it is an acknowledgment in the language of deeds [*iqrār bi-nutq ʿamaliy*]" (II:50: 70). See Scheindlin, *Gazelle*, 199; Schirmann, *Ha-shirah ha-ʿivrit* I:516; *Diwān*, ed. Brody, 2:296; Komem, *Ben shirah li-nevuah*, 683ff., 687–90, 694–95.

Conclusions

1. See Yehudah Ratzaby, "Borrowed Elements."

2. "So you are My witnesses," declares the Lord, "and I am God" (Isaiah 43:12). R. Shimʿon bar Yoḥai taught: "If you are My witnesses, I am God, and if you are not My witnesses, I am, as it were, not God." *Pesiqta de-Rav Kahana*, ed. S. Buber (Llyck, 1868; New York, 1949), 12:49, 103b; *Sifre Devarim*, ed. L. Finkelstein (Berlin, 1939; New York, 1969) 3:46, 403.

3. On this point, see the illuminating studies of Eliezer Schweid, "The Literary Structure of the First Book of the *Kuzari*," and *Ṭaʿam ve-haqasha.*

4. Compare with Maimonides, *Shemonah Peraqim,* chapter 4; *Mishneh Torah, "Hilkhot Deʿot,"* chapters 1 and 2.

5. The *Ḥaver* perhaps also echoes this passage when he says that the prophet sees the Glory as a great, fearsome form which points to (*tadullu*—from *d-l-l*) realities (truths) about which there is no doubt (IV:3: 155).

6. Davidson, Ivry, and others have stressed, correctly I believe, direct divine causality as one of Ha-Levi's cardinal principles. See Davidson's landmark article, "Cuzari," 374–81, 392–95. Davidson, in fact, interprets the *ʾamr ilāhī* as Ha-Levi's expression for direct divine causality (395). See also idem, *Intellect*, 190–95; Wolfson, "Hallevi and Maimonides on Design, Chance, and Necessity," *PAAJR* II (New York, 1941), 159.

7. For Saʿadya's use of *kalām* arguments, see Wolfson, *The Kalām*, 85, 87, passim; idem, *Repercussions of the Kalām in Jewish Philosophy* (Cambridge, 1979), passim. Wolfson notes that Saʿadya modified some of the *kalām* arguments he uses, rejecting such Muʿtazilite ideas as the existence of modes in God and the theory of atoms.

8. Saʿadya, *Amānāt*, Introduction, Qafih, 7; Rosenblatt, 9.

9. See above, 75–78 and below 171–174.

10. As Isaak Heinemann points out, the dialogue's avowed purpose is a "defense of the despised religion," and not a general theological presentation. Heinemann, *Rabi Yehudah Ha-Levi: Ha-'ish ve-hogeh ha-deʿot*, 132.

11. Strauss points out that *kalām* by its very nature is apologetic; its goal is to defend religion and—in Ha-Levi's words—to refute the heretic. Strauss characterizes the *Kuzari* itself as a work of *kalām*; however, it is doubtful that Ha-Levi would concur, given his attacks on *kalām* in V:1 and V:16. See Motzkin, "On Ha-Levi's *Kuzari*," 122 n.22. As we noted above (75 and notes), this was an internal Muslim critique of *kalām*, one which Maimonides echoes in I:71 of the *Guide*.

12. Contrast Maimonides' intellectual notion of ascending to levels of metaphysical study for which one is unprepared. See, for example, *Guide* I:32. On this point, see now Howard Kreisel, "Judah Halevi's Influence on Maimonides," in *Maimonidean Studies II*, ed. Arthur Hyman, 111.

13. *Amānāt*, Qafih, 111; Rosenblatt, 130; Altmann, "Saadya's Theory of Revelation," 19.

14. This assessment holds true even if there may have been original Sufi influence on the ideas of the gaonim. For possible Sufi influence on the gaonim, see Wolfson, "Merkavah" 219 and sources in n.24.

15. The one instance in which Saʿadya does not give a conservative rendering of the verb *d-b-q* is in the admonition (or promise) "and you will cling to him [*u-ledovqa bo*]" (Deuteronomy 11:22). Here, Saʿadya uses the same verb, but without the object *obedience* (*ṭāʿa*), translating simply *lazimahu*. However, perhaps he is relying on the previous phrase which speaks of "walking in all His ways," to interpret the language of clinging as metaphorical. See above, 198 n.97.

16. *Ishārāt*, ch. 9; Ibn Ṭufayl, *Ḥayy*, Gauthier, 7; Goodman, 97.

17. See above, p. 242 n.8.

18. Fenton affirms that the *Ḥaver*'s "criticism of ascetic solitude in the *Kuzari*, III:1 . . . is most certainly directed against Sufism." Fenton, *The Treatise of the Pool* 54, n.3.

19. Note that Baḥya praises the benefits of Saʿadya's works with as much enthusiasm as does Saʿadya (see p. 166 above): "Understand from the Book of your Lord that to which I have called your attention, and help yourself in that through the works of our Rabbi Saʿadya Gaon, for they bring light to the heart, sharpen the mind, direct the careless, and arouse the idle." Baḥya, *al-Hidāya*, Qafih, 42.

20. See Wolfson, *Kalām*, 85, 87. Wolfson notes that Baḥya, like Saʿadya before him in the East, used modified forms of the *kalām* arguments for the creation of the world and the existence of God, ones which eliminate the theory of atoms. See also Menahem Mansoor, "Translator's Introduction," *Book of Direction*, 25–29, 38–39.

21. Cf. Bernard Septimus, *Hispano-Jewish Culture in Transition*, 61–62 and nn.3, 11; Baneth, "Autographs," 300.

22. In this, Baḥya follows Sufis like Qushayri who also denounced *taqlīd*. See above, 207 n.74.

23. Baḥya, *Al-Hidāja*, ed. Yahuda, 379; tr. Qafih, 410; tr. Ibn Tibbon, Hyamson, 342–43.

24. Some in the Islamic world did reject *ilhām* as a source of valid knowledge. See Van Ess, *Erkentisslehre*, 121ff.

25. These are at least the *Ḥaver*'s avowed opponents. If Ha-Levi was indeed aware of Saʿadya's views on *waḥy* and *ilhām*, as seems likely, he might also have the Karaites in mind in I:87, although he does not make this explicit.

26. See Baneth, "Halevi," 312. Kaufmann comments, for example, that "the statements of Yehudah Ha-Levi sound like a translation from Ghazzālī." *Attributenlehre*, 128.

27. See Ghazzālī, *Iḥyā' 'ulūm al-dīn* (Bulaq, 1872–73), I:22; *The Book of Knowledge*, tr. Faris, 54–55. For Ghazzālī on *kalām*, see also *Munqidh*, 80–83; Watt, 27–29; McCarthy, 68–69.

28. Ironically, thinkers often themselves exhibit some of the traits against which they polemicize. Just as Leo Strauss saw the resemblance between the *Kuzari* and *kalām* literature, so David Baneth suggests that Ghazzālī's *Tahafūt al-falāsifa* shares some (negative) traits of works of *kalām*. See Baneth, "Halevi ve-al-Ghazzālī," 313.

29. The *Ḥaver* at the end of IV:25 tells the King: "I communicated these principles to you lest the philosophers confuse you, and you might think that if you follow them, your soul would find rest in satisfactory proof [*la-araḥat nafsuka bi-l-burhān al-shāfī*]" (IV:25: 183).

And in IV:17, the *Ḥaver* says: "All who follow the divine law [*al-nāmūs al-ilāhī*] follow the people of this seeing [*baṣar*]. Their souls find pleasantness [*taṭayyaba*] in *taqlīd* upon them, [despite] the simplicity of their speech and the coarseness of their examples, a pleasantness they do not find in *taqlīd* on the philosophers, [despite] the fineness of their examples, and the fine order of their compositions, and the proof [*burhān*] that appears to them. Nevertheless the masses do not follow them" (IV:17: 169).

30. Cf. Kaufmann, *Attributenlehre*, 126–28; Baneth, "Ha-Levi ve-al-Ghazzālī," 315–16.

31. There are, of course, significant differences between the two thinkers' use of this image. Ghazzālī appears to draw upon both a Neo-Platonic, intellectual concept of inner vision and a Sufi, mystical or intuitive concept. Ha-Levi, in contrast, sharply contrasts prophetic vision with intellectual knowledge. However, like Ha-Levi, who describes the inner eye as an "internal sense," Ghazzālī firmly believes that the inner eye sees what is not available to the ordinary intellect.

32. Ghazzālī, *Munqidh*, 139–40; McCarthy, 98–99; Watt, 65–66.

33. See, for example, IV:3, V:14, II:66, III:41. Note that Ghazzālī attributes knowledge to *ilhām*—a controversial assertion, as we saw in Part Four.

34. Ghazzālī, *Mishkāt al-anwār* (*The Niche for Lights*), ed. A. Affīfī (Cairo, 1964), 78; tr. W. H. T. Gairdner (London, 1924), 82–83; cited by Efros, "Mysticism," 148.

35. Efros, ibid.

36. Ghazzālī, ibid.

37. *Munqidh*, 137–40; McCarthy, 96–99; Watt, 63–67; Lazarus-Yafeh, *Studies*, 295–306.

38. *Munqidh*, 136; McCarthy, 95; Watt, 64.

39. See Lazarus-Yafeh, "Place of the Religious Commandments in the Philosophy of Al-Ghazzālī," *The Muslim World* 51 (1961), 173 reprinted in idem, *Studies*, 413. Baneth, on the other hand, believes that the commandments are merely propaeduetic for Ghazzālī. See Baneth, "Halevi ve-al-Ghazzālī," 326–27.

40. *Kuzari* I:98: 32; cf. II:46: 68. Lazarus-Yafeh, "Place of the Religious Commandments," *The Muslim World*, 177. While the article is reprinted in *Studies in al-Ghazzālī*, this quote has been omitted.

41. I have been enriched on the subject of dialogue through conversations with Joel Rosenberg.

Bibliography

Primary Texts

(Modern translations are listed under Secondary Literature)

Editions of the Kuzari

Judah b. Samuel Ha-Levi.
———. *Kitāb al-radd wa'l-dalīl fī'l-dīn al-dhalīl (al-kitāb al-khazarī)*. Edited by David H. Baneth and Haggai Ben-Shammai. Jerusalem: Magnes Press, 1977.
———. *Le Kuzari: Apologie de la religion méprisée*. Translated by Charles Touati. Paris: Verdier, 1994.
———. *Sefer ha-Kuzari: Maqor ve-targum*. Translated by Joseph Qafih. Kiryat Ono, 1997.
———. *Sefer ha-kuzari*. Translated by Judah Ibn Tibbon. Edited by A. Zifroni. Maḥbarot le-Sifrut, 1948.
———. *Das Buch Al-Chazari des Abū-l-Ḥasan Jehuda Hallewi im Arabischen Urtext sowie in der Hebräischen Ubersetzung des Jehuda Ibn Tibbon. Herausgegeben von Hartwig Hirschfeld*. Leipzig: Otto Schulze, 1887.

Other Primary Texts

'Abd al-Rāzzāq. *Iṣṭilāḥāt al-ṣūfīya* (Dictionary of the Technical Terms of the Sufies). Edited by Aloys Sprenger. Calcutta, 1845.
Abraham ben Meir Ibn Ezra. *Perushe ha-Torah le-Rabbenu Avraham Ibn Ezra*. Edited by Asher Weiser. Three vols. Jerusalem: Mossad Harav Kook, 1976.
Avot de Rabbi Natan. Edited by Solomon Schechter. Vienna, 1887. New York: Feldheim, 1967.

Baḥya Ibn Paqūda. *Kitāb al-hidāja 'ilā farā'iḍ al-qulūb*. Edited by Abraham S. Yahuda. Leiden: E. J. Brill, 1912.

———. *Kitāb al-hidāya ilā farā'iḍ al-qulūb* (*Torat ḥovot ha-levavot*). Edited and translated by Joseph Qafih. Jerusalem, 1973.

Abū-Naṣr al-Fārābī. *Falsafat Aflatūn*. Edited by Frank Rosenthal and Richard Walzer. London, 1943.

———. *Fuṣūl al-madanī*. Edited by D. Dunlop. Cambridge, 1961.

———. *Kitāb al-milla*. Edited by Muhsin Mahdi. Beirut: DarEl-Machreq, 1967.

———. *Mabādi' ārā' ahl al-madīna al-fāḍila*. Published as *Al-Fārābī on the Perfect State: Abū Naṣr al-Fārābī's Mabādi' ārā' ahl al-madīna al-fāḍila*. A revised text with introduction, translation, and commentary by Richard Walzer. Oxford: Clarendon Press; New York: Oxford University Press, 1985. Published by Friedrich Dieterici as *Der Musterstaat von Alfarabi*. Leiden: E. J. Brill, 1900.

———. *Al-siyāsa al-madaniyya*. Edited by F. Najjar. Beirut, 1964.

Abū Ḥāmid al-Ghazzālī. *Iḥyā' 'ulūm al-dīn*. (The Revival of the Religious Sciences). Bulaq, 1872–73.

———. *Iḥyā' 'ulūm al-dīn*. Cairo, 1356/57 A.H.

———. *Mishkāt al-anwār*. Edited by A. Afifi. Cairo, 1964.

———. *Mizān al-'amal*. Cairo, 1328 A.H.

———. *Mizān al-'amal*. Translated by R. Abraham Ibn Ḥasdai as *Mozne Tsedeq*. Edited by Jacob Godenthal. Leipzig: Gebhardt and Reisland, 1839.

———. *Al-Munqidh min al-ḍalāl*. Damascus, 1939.

———. *Tahāfut al-falāsifa*. Edited by Maurice Bouyges and published as *AlGazel: Tahāfot al-falāsifa*. Beirut: Imprimerie Catholique, 1927.

Ibn Bājja. *Tadbīr al-mutawḥḥid* (*Governance of the Solitary*). In *Opera Metaphysica*. Edited by M. Fakhry. Beirut: Dār al-Nahār, 1968.

Ibn Khaldun. *Al-Muqāddima. Prolegomènes d'Ebn-Khaldoun*. Texte Arabe par E. Quatremere. Notices et Extraits des manuscrits de la Bibliotheque Imperiale (Academie des Inscriptions et Belles-Lettres), vols. xvi-xviii. Paris, 1858.

———. *Ibn Khaldun: The Muqāddimah; An Introduction to History*. Translated by Franz Rosenthal. Three vols. New York: Pantheon Books, 1958.

Ibn Sīnā (Avicenna). *Fī-ithbāt al-nubuwwāt*. Edited by Michael Marmura. Beirut, 1968.

———. *Kitāb al-ishārāt wa-l-tanbīhāt*. Edited by Jacques Forget. Leiden: E. J. Brill, 1892.

———. *Kitāb al-mubāhathāt*. In *Arisṭū 'ind al-'Arab*. Edited by 'Abd al-Raḥmān Badawi. Cairo, 1947.

———. *Al-najāt*. Cairo, 1938.

———. "Die Psychologie des Ibn Sīnā." Published by S. Landauer. *Zeitschrift der deutschen morgenlandischen Gesellschaft* 29 (1876).

———. *Sharh kitāb uthūlūjiya al-mansūb 'ilā Arisṭū li-'ibn Sīnā* (Glosses on the Theology of Aristotle) in *Arisṭū 'ind al-'arab*, ed. 'Abd al-Raḥmān Badawi (Cairo, 1947)

———. *Shifā': De Anima*. Published as *Avicenna's De Anima* (*Arabic Text*). *Psychological Part of Kitāb al-Shifā'*. Edited by Fazlur Rahman. London: Oxford University Press, 1959.

———. *Shifā': Ilāhiyyāt*. Edited by George Anawati and S. Zayed. Cairo. 1960.

Ibn Ṭufayl. *Ḥayy Ibn Yaqẓan*. Edited by Leon Gauthier. *Ḥayy ben Yaqdhān: Roman philosophique d'Ibn Thofaïl*. Beirut: Imprimerie Catholique, 1936.
Ikhwān al-Ṣafā'. *Rasā'īl Ikhwān al-ṣafā'*. Four vols. Beirut, 1957.
———. *Rasa'īl Ikhwān al-Ṣafā'*. Four vols. Cairo, 1928.
Isaac Israeli. *The Mantua Text* (The Chapter on the Elements). Published by Alexander Altmann. "Isaac Israeli's *Chapter on the Elements*." *Journal of Jewish Studies* 7 (1956).
———. *Sefer ha-Yesodot* (The Book of Elements). Drogobych: A. H. Zupniq, 1900.
Judah Ha-Levi. *Selected Poems of Yehudah Halevi*. Edited by Heinrich Brody and translated by Nina Salaman. Philadelphia: Jewish Publication Society of America, 1928.
———. *Dīwān des Abū-l-Ḥasan Jehuda ha-Levi*. Edited by Heinrich Brody. Berlin: Mekize Nirdamim, 1894–1930.
———. *Kitāb al-radd wa'l-dalīl fī'l-dīn al-dhalīl* (*al-kitāb al-khazarī*). Edited by David H. Baneth and Haggai Ben-Shammai (Jerusalem: Magnes Press, 1977).
———. *Selected Poems*. Edited by Heinrich Brody and translated by Nina Salaman. Philadelphia: Jewish Publication Society of America, 1928.
———. *Shire ha-qodesh le-rabi Yehuda ha-Levi* (The Liturgical Poetry). Four vols. Edited by Dov Yarden. Jerusalem, 1978–85.
Judah b. Barzilai. *Perush Sefer Yetsirah*. Edited by S. Halberstam. Breslau, 1885.
al-Jurjānī, 'Ali ibn Muhammad al-Sayyid al-Sharif. *Kitāb al-Ta'rifāt* (Definitiones). Edited by Gustavus Flugel. Leipzig, 1845.
al-Makkī, Abū Tālib. *Qūt al-qulūb fi mu'āmalāt al-maḥbūb*. Cairo, 1892–93/1310.
Mekhilta de Rabbi Ishmael. Edited by H. S. Horovitz and I. A. Rabin. Frankfurt, 1928–31. Edited by J. Z. Lauterbach. Three vols. Philadelphia: Jewish Publication Society, 1933–35.
Midrash Bereshit Rabbah. Edited by J. Theodor and C. Albeck. Two vols. Berlin, 1912–31.
Midrash Rabbah. Two vols. Warsaw, 1876.
Midrash Tehillim (*Shoḥer ṭov*). Edited by Solomon Buber. Vilna, 1891.
Moses ben Maimon (Maimonides). *Dalālat al-ḥa'irīn*. Edited by Salomon Munk. Jerusalem, 1929.
———. *Mishnah 'im perush rabbenu Moshe ben Maimon*. Edited and translated by Josef Qafih. Jerusalem: Mossad Harav Kook, 1964–68.
———. *Mishneh Torah*. Warsaw, 1881.
———. *Sefer moreh ha-nevukhim*. Translated by Samuel Ibn Tibbon. Notes by Yehudah Even-Shemuel. Jerusalem: Mossad Harav Kook, 1981.
———. *Shemonah Peraqim* (*Haqdamah le-masekhet Avot*). Edited and translated by Yitzhaq Sheilat. In idem, *Haqdamot ha-Rambam la-Mishnah*, 227–56 (Hebrew); 375–99 (Arabic). Jerusalem, 1994.
Moses ben Nahman (Nahmanides). *Perushe ha-Torah le-Rabbenu Moshe ben Nahman* (*Ramban*). 2d ed. Edited by C. Chavel. Two vols. Jerusalem: Mossad Harav Kook, 1980.
Nathan of Rome. *'Arukh Completum* (*Ha-'Arukh ha-shalem*). Edited by Alexander Kohut. Vienna: Menorah, 1926.

Nissim ben Jacob of Kairouan. "Extracts from the Book Megillat Setarim of Rabbi Nissim ben Jacob of Kairouan" (Hebrew). Published by Samuel A. Poznanski. *Ha-Tsofeh le-Ḥokhmat Yisrael* 5 (1921): 177–84.

Pesiqta de-Rav Kahana. Edited by Solomon Buber. Lyck, 1868. Reproduced by Om Publishing Company, New York, 1949.

Pesiqta Rabbati. Edited by M. Friedmann. Vienna, 1880.

Philo. *Philo in Ten Volumes*. Translated by F. H. Colson, G. H. Whitaker, and Ralph Marcus. Loeb Classics Series. Cambridge: Harvard University Press, 1929–62.

Plotini Opera. Edited by Paul Henry and Hans-Rudolf Schwyzer. Paris: Désclée de Brouwer, 1959.

Plotinus. *Enneads*. Translated by A. H. Armstrong. Loeb Classics Series. Cambridge, Mass.: Harvard University Press, 1984.

Plotinus apud arabes. Edited by ʿAbd al-Raḥmān Badawī. Cairo, 1955.

al-Qirqisānī, Yaʿqūb Yusuf. *Kitāb al-anwār wa-l-marāqib*, ed. Leon Nemoy. New York: Alexander Kohut Memorial Foundation, 1939.

al-Qushayri, ʿAbd al-Karīm ibn Hawazim. *Al-risāla al-Qushayrīya*. Edited by Mahmud and Sharif. Two vols. Cairo, 1966.

Saʿadya ben Yosef al-Fayyumi Gaon. *Commentaire sur le sefer yetsira par le Gaon Saadya de Fayyoum*. Edited and translated by Meyer Lambert. Paris: Emile Bouillon, 1891.

———. *Daniel im Targum u-ferush Rabenu Saʿadya Ben Yosef Fayyumi u-ferush Tanhum ha-Yerushalmi*. Translated by Joseph Qafih. Jerusalem, 1980–81.

———. *Ha-egron (Kitāb uṣūl al-shiʿr al-ʿibrānī) me-et Rav Saʿadya Ga'on*. Edited by N. Allony. Jerusalem: The Academy of the Hebrew Language, 1969.

———. *Iyov ʿim targum u-ferush ha-Gaon Rabenu Saʿadya ben Yosef Fayyumi*. Translated by Joseph Qafih. Jerusalem, 1972–73.

———. *Kitāb al-mukhtār fī'l-āmānāt wa'l-iʿtiqādāt*. Translated and edited by Joseph Qafih. Jerusalem: Sura Institute for Research and Publication, 1970.

———. *Perushe Rav Saʿadya Gaon li-Vereshit*. Translated by Moshe Zucker. New York: Jewish Theological Seminary, 1984.

———. *Sefer ha-galui*. In *Ha-sharid ve-ha-palit mi-sefer ha-igron ve-sefer ha-galui*. Edited by Elhanan Harkavy. St. Peterbourg, 1892.

———. *Tehillim ʿim targum u-ferush ha-gaon rabbenu Saʿadya ben yosef fayyumi*. Edited and translated by Joseph Qafih.

———. *Version arabe du pentateuque*. Edited by Jacques Derenbourg.

al-Sarrāj, Abu Nasr ʿAbdallah b. ʿAli. *Kitāb al-luma' fi'l-taṣawwuf*. Edited by Reynold A. Nicholson. Leiden and London: Gibb Memorial Series, no. 22, 1914.

Shemot Rabbah. Vilna, 1887.

Shir ha-Shirim Rabbah. Warsaw, 1876.

Sifré debé Rab. Edited by M. Friedmann. Vienna, 1864.

Siphre ad Deuteronomium. Edited by Louis Finkelstein. Berlin, 1939. Reproduced New York: Jewish Theological Seminary of America, 1969.

Al-Ṭabarī, Abū Ja'far Muḥammad ibn Jarīr. *Jāmiʿ al-bayān ʿan ta'wīl al-Qur'ān*. Cairo, 1954.

Al-Tabarsi. *Majmaʿ al-bayān fī tafsīr al-Qur'ān*. Beirut, 1955.

Kitāb Uthulūjiya Aristatalis (*Die Sogenannte Theologie des Aristoteles*). Edited by Friedrich Dieterici. Leipzig: J. C. Hinrichs'sche Buchhandlung, 1883.

Yalqut Shim'oni. Edited by Arthur B. Hyman. Jerusalem: Mossad Harav Kook, 1991.

Yefet b. 'Elī. Commentary to Exodus 21. British Museum Manuscript 2468.

al-Zamakhsharī, Jadullah Mahmud ibn 'Umar. *Tafsīr al-kashshāf 'an ḥaqā'iq ghawāmid al-tanzīl wa-'uyūn al-'aqāwil fī wujūḥ al-ta'wīl*. Edited by Mustafa Husain Ahmad. Four vols. 2d ed. Cairo, 1953–55.

Secondary Literature

'Abd al-Razzāq al-Qāshānī. *A Glossary of Sufi Technical Terms*. Translated by Nabil Safwat. London: Octagon Press, 1991.

Abramson, Shraga. "R. Judah Ha-Levi's Letter on His Emigration to the Land of Israel" (Hebrew). *Kiryat Sefer* 29 (1953–54): 133–44.

Aloni, Nehemiah. "*The Kuzari*: an Anti-Arabiyyah Polemic [Hebrew]." *Eshel Be'er Sheva, 2: 119–44*

Altmann, Alexander. "Moses Narboni's 'Epistle on *Shi'ur Qomah*." In *Studies in Religious Philosophy and Mysticism*. Ithaca: Cornell University Press, 1969.

———. "Saadya's Theory of Revelation: Its Origin and Background." In *Saadya Studies*, ed. E. I. J. Rosenthal, 4–25. Manchester: Manchester University Press, 1943.

———. "Ibn Bājja on Man's Ultimate Felicity." In *H. A. Wolfson Jubilee Volume* (English Section). Vol. 1. 47–88. Jerusalem: American Adademy for Jewish Research, 1965. Reprinted in Alexander Altmann, *Studies in Religious Philosophy and Mysticism*, 73–107. Ithaca: Cornell University Press, 1969.

———. "The Climatological Factor in Yehuda Ha-Levi's Theory of Prophecy [Hebrew]." *Melilah* 1 [1944]: 1–17.

———. "Maimonides and Thomas Aquinas: Natural or Divine Prophecy?" *Association for Jewish Studies Review*, Volume III (1978), 1–19. Reprinted in, *Essays in Jewish Intellectual History* (Hanover, N.H.: University Press of New England for Brandeis University, 1981), 77–96.

———. *Saadya Gaon: The Book of Doctrines and Beliefs*. Oxford: East and West Library, 1946; reprint in *Three Jewish Philosophers*. New York: Atheneum, 1977.

———, and S. M. Stern. *Isaac Israeli: A Neoplatonic Philosopher of the Early Tenth Century*. London: Oxford University Press, 1958.

Ankori, Zvi. *Karaites in Byzantium*. New York: Columbia University Press/Jerusalem: Weizmann Science Press, 1959.

Arberry, Arthur J. *Avicenna on Theology*. London: John Murray, 1951.

———. "Fārābī's Canons of Poetry," *Revista degli Studi Orientali* XVII (1937).

———. *Sufism: An Account of the Mystics of Islam*. London: G. Allen and Unwin, 1968.

Ariel, David S. "'The Eastern Dawn of Wisdom': The Problem of the Relation between Islamic and Jewish Mysticism." In *Approaches to Judaism in Medieval Times,* vol. 2. Edited by David R. Blumenthal. Chico, Ca.: Scholars' Press, 1985: 149–67.

Baḥya ibn Paqūda. *The Book of Direction to the Duties of the Heart.* Translated by Menahem Mansoor with Sara Arenson and Shoshana Dannhauser. London: Routledge & Kegan Paul, 1973.

———. *Duties of the Heart.* Translated into Hebrew by Yehuda Ibn Tibbon. With English translation by Moses Hyamson. New York: Feldheim, 1962.

———. *Torat ḥovot ha-levavot: maqor ve-targum.* Translated by Josef Qafih. Jerusalem, 1973.

Baneth, David H. "*R. Yehudah Ha-Levi ve-al-Ghazzālī.*" *Keneset* 7:312–29; "Judah Halevi and al-Ghazali." Translated by G. Hirschler. In *Studies in Jewish Thought: An Anthology of German Jewish Scholarship.* Edited by Alfred Jospe, 181–99. Detroit: Wayne State University Press, 1981.

———."Some Remarks on the Autographs of Yehudah Hallevi and the Genesis of the Kuzari." (Hebrew). *Tarbiz* 26 (1957): 297–303.

Bell, Joseph Norment. *Love Theory in Later Hanbalite Islam.* Albany: State University of New York Press, 1979.

Ben-Shammai, Haggai. "On a Polemical Element in R. Sa'adya Gaon's Theory of Prophecy." *Jerusalem Studies in Jewish Thought,* Vol. 7 (*Jubilee Volume Dedicated to Shlomo Pines,* 1971–72, Part One), 127–46.

———. Review of Uriel Simon, *Four Approaches to the Book of Psalms* in *Kiryat Sefer* 58:1 400–406.

———. *Shiṭot ha-maḥshavah ha-datit shel Abū Yūsuf Ya'qūb al-Qirqisānī ve-Yefet ben 'Elī.* Jerusalem: Hebrew University, 1977.

Berger, Michael. "Toward a New Understanding of Judah Halevi's *Kuzari.*" *Journal of Religion* 72 (2) (1992): 210–28.

Birnbaum, Ellen. *The Place of Judaism in Philo's Thought: Israel, Jews, and Proselytes.* Atlanta: Scholars' Press, 1996.

Brann, Ross. *The Compunctious Poet: Cultural Ambiguity and Hebrew Poetry in Muslim Spain.* Baltimore: Johns Hopkins University Press, 1991.

Cohen, Gerson. *Abraham Ibn Daud: The Book of Tradition* (*Sefer ha-qabbalah*). Philadelphia: Jewish Publication Society, 1967.

Coulson, Noel J. *A History of Islamic Law.* Edinburgh: Edinburgh University Press, 1964.

Davidson, Herbert. "The Active Intellect in the Kuzari and Hallevi's Theory of Causality." *Révue des études juives* 131 (1973): 351–96.

———. *Alfarabi, Avicenna, and Averroes, on Intellect.* Oxford and New York: Oxford University Press, 1992.

———. "Alfarabi and Avicenna on Active Intellect." *Viator* 3 (1972).

Dozy, Reinhart. *Supplément aux dictionnaires arabes.* Leiden: E. J. Brill, 1967.

Efros, Israel. "Sa'adya's Theory of Knowledge." In *Studies in Medieval Jewish Philosophy.* New York and London: Columbia University Press, 1974.

———. "Some Aspects of Yehudah Ha-Levi's Mysticism." *Studies in Medieval Jewish Philosophy.* New York and London: Columbia University Press, 1974, 143–54.

Eisen, Robert. "The Problem of the King's Dream and Non-Jewish Prophecy in

Judah Halevi's *Kuzari.*" *Jewish Thought and Philosophy* 3 (1994): 231–247.
Ernst, Carl. *Words of Ecstasy in Sufism*. Albany: State University of New York Press, 1985.
Al-Fārābī. Al-Fārābī on the Perfect State: Abū Naṣr al-Fārābī's *Mabādi' ārā' ahl al-madīna al-fādila*. Revised text with introduction, translation, and commentary by Richard Walzer. Oxford: Clarendon Press; New York: Oxford University Press, 1985.
———. *The Philosophy of Plato and Aristotle*, Edited by Muhsin Mahdi, pp. 64–65.
———. "Treatise on the Canons of the Art of Poetry." Translated by Arthur Arberry. In Arthur Arberry, "Fārābī's Canons of Poetry," *Revista degli Studi Orientali* XVII (1937).
Feldman, Seymore. "Review Essay: Judah Halevi's *The Kuzari* in French." Review of Charles Touati, trans. *Le Kuzari: Apologie de la religion méprisée, AJS Review* 21:1 (1996): 119–23.
Fenton, Paul, ed. *'Obadyāh b. Abraham b. Moses Maimonides' The Treatise of the Pool* (*al-Maqāla al-ḥawḍiyya*). London: Octagon Press, 1981.
Gardet, Louis. *La Pensée réligieuse d'Avicenne*. Paris: Librairie Philosophique J. Vrin, 1951.
Gartner, Ya'aqov. "*Hashpa'atam shel avale tsion 'al minhage tish'a be-Av bi-tequfat ha-gaonim.*" *Annual of Bar-Ilan University: Studies in Judaica and Humanities* 20–21, 1983: 128–44.
Gatje, Helmut. *The Qur'ān and Its Exegesis: Selected Texts with Classical and Modern Muslim Interpretations*. London and Henley: Routledge and Kegan Paul, 1971.
Gauthier, Leon. *Ḥayy ben Yaqdhān: Roman philosophique d'Ibn Thofaïl*. Beirut: Imprimerie Catholique, 1936.
Al-Ghazzālī. *Al-Ghazzālī's Mishkāt Al-Anwār* ("*The Niche for Lights*"). Edited by W. H. T. Gairdner. Lahore: Sh. Muhammad Ashraf, 1952.
———. *The Book of Knowledge*. Translation with notes of the *Kitāb al-'ilm of Al-Ghazzālī's Iḥyā' 'ulūm al-dīn* by Nabi Amin Faris. Lahore: Sh. Muhammad Ashraf, 1962.
———. *Al-Ghazali's Tahāfut al-falāsifa* (*Incoherence of the Philosophers*). Translated by Sabih Ahmad Kamali. Lahore: Pakistan Philosophical Congress, 1958.
Giffen, Lois Anita. *Theory of Profane Love among the Arabs: The Development of the Genre*. New York: New York University Press, 1971.
Goichon, A.-M. *Lexique de la langue philosophique d'ibn Sīnā* (*Avicenne*). Paris: Désclée de Brouwer, 1938.
———, translator. *Livre des directives et remarques d'Avicenne* (*Kitāb al-isharāt wa'l-tanbihāt*). Paris: Librarie Philosophique J. Vrin, 1951.
Goitein, Shlomo Dov. *A Mediterranean Society*. Vol. 5. Berkeley and Los Angeles: University of California Press, 1988.
———. "Autographs of Yehuda Hallevi." *Tarbiz* 25 (1955–56): 393–412 (Hebrew).
———. "The Biography of Rabbi Judah Ha-Levi in Light of the Cairo Genizah Documents." *Proceedings of the American Academy of Jewish Research* 28 (1959): 41–56.
Goldreich, Amos. "Possible Arabic Sources for the Distinction Between 'Duties of the Heart' and 'Duties of the Limbs.'" (Hebrew). *Te'udah* 6 (1988): 179–208.

Goldziher, Ignaz. "*Mélanges judéo-arabes: Le 'Amr ilāhī (ha-'inyan ha-'elohi) chez Juda Halevi*," *Révue des études juives* 50 (1905): 32–41.
———. *Muslim Studies*. Edited by S. M. Stern. Chicago: Aldine Atherton 1967–71.
———. *The Ẓāhirīs: Their Doctrine and Their History*. Translated by Wolfgang Behn. Leiden: E. J. Brill, 1971.
Goodman, Lenn. "Ibn Bajjah." In History of Islamic Philosophy. Edited by S. H. Nasr. London: Routledge, 1995: 294–312.
———. *Ibn Ṭufayl's Ḥayy Ibn Yaqẓān*. Los Angeles: Gee Tee Bee, 1983.
———. "Judah Halevi." In *History of Jewish Philosophy*, Edited by D. Frank and O. Leaman. London: Routledge, 1996.
Groner, Tsvi. *The Legal Methodology of Hai Gaon*. Chico, Calif.: Scholars Press, 1985.
Grunebaum. G. E. von. "The Logical Structure of Islamic Theology." *Logic in Classical Islamic Culture*. Wiesbaden: O. Harrassowitz, 1970.
Gutas, Dimitri. *Avicenna and the Aristotelian Tradition: An Introduction to Reading Avicenna's Philosophical Works*. Leiden: E. J. Brill, 1988.
Guttmann, Julius. "*Ha-dat ve-ha-mada' ba-maḥshavat yeme-ha-benayim ve-ha-'et ha-ḥadasha*." In *Dat u-mada': kovets ma'amarim ve-hartsa'ot*. Jerusalem: Magnes Press, 1955.
Halkin, Abraham S. "*Mi-petiḥat Rav Sa'adya Gaon le-ferush ha-Torah*." In *Sefer ha-Yovel Li-khevod Levi Ginzberg*. New York, 1945.
Hallaq, Wael B. "Was Shafi'i the Master Architect of Islamic Jurisprudence?" In *International Journal of Middle East Studies* 25 (1993), 587–605.
———. "Was the Gate of Ijtihād Closed?" In *International Journal of Middle East Studies* 16 (1984), 3–4: 3–41.
Halperin, David J. "A New Edition of the Heikhalot Literature," *Journal of the American Oriental Society* 104, no. 3 (1984): 544, 547, 550–51.
———. *The Merkavah in Rabbinic Literature*. New Haven, Conn.: American Oriental Society, 1980.
Harris, Jay. *How Do We Know This? Midrash and the Fragmentation of Modern Judaism*. Albany: State University of New York Press, 1994.
Harkavy, Elhanan. *Ha-sharid ve-ha-paliṭ mi-sefer ha-'igron ve-sefer ha-galui*. St. Peterbourg, 1892.
Harvey, Steven. "The Place of the Philosopher in the City According to Ibn Bājjah." In *The Political Aspects of Islamic Philosophy: Essays in Honor of Muhsin S. Mahdi*. Edited by C. Butterworth. Cambridge, Mass.: Harvard, 1992: 199–233.
Harvey, Warren Zev. "Judah Halevi's Synthetic Theory of Prophecy and a note on the Zohar" (in Hebrew). *Jerusalem Studies in Jewish Thought* 13 (1996) (Rivkah Schatz-Uffenheimer Memorial Volume). Edited by R. Elior and J. Dan: 141–56.
Heinemann, Isaak. "*Helekh ha-ra'yonot shel hatḥalat sefer ha-Kuzari*." In *Rabi Yehudah Halevi: kovets meḥkarim ve-ha'arakhot*, edited by Israel Zemorah. Tel Aviv: *Maḥbarot le-sifrut*, 1950.
———."*Rabbi Yehudah Halevi: ha-'ish ve-hogeh* ha-*de'ot*." In *Qovets Rabbi Yehudah Ha-Levi*, edited by Israel Zemorah, 131–65. Tel Aviv: Mahbarot le-Sifrut, 1950.
———. "*Ha-pilosof ha-meshorer: be'ur le-mivhar piyyutim shel Rabbi Yehudah Ha-*

Levi." In *Qovets Rabbi Yehudah Halevi*, edited by Israel Zemorah, 166–235. Tel Aviv: Maḥbarot le-sifrut, 1950.

Heinrichs, Wolfhart. "The Meaning of Mutanabbī." In *Poetry and Prophecy*. Edited by James Kugel. Ithaca and London: Cornell University Press, 1990.

Al-Hujwīrī, ʿAli ibn ʿUthman al-Jullībī, *Kashf al-Maḥjūb: The Oldest Persian Treatise on Sufism*. Translated by Reynold A. Nicholson. Leiden: E. J. Brill, 1911; London: Luzac, 1936.

Ibn ʿArabī, Muhyī al-Dīn. *Sufis of Andalusia: The Rūh al-quds and al-Durrat al-fākhirah of Ibn ʿArabī*. Translated by R. W. J. Austin. London: George Allen & Unwin, 1971.

Ibn Sīnā. *Livre de directives et remarques*. Translated by A.- M. Goichon. Paris: Librarie philosophique J. Vrin, 1951.

———. *Remarks and Admonitions*. Translated by Shams Constantine Inati. Toronto: Pontifical Institute of Mediaeval Studies, 1984.

Idel, Moshe. "*Hitbodedut* as Concentration." In *Studies in Ecstatic Kabbalah*. Albany: State University of New York Press, 1988.

———. *Kabbalah: New Perspectives*. New Haven and London: Yale University Press, 1988.

———. "The World of Angels in Human Form" (Hebrew). In *Studies in Philosophy, Mysticism, and Ethical Literature presented to Isaiah Tishby on His Seventy-fifth Birthday*. Jerusalem: Magnes Press, 1986.

Inati, Shams Constantine, translator. *Remarks and Admonitions*. Toronto: Pontifical Institute of Mediaeval Studies, 1984.

Ivry, Alfred. "Averroes on Intellection and Conjunction." *Journal of the American Oriental Society*, 86, 2 (April-June): 1966, 76–85.

———. "Moses of Narbonne's 'Treatise on the Perfection of the Soul,' A Methodological and Conceptual Analysis," *JQR* 57 (1966): 271–97.

———. "Neoplatonic Currents in Maimonides' Thought." In *Perspectives on Maimonides*, edited by Joel L. Kraemer. Oxford: University Press for The Littman Library, 1991, 115–40.

———. "The Philosophical and Religious Arguments in Rabbi Yehuda Halevy's Thought" (Hebrew). In *Thought and Action: Essays in Memory of Simon Rawidowicz on the Twenty-fifth Anniversary of His Death*. Edited by Abraham Greenbaum and Alfred Ivry. Tel Aviv, 1983.

Judah b. Samuel Ha-Levi. *The Kosari of R. Yehudah Halevi* (Hebrew). Translated by Yehudah Even-Shemuel. Second edition. Tel Aviv: Dvir, 1972.

———. *Judah Hallevi's Kitāb al-Khazari*. Translated by Hartwig Hirschfeld. London: Routledge, 1905.

———. *Kuzari: The Book of Proof and Argument*. Translated by Isaak Heinemann. Oxford: East and West Library, 1947. Reprinted in *Three Jewish Philosophers*. New York: Atheneum, 1977.

Kaufmann, David. "R. Yehuda Ha-Levi." In *Rabbi Yehudah Ha-Levi*, edited by J. L. Fishman. Jerusalem: Mosad ha-Rav Kook, 1940–41 (Hebrew): .

———. *Geschichte der Attributenlehre in der jüdischen Religionsphilosophie von Saadia bis Maimûni*. Gotha: F. A. Perthes, 1877.

———. *Meḥqarim ba-sifrut ha-ʿivrit shel yeme ha-benayyim*. (*Studies in the Hebrew Literature of the Middle Ages*). Translated by Israel Eldad. Jerusalem: Mosad ha-Rav Kook, 1962.

Kogan, Barry. "Judah Halevi." In *A History of Islamic Philosophy*, edited by M. Fakhry. London: Routledge, 1996.

Komem, Aharon. "*Ben shirah li-nevuah*." *Molad* 25 (1969): 676–97.

Kreisel, Howard. "Judah Halevi's Influence on Maimonides." *Maimonidean Studies II*. Edited by A. Hyman. New York: Yeshiva University, 1991.

———. *Theories of Prophecy in Medieval Jewish Philosophy*. Ann Arbor: University Microforms, Brandeis University, 1981.

Kugel, James, editor. *Poetry and Prophecy*. Ithaca and London: Cornell University Press, 1990.

Landauer, S. "Die Psychologie des Ibn Sīnā." *Zeitschrift der deutschen morgenlandischen Gesellschaft* 29 (1876).

Lasker, Daniel J. "Islamic influences on Karaite Origins," in *Studies in Islamic and Judaic Traditions*, II. Edited by William M. Brinner and Stephen D. Ricks.

———."Judah Halevi and Karaism." In *From Ancient Israel to Modern Judaism Essays in Honor of Marvin Fox*. Edited by Jacob Neusner, and Ernest S. Fredrichs, Nahum M. Sarna. Atlanta: Scholars' Press, 1989. Volume III: 111–25

———."Karaites in Twelfth-Century Spain." In *Jewish Thought and Philosophy*. Volume 1, no. 2 (1992): 179–95.

———. "*Munaḥim ʿaraviʾim filosofiim be-sefer ha-kuzari le-rabbi Yehudah ha-Levi*." *Proceedings of the Judaeo-Arabic Society*. Bar Ilan, forthcoming.

———. "The Philosophy of Judah Hadassi the Karaite." In *Shlomo Pines Jubilee Volume* Part I (*Jerusalem Studies in Jewish Thought* 7), 1988.

———. "Proselyte Judaism, Christianity, and Islam in the Thought of Judah Halevi." *Jewish Quarterly Review*, 81,1–2 (July-October, 1990): 75–92.

Lazaroff, Allan. "Baḥya's Asceticism against Its Rabbinic and Islamic Background." *Journal of Jewish Studies* 21 (1970): 11–38.

Lazarus-Yafeh, Hava. "Place of the Religious Commandments in the Philosophy of Al-Ghazzālī." In *The Muslim World* 51 (1961): 173–84.

———. *Studies in Al-Ghazzālī*. Jerusalem: Magnes Press, 1975.

Leaman, Oliver. "Maimonides, Imagination, and the Objectivity of Prophecy." *Religion* 18 (1988).

Lerner, Ralph, and Mahdi Muhsin. *Medieval Political Philosopy: A Sourcebook*. Columbia: Columbia University Press, 1963.

Levinger, Yaʿaqov. "*Ahavah ke-bitui la-ḥavayyah ha-datit etsel Rabi Yehudah Ha-Levi*." In *Mishnato ha-hagutit shel Rabi Yehudah Ha-Levi*. Jerusalem: Ministry of Education and Culture.

Lobel, Diana. *Between Mysticism and Philosophy: Arabic Terms For Religious Experience in R. Yehudah Ha-Levi's Kuzari*. Ann Arbor: University Microfilms, 1995.

Macy, Jeffrey. "Prophecy in al-Fārābī and Maimonides: The Imaginative and Rational Faculties." In *Maimonides and Philosophy*. Edited by S. Pines and Y. Yovel. Dordrecht: Martinus Nijhoff Publishers, 1986.

Mansoor, Menahem, translator (with Sara Arenson and Shoshana Dannhauser).

Baḥya Ibn Paqūda: The Book of Direction to the Duties of the Heart. London: Routledge and Kegan Paul, 1973.

Marmura, Michael E. "Plotting the Course of Avicenna's Thought." *Journal of the American Oriental Society* 111, 2 (1991): 333–42.

Marqet, Yves. *La philosophie des Ihwān al-Ṣafā'*. Alger, 1973.

———. "Révélation et vision véridique chez les Ikhwān al-Ṣafā'." *Révue des études islamiques* (1964).

Massignon, Louis. *Essai sur les origines du lexique technique de la mystique musulmane.* Paris, 1922.

McAuliffe, Jane Dammen. *Qu'rānic Christians.* Cambridge: Cambridge University Press, 1991.

McCarthy, Richard Joseph, S.J. *Freedom and Fulfillment: An Annotated Translation of Al-Ghazālī's al-Munqidh min al-Dalāl and Other Relevant Works of al-Ghazzālī.* Boston: Twayne Publishers, 1980.

Mirsky, Aharon. *From Duties of the Heart to Songs of the Heart.* (Hebrew). Jerusalem: Magnes Press, 1992.

Monroe, James T., trans. *The Shu'ūbiyya in Al-Andalus: the Risāla of Ibn Garcia and Five Refutations.* Berkeley: University of Califorina Press, 1970.

Motzkin, Aryeh. "On Halevi's *Kuzari* as a Platonic Dialogue." *Interpretation* 9.1 (1980): 111–24.

Nasr, Seyyed Hossein. "The Spiritual States in Sufism." In *Sufi Essays.* Albany: State University of New York Press, 1991.

Neumark, David. *Judah Halevi's Philosophy in Its Principles.* Cincinatti: Hebrew Union College Press, 1908.

Nicholson, Reynold A. "The Perfect Man." In *Studies in Islamic Mysticism.* Cambridge: Cambridge University Press, 1921, 77–148.

Peters, J.R.T.M. *God's Created Speech: A Study in the Speculative Theology of the Mu'tazilī Qaḍi l-Quḍat Abū l-Ḥasan 'Abd al-Jabbār ibn Aḥmad al-Hamadānī.* Leiden: E. J. Brill, 1976.

Philo in Ten Volumes. Translated by F. H. Colson, G. H. Whitaker, and Ralph Marcus. Loeb Classics Series. Cambridge: Harvard University Press, 1929–62.

Pines, Shlomo. "The Arabic Recension of *Parva Naturalia* and the Philosophical Doctrine concerning Veridical Dreams According to *al-Risāla al-manāmiyya and Other Sources,*" *Israel Oriental Studies* 4 (1974): 104–53.

———. "The Limitations of Human Knowledge According to Al-Fārābī, ibn Bājja, and Maimonides." In *Studies in Medieval Jewish History and Literature.* Edited by Isadore Twersky, 82–109. Cambridge, Mass.: Harvard University Press, 1979.

———. "On the Term *Ruḥaniyyut* and Its Origin, and on Judah Ha-Levi's Doctrine." (Hebrew), *Tarbiz* 57 (1988): 511–34.

———. "Shī'ite Terms and Conceptions in Judah Halevi's *Kuzari.*" *Jerusalem Studies in Arabic and Islam* 2 (1980): 165–251.

———, translator. *Moses Maimonides: The Guide of the Perplexed.* Chicago and London: University of Chicago Press, 1963.

Plotinus. *Enneads.* Translated by A. H. Armstrong. Cambridge, Mass.: Harvard University Press, 1984.

Poznanski, Samuel A. "Anan et ses écrits," *Révue des études juives* 44 (1902).

———. "Extracts from the Book Megillat Setarim of Rabbi Nissim ben Jacob of Kairouan" (Hebrew). *Ha-Tsofeh le-Ḥokhmat Yisra'el* 5 (1921): 177–84.

al-Qirqisānī, Ya'qub Yūsuf. *Kitab al-anwār wa-l-marāqib*. Edited by Leon Nemoy. New York: Alexander Kohut Memorial Foundation, 1939.

Rahman, Fazlur. *Prophecy in Islam: Philosophy and Orthodoxy*. London: Allen and Unwin, 1958.

Ravitsky, Aviezer. "The Anthropological Theory of Miracles." *Studies on Medieval Jewish History and Literature, vol. II*. Edited by Isadore Twersky. Cambridge, Mass.: Harvard University Press, 1984, 231–72.

Razhaby, Yehudah. "Borrowed Elements in the Poems of Yehuda Halevi from Arabic Poetry and Philosophy" (Hebrew), *Molad* 5 (1975):173–83.

———. *A Dictionary of Judaeo-Arabic in R. Saadya's Tafsīr* (Hebrew). Ramat Gan: Bar Ilan University Press, 1985.

Rosenblatt, Samuel. *Saadia Gaon: The Book of Beliefs and Opinions*. New Haven, Conn.: Yale University Press, 1948.

Rosenthal, Franz. "A Judaeo-Arabic Work under Sufi Influence." *Hebrew Union College Annual* 15 (1940): 433–84.

Safran, Bezalel. "Baḥya Ibn Paqūda's Attitude toward the Courtier Class." In *Studies in Medieval Jewish History and Literature*. Vol. I. Cambridge: Harvard University Press, 1979.

———. "Rabbi Azriel and Nahmanides: Two Views of the Fall of Man." In *Rabbi Moses Nahmanides (Ramban): Explorations in His Religious and Literary Virtuosity*. Edited by Isadore Twersky. Cambridge: Harvard University Press, 1983, 75–106.

Salisbury, Edward E. "Contributions from Original Sources to Our Knowledge of the Science of Muslim Tradition." In *Journal of the American Oriental Society* VII.

Saperstein, Marc. "The Aggadah: Problem and Challenge." In *Decoding the Rabbis: A Thirteenth-Century Commentary on the Aggadah*. Cambridge, Mass.: Harvard University Press, 1980.

Schacht, Joseph. *An Introduction to Islamic Law*. Oxford: Oxford University Press, 1964.

———. *The Origins of Muhammadan Jurisprudence*, 4th ed. Oxford: Oxford University Press, 1967.

Scheindlin, Raymond. *The Gazelle: Medieval Hebrew Poems on God, Israel, and the Soul*. Philadelphia: Jewish Publication Society, 1991.

———. "Ibn Gabirol's Religious Poetry and Sufi Poetry," *Sefarad LIV* (1994): 110–42.

———. *Wine, Women, and Death: Medieval Hebrew Poems on the Good Life*. Philadelphia: Jewish Publication Society, 1986.

Schimmel, Annemarie. *As through a Veil: Mystical Poetry in Islam*. New York: Columbia University Press, 1982.

———. *Mystical Dimensions of Islam*. Chapel Hill: University of North Carolina Press, 1975.

Schirmann, Hayyim. "The Life of Jehuda Halevi" (Hebrew), *Tarbiz* 9 (1937–39): 35–54, 219–40, 284–305; 10 (1938–39):237–39; 11 (1939–40):125.

———. *Ha-shirah ha'ivrit bi-sefarad u-ve-provans* (Hebrew Poetry in Spain and Provence). Jerusalem and Tel Aviv: Bialik Institute and Dvir Company, 1960–61.

Scholem, Gershom. "*Devekut* or Communion with God." In *The Messianic Idea in Judaism*. London: George Allen and Unwin, 1971.

———. *Kabbalah*. Jerusalem: Keter, 1974.

———. *On the Kabbalah and Its Symbolism*. Translated by Ralph Manheim. New York: Schocken Books, 1965.

———. *Major Trends in Jewish Mysticism*. New York: Schocken Books, 1961.

Schweid, Eliezer. "The Literary Structure of the First Book of the *Kuzari*" (Hebrew), *Tarbiz* 30 (1961): 257–72.

———. *Ta'am ve-haqashah*. Ramat Gan: Bar Ilan University Press, 1970.

Septimus, Bernard. *Hispano-Jewish Culture in Transition: The Career and Controversies of Ramah*. Cambridge: Harvard University Press, 1982.

———. "On the Use of Talmudic Literature in Spanish-Hebrew Poetry" (Hebrew), *Tarbiz* 53 (1984): 607–14.

Shinn, Larry D. *Two Sacred Worlds: Experience and Structure in the World's Religions*. Nashville: Abingdon, 1977.

Silman, Yochanan. "The Visual Experience in the *Kuzari*." In *Yearbook for Religious Anthropology: Ocular Desire*. Berlin: Academie Verlag (1994): 117–26.

———. *Ben filosof le-navi: hitpatḥut haguto shel Rabi Yehudah Ha-Levi be-Sefer ha-Kuzari*. Ramat Gan: Bar Ilan University Press, 1985. *Philosopher and Prophet: Judah Halevi, the Kuzari, and the Development of His Thought*. Translated by L. Schramm. Albany: State University of New York Press, 1995.

———. "*Yiḥudo shel ha-ma'amar ha-shelishi ba-sefer ha-Kuzari*." *Eshel Be'er-Sheva'*, vol. 1 Be'er Sheva: Ben-Gurion University, 1976, 94–119.

Simon, Uriel. *Four Approaches to the Book of Psalms* (Hebrew). Ramat Gan: Bar-Ilan University Press, 1982. Translated by Lenn J. Schramm. Albany: State University of New York Press, 1991.

Sirat, Colette. *A History of Jewish Philosophy in the Middle Ages*. Cambridge: Cambridge University Press, 1985.

———. *Les théories des visions surnaturelles dans la pensée juive du Moyen Age*. Leiden, 1969.

Sklare, David. *Samuel ben Hofni Gaon and his Cultural World: Texts and Studies*. Leiden: Brill, 1996.

Smith, Margaret. *The Way of the Mystics: The Early Christian Mystics and the Rise of the Sufis*. London: Sheldon Press, 1976.

Sokolow, Moshe. "Saadiah Gaon's Prolegomenon to Psalms." *Proceedings of the American Academy of Jewish Research* 51 (1984).

Strauss, Leo. "The Law of Reason in the *Kuzari*." In *Persecution and the Art of Writing*. Glencoe: Free Press, 1952; Chicago: University of Chicago Press, 1988, 95–141.

———. "The Philosophical Grounding of the Law." In *Philosophy and Law: Essays toward the Understanding of Maimonides and His Predecessors*. Translated by Fred Baumann. Philadelphia: Jewish Publication Society, 1987

The Theology of Aristotle. Translated by Geoffrey Lewis. In *Plotini Opera*. Edited by Paul Henry and Hans-Rudolf Schwyzer. Paris: Desclee de Brouwer, 1959.

Twersky, Isadore. *Introduction to the Code of Maimonides (Mishneh Torah)*. New Haven, Conn.: Yale University Press, 1980.

———. "Some Non-Halakhic Aspects of the *Mishneh Torah*. In *Jewish Medieval and Renassance Studies*, 95–118.

Urbach, Ephraim. "*Ha-mesorot ʿal torat ha-sod bi-tequfat ha-Tannaim*." *Studies in Mysticism and Religion Presented to Gershom Scholem*. Jerusalem, 1969, 1–28.

———. "*Matai paskah ha-nevuah?*" *Tarbiz* 17: 1–11.

———. *The Sages: Their Concepts and Beliefs*. Translated by Israel Abrahams. Jerusalem: Magnes Press, 1965. Cambridge, Mass.: Harvard University Press, 1979.

Vajda, Georges. *L'amour de dieu dans la théologie juive du moyen age*. Paris: Librarie philosophique J. Vrin, 1957.

———. "Le commentaire kairouanais sur le *Livre de la Création*," *Révue des études juives* 107 (1946–47): 99–156

———. "Le dialogue de l'âme et de la raison dans Les Devoirs des Coeurs de Baḥya Ibn Paqūda." In *Révue des études juives* 102 (1937): 93–104.

———. "Glosses sur la Théologie d'Aristu par ibn Sīnā," *Révue Thomiste* 51 (1951): 346–406.

———. "Jewish Mysticism and Muslim Mysticism." Translated by Paul Fenton. Conference June 20, 1966; compiled by Hananya Goodman for forthcoming issue of *Kabbalah: A Journal of Jewish Mysticism*.

———. "Nouveaux fragments arabes du commentaire de Dunash b. Tamim sur le *Livre de la Création*," *Révue des études juives* 113 (1954):37–61.

———. *La théologie ascetique de Baḥya ibn Paqūda*. Paris: Cahiers de la Societe Asiatique 7, 1947.

Van Ess, Joseph. *Die Erkentnisslehre des ʿAḍudaddīn al-Icī (Ubersetzung und Kommentar des 11. Buches seiner Mawaqif)*. Wiesbaden: Steiner, 1966.

———. "The Logical Structure of Islamic Theology," in *Logic in Classical Islamic Culture*. Edited by Gustave E. von Grunebaum. Wiesbaden: O. Harrassowitz, 1970, 21–50.

Walzer, Michael. "Al-Fārābī's Theory of Divination." In *Greek into Arabic: Essays on Islamic Philosophy*. Cambridge, Mass.: Harvard University Press, 1962.

Wansbrough, John. *Qur'ānic Studies: Sources and Methods of Scriptural Interpretation*. Oxford: Oxford University Press, 1977.

Wasserstrom, Steven M. Review of Yochanan Silman, *Philosopher and Prophet. Judah Halevi, the Kuzari, and the Evolution of His Thought*. Translation from the Hebrew by Lenn J. Schramm. In *Medieval Encounters*, vol. 4, number 2 (1998).

Watt, William Montgomery. "The Closing of the Door of Igtihād." *Orientalia Hispanica* I. Leiden: E. J. Brill, 1964.

———. *The Faith and Practice of Al-Ghazali*. London: George Allen and Unwin, 1953.

———. *Muslim Intellectual: A Study of al-Ghazali*. Edinburgh: Edinburgh University Press, 1963.

Wegner, Judith Romney. "Islamic and Talmudic Jurisprudence: The Four Roots of Islamic Law and Their Talmudic Counterparts." In *The American Journal of Legal History*, 26 (1982): 44–45.

Wensinck, A. J. "On the Relation between Ghazali's Cosmology and His Mysticism." *Mededeelingen der Koninklijke Akademie van Wetenschappen, Afdeeling Letterkunde*, Deel 75, Serie A, No. 6. Amsterdam, 1933.

———. *The Muslim Creed*. Cambridge: Cambridge University Press, 1932.

Wieder, Naphtali. *The Judean Scrolls and Karaism*. London: East and West Library, 1962.

Wolfson, Elliot. "Merkavah Traditions in Philosophical Garb: Judah Halevi Reconsidered." *Proceedings of the American Academy of Jewish Research* (1990–91): 179–242.

———. "The Hermeneutics of Visionary Experience: Revelation and Interpretation in the *Zohar.*" *Religion* 18 (1988).

———. *Through a Speculum That Shines: Vision and Imagination in Medieval Jewish Mysticism*. Princeton: Princeton University Press, 1994.

Wolfson, Harry A. "Hallevi and Maimonides on Prophecy," *Studies in Religious Philosophy*, edited by Isadore Twersky and George H. Williams. Cambridge, Mass.: Harvard University Press, 1973–79: 60–119.

———. "The Internal Senses in Latin, Arabic, and Hebrew Philosophic Texts." In *Studies in Religious Philosophy,* vol. 1. Edited by Isadore Twersky and George H. Williams. Cambridge: Harvard University Pres, 1973–79.

———. *The Philosophy of the Kalām*. Cambridge, Mass.: Harvard University Press, 1962.

———. *Repercussions of the Kalām in Jewish Philosophy*. Cambridge, Mass.: Harvard University Press, 1979.

Zucker, Moshe. "Fragments from Rav Sa'adya Gaon's Commentary to the Pentateuch from Mss, *Ṣūra* 2 (1955–56) (Hebrew).

———. "Notes on Saadiah's Introduction to Psalms," *Leshonenu* 33 (1969).

———. *Perushe Rav Saadia Gaon le-Vereshit*. Jerusalem: Jewish Theological Seminary, 1984.

———. "*Qeta'im mi-kitāb taḥsīl al-sharā'i al-sam'iyya li-Rav Sa'adya Gaon,*" *Tarbiz* 41 (1971–72):

———. *Teguvot li-tenu'at avale Zion ha-Qar'iyim be-sifrut ha-rabbanit.*" In *Sefer ha-Yovel li-Rabbi Hanokh Albeck*. Jerusalem: Mossad Harav Kook, 1963, 378–401.

Zysow, Aron. *The Economy of Certainty: An Introduction to the Typology of Islamic Legal Theory*. Ann Arbor, Mich.: University Microfilms, 1984.

Index

Passages from Judah Ha-levi's *Kuzari*